CICERO

XXVIII

LETTERS TO QUINTUS, BRUTUS, AND OTHERS

462

CICERO

IN TWENTY-EIGHT VOLUMES

XXVIII

THE LETTERS TO
HIS BROTHER QUINTUS
Translated by W. GLYNN WILLIAMS, M.A.

THE LETTERS TO BRUTUS
Translated by M. CARY, D.Litt.

HANDBOOK OF
ELECTIONEERING

LETTER TO OCTAVIAN
Translated by MARY HENDERSON, M.A.

CAMBRIDGE, MASSACHUSETTS
HARVARD UNIVERSITY PRESS
LONDON
WILLIAM HEINEMANN LTD
MCMLXXIX

American
ISBN 0-674-99509-0

British
ISBN 0 434 99462 6

First printed 1954
Reprinted 1960, 1965
Reprinted with additions 1972, 1979

Printed in Great Britain

CONTENTS OF VOLUME IV

LETTERS TO HIS BROTHER QUINTUS

BOOK I

BOOK II

BOOK III

LETTERS TO BRUTUS

CONTENTS

vi

LIST OF CICERO'S WORKS

SHOWING THEIR DIVISION INTO
VOLUMES IN THIS
EDITION

LIST OF CICERO'S WORKS

LIST OF CICERO'S WORKS

LIST OF CICERO'S WORKS

PREFACE

VOLUME XXVII of Cicero's works (Vol. III of the Letters) in the Loeb Classical Library consisted until 1972 of Books xiii-xvi of Cicero's *Letters to his Friends* ; his *Letters to his Brother Quintus* ; and his *Letters to M. Brutus*. The Library has decided (i) to divide this volume into two so that Vol. XXVII of Cicero's works (Vol. III of the Letters) shall comprise only Books xiii-xvi of Cicero's *Letters to His Friends* ; and (ii) to form a new volume XXVIII of the works (Volume IV of the Letters) containing (*a*) the *Letters to his Brother Quintus* and the *Letters to M. Brutus* ; and (*b*) two " Ciceronian " works not hitherto included in the Loeb series—the *Handbook of Electioneering* (*Commentariolum Petitionis*) and the *Letter to Octavian* (*Epistula ad Octavianum*).

For the *Letters to Quintus* and the *Letters to Brutus* we now have, in the Oxford Classical Texts, *M. Tulli Ciceronis Epistulae* Vol. III, excellently edited by W. S. Watt, Oxford, 1958, which contains also, in an Appendix, the *Commentariolum Petitionis* and the *Epistula ad Octavianum*. The Loeb Classical Library is able to avail itself of the translation (with scholarly commentary and introductions) of the *Commentariolum* and of the *Epistula* by Mrs. Mary Isobel Henderson, M.A. (she was Vice-Principal and fellow of Somerville College, Oxford, and University Lecturer in

PREFACE

Ancient History). At the time of her death, her translation and commentaries were finished. So were her introductions except in so far as they did not include an account of the manuscripts and also needed some bringing up to present date. Her translations, which lacked a final revision, have been altered in a number of passages which were inadequate, imperfect or incomplete. On the other hand she submitted no text or critical notes, but obviously used Watt's edition. Therefore, in this supplement to our new volume, the text, critical notes and parts of the introductions have been added by myself. The Loeb Classical Library and its editor are grateful to Professor Watt for help given, and to him and the Clarendon Press, Oxford, for permission to make use of their text of the two works concerned. In order not to delay further the publication of Mrs. Henderson's works, we have joined it meanwhile to the unaltered remainder of our original issue of the Letters to Quintus and to Brutus.

E. H. WARMINGTON
EDITOR, LOEB CLASSICAL LIBRARY

A CHRONOLOGICAL SUMMARY

OF THE PRINCIPAL EVENTS IN
THE LIFE OF CICERO

63 B.C.

§ 1. Cicero, being now consul, successfully opposes the agrarian law of the tribune P. Servilius Rullus, which was in the interests of Caesar and Crassus, and

intended to check the growing power of Pompey.
Caesar is elected Pontifex Maximus. Cicero carries
in the Senate the proposal of a *supplicatio* of
unusual length to Pompey in honour of his eastern
triumphs.

§ 2. Having conciliated his colleague C. Antonius
by resigning to him the governorship in 62 of the
rich province of Macedonia, Cicero felt himself
able in the autumn of 63 to oppose the treasonable
designs of L. Sergius Catilina, of which he had full
information from the spy, L. Curius. In the consular
elections for 62 Catiline was again defeated. On
October 21 Cicero foretold the rising of the Catilinarian Manlius in Etruria on the 27th. Martial law
was proclaimed, and the conspirators failed in an
attempt to seize Praeneste on November 1, and
another plot to murder Cicero was exposed. But
Catiline had the audacity to appear in the Senate on
November 8, when Cicero so crushingly denounced
him that he left Rome to take command of the
insurgents in Etruria.

§ 3. Certain envoys of the Allobroges, having been
approached by the conspirators to supply Catiline
with cavalry, were arrested, and on the strength of
incriminating letters found upon them the following
five conspirators were seized and imprisoned — P.
Lentulus Sura (praetor), C. Cethegus (senator), L.
Statilius, P. Gabinius Cimber, and M. Caeparius ;
and at a meeting of the Senate on December 5,
mainly at the instance of M. Cato, though Caesar,
then praetor elect, was opposed to it, a decree was
carried that the five conspirators arrested should be
put to death, and that same evening they were
strangled under Cicero's supervision.

CHRONOLOGICAL SUMMARY

§ 4. On December 29 the tribune Q. Metellus Nepos vetoed Cicero's address to the people on going out of office, alleging that "he had put citizens to death without a trial"; but Cicero's declaration that he had thereby saved his country was received with applause. This Metellus was one of Pompey's officers and was probably instigated by his general, who was chagrined that Cicero, and not he, should have quelled the conspiracy.

62 B.C.

Consuls : D. Junius Silanus and L. Licinius Murena

§ 1. Catiline, making for Cisalpine Gaul with Manlius's army, is met by Metellus Celer and thrown back on the army of C. Antonius. In a battle near Pistoria the insurgents were utterly and finally defeated, and Catiline slain.

§ 2. Cicero resents Pompey's lukewarm appreciation of his services to the Republic (v. 7).

§ 3. In December P. Claudius Pulcher, commonly known as Clodius, "one of the most profligate characters of a profligate age," disguised as a female musician profaned the mysteries of the Bona Dea, which were being celebrated by Roman matrons at the house of Caesar. He was discovered and brought to trial in 61.

61 B.C.

Consuls : M. Pupius Piso and M. Valerius
Messalla Niger

§ 1. Pompey, having returned from the east and disbanded his army in the preceding December,

addressed the Roman people in January of this year, but failed to create a good impression. He disapproved of the bill for Clodius's prosecution, and being distrusted by the extremists in the Senate, found himself so isolated that he made overtures to Cicero.

§ 2. The consul Pupius Piso also opposed the bill for an inquiry into Clodius's affair, but the trial ultimately came on, with the result that by means of the grossest bribery Clodius was acquitted. Cicero had given evidence cancelling an alibi put up by Clodius, who swore to be avenged upon him, and proved to be a formidable foe, owing to his family connexions, and his influence over the city populace.

60 B.C.

*Consuls : L. Afranius and Q. Caecilius
Metellus Celer*

§ 1. Led by the consul Metellus Celer, now at enmity with Pompey for having divorced his half-sister Mucia, the Senate, by obstinately opposing Pompey's plans in Asia and grants of land to his veterans, completely alienated him, and by refusing all concessions to the *publicani* in Asia offended the *equites* from among whom the *publicani* were mainly drawn. Pompey was ultimately forced into a coalition with Caesar, who returned to Rome in June to canvass for the consulship, which by the aid of Pompey and Crassus he secured.

§ 2. The *optimates*, however, brought about by bribery the election as Caesar's colleague of

M. Calpurnius Bibulus, a staunch aristocrat, but a *fainéant* consul.

§ 3. Caesar, having effected the reconciliation of Pompey and Crassus, now invited Cicero to join them, but he preferred to retain his independence, and the coalition (incorrectly called the first triumvirate) of Caesar, Pompey, and Crassus, to which he might have belonged, was established without him.

59 B.C.

Consuls : C. Julius Caesar and M. Calpurnius Bibulus

§ 1. Caesar, having failed to carry through the Senate an agrarian law providing *inter alia* for Pompey's veterans, brought another law before the assembly of the people distributing the *ager Campanus* among those veterans, and this law was carried despite the opposition of the consul Bibulus and some of the tribunes.

§ 2. P. Vatinius, one of the most unprincipled men of the time, was a humble hireling of Caesar, and now as tribune he carried the famous Lex Vatinia, which gave Caesar the command of Cisalpine Gaul and Illyricum with three legions for five years ; and the Senate, on the motion of Pompey (now, by his marriage with Julia, Caesar's son-in-law), added Transalpine Gaul to his command, with a fourth legion.

§ 3. In March Cicero, in defending his former colleague C. Antonius, who was accused of extortion as proconsul of Macedonia, attacked the triumvirate, causing grave offence to Caesar, who immediately

retaliated by sanctioning the adoption into a plebeian family of Cicero's enemy Clodius, thus making him eligible for the tribunate, where he would be in a stronger position to wreak his vengeance on Cicero.

58 B.C.

Consuls : L. Calpurnius Piso Caesoninus and Aulus Gabinius

§ 1. Clodius, who had been elected tribune in the preceding October, having carried some very popular measures in January, further established his position in February by promulgating a law assigning to the consuls on their going out of office the provinces they most desired—Syria to Gabinius, and Macedonia with Achaia to Piso,—but he made the law contingent upon the passing of two other measures which were subsequently carried—(1) a commission giving to Cato the annexation of Cyprus, and (2) an enactment " that anyone who had put Roman citizens to death without a trial should be forbidden fire and water."

§ 2. Cicero, realizing that the enactment was aimed at himself, put on mourning and threw himself on the mercy of the people. The senators and *equites* also went into mourning, but were compelled by an edict of the consuls to dress as usual. Caesar stated in public that he thought Cicero had acted illegally in putting Lentulus Sura to death, and Pompey, on being appealed to, referred Cicero to the consuls, who had already shown their hostility. Finally Cicero, at the instance of his family and Hortensius, left Rome and went into exile at the end of March. He was immediately declared an outlaw by Clodius,

and his house on the Palatine and villas at Formiae and Tusculum were pillaged and dismantled.

§ 3. Cicero went to Brundisium and thence to Thessalonica, where he sojourned for seven months at the house of his friend, the quaestor Cn. Plancius. As the year went on the situation at Rome became brighter for him ; Clodius had offended Pompey by aiding the escape from Rome of the Armenian prince Tigranes whom Pompey had captured, by defeating the consul Gabinius in a street riot, and even forcing Pompey to shut himself up in his house. Moreover, Lentulus Spinther, one of the consuls elected, was personally devoted to Cicero, and the other, Metellus Nepos, a friend of Pompey ; while among the new tribunes T. Annius Milo, T. Fadius, and P. Sestius strenuously advocated Cicero's recall. His son-in-law also, C. Calpurnius Piso, who had married Cicero's daughter Tullia in 63, and was now quaestor, exercised what influence he had in the interests of his father-in-law.

57 B.C.

*Consuls : P. Cornelius Lentulus Spinther
and Q. Caecilius Metellus Nepos*

§ 1. No sooner had the consul Lentulus entered into office on January 1 than he brought before the Senate, with the approval of Pompey, the question of Cicero's recall ; and despite the obstruction of two of the tribunes, the people, led by Fabricius and all the praetors (except Appius Claudius Pulcher, Clodius's brother), passed in their Assembly (the *comitia centuriata*) on January 23 a provisional decree recalling Cicero. The Senate thanked Cn. Plancius and others for sheltering Cicero in his

banishment, and summoned the Italians to vote finally for his recall in the Assembly, and the bill was carried with enthusiastic unanimity on August 4, the voters being protected from Clodius and his armed ruffians by troops under the command of Milo.

§ 2. Cicero, who had come down to Dyrrachium in the preceding autumn, now crossed over to Brundisium, where he was informed by his brother Quintus of the passing of the decree for his recall, and, after a triumphal progress homeward, re-entered Rome amid universal rejoicings on September 4.

§ 3. Later on, on the motion of Cicero, Pompey is granted the *imperium* in the form of the control of the corn supply (*curatio rei annonariae*) for five years ; and on the expiry of their terms of office Lentulus receives Cilicia, and Nepos Hither Spain, as his province.

§ 4. Ptolemy Auletes (the Flute-player), king of Egypt, father of Cleopatra, having been expelled by his subjects, comes to seek the assistance of Rome, and the Senate decrees that his restoration should be entrusted to the next governor of Cilicia, *i.e.* the then consul, Lentulus Spinther.

56 B.C.

Consuls : Cn. Cornelius Lentulus Marcellinus, who supported the optimates *and opposed the triumvirs ; and L. Marcius Philippus, who later married Atia, widow of C. Octavius, and so became the stepfather of Augustus*

§ 1. In January the question of the restoration of Ptolemy Auletes is reopened and hotly debated in the Senate, and Cicero sends Lentulus, now proconsul of Cilicia, a full account of the voting. Pompey,

though ostensibly supporting the claims of Lentulus to effect the restoration, was anxious to secure for himself a commission which would not only be highly lucrative, but would give him a fleet, an army, and a base in Egypt. Cicero felt bound to support his benefactor Lentulus, and the majority of the Senate were afraid or jealous of Pompey, when, very opportunely for them, the tribune C. Cato discovered a Sibylline oracle, forbidding the restoration of Ptolemy by anyone *cum multitudine hominum* (" with a host of men "). This is the *religio* referred to in Bk. i. 2 and 3. The wranglings in the Senate ended in no settlement, but Ptolemy was ultimately restored by A. Gabinius in 55.

§ 2. Clodius, who still lorded it in the streets of Rome, escaped being prosecuted by Milo by being elected curule aedile, and turned the tables on Milo by accusing him in February of *vis* (breach of the peace). Pompey, when defending Milo, was shouted down by Clodius's ruffians, who declared that Crassus, and not Pompey, should restore Ptolemy. This led Pompey to suspect that Crassus was aiding and abetting the rioters. The result of the trial was the closer alliance of Pompey and Milo, and the more definite support of Clodius by the extreme aristocrats—Curio, Bibulus, Favonius, and others.

§ 3. Later in February, Cicero, in defending P. Sestius, who had strongly favoured his recall, and was now accused of *vis*, made his speech (as Watson describes it) " a regular political manifesto," and converted his *interrogatio* (cross-examination) of P. Vatinius, now a witness for the prosecution, into a bitter attack upon him as the author of the Lex Vatinia in 59 (see 59 B.C., § 2). The acquittal

of Sestius encouraged Cicero to hope for the restoration of the Republic, or at any rate the dissolution of the coalition, Pompey being still at feud with Crassus (§ 2) and jealous of Caesar.

§ 4. Cicero therefore, partly with a view of widening the breach between Pompey and Caesar, proposed the suspension of Caesar's law about the *ager Campanus* (see 59 B.C., § 1) on the grounds that the State could not afford any more allotments. This would not affect Pompey, whose veterans had already been provided for, whereas Caesar would be precluded from using the remaining land for his own veterans. He also saw that the repeal of the agrarian law would be followed by that of the Vatinian.

§ 5. Having therefore previously interviewed Crassus at Ravenna, Caesar took him with him to join Pompey at Luca, a town of Liguria in N. Italy ; and here the coalition of 60 (see 60 B.C., § 3) was not only renewed but developed into an omnipotent triumvirate who could settle the affairs of the State at their own discretion.

§ 6. This to Cicero, the Republican, and lifelong advocate of *concordia ordinum* ("the harmony of the senatorial and equestrian orders"), was a crushing political calamity, but he had to bow to the inevitable, and the famous letter 9 in Bk. I. is his *apologia* for his change of front. Withdrawing his motion on the *ager Campanus*, he supported a motion in the Senate to provide pay for Caesar's troops and allowing him to appoint ten *legati*. This was followed by his brilliant speech *De provinciis consularibus*, practically a panegyric upon Caesar and his achievements in Gaul.

CHRONOLOGICAL SUMMARY

§ 7. Clodius's turbulence in 56–57 had estranged Pompey, who now leaned to the side of Milo, but the extreme *optimates* (including M. Cato, who was indebted to Clodius for a commission to settle the affairs of Cyprus in 58) showed such fulsome partiality for Clodius, that Cicero, being earnestly requested by Caesar, whom he could not now disobey, to undertake the defence of Vatinius, whom he particularly detested, adroitly converted his predicament into a means of annoying the *optimates* saying that "if *they* coquetted with one Publius (viz. Clodius), *he* would coquet with another Publius (viz. Vatinius) by way of reprisal" (i. 9. 19).

55 B.C.

Consuls (after an "interregnum" in January caused by the tribune C. Cato): Cn. Pompeius and M. Licinius Crassus, both for the second time, having been consuls together in 70

§ 1. Crassus carries his *Lex Licinia* for the suppression of *sodalicia* ("political combinations"). Pompey opens his new theatre with shows of unparalleled magnificence, but his wholesale slaughter of elephants disgusts not only Cicero, but the people generally.

§ 2. Cicero finishes his *De oratore*. Crassus sets out for Syria, and his departure, together with the death of Pompey's wife Julia, Caesar's daughter, put an end to even the semblance of friendship between Pompey and Caesar.

§ 3. Gabinius marches into Egypt, occupies Alexandria, and restores the ex-king Ptolemy Auletes.

54 B.C.

Consuls: L. Domitius Ahenobarbus, an optimate, who married M. Crassus's sister Porcia, and fell at Pharsalia in 48, and Appius Claudius Pulcher

§ 1. Cicero helps to secure the acquittal of his former enemy, P. Vatinius, who requited his kindness after Pharsalia and later, and at Pompey's instance defends, though unsuccessfully, his former enemy, A. Gabinius ; and also defends successfully his old friend Cn. Plancius, charged with *ambitus*, in his famous speech *Pro Plancio*.

§ 2. His brother, Q. Cicero, goes over from Pompey to Caesar as his legate, and serves him with distinction in Britain and Gaul ; and this leads to a *rapprochement* between Cicero and Caesar.

53 B.C.

Consuls, after disorder lasting till July : Cn. Domitius Calvinus and M. Valerius Messalla

Defeat and murder of M. Crassus in June, near Carrhae. Cicero is more deeply affected by the death, a little earlier, of M. Crassus's son, Publius (v. 8. 4). Cicero succeeds Crassus as augur, and supports Milo's candidature for the consulship, recommending him to C. Scribonius Curio, to whom he writes a series of letters (ii. 1-7).

52 B.C.

About the middle of January Clodius is slain near Bovillae by the retainers of Milo ; his body is buried by his supporters in the forum, when the senate-house caught fire and was destroyed ; martial law

xxiv

is proclaimed, and finally Pompey is made sole consul, being allowed to retain the government of Spain. Milo is accused of *vis* and condemned. He goes into exile at Massilia.

51 B.C.

Consuls: Servius Sulpicius Rufus and M. Claudius Marcellus

Cicero goes to Cilicia as proconsul, succeeding Appius Claudius, who had succeeded Lentulus in 54, and M. Calpurnius Bibulus goes to Syria. Cicero is kept fully informed of what occurs in Rome by his friend M. Caelius Rufus (Bk. VIII. of these Letters).

50 B.C.

Consuls: C. Claudius Marcellus, cousin of the consul for 51, and L. Aemilius Paullus

§ 1. Cicero, after a satisfactory tenure of office, quits his province, leaving C. Caelius Caldus, his quaestor, in charge, and reaches Rome in December. He is anxious about the honours due to his Cilician successes, having so far only had a *supplicatio* voted him, but no triumph; he is also embarrassed about the marriage of his daughter Tullia with P. Cornelius Dolabella, who was prosecuting for treason Appius Claudius Pulcher, with whom Cicero desired a reconciliation.

§ 2. A motion in the Senate, that Caesar's candidature for the consulship should be considered in his absence, having been rejected, the tribune Scribonius Curio demands the disbanding of Pompey's army, which the Senate would have passed but for

the opposition of the consul Marcellus. Curio openly declares for Caesar, whom he joins at Ravenna, thus, according to Lucan, turning the scales against the Pompeian party (*momentumque fuit mutatus Curio rerum*).

49 B.C.

Consuls : L. Cornelius Lentulus Crus and C. Claudius Marcellus, cousin of his namesake, the consul for 50, and brother of the consul for 51

The tribunes M. Antonius and Q. Cassius, accompanied by Caelius Rufus, leave Rome and join Caesar, who on January 11 crosses the Rubicon, and thereby declares war upon the Republic, and marching southwards finally besieges Pompey in Brundisium. On March 17 Pompey escapes to Dyrrachium, whither the consuls had gone with the bulk of his army on March 4. Cicero vacillates as to his future policy, but finally decides to throw in his lot with Pompey.

48 B.C.

Consuls : C. Julius Caesar (for the second time) and P. Servilius Isauricus

Cicero spends the first half of the year in Pompey's camp at Dyrrachium, where he conceives a poor opinion of Pompey's army ; he is still there when he hears of the utter defeat of Pompey by Caesar near Pharsalus on August 7 and his flight to Egypt. Crossing with the Pompeians from Dyrrachium to Corcyra, Cicero is threatened with death by young Cn. Pompey for refusing to take the command as senior consul. In October he returns to Italy and settles in Brundisium.

xxvi

CHRONOLOGICAL SUMMARY

47 B.C.

Consuls : Q. Fufius Calenus and P. Vatinius, but only for Oct., Nov., and Dec.

§ 1. Though allowed to remain in Italy when all other Pompeians were driven out, Cicero was not happy ; he had broken with his brother Quintus, and Terentia (he alleged) had mismanaged his financial affairs in his absence ; while Dolabella, his son-in-law, was so notoriously unfaithful to Tullia as to make a divorce inevitable.

§ 2. He was consoled, however, by a reassuring letter from Caesar in Egypt, who permitted him to retain his lictors and the title of *imperator* ; on Caesar's return Cicero met him and was cordially received, and being given leave to live wherever he liked, he chose Tusculum, so as to be near Rome.

§ 3. Dolabella, now tribune, agitating for the abolition of debts, is opposed by his colleague, Trebellius, and the ensuing riots had to be quelled by troops under M. Antonius.

§ 4. Towards the end of the year, through Caesar's influence, Q. Fufius Calenus and P. Vatinius are elected consuls.

46 B.C.

Consuls : C. Julius Caesar (third time) and M. Aemilius Lepidus

§ 1. Caesar defeats the Pompeian army under Scipio at Thapsus in Africa, and M. Cato, preferring death to slavery, commits suicide at Utica.   Returning to Rome and celebrating four triumphs in August

for his victories in Gaul, Egypt, Pontus, and Africa, Caesar is made Dictator for the year.

§ 2. Cicero's letters now show a more cheerful spirit ; he had now divorced Terentia, and after a short interval married his young and wealthy ward, Publilia ; the marriage, however, was an unhappy one.

§ 3. Cicero wrote this year his *Partitiones oratoriae*, *Brutus*, and *Orator*.

45 B.C.

Consul (fourth time) : C. Julius Caesar

§ 1. In February Tullia, shortly after her divorce from Dolabella, died in childbed. Cicero, who had loved her devotedly, refused to be comforted and sought refuge in the solitude of Astura.

§ 2. Caesar now openly aimed at monarchy, and Cicero especially resented, as an insult to the senatorial order, the election as consul for one day of Caninius Rebilus.

44 B.C.

§ 1. Caesar, now consul for the fifth time and dictator for the fourth, had already by his arrogance and ill-concealed ambition aroused the opposition of the republicans, and a conspiracy had long been maturing which culminated in his assassination on March 15 at the foot of Pompey's statue in the senate-house. By his will he adopted C. Octavius and made him his chief heir.

§ 2. On the 17th, at a meeting of the Senate in the temple of Tellus, Cicero proposed an amnesty, which the Senate passed, but at the same time ratified all Caesar's acts. After this he retired into private life for six months.

CHRONOLOGICAL SUMMARY

§ 3. He had already completed his *Tusculan Disputations* and *De natura deorum*, and during the remainder of the year composed his *De amicitia, De senectute, De officiis*, and several other works.

43 B.C.

Consuls : C. Vibius Pansa and A. Hirtius

After a series of events too complicated even to summarize here,[a] C. Octavius, by then called Octavianus, formed a triumvirate with Antony and Lepidus, who removed their chief opponents by *proscriptio*. Among the proscribed was Cicero, who was slain on December 7th, when he was approaching the end of his sixty-fourth year.

[a] A full note on the Cisalpine Campaign will be found at the beginning of Book X.

CICERO'S
LETTERS TO HIS BROTHER QUINTUS

WITH AN ENGLISH TRANSLATION BY
W. GLYNN WILLIAMS, M.A.

FORMERLY SCHOLAR OF ST. JOHN'S COLLEGE, CAMBRIDGE
AND HEADMASTER OF FRIARS SCHOOL, BANGOR

A SHORT LIFE OF QUINTUS TULLIUS CICERO

Quintus Tullius Cicero was born in 102 B.C., and was therefore four years younger than his brother Marcus, the orator. The two brothers were brought up together at Arpinum, until their father, recognizing their intellectual ability, and desiring better educational opportunities for them, moved with his family to Rome, where one of the boys' teachers was the poet Archias of Antioch.

In 67 B.C., at the age of thirty-five, Quintus became aedile, and in 62 praetor, and for the next three years governed the province of Asia as propraetor. It was during this time that Marcus wrote Book I. of his letters, *Ad Quintum Fratrem.* Returning to Rome in 58, Quintus exerted himself to procure his brother's recall from banishment, though he had enemies of his own who threatened to prosecute him for malpractices. In 56 he went to Sardinia on the staff of Pompey, who had been appointed *curator annonae,* " Minister of the Corn Supply "; and in 55 joined Caesar as his *legatus* in Gaul, where he greatly distinguished himself by gallantly resisting with one legion a vastly superior force of Gauls in the country of the Nervii. In 51 he accompanied his brother as one of his *legati* to Cilicia. When the civil

war broke out in 49 he joined Pompey. After the battle of Pharsalia, Caesar, who had a high regard for him, treated him with great leniency and kindness, as indeed he did Marcus. Just at this time, when visiting Patrae in Achaia in Marcus's company, Quintus, for some reason unknown to us, developed a bitter hostility to his brother, who shortly afterwards at Brundisium intercepted a packet of Quintus's letters, addressed to various friends, full of malicious reflections upon himself, and threatening to denounce him to Caesar. So far from taking action against Quintus for his treachery, Marcus actually wrote to Caesar, absolving Quintus from any suspicion of having instigated his own opposition to Caesar, and begging of him to befriend the brother who had behaved so badly to himself. " It seems to us," as Tyrrell rightly remarks, " that this is an act of large nobleness and truly chivalrous feeling, quite startling when we remember the times in which Cicero lived "; indeed we cannot but be impressed with the more than paternal gentleness and patience with which Cicero treated his impulsive and irascible younger brother as long as they lived; and " in death they were not divided," for Quintus, together with his son, was proscribed by the last Triumvirate (Octavian, Antony, and Lepidus) and put to death in Rome a few days before the murder of Marcus in December, 43.

Quintus was a man of ungovernable temper and harshly over-bearing in his treatment of those under his authority, but just, honest, and free from all taint of self-seeking as administrator of a province, while his gallantry as a soldier was proved beyond all question in Gaul. Apart from the unpleasant episode after Pharsalia, his attitude towards Marcus was, in the

main, one of loyalty and affection. He wrote much (including four tragedies, said to have been written in sixteen days), but all that has come down to us is his *brochure* to his brother, *De petitione consulatus.* He married Pomponia, a sister of Atticus, a somewhat arrogant person. Their married life was not a happy one, and ended in his divorcing her.

M. TULLI CICERONIS
EPISTULARUM AD QUINTUM FRATREM

LIBER PRIMUS

I

M. C. S. D. Q. FRATRI

Romae, A.U.C. 694.

1   I. Etsi non dubitabam, quin hanc epistulam multi
nuntii, fama denique esset ipsa sua celeritate supera-
tura, tuque ante ab aliis auditurus esses, annum
tertium accessisse desiderio nostro, et labori tuo,
tamen existimavi a me quoque tibi huius molestiae
nuntium perferri oportere. Nam superioribus litteris, non unis, sed pluribus, cum iam ab aliis desperata
res esset, tamen ego tibi spem maturae decessionis
afferebam, non solum, ut quam diutissime te iucunda
opinione oblectarem, sed etiam quia tanta adhibe-
batur et a nobis et a praetoribus contentio, ut rem
2 posse confici non diffiderem. Nunc quoniam ita
accidit, ut neque praetores suis opibus, neque nos
nostro studio quidquam proficere possemus, est omni-

---

    a Who was now at the beginning of his third year as pro-
praetor of Asia.
    b A vacancy in provincial government was of interest to the
praetors, one of whom might get the appointment.

388

CICERO'S LETTERS TO HIS BROTHER QUINTUS

BOOK I

I

CICERO TO QUINTUS [a]

Rome, end of 60 B.C.

I. Although I have no doubt that many a messen- 1
ger, and indeed rumour itself with its usual rapidity, is
likely to outstrip this letter, and that you are likely to
be told by others of the addition of a third year to my
longing for you, and to the period of your work, yet
I thought it right that I too should convey to you
the news of this annoying fact. For in my previous
letters, not in one, but several, though others had by
that time despaired of such a possibility, I still per-
severed in feeding you with the hope of quitting your
province at an early date, not only that I might keep
on cheering you as long as possible with an agreeable
expectation, but also because both the praetors and I
were making such strenuous efforts that I never lost
faith in the possibility of the arrangement.

As it is, since it has so happened that neither the 2
praetors [b] with all their influence, nor I with all my
zeal, have been able to do any good, it is indeed hard

389

no difficile non graviter id ferre ; sed tamen nostros
animos maximis in rebus et gerendis et sustinendis
exercitatos frangi et debilitari molestia non oportet.
Et quoniam ea molestissime ferre homines debent,
quae ipsorum culpa contracta sunt, est quiddam in
hac re mihi molestius ferendum, quam tibi. Factum
est enim mea culpa, contra quam tu mecum et proficiscens et per litteras egeras, ut priore anno non
succederetur. Quod ego, dum sociorum saluti con-
sulo, dum impudentiae nonnullorum negotiatorum
resisto, dum nostram gloriam tua virtute augeri
expeto, feci non sapienter, praesertim cum id com-
miserim, ut ille alter annus etiam tertium posset
3 adducere. Quod quoniam peccatum meum esse
confiteor, est sapientiae atque humanitatis tuae
curare et perficere, ut hoc, minus sapienter a me
provisum, diligentia tua corrigatur. Ac si te ipse
vehementius ad omnes partes bene audiendi excitaris,
non ut cum aliis, sed ut tecum iam ipse certes, si
omnem tuam mentem, curam, cogitationem ad ex-
cellentem omnibus in rebus laudis cupiditatem in-
citaris, mihi crede, unus annus additus labori tuo,
multorum annorum laetitiam nobis, immo vero etiam
4 posteris nostris afferet. Quapropter hoc te primum
rogo, ne contrahas ac demittas animum, neve te
obrui, tamquam fluctu, sic magnitudine negoti
sinas, contraque erigas ac resistas sive etiam ultro

---

a The *socii* are the provincials, as opposed to the *cives*,
Romans dwelling in the province, such as *publicani* and
negotiatores.
  b Certain bankers, who out of private animosity opposed
the reappointment of Quintus, probably Paconius and
Tuscenius referred to in § 19.

not to resent it ; but, for all that, it is not right that
our minds, trained as they have been in the management and maintenance of affairs of the utmost importance, should be crushed and weakened by a mere
sense of annoyance. And since men ought to feel
most annoyed with what has been brought about by
their own fault, there is an element in this business
which should cause me more annoyance than you.
For it was entirely my fault—and you pleaded with
me against it both on your departure and subsequently by letter—that you were not given a successor
last year. And in that, in my anxiety to promote the
interests of the allies,[a] and to resist the shameless
policy of certain dealers,[b] and in my strong desire to
see our country's glory enhanced by your excellent
rule, I acted unwisely, especially since by my mistake
I made it possible for that second year to bring a
third also in its train.

And now that I admit that the error was mine, it 3
lies with you, in your wisdom and humanity, to see to
it and ensure that this lack of wise foresight on my
part is rectified by your careful administration. Indeed, if you rouse yourself in all earnestness to win
golden opinions in all quarters—not in order to rival
others, but to be henceforth your own rival—if you
direct your whole mind, your every care and thought,
into a predominating desire to be well spoken of in
every respect, then, take my word for it, one single
year added to your labours will bring us, and indeed
those who come after us also, many a year of joy.

For that reason I beg of you, first and foremost, not 4
to let your heart shrink or sink, and not to allow yourself to be overwhelmed, as by a wave, by the great-
ness of your task, but, on the contrary, to lift up your

occurras negotiis. Neque enim eiusmodi partem
reipublicae geris, in qua fortuna dominetur, sed in
qua plurimum ratio possit et diligentia. Quod si
tibi, bellum aliquod magnum et periculosum ad-
ministranti, prorogatum imperium viderem, tre-
merem animo, quod eodem tempore esse intellegerem
5 etiam fortunae potestatem in nos prorogatam. Nunc
vero ea pars tibi reipublicae commissa est, in qua aut
nullam, aut perexiguam partem fortuna tenet, et
quae mihi tota in tua virtute ac moderatione animi
posita esse videatur. Nullas, ut opinor, insidias
hostium, nullam proeli dimicationem, nullam de-
fectionem sociorum, nullam inopiam stipendi aut rei
frumentariae, nullam seditionem exercitus per-
timescimus, quae persaepe sapientissimis viris acciderunt, ut, quemadmodum gubernatores optimi vim
tempestatis, sic illi fortunae impetum superare non
possent. Tibi data est summa pax, summa tran-
quillitas ; ita tamen, ut ea dormientem gubernatorem
6 vel obruere, vigilantem etiam delectare possit. Con-
stat enim ea provincia primum ex eo genere sociorum,
quod est ex hominum omni genere humanissimum ;
deinde ex eo genere civium, qui aut, quod publicani
sunt, nos summa necessitudine attingunt, aut, quod
ita negotiantur, ut locupletes sint, nostri consulatus
beneficio se incolumes fortunas habere arbitrantur.

---

* See note *a* on § 2.

heart and to face, or even hurry forward to meet, your responsibilities. As a matter of fact, the department of the State you are administering is not one in which fortune plays a ruling part, but one in which a reasoned policy combined with assiduity carries the greatest power; whereas if I saw that the prolongation of your government happened during your management of some great and dangerous war, I should shudder in spirit because it would be evident to me that at the same time fortune's power over us had been prolonged.

As it is, however, you have been entrusted with a 5 department of the State in which fortune holds no part, or a very insignificant one, and which, it would seem to me, depends entirely upon your own virtue and self-control. We need fear, I take it, no ambuscades of enemies, no clash of swords in battle, no revolt of allies, no lack of tribute or corn-supply, no mutiny in the army,—evils which have befallen the wisest of men, so that, just as the best of helmsmen cannot defy the violence of a tempest, neither can they defy the assault of fortune. What has been granted you is perfect peace, perfect tranquillity, with the reservation, however, that such a calm can even overwhelm the helmsman if he sleeps, while it can give him positive pleasure if he keeps awake.

For your province consists, in the first place, of that 6 type of ally [a] which of all types of humanity is the most civilized; and secondly, of that type of citizen [a] who, either because they are *publicani*, are attached to us by the closest ties, or, because their trade is such that they have amassed riches, consider that the security of the fortunes they enjoy is due to the blessing of my consulship.

7 II. At enim inter hos ipsos exsistunt graves contro-
versiae, multae nascuntur iniuriae, magnae contentiones consequuntur. Quasi vero ego id putem,
non te aliquantum negoti sustinere. Intellego, permagnum esse negotium et maximi consili. Sed
memento, consili me hoc negotium esse magis aliquanto, quam fortunae, putare. Quid est enim
negoti, continere eos, quibus praesis, si te ipse con-
tineas? Id autem sit magnum et difficile ceteris,
sicut est difficillimum ; tibi et fuit hoc semper
facillimum, et vero esse debuit, cuius natura talis
est, ut etiam sine doctrina videatur moderata esse
potuisse : ea autem adhibita doctrina est, quae vel
vitiosissimam naturam excolere possit. Tu cum
pecuniae, cum voluptati, cum omnium rerum cupiditati resistes, ut facis, erit, credo,* periculum, ne
improbum negotiatorem, paullo cupidiorem publica-
num comprimere non possis! Nam Graeci quidem
sic te ita viventem intuebuntur, ut quemdam ex
annalium memoria, aut etiam de caelo divinum
8 hominem esse in provinciam delapsum putent. Atque haec nunc, non ut facias, sed ut te facere et
fecisse gaudeas, scribo. Praeclarum est enim, summo
cum imperio fuisse in Asia triennium, sic ut nullum
te signum, nulla pictura, nullum vas, nulla vestis,
nullum mancipium, nulla forma cuiusquam, nulla

---

* *Credo* marks the statement as ironical.

II. "Ah! but," it may be objected, "among these 7 very men serious disputes arise, numerous wrongs spring up, and great conflicts are the result." As though I supposed for a moment that you had not a lot of trouble on your shoulders! I fully understand that your trouble is very great, and calls for the soundest possible judgment. But remember that, in my opinion, this trouble of yours depends far more upon judgment than upon fortune. For what trouble is it to control those whom you rule, if you control yourself? For others, I grant, that may be a great and difficult thing to do, and it is indeed most difficult; but for you it has always been the easiest thing in the world, and indeed was bound to be so, since your nature is such that I think it would have been capable of self-restraint even without education; but you have had such an education as might well ennoble the most depraved nature. While you yourself still resist money, and pleasure, and every form of desire, as you do resist them, there will, I imagine,[a] be danger of your being unable to restrain some unscrupulous trader or some rather too rapacious tax-collector! For as to the Greeks, living as you do, they will so gaze upon you as to deem you someone celebrated in their own annals, or even think that a deified mortal has dropped down from heaven into their province.

And I write thus not to make you act, but to make 8 you rejoice that you are acting, and have acted, in this way. It is a glorious thought that you should have been three years in Asia in supreme command, and not been tempted by the offer of any statue, picture, plate, garment, or slave, by any fascination of human beauty, or any pecuniary proposals—

condicio pecuniae (quibus rebus abundat ista provincia) ab summa integritate continentiaque de-
9 duxerit. Quid autem reperiri tam eximium, aut
tam expetendum potest, quam istam virtutem,
moderationem animi, temperantiam, non latere in
tenebris, neque esse abditam, sed in luce Asiae, in
oculis clarissimae provinciae, atque in auribus omnium
gentium ac nationum esse positam ? non itineribus
tuis perterreri homines ? non sumptu exhauriri ?
non adventu commoveri ? esse, quocumque veneris,
et publice et privatim maximam laetitiam, cum urbs
custodem, non tyrannum, domus hospitem, non ex-
pilatorem, recepisse videatur ?

10   III. His autem in rebus iam te usus ipse profecto
erudivit, nequaquam satis esse ipsum hasce habere
virtutes, sed esse circumspiciendum diligenter, ut in
hac custodia provinciae non te unum, sed omnes
ministros imperi tui, sociis, et civibus, et reipublicae
praestare videare. Quamquam legatos habes eos,
qui ipsi per se habituri sint rationem dignitatis suae ;
de quibus honore, et dignitate, et aetate praestat
Tubero, quem ego arbitror, praesertim cum scribat
historiam, multos ex suis annalibus posse deligere,
quos velit et possit imitari ; Allienus autem noster
est cum animo et benevolentia, tum vero etiam
imitatione vivendi. Nam quid ego de Gratidio

---

a L. Aelius Tubero was highly esteemed for his literary
ability by Cicero, who refers to him in *Pro Plancio* as *neces-
sarius meus.*
396

temptations with which that province of yours abounds—to deviate from the path of strict integrity and sobriety of conduct.

But what can one find so excellent or so desirable 9 as that your virtue, your restraint of passion, and your self-control, should not lurk in the shadows or be hidden out of sight, but set in the light of Asia, before the eyes of a most distinguished province, to ring in the ears of all the nations and tribes of the earth ? That men are not trampled underfoot in your progresses, not drained by expenditure, not struck with panic at your approach ? That, wheresoever you come, there is an ecstasy of joy, both in public and in private, since it would seem that the city has taken unto herself no tyrant, but a guardian, the home no plunderer, but a guest ?

III. In these matters, however, experience itself 10 has by this time taught you that it is by no means sufficient to possess these virtues yourself, but that you must keep diligent watch around you so that in this guardianship of your province it may appear that you are responsible to the allies, the citizens, and the State, not for yourself alone, but for all the officials of your government. And yet you have as *legati* men who are likely to consider their reputation on their own account ; and of them, in rank, position, and age, Tubero [a] stands first ; and I imagine, especially as he writes history, that he can select many characters from his own annals whom he would wish and be able to emulate. Allienus [b] moreover is our good friend in spirit and friendly feeling as well as in his adaptation of himself to our rules of life. About

[b] A. Allienus, praetor in 49, and proconsul in Sicily in 46. *Fam.* viii. 78 and 79 are addressed to him.

dicam ? quem certo scio ita laborare de existimatione sua, ut propter amorem in nos fraternum etiam
11 de nostra laboret. Quaestorem habes, non tuo
iudicio delectum, sed eum, quem sors dedit. Hunc
oportet et sua sponte esse moderatum et tuis institutis ac praeceptis obtemperare. Quorum si quis
forte esset sordidior, ferres eatenus, quoad per se
neglegeret eas leges, quibus esset astrictus, non ut
ea potestate, quam tu ad dignitatem permisisses, ad
quaestum uteretur. Neque enim mihi sane placet,
praesertim cum hi mores tantum iam ad nimiam
lenitatem et ad ambitionem incubuerint, scrutari te
omnes sordes, excutere unum quemque eorum, sed,
quanta sit in quoque fides, tantum cuique committere. Atque inter hos, eos, quos tibi comites et
adiutores negotiorum publicorum dedit ipsa res-
publica, dumtaxat finibus his praestabis, quos ante
12 praescripsi. IV. Quos vero aut ex domesticis con-
victionibus aut ex necessariis apparitionibus tecum
esse voluisti, qui quasi ex cohorte praetoris appellari
solent, horum non modo facta, sed etiam dicta omnia
praestanda nobis sunt. Sed habes eos tecum, quos
possis recte facientes facile diligere, minus con-

---

a M. Gratidius was a brother of Cicero's grandmother
Gratidia. If the Gratidius here mentioned was M. Gratidius's
grandson, he would be Cicero's cousin (*frater* is often used for
cousin).

b His name is unknown.

Gratidius[a] I need say nothing ; I am well assured that he is so anxious about his own reputation that, if only out of cousinly affection for us, he is anxious about ours. Your quaestor[b] is not a man of your own deliberate selection, but one assigned you by lot. He ought to be a man of instinctive self-control, and should also comply with your policy and instructions.

Among these men, should it happen that anyone could not show a clean sheet of conduct, you would put up with him so long as he defied the regulations which bound him in his private capacity only, and not to the extent of abusing for purposes of private lucre the powers you had vouchsafed him for the maintenance of his public position. For it does not at all commend itself to me (especially in view of the distinct bias of modern morality in favour of undue laxity of conduct, and even of self-seeking) that you should investigate every ugly charge, and turn every single one of the charged inside out ; no, but that you should apportion your confidence in every case to the trustworthiness of the man to whom you give it. And among all these you will be responsible for those whom the State itself has assigned to you as your *attachés* and assistants in public business, at least within the limits I have laid down above.

IV. As for those, however, whom you have chosen to be about you, either in your domestic *entourage* or on your train of personal attendants, generally spoken of as a sort of " praetor's retinue," in *their* case we have to be responsible not only for their every act, but for their every word. But you have with you the kind of men whom you may easily make friends of when they act aright, and very easily check when they show

399

sulentes existimationi tuae, facillime coercere : a
quibus, rudis cum esses, videtur potuisse tua liberalitas decipi ; nam ut quisque est vir optimus, ita
difficillime esse alios improbos suspicatur ; nunc vero
tertius hic annus habeat integritatem eamdem,
quam superiores, cautiorem etiam ac diligentiorem.

13 Sint aures tuae eae, quae id, quod audiunt, existi-
mentur audire, non in quas ficte et simulate quaestus
causa insusurretur. Sit anulus tuus non ut vas aliquod, sed tamquam ipse tu, non minister alienae voluntatis, sed testis tuae. Accensus sit eo etiam
numero, quo eum maiores nostri esse voluerunt ; qui
hoc non in benefici loco, sed in laboris ac muneris, non
temere nisi libertis suis deferebant, quibus illi quidem
non multo secus ac servis imperabant. Sit lictor
non suae, sed tuae lenitatis apparitor ; maioraque
praeferant fasces illi ac secures dignitatis insignia,
quam potestatis. Toti denique sit provinciae cognitum, tibi omnium, quibus praesis, salutem, liberos,
famam, fortunas esse carissimas. Denique haec
opinio sit, non modo iis, qui aliquid acceperint, sed
iis etiam, qui dederint, te inimicum (si id cognoveris)
futurum. Neque vero quisquam dabit, cum erit hoc
perspectum, nihil per eos, qui simulant se apud te

14 multum posse, abs te solere impetrari. Nec tamen

---

a The *accensus* was an official of low rank who attended
upon a consul, proconsul, or praetor, at Rome or abroad;
his duties were to summon parties to court, and maintain
order there. He was generally the freedman of the magistrate he served.

b This is a warning to Quintus against the undue ascendancy of his freedman Statius.

c Cicero alludes to the lictors' practice of taking bribes to
mitigate the severity of the punishment it was their duty to
inflict. Tyrrell.

too little consideration for your good name—men who might very likely have taken you in, when you were a mere novice, generous soul that you are (for the better a man is, the more difficult it is for him to sus- pect others of being unscrupulous), but, as it is, let the third year show the same standard of integrity as the preceding two, but even an increase in caution and in diligence.

Let your ears be such as are reputed to hear only **13** what they do hear, and not such as are open to false and interested whispers prompted by the hope of profit.   Let not your signet-ring be a sort of utensil, but, as it were, your very self—not the servant of another's will, but the witness of your own.   Let your beadle [a] hold the rank which he was intended to hold by our ancestors, who, regarding that post not as a lucrative sinecure but as one of work and duty, were slow to confer it upon any but their own freedmen, over whom they exercised much the same authority as over their slaves.[b]   Let your lictor be the dis- penser not of his own, but of your clemency,[c] and let the *fasces* and axes they carry before them be more the symbols of rank than of power.   In a word, let it be recognized by the whole province that the welfare, children, reputation, and fortunes of all whom you govern are most precious to you.   Finally, let it be the general impression that you will regard with dis- favour not only those who have taken a bribe, but also those who have given one, if ever you get to know of it.   And, as a matter of fact, there will be no giving of bribes when it is made perfectly clear that, as a rule, nothing is got out of you through the machinations of persons pretending to have great influence with you.

est haec oratio mea huiusmodi, ut te in tuos aut durum esse nimium, aut suspiciosum velim. Nam si quis est eorum, qui tibi bienni spatio numquam in suspicionem avaritiae venerit, (ut ego Caesium et Chaerippum et Labeonem et audio, et, quia cognovi, existimo,) nihil est, quod non et iis, et si quis est alius eiusdemmodi, et committi et credi rectissime putem. Sed si quis est, in quo iam offenderis, de quo aliquid senseris, huic nihil credideris, nullam 15 partem existimationis tuae commiseris. V. In provincia vero ipsa, si quem es nactus, qui in tuam familiaritatem penitus intrarit, qui nobis ante fuerit ignotus, huic quantum credendum sit, vide ; non quin possint multi esse provinciales viri boni, sed hoc sperare licet, iudicare periculosum est. Multis enim simulationum involucris tegitur, et quasi velis quibusdam obtenditur unius cuiusque natura ; frons, oculi, vultus persaepe mentiuntur, oratio vero saepissime. Quamobrem, qui potes reperire ex eo genere hominum, qui pecuniae cupiditate adducti careant his rebus omnibus, a quibus nos divulsi esse non possumus, te autem, alienum hominem, ament ex animo, ac non sui commodi causa simulent ? Mihi quidem permagnum videtur ; praesertim si iidem homines privatum non fere quemquam, praetores

---

^a *i.e.*, the delights of life and society in Rome.

And yet by this discourse I do not mean that I 14 would have you be either unduly harsh or suspicious in dealing with your subordinates. For if anyone of them in the course of two years has never given you reason to suspect him of rapacity (and I am not only told this, but, because I know them, believe it of Caesius and Chaerippus and Labeo), I should think that there is nothing which might not be most properly entrusted or confided to them, or anybody else of the same sort. But if there is anyone whom you have already found reason to suspect, or about whom you may have discovered something, put no confidence in that man, entrust him with no fraction of your reputation.

V. In the province itself, however, if you have 15 found anyone who has become thoroughly intimate with you without our having known him before, take care how far you give him your confidence ; not that many provincials may not be quite good men, but while we may hope so, it is dangerous to be positive. For there are many wrappings and pretences under which each individual's nature is concealed and overspread, so to speak, with curtains ; the brow, the eye, and the face very often lie, but speech most often of all. How, therefore, among that class of men who, tempted by their greed for money, are ready to dispense with all the amenities [a] from which *we* cannot tear ourselves, how, I ask, can you discover any who yet have a sincere affection for you, a mere stranger, and are not simply pretending to have it in order to gain their own ends ? I think you would find it extremely hard, especially when those same persons show affection for hardly anybody who is not in office, but are always at one in

semper omnes amant. Quo ex genere si quem forte
tui cognosti amantiorem (fieri enim potuit) quam
temporis, hunc vero ad tuorum numerum libenter
ascribito; sin autem id non perspicies, nullum erit
genus in familiaritate cavendum magis, propterea
quod et omnes vias pecuniae norunt, et omnia
pecuniae causa faciunt, et, quicum victuri non sunt,
16 eius existimationi consulere non curant. Atque
etiam e Graecis ipsis diligenter cavendae sunt quaedam familiaritates, praeter hominum perpaucorum,
si qui sunt vetere Graecia digni. Isti[1] vero fallaces
sunt permulti et leves, et diuturna servitute ad
nimiam assentationem eruditi; quos ego universos
adhiberi liberaliter, optimum quemque hospitio
amicitiaque coniungi dico oportere; nimiae familiaritates eorum neque tam fideles sunt, (non enim audent
adversari nostris voluntatibus,) et invident non nostris
17 solum, verum etiam suis. VI. Iam qui in eiusmodi
rebus, in quibus vereor etiam ne durior sim, cautus
esse velim ac diligens, quo me animo in servos esse
censes? quos quidem cum omnibus in locis, tum
praecipue in provinciis regere debemus. Quo de
genere multa praecipi possunt; sed hoc et brevis-
simum est, et facillime teneri potest, ut ita se gerant

---

[1] *Tyrrell*: sic MSS.

their affection for praetors. But if you happen to
have found any member of the class to be fonder of
you (and it might have occurred) than of your position at the moment, by all means gladly add him to
the list of your friends ; if however you are not quite
certain about it, there is no class of man you will have
to be more on your guard against in the matter of
intimacy, for the simple reason that they are up to all
the ways of making money, and stick at nothing to
make it, and have no consideration for the good name
of one with whom they are not going to spend their
lives.

And further among the Greeks themselves there are 16
certain intimacies against which you must be strictly
on your guard, except intimacy with the very few, if
any, who are worthy of ancient Greece. In your
province, however, there are a great many who are
deceitful and unstable, and trained by a long course
of servitude to show an excess of sycophancy. What
I say is, that they should all of them be treated as
gentlemen, but that only the best of them should be
attached to you by ties of hospitality and friendship ;
unrestricted intimacies with them are not so much to
be trusted, for they dare not oppose our wishes, and
they are jealous not only of our countrymen, but even
of their own.

VI. And now, since in matters of this kind, in 17
which, though I would be merely cautious and careful, I am afraid I am somewhat too strict, what do
you suppose are my sentiments in regard to slaves ?
Well, it is our duty to keep them in hand everywhere,
but particularly in the provinces. In this connexion
a number of rules may be laid down, but the shortest
as well as the easiest to remember is this—let them

in istis Asiaticis itineribus, ut si iter Appia via
faceres ; neve interesse quidquam putent, utrum
Tralles an Formias venerint. At, si quis est ex
servis egregie fidelis, sit in domesticis rebus, et
privatis ; quae res ad officium imperi tui atque ad
aliquam partem reipublicae pertinebunt, de his rebus
ne quid attingat. Multa enim, quae recte committi
servis fidelibus possunt, tamen sermonis et vitupera-
18 tionis vitandae causa committenda non sunt. Sed,
nescio quo pacto, ad praecipiendi rationem delapsa
est oratio mea, cum id mihi propositum initio non
fuisset. Quid enim ei praecipiam, quem ego in hoc
praesertim genere intellegam prudentia non esse
inferiorem quam me, usu vero etiam superiorem ?
Sed tamen si ad ea, quae faceres, auctoritas accederet
mea, tibi ipsi illa putavi fore iucundiora. Quare sint
haec fundamenta dignitatis tuae, tua primum in-
tegritas et continentia ; deinde omnium, qui tecum
sunt, pudor ; delectus in familiaritatibus, et pro-
vincialium hominum et Graecorum, percautus et
diligens ; familiae gravis et constans disciplina.
19 Quae cum honesta sint in his privatis nostris quo-
tidianisque rationibus, in tanto imperio, tam de-
pravatis moribus, tam corruptrice provincia, divina
videantur necesse est. Haec institutio atque haec

---

^a A commercial town of Lydia in Asia Minor, used here of
any " out-of-the-way " foreign place, as in Juv. i. 3. 70 (" hic
Trallibus aut Alabandis ").
^b See note a on § 2.

conduct themselves on your progresses in Asia exactly as if they were travelling by the Appian Way, and don't let them imagine that it makes any difference whether their destination is Tralles [a] or Formiae. Of course, if anyone of your slaves stands above the rest in trustworthiness, employ him in your domestic and private affairs ; but with matters belonging to your office as governor, or with any State department, —with such matters don't let him meddle. For there are many things which may quite properly be entrusted to honest slaves, but which, for all that, in order to avoid tittle-tattle and fault-finding, should not be so entrusted.

But somehow or other my discourse has dropped 18 into a scheme of instruction, though that is not what I had in view when I began. For why should I instruct one who, especially in this department, is, I well know, not inferior to myself in wisdom, and in experience my superior also ? But I thought, nevertheless, that if your actions had the additional ratification of my approval, you yourself would find a deeper satisfaction in them. Let these, therefore, be the foundations of your public position,—first of all, your own integrity and self-restraint ; secondly, the respectful treatment of those about you, an extremely cautious and careful choice, in the matter of intimacy, of both provincials [b] and Greeks, and a strict and consistent system of discipline in dealing with slaves.

Such characteristics are honourable even in our 19 private and daily business here at home ; in so important a command, where morals are so debased, and provincial life so corrupting, they must needs seem godlike. The establishment of such principles,

disciplina potest sustinere in rebus statuendis de-
cernendisque eam severitatem, qua tu in iis rebus
usus es, ex quibus nonnullas simultates cum magna
mea laetitia susceptas habemus. Nisi forte me
Paconi nescio cuius, hominis ne Graeci quidem, at
Mysii aut Phrygis potius, querellis moveri putas, aut
Tusceni, hominis furiosi ac sordidi, vocibus, cuius tu
ex impurissimis faucibus inhonestissimam cupiditatem
20 eripuisti summa cum aequitate. VII. Haec, et
cetera plena severitatis, quae statuisti in ista provincia, non facile sine summa integritate sustinere-
mus. Quare sit summa in iure dicundo severitas,
dummodo ea ne varietur gratia, sed conservetur
aequabilis. Sed tamen parvi refert abs te ipso ius
dici aequabiliter et diligenter, nisi idem ab iis fiet,
quibus tu eius muneris aliquam partem concesseris.
Ac mihi quidem videtur non sane magna varietas
esse negotiorum in administranda Asia, sed ea tota
iurisdictione maxime sustineri. In qua scientiae
praesertim provincialis ratio ipsa expedita est ; constantia est adhibenda et gravitas, quae resistat non
21 solum gratiae, verum etiam suspicioni. Adiungenda
etiam est facilitas in audiendo, lenitas in decernendo,
in satisfaciendo ac disputando diligentia. His rebus
nuper C. Octavius iucundissimus fuit, apud quem

---

[a] See note *b* on § 2.
[b] The father of Augustus, now praetor in Macedonia, but
the above passage refers to what he did when praetor at Rome
before he left for Macedonia.
408

and such discipline, may well justify that severity in the settlement and decision of affairs which you yourself have practised in certain matters, in consequence of which we have incurred several personal animosities with no little happiness to myself,—unless of course you imagine that I pay any heed to the complaints of some Paconius [a] or other, a fellow who is not even a Greek, but more of a Mysian or Phrygian, or to the ejaculations of Tuscenius,[a] a crazy fellow of the baser sort, from whose disgustingly filthy jaws you snatched the prey of his most discreditable cupidity ; and you were absolutely right.

VII. These and all the other precedents of notable 20 severity you have established in your province we should not easily justify except by the most perfect probity. For that reason be as severe as you please in administering justice, provided that your severity is not varied by partiality, but kept on the same level of consistency. However, it is of little importance that your own administration of justice is consistent and careful, unless it be so administered by those also to whom you have yielded any portion of that duty. And indeed it seems to me that there is no great variety of transactions in the government of Asia, but that the entire government mainly depends upon the administration of justice ; and, being thus limited, the theory of government itself, especially in the provinces, presents no difficulty ; you only need show such consistency and firmness as to withstand not only favouritism, but the very suspicion of it.

In addition to this there must be civility in hearing, 21 clemency in deciding, a case, and careful discrimination in the satisfactory settlement of disputes. It was by acting thus that C. Octavius [b] lately made himself

primum[1] lictor quievit, tacuit accensus, quoties quisque voluit, dixit, et quam voluit diu. Quibus ille rebus fortasse nimis lenis videretur, nisi haec lenitas illam severitatem tueretur. Cogebantur Sullani homines, quae per vim et metum abstulerant, reddere. Qui in magistratibus iniuriose decreverant, eodem ipsis privatis erat iure parendum. Haec illius severitas acerba videretur, nisi multis condimentis 22 humanitatis mitigaretur. Quod si haec lenitas grata Romae est, ubi tanta arrogantia est, tam immoderata libertas, tam infinita hominum licentia, denique tot magistratus, tot auxilia, tanta vis populi, tanta senatus auctoritas, quam iucunda tandem praetoris comitas in Asia potest esse, in qua tanta multitudo civium, tanta sociorum, tot urbes, tot civitates unius hominis nutum intuentur ? ubi nullum auxilium est, nulla conquestio, nullus senatus, nulla contio ? Quare cum semper[2] magni hominis est, et cum ipsa natura moderati, tum vero etiam doctrina atque optimarum artium studiis eruditi, sic se adhibere in tanta potestate, ut nulla alia potestas ab iis, quibus ipse 23 praesit, desideretur. VIII. Cyrus ille a Xenophonte non ad historiae fidem scriptus, sed ad effigiem iusti

---

[1] *Malaspina*: primus MSS.
[2] *Boot*: cum permagni *M*.

---

[a] *Sullani homines* or *Sullani possessores* was the regular term for the illegal proprietors of land confiscated by Sulla— men who had obtained possession of the land by buying it from the soldiers to whom it had been assigned, or encroached on any land unassigned ; for Sulla had confiscated more land than was necessary to satisfy the soldiers.

most popular ; it was in his court, for the first time, that the lictor made no fuss, and the beadle held his tongue, while everyone spoke as often as he pleased, and as long as he pleased. It is possible that by so doing he gave one the impression of being too gentle, were it not that this very gentleness served to counteract such an instance of severity as the following : certain "men of Sulla"[a] were compelled to restore what they had carried off by violence and intimidation, and those who, when in office, had passed unjust decrees, were themselves, when private citizens, obliged to bow to the same rulings. This severity on his part might seem a bitter pill to swallow, were it not coated with the honey of many a kindness.

But if this gentleness is popular at Rome, where such arrogance is to be found, such unrestricted liberty, such unbounded licence on every side, and in short, so many magistrates, so many sources of aid, such power in the people, such authority in the Senate, how welcome, I ask you, must the courteousness of a praetor be in Asia, where so vast a multitude of citizens and allies, so many cities and communities concentrate their gaze upon the nod of a single man ; where there is no succour for the oppressed, no facility for protest, no senate, no popular assembly ? It must, therefore, ever be the privilege of some great man, and a man not only instinctively self-controlled, but also refined by learning and the study of all that is best in the arts, so to conduct himself in the possession of so vast a power that the absence of any other power may never be regretted by his subjects.

VIII. The great Cyrus was portrayed by Xenophon not in accord with historical truth, but as a model of

imperii ; cuius summa gravitas ab illo philosopho
cum singulari comitate coniungitur ; (quos quidem
libros non sine causa noster ille Africanus de manibus
ponere non solebat ; nullum est enim praetermissum
in his officium diligentis et moderati imperi ;) eaque,
si sic coluit ille, qui privatus futurus numquam fuit,
quonam modo retinenda sunt iis, quibus imperium
ita datum est, ut redderent, et ab his legibus datum
24 est, ad quas revertendum est ? Ac mihi quidem
videntur huc omnia esse referenda iis, qui praesunt
aliis, ut ii, qui erunt eorum in imperio, sint quam
beatissimi ; quod tibi et esse antiquissimum, et ab
initio fuisse, ut primum Asiam attigisti, constante
fama atque omnium sermone celebratum est. Est
autem non modo eius, qui sociis et civibus, sed etiam
eius, qui servis, qui mutis pecudibus praesit, eorum,
25 quibus praesit, commodis utilitatique servire. Cuius
quidem generis constare inter omnes video abs te
summam adhiberi diligentiam ; nullum aes alienum
novum contrahi civitatibus ; vetere autem magno et
gravi multas abs te esse liberatas ; urbes complures,
dirutas ac paene desertas, (in quibus unam Ioniae
nobilissimam, alteram Cariae, Samum et Halicarnas-
sum,) per te esse recreatas ; nullas esse in oppidis

just government, and the impressive dignity of his character is combined in that philosopher's description of him with a matchless courtesy ; and indeed it was not without reason that our great Africanus did not often put those books out of his hands, for there is no duty belonging to a painstaking and fair-minded form of government that is omitted in them. And if Cyrus, destined as he was never to be a private citizen, so assiduously cultivated those qualities, how carefully, I ask, should they be preserved by those to whom supreme power is only given on the condition that it must be surrendered, and given too by those very laws to the observance of which those rulers must return ?

And my personal opinion is, that those who govern 24 others must gauge their every act by this one test— the greatest possible happiness of the governed ; and that this principle is and has been from the beginning, from the moment you set foot in Asia, of primary importance in your eyes is a fact bruited abroad by unvarying report and the conversation of all. And indeed it is the duty not only of one who governs allies and citizens, but also of one who governs slaves and dumb animals, to be himself a slave to the interests and well-being of those he governs.

And in this respect I see that there is universal 25 agreement as to the extraordinary pains you are taking ; I see that no new debt is being contracted to burden the states, whereas many of them have been relieved by you of a big and heavy debt of long standing ; that several cities, dismantled and almost deserted (one of them the most famous city in Ionia, the other in Caria—Samos and Halicarnassus) have been rebuilt through your instrumentality ; that

413

seditiones, nullas discordias ; provideri abs te, ut
civitates optimatium consiliis administrentur ; sublata Mysiae latrocinia ; caedes multis locis repressas ;
pacem tota provincia constitutam ; neque solum illa
itinerum atque agrorum, sed multo etiam plura et
maiora oppidorum et fanorum furta et latrocinia esse
depulsa ; remotam a fama et a fortunis et ab otio
locupletum illam acerbissimam ministram praetorum
avaritiae, calumniam : sumptus et tributa civitatum
ab omnibus, qui earum civitatum fines incolant,
tolerari aequabiliter ; facillimos esse aditus ad te ;
patere aures tuas querellis omnium, nullius inopiam
ac solitudinem, non modo illo populari accessu ac
tribunali, sed ne domo quidem et cubiculo esse
exclusam ; tuo toto denique imperio nihil acerbum
esse, nihil crudele, atque omnia plena clementiae,
mansuetudinis, humanitatis.

26   IX. Quantum vero illud est beneficium tuum, quod
iniquo et gravi vectigali aedilicio, magnis nostris
simultatibus, Asiam liberasti ! Enimvero, si unus
homo nobilis queritur palam, te, quod edixeris, NE
AD LUDOS PECUNIAE DECERNERENTUR, HS cc. sibi eri-
puisse, quanta tandem pecunia penderetur, si om-

---

^a *i.e.*, taxation imposed by the aediles to defray the expenses
of the games.

there are no insurrections, no civil discords in the towns ; that you are providing for the government of the states by councils of their leading men ; that brigandage has been exterminated in Mysia, murder suppressed in various places, and peace established throughout the province ; that thefts and robberies, not only those on the highways and in the country, but also those (and they are far more frequent and serious) in towns and temples, have been effectually checked ; that the good name, the possessions, and the peace of mind of the rich has been delivered from that most pernicious instrument of praetorian greed— prosecution on a false charge ; that the incidence of expenditure and taxation in the states bears in equal proportion upon all those who dwell within the boundaries of those states ; that it is the easiest thing in the world to get access to you ; that your ears are open to the complaints of all ; that no man's lack of means or of friends has ever shut him out, nor ever will, from approaching you, not only in public and on the tribunal, but even in your very house and bed-chamber ; in short, that in the whole sphere of your command there is nothing harsh, nothing brutal, and, look where we will, we see nothing but clemency, gentleness, and kindness of heart.

IX. But what am I to say of the service you have **26** done us in freeing Asia from the heavy and iniquitous tribute imposed by the aediles,[a] though it cost us some bitter animosities ! For to speak plainly, if a single man of noble rank complains without any concealment that by your edict, " *that no sums of money should be voted for the games,*" you actually robbed him of 200,000 sesterces, how much money, I should like to know, would be paid if a grant were made to the

nium nomine, quicumque Romae ludos facerent, quod erat iam institutum, erogaretur? Quamquam has querellas hominum nostrorum illo consilio oppressimus, quod in Asia nescio quo modo, Romae quidem non mediocri cum admiratione laudatur, quod, cum ad templum monumentumque nostrum civitates pecunias decrevissent; cumque id et pro magnis meis meritis, et pro tuis maximis beneficiis summa sua voluntate fecissent, nominatimque lex exciperet, UT AD TEMPLUM MONUMENTUMQUE CAPERE LICERET; cumque id, quod dabatur, non esset interiturum, sed in ornamentis templi futurum, ut non mihi potius, quam populo Romano ac dis immortalibus datum videretur; tamen id, in quo erat dignitas, erat lex, erat eorum, qui faciebant, voluntas, accipiendum non putavi, cum aliis de causis, tum etiam, ut animo aequiore ferrent ii, quibus nec deberetur

27 nec liceret. Quapropter incumbe toto animo et studio omni in eam rationem, qua adhuc usus es, ut eos, quos tuae fidei potestatique senatus populusque Romanus commisit et credidit, diligas, et omni ratione tueare, ut esse quam beatissimos velis. Quod si te sors Afris aut Hispanis aut Gallis praefecisset, immanibus ac barbaris nationibus, tamen esset humanitatis tuae, consulere eorum commodis,

account of everyone who gave games at Rome—a
practice that had already become established ?   Anyhow our good friends had their complaints forced down
their throats by what I decided to do—a decision
which, however it is received in Asia, meets with no
little admiration and applause at Rome—I mean that
when the states had voted their contributions to a
temple and monument in our honour, and though
they had done so with the heartiest goodwill in view
of my great deserts and your even greater services,
and though the law contained a specific exception
legalizing " the receipt of funds for a temple and a
monument," and though the money offered was not
going to be thrown away, but was to be spent on the
ornamentation of a temple, so that the offer seemed
to be made not so much to myself as to the people of
Rome and the immortal gods,—in spite of all that I
did not consider that such an offer, justified as it was
by meritorious achievement, by the law, and by the
goodwill of those who made it, should after all be
accepted.   And I did this for other reasons, but
especially in order that those, in whose case such an
honour was neither due nor legal, might bear their
disappointment with greater resignation.

Therefore throw your whole heart and soul into the 27
policy you have hitherto adopted, treating as friends
those whom the Senate and people of Rome have
committed and entrusted to your honour and
authority, protecting them in every possible way, and
desiring their greatest possible happiness.   Why, if
the drawing of lots had given you the government of
the Africans or the Spaniards or the Gauls, uncouth
and barbarous nations, it would still be incumbent
upon a man of your humane character to study their

417

et utilitati salutique servire. Cum vero ei generi
hominum praesimus, non modo in quo ipsa sit, sed
etiam a quo ad alios pervenisse putetur humanitas,
certe iis eam potissimum tribuere debemus, a quibus
28 accepimus. Non enim me hoc iam dicere pudebit,
praesertim in ea vita atque iis rebus gestis, in quibus
non potest residere inertiae aut levitatis ulla suspicio, nos ea, quae consecuti sumus, his studiis et
artibus esse adeptos, quae sint nobis Graeciae monumentis disciplinisque traditae. Quare praeter communem fidem, quae omnibus debetur, praeterea nos
isti hominum generi praecipue debere videmur, ut,
quorum praeceptis eruditi simus, apud eos ipsos,
29 quod ab iis didicerimus, velimus expromere. X. Atque ille quidem princeps ingeni et doctrinae, Plato,
tum denique fore beatas respublicas putavit, si aut
docti ac sapientes homines eas regere coepissent,
aut, qui regerent, omne suum studium in doctrina
ac sapientia collocassent. Hanc coniunctionem videlicet potestatis ac sapientiae saluti censuit civitatibus esse posse. Quod fortasse aliquando universae
reipublicae nostrae, nunc quidem profecto isti provinciae contigit, ut is in ea summam potestatem
haberet, cui in doctrina, cui in virtute atque humanitate percipienda plurimum a pueritia studi fuisset et
30 temporis. Quare cura, ut hic annus, qui ad laborem
tuum accessit, idem ad salutem Asiae prorogatus
esse videatur. Quoniam in te retinendo fuit Asia

---

a Weaknesses not unknown in the Greek character, which
Cicero claims to have avoided.
b *De Rep.* 473 D.

interests, and consider their welfare and security. But seeing that we are governing that race of mankind in which not only do we find real civilization, but from which it is also supposed to have spread to others, it is at any rate our duty to bestow upon them, above all things, just that which they have bestowed upon us.

For at this point, especially as my life and achieve- 28 ments leave no room for the slightest suspicion of indolence or frivolity,[a] I shall not be ashamed to assert that I am indebted for whatever I have accomplished to the arts and studies transmitted to us in the records and philosophic teachings of Greece. And that is why, over and above the common honesty due to all, yes, over and above that, it seems to me that we owe a special debt to that race of men, and that is, among those very people whose precepts have rescued us from barbarism, to be the willing exponents of the lessons we have learnt from them.

X. And indeed Plato, that foremost of men in 29 genius and learning, thought that states would only then be prosperous when learned and wise men began to rule them, or when those who ruled them devoted all their mental energies to learning and wisdom.[b] He was evidently of opinion that this combination of power and wisdom would be the salvation of states — a blessing which some day perhaps will befall our whole Republic, as it has assuredly now befallen your province, in that it has as its supreme ruler one who had from his very boyhood devoted the maximum of zeal and time to absorbing the principles of philosophy, of virtue, and of philanthropy.

See to it, then, that this year which has been added 30 to your period of work may be regarded as having been a prolongation of welfare to Asia. Since Asia

felicior, quam nos in deducendo, perfice, ut laetitia
provinciae desiderium nostrum leniatur. Etenim si
in promerendo, ut tibi tanti honores haberentur,
quanti haud scio an nemini, fuisti omnium diligentissimus, multo maiorem in his honoribus tuendis ad-
31 hibere diligentiam debes. Et quidem de isto genere
honorum quid sentirem, scripsi ad te ante. Semper
eos putavi, si vulgares essent, viles, si temporis causa
constituerentur, leves ; si vero (id quod ita factum
est) meritis tuis tribuerentur, existimabam multam
tibi in his tuendis operam esse ponendam. Quare
quoniam in istis urbibus cum summo imperio et
potestate versaris, in quibus tuas virtutes consecratas
et in deorum numero collocatas vides, in omnibus
rebus, quas statues, quas decernes, quas ages, quid
tantis hominum opinionibus, tantis de te iudiciis,
tantis honoribus debeas, cogitabis. Id autem erit
eiusmodi, ut consulas omnibus, ut medeare incommodis hominum, provideas saluti, ut te parentem
32 Asiae et dici et haberi velis. XI. Atqui huic tuae
voluntati ac diligentiae difficultatem magnam afferunt
publicani ; quibus si adversamur, ordinem de nobis optime meritum et per nos cum republica coniunctum
et a nobis et a republica diiungemus ; sin autem

has been more successful in keeping her hold on you than I have in bringing you home, so manage matters that my own sense of loss may be lightened by the rejoicings of the province. For if, in earning the bestowal upon you of such honours as, I am inclined to think, have been bestowed upon no other, you have been the most assiduous of men, far greater is the assiduity you ought to display in justifying those honours.

And what I feel about honours of that sort I have **31** told you in previous letters ; if given indiscriminately, I have always thought them cheap ; if designed to meet some difficulty of the moment, paltry ; if on the other hand, as in this case, they were a tribute to your deserts, I have always thought that you were bound to take particular pains to justify them. Therefore, now that you are engaged in a position of supreme command and authority in cities where, as you see, your virtues are hallowed and held up as being nothing less than divine, well then, in all your decisions, decrees, and official acts, you will, I am sure, consider what you owe to the high opinions men have of you, to their flattering judgments about you, and to the distinguished honours conferred upon you. And what you owe is just this—to bear in mind the interests of all, to redress the ills of men, to provide for their welfare, and to make it your ambition to be not only entitled, but also esteemed, " the father of Asia."

XI. And yet to all your goodwill and devotion to **32** duty there is a serious obstacle in the *publicani*; if we oppose them, we shall alienate from ourselves and from the commonwealth an order that has deserved extremely well of us, and been brought through our instrumentality into close association with the

omnibus in rebus obsequemur, funditus eos perire
patiemur, quorum non modo saluti, sed etiam commodis consulere debemus. Haec est una (si vere
cogitare volumus) in toto imperio tuo difficultas.
Nam esse abstinentem, continere omnes cupiditates,
suos coercere, iuris aequabilem tenere rationem,
facilem se in rebus cognoscendis, in hominibus
audiendis admittendisque praebere, praeclarum
magis est, quam difficile. Non est enim positum in
labore aliquo, sed in quadam inductione animi atque
33 voluntate. Illa causa publicanorum quantam acerbitatem afferat sociis, intelleximus ex civibus, qui nuper
in portoriis Italiae tollendis, non tam de portorio,
quam de nonnullis iniuriis portitorum querebantur.
Quare non ignoro, quid sociis accidat in ultimis terris,
cum audierim in Italia querellas civium. Hic te ita
versari, ut et publicanis satisfacias, praesertim publicis male redemptis, ac socios perire non sinas,
divinae cuiusdam virtutis esse videtur, id est, tuae.
Ac primum Graecis, id quod acerbissimum est, quod
sunt vectigales, non ita acerbum videri debet, propterea quod sine imperio populi Romani, suis institutis,
per se ipsi ita fuerunt. Nomen autem publicani

---

^a By Q. Metellus Nepos.
^b Employed by the *publicani* to collect their dues.
^c The syndicate which had bought the right to farm the
taxes of Asia had made an excessive bid for them; indeed
Cicero tells Atticus that they actually "demanded a can-
cellation of the assignment" ("ut induceretur locatio postulaverunt"), *Att.* i. 17. 9.

commonwealth; and yet, if we yield to them in every-thing, we shall be acquiescing in the utter ruin of those whose security, and indeed whose interests, we are bound to protect. This is the one outstanding difficulty (if we would face the question honestly) in the whole sphere of your command. For as to one's being unselfish, curbing all one's passions, keeping one's staff in check, maintaining a consistently uni-form policy in legal proceedings, conducting oneself with kindly courtesy in investigating cases and in giving audience to suitors and not shutting one's door to them,—all that is magnificent rather than difficult to do ; for it depends not upon any strenuous exer-tion, but upon making up one's mind, and setting one's will in a certain direction.

What bitterness of feeling this question of the *publicani* causes the allies we have gathered from those citizens who recently, on the abolition of port-dues in Italy,[a] complained not so much of that duty itself as of certain malpractices on the part of the custom-officers.[b] I therefore know pretty well what happens to allies in distant lands from the complaints I have heard from citizens in Italy. So to conduct yourself in this connexion as to satisfy the *publicani*, especially when they took over the collection of taxes at a loss,[c] and at the same time not to permit the ruin of the allies, seems to demand a sort of divine ex-cellence—in other words, an excellence such as yours. Let us take the Greeks first ; their greatest grievance is that they are subject to taxation ; but they should not regard that as so very much of a grievance, for the simple reason that they put themselves in that position of their own free will by their own enactment, quite apart from the rule of the Roman people. More-

aspernari non possunt, qui pendere ipsi vectigal sine publicano non potuerunt, quod his aequaliter Sulla descripserat. Non esse autem leniores in exigendis vectigalibus Graecos, quam nostros publicanos, hinc intellegi potest, quod Caunii nuper, omnesque ex insulis, quae erant ab Sulla Rhodiis attributae, confugerunt ad senatum, nobis ut potius vectigal, quam Rhodiis penderent. Quare nomen publicani neque ii debent horrere, qui semper vectigales fuerunt, neque ii aspernari, qui per se pendere vectigal non potuerunt, neque ii recusare, qui postulaverunt.

34 Simul et illud Asia cogitet, nullam a se neque belli externi, neque discordiarum domesticarum calamitatem abfuturam fuisse, si hoc imperio non teneretur. Id autem imperium cum retineri sine vectigalibus nullo modo possit, aequo animo parte aliqua suorum fructuum pacem sibi sempiternam redimat atque otium.

35 XII. Quod si genus ipsum et nomen publicani non iniquo animo sustinebunt, poterunt iis, consilio et prudentia tua, reliqua videri mitiora. Possunt in pactionibus faciendis non legem spectare censoriam, sed potius commoditatem conficiendi negoti et liberationem molestiae. Potes etiam tu id facere, quod

---

a Caunus was one of the chief cities of Caria, on its south coast, founded by the Cretans, but made subject to the Rhodians in 300 B.C. It was unhealthily situated, but famous for its dried figs.

b These words are strikingly applicable to India under British rule.

c The provincials might make special arrangements, not in strict accord with the censorian law, with the *publicani*; they might, for instance, substitute an immediate payment of the tax for that enjoined by the law, and thereby facilitate business, and escape the constant dunning of the tax-farmers. Tyrrell.

over they cannot afford to disdain the name of *publicanus*, since without the aid of that *publicanus* they themselves could never have paid the assessment imposed by Sulla as a poll-tax on all alike. But that the Greek collectors are no more gentle in enforcing the payment of taxes than our own *publicani* may be inferred from the fact that the Caunians [a] and all the islands that had been made tributary by Sulla to the Rhodians quite recently fled for protection to our Senate, begging that they might pay to us rather than to the Rhodians. It follows, therefore, that neither ought those who have always been subject to the tax to shudder at the name of a *publicanus*, nor those to disdain it who have been unable to pay the tax by themselves, nor those to reject his services who have applied for them.

Let Asia at the same time bear this in mind, that 34 were she not under our government, there is no disaster in the way of either foreign war or intestine discords which she would have been likely to escape.[b] Seeing, however, that such government cannot possibly be maintained without taxes, she should not resent having to pay for perpetual peace and tranquillity with some portion at least of what her soil produces.

XII. If they will but accept without resentment 35 the mere existence of such a class, and the name *publicanus*, all else, owing to your counsel and wisdom, may possibly seem to them less oppressive. They have the power in making agreements not to regard the *lex censoria* so much as convenience in the settlement of the business and freeing themselves from annoyance.[c] You too are able to do what you

425

et fecisti egregie et facis, ut commemores, quanta
sit in publicanis dignitas, quantum nos illi ordini
debeamus, ut remoto imperio ac vi potestatis et
fascium publicanos cum Graecis gratia atque auctoritate coniungas, et ab iis, de quibus optime tu meritus
es, et qui tibi omnia debent, hoc petas, ut facilitate sua nos eam necessitudinem, quae est nobis
cum publicanis, obtinere et conservare patiantur.
36 Sed quid ego te haec hortor, quae tu non modo
facere potes tua sponte sine cuiusquam praeceptis,
sed etiam magna iam ex parte perfecisti ? Non
enim desistunt nobis agere quotidie gratias hone-
stissimae et maximae societates ; quod quidem mihi
idcirco iucundius est, quod idem faciunt Graeci.
Difficile est autem, ea, quae commodis, utilitate et
prope natura diversa sunt, voluntate coniungere. At
ea quidem, quae supra scripta sunt, non ut te insti-
tuerem, scripsi, (neque enim prudentia tua cuiusquam praecepta desiderat,) sed me in scribendo
commemoratio tuae virtutis delectavit ; quamquam
in his litteris longior fui, quam aut vellem, aut quam
37 me putavi fore. XIII. Unum est, quod tibi ego
praecipere non desinam, neque te patiar (quantum
in me erit) cum exceptione laudari. Omnes enim,

---

* *i.e.*, of *publicani*.

have done, and are doing, in the most admirable way,—you can remind everybody of the high responsibilites imposed upon the *publicani*, and our own great indebtedness to that order, so that, waiving your official command and the might of your power with all its symbols, you may unite the *publicani* with the Greeks by means of the regard and respect they have for you personally, and entreat those Greeks whom you have so admirably served, and who owe you everything, to allow us, by showing a compliant temper, to maintain and preserve the intimate connexion which already subsists between us and the *publicani*.

But why am I thus urging you to do what you can **36** not only do on your own initiative without anybody's instructing you, but have also to a large extent succeeded in doing ? For the most honourable and important companies *a* never cease expressing their gratitude to me day after day ; and that gives me all the more pleasure because the Greeks do the same. And it is no easy task to harmonize in mutual goodwill elements in respect of interests and expediency, and indeed almost intrinsically, irreconcilable.

All, however, that I have written above I have not written for the purpose of instructing you—for your good sense needs no schooling by anybody—but the rehearsal of your virtues in writing has been a pleasure to me, though I have certainly been more prolix in this letter than I could have wished to be, or ever thought I should be.

XIII. There is one lesson I shall never cease to **37** impress upon you, and (so far as in me lies) I am not going to allow your praises to be qualified by a single reservation. The fact is that all who come from your

qui istinc veniunt, ita de tua virtute, integritate,
humanitate commemorant, ut in tuis summis laudibus
excipiant unam iracundiam.   Quod vitium cum in
hac privata quotidianaque vita levis esse animi atque
infirmi videtur, tum vero nihil est tam deforme,
quam ad summum imperium etiam acerbitatem
naturae adiungere. Quare illud non suscipiam, ut,
quae de iracundia dici solent a doctissimis hominibus,
ea tibi nunc exponam, cum et nimis longus esse
nolim, et ex multorum scriptis ea facile possis cognoscere ; illud, quod est epistulae proprium, ut is,
ad quem scribitur, de iis rebus, quas ignorat, certior
38 fiat, praetermittendum esse non puto.   Sic ad nos
omnes fere deferunt, nihil, cum absit iracundia, te
fieri posse iucundius ; sed cum te alicuius im-
probitas perversitasque commoverit, sic te animo
incitari, ut ab omnibus tua desideretur humanitas.
Quare quoniam in eam rationem vitae nos non tam
cupiditas quaedam gloriae, quam res ipsa ac fortuna
deduxit, ut sempiternus sermo hominum de nobis
futurus sit, caveamus, quantum efficere et consequi
possumus, ut ne quod in nobis insigne vitium fuisse
dicatur. Neque ego hoc nunc contendo, quod
fortasse cum in omni natura, tum iam in nostra
aetate difficile est, mutare animum et, si quid est
penitus insitum moribus, id subito evellere ; sed te
illud admoneo, ut, si hoc plane vitare non potes,
quod ante occupatur animus ab iracundia, quam pro-

province, while they dwell upon your virtues, your integrity, and your kindliness, do make one reservation, and that is your irascibility. Now not only does that failing seem to betray a capricious and feeble mind, in this private and everyday life of ours, but there is nothing so repulsive as this intrusion into supreme command of acerbity of temper. I shall not therefore take upon myself to lay before you now the repeated utterances of the greatest philosophers on the subject of irascibility, as I should not like to be tedious, and you can easily discover them in many writers ; but the special purpose of a letter—the enlightenment of the recipient on matters of which he has no knowledge—that purpose, I think, should not be overlooked.

Well, what practically everybody reports of you is 38 this—that, as long as you keep your temper, they find you the pleasantest person in the world ; but when you are upset by some fellow's rascality or wrong-headedness, you become so exasperated that everybody sighs for your vanished kindliness. Therefore, since we have been brought, not so much by any kind of desire for glory as by the mere force of circumstances and by fortune, into such a position of life that men are likely to talk about us for all time, let us be careful, to the best of our ability and power, to avoid its being said of us that we had any particularly notorious failing. And I am not now urging you to do what is perhaps difficult in human nature at any time, but especially at our time of life, and that is to change one's disposition and suddenly to pluck out some evil deeply ingrained in the character ; but this much advice I do give you, that if you cannot possibly avoid it, because anger takes possession of the mind

videre ratio potuit, ne occuparetur, ut te ante compares, quotidieque meditere, resistendum esse iracundiae ; cumque ea maxime animum moveat, tum
tibi esse diligentissime linguam continendam ; quae
quidem mihi virtus non interdum minor videtur,
quam omnino non irasci. Nam illud non solum est
gravitatis, sed nonnumquam etiam lentitudinis ;
moderari vero et animo et orationi, cum sis iratus,
aut etiam tacere et tenere in sua potestate motum
animi et dolorem, etsi non est perfectae sapientiae,
39 tamen est non mediocris ingeni. Atque in hoc
genere multo te esse iam commodiorem mitiorem-
que nuntiant. Nullae tuae vehementiores animi
concitationes, nulla maledicta ad nos, nullae contumeliae perferuntur ; quae cum abhorrent a litteris, ab humanitate, tum vero contraria sunt imperio
ac dignitati. Nam si implacabiles iracundiae sint,
summa est acerbitas ; sin autem exorabiles, summa
levitas ; quae tamen (ut in malis) acerbitati ante-
40 ponenda est. XIV. Sed quoniam primus annus
habuit de hac reprehensione plurimum sermonis,
credo propterea, quod tibi hominum iniuriae, quod
avaritiae, quod insolentia praeter opinionem accide-
bat et intolerabilis videbatur, secundus autem multo
lenior, quod et consuetudo et ratio et (ut ego arbitror)

before reason has been able to prevent its being so
possessed, in that case you should prepare yourself
beforehand, and reflect daily that what you have to
fight against is anger, and that when the mind is most
under its influence is just the time when you should be
most careful to bridle your tongue ; and indeed I
sometimes think that this is as great a virtue as not
feeling anger at all.   For the latter is not exclusively
a sign of strength of character, but also occasionally
of a phlegmatic habit of mind ; while to govern one's
mind and speech when angry, or even to hold one's
tongue and retain one's sway over mental perturba-
tion and resentment, that, though not a proof of
perfect wisdom, is at any rate a mark of no slight
natural ability.

And even in this respect they tell me that you are 39
now far more amenable and mild. I receive no reports
of any unduly violent outbursts of temper on your
part, of any abusive or insulting language, which, while
inconsistent with literary culture and refinement, are
utterly incompatible with a position of high command.
For where paroxysms of anger cannot be pacified, you
will there find extreme harshness ; where they yield
to remonstrances, an extremely changeable mind ;
though of course the latter, as a choice of evils, is to
be preferred to harshness.

XIV. But since it was in your first year that there 40
was the most talk about this subject of censure (I
suppose because the cases of injustice and rapacity
and the general insolence you came across took you
by surprise, and struck you as intolerable), while your
second year was much milder, because you improved
in tolerance and mildness as the result of getting used
to things and reasoning things out, and also, I do

meae quoque litterae te patientiorem lenioremque
fecerunt, tertius annus ita esse debet emendatus,
ut ne minimam quidem rem quisquam possit ullam
41 reprehendere. Ac iam hoc loco non hortatione
neque praeceptis, sed precibus tecum fraternis ago,
totum ut animum, curam, cogitationemque tuam
ponas in omnium laude undique colligenda. Quod si
in mediocri statu sermonis ac praedicationis nostrae
res essent, nihil abs te eximium, nihil praeter aliorum
consuetudinem postularetur. Nunc vero, propter
earum rerum, in quibus versati sumus, splendorem
et magnitudinem, nisi summam laudem ex ista
provincia assequimur, vix videmur summam vitu-
perationem posse vitare. Ea nostra ratio est, ut
omnes boni cum faveant, tum etiam a nobis omnem
diligentiam virtutemque et postulent et exspectent,
omnes autem improbi (quod cum his bellum suscepi-
mus sempiternum) vel minima re ad reprehendendum
42 contenti esse videantur. Quare quoniam eiusmodi
theatrum tuis virtutibus est datum, celebritate refer-
tissimum, magnitudine amplissimum, iudicio erudi-
tissimum, natura autem ita resonans, ut usque
Romam significationes vocesque referantur, contende,
quaeso, atque elabora, non modo ut his rebus dignus
fuisse, sed etiam ut illa omnia tuis artibus superasse
43 videare. XV. Et quoniam mihi casus urbanam in

believe, of reading my letters, well, then, your third year ought to be so free from blemish that nobody could possibly find the slightest fault with it.

And here I no longer plead with you by exhortation 41 and precept, but by beseeching you in brotherly fashion to devote all your mind, attention, and meditation to the winning of praise from every man's lips in every quarter. Now if our sphere of action were so limited as to elicit no more than ordinary talk and comment, nothing extraordinary, nothing beyond the common practice of others, would be demanded of you. As it is, however, owing to the splendour and magnitude of the affairs in which we have had a hand, if we fail to secure the highest praise for the administration of your province, it seems hardly possible for us to escape the bitterest vituperation. We are in such a position that all loyal men, though they support us, at the same time demand and expect of us every devotion to duty and every virtue, while all the disloyal on the other hand, since with them we are engaged in a war that knows no ending, seem to be satisfied with the most trivial pretext for censuring us.

Since, therefore, you have been assigned a theatre 42 such as this, crowded with such multitudes, so ample in its grandeur, so subtle in its criticism, and by nature possessed of such an echo that its manifestations of feeling and ejaculations reach Rome itself, for that reason, I implore you, struggle and strive with all your might, not merely to prove yourself to have been worthy of the task allotted to you, but also to prove that by the excellence of your administration you have surpassed all that has ever been achieved in Asia.

XV. And now that fortune has assigned the 43

magistratibus administrationem reipublicae, tibi pro-
vincialem dedit, si mea pars nemini cedit, fac ut
tua ceteros vincat. Simul et illud cogita, nos non
de reliqua et sperata gloria iam laborare, sed de
parta dimicare, quae quidem non tam expetenda
nobis fuit, quam tuenda est. Ac si mihi quidquam
esset abs te separatum, nihil amplius desiderarem
hoc statu, qui mihi iam partus est. Nunc vero res
sic sese habet, ut, nisi omnia tua facta atque dicta
nostris rebus istinc respondeant, ego me meis tantis
laboribus tantisque periculis, quorum tu omnium
particeps fuisti, nihil consecutum putem. Quod si,
ut amplissimum nomen consequeremur, unus praeter
ceteros adiuvisti, certe idem, ut id retineamus, praeter ceteros elaborabis. Non est tibi his solis utendum
existimationibus ac iudiciis, qui nunc sunt, hominum,
sed iis etiam, qui futuri sunt ; quamquam illorum erit
verius iudicium, obtrectatione et malevolentia libera-
44 tum. Denique illud etiam debes cogitare, non te
tibi soli gloriam quaerere ; quod si esset, tamen non
neglegeres, praesertim cum amplissimis monumentis
consecrare voluisses memoriam nominis tui ; sed
ea tibi est communicanda mecum, prodenda liberis
nostris. In qua cavendum est, ne, si neglegentior

---

a Though Cicero does not appear to have held any
particular public office this year, his influence in the Senate
and Forum was such that he might, had he so desired, have
joined the famous coalition of Pompey, Caesar, and
Crassus. See Chron. Sum. for 60 B.C.

434

management of public affairs to me among the magistrates in the city,[a] and to you in a province, if I yield to no man in the part I have to play, see to it that you excel all others in yours. At the same time bear in mind that we are not now striving after a glory that remains to be won, and that we but hope to win, but fighting for a glory already ours—a glory which it was not so much our object to gain in the past, as it is to defend in the present. And indeed, if I could possess anything apart from you, I should desire nothing greater than the position which I have already won. As it is, however, the case stands thus : unless your every act and word in your province is in exact accord with my achievements, I consider that, great as have been my labours and dangers (and you have shared them all), they have brought me no gain whatever. But if it was you who helped me more than any other living man to win a highly honoured name, you will surely also exert yourself more than others to enable me to preserve that name. You must not only take the opinion and judgments of the present generation, but those also of the generations to come ; though the verdict of the latter will be the more accurate because it has got rid of disparagement and malice.

Finally, you should also bear in mind that you are 44 not seeking glory for yourself alone—though even so you would not be regardless of it, especially since it has ever been your desire to hallow the memory of your name with the most magnificent memorials— but you have to share that glory with me, and bequeath it to our children. And in that connexion you must beware lest, by your undue heedlessness, you create the impression that you have not only been

fueris, non solum tibi parum consuluisse, sed etiam
45 tuis invidisse videaris. XVI. Atque haec non eo
dicuntur, ut te oratio mea dormientem excitasse, sed
potius, ut currentem incitasse videatur. Facies enim
perpetuo, quae fecisti, ut omnes aequitatem tuam,
temperantiam, severitatem integritatemque lauda‧
rent. Sed me quaedam tenet, propter singularem
amorem, infinita in te aviditas gloriae ; quamquam
illud existimo, cum iam tibi Asia, sicut uni cuique
sua domus, nota esse debeat, cum ad tuam summam
prudentiam tantus usus accesserit, nihil esse, quod
ad laudem attineat, quod non tu optime perspicias
et tibi non sine cuiusquam hortatione in mentem
veniat quotidie. Sed ego, qui, cum tua lego, te
audire, et qui, cum ad te scribo, tecum loqui videor,
idcirco et tua longissima quaque epistula maxime
delector, et ipse in scribendo saepe sum longior.
46 Illud te ad extremum et oro et hortor, ut, tamquam
poetae boni et actores industrii solent, sic tu in
extrema parte et conclusione muneris ac negoti tui
diligentissimus sis, ut hic tertius annus imperi tui,
tamquam tertius actus, perfectissimus atque orna-
tissimus fuisse videatur. Id facillime facies, si me
(cui semper uni magis, quam universis, placere

neglectful of your own interests, but also to have
cast an evil eye on those of your friends.

XVI. And I do not speak thus to make it appear 45
that my discourse has roused you from sleep, but
rather that it has spurred you on in your career.
For you will never cease to act as you have done, in
such a way as to win all men's praise for your fairness,
self-restraint, strictness, and integrity. Indeed, such
is my extraordinary affection for you that I am possessed by a sort of insatiable desire for your glory ;
and yet it is my belief that since Asia ought now to
be as well known to you as his own house is known
to every man, and since so long an experience has now
been added to the consummate wisdom you have
always shown, it is my belief, I say, that there is
nothing appertaining to a high reputation of which
you have not the clearest apprehension, and which
does not occur daily to your mind without the aid of
anybody's exhortation.

But I, who seem to be listening to you whenever
I read your communications, and to be talking to
you whenever I write to you, for that very reason
am more pleased the longer every letter of yours is,
and am myself often somewhat prolix in writing
to you.

I end my letter by imploring and urging you that 46
—after the fashion of good poets and hard-working
actors—you should take particular pains with the
last phase and *finale* of your office and employment ;
so that this third year of your rule may, like the third
act of a play, be recognized as having been the most
highly finished and brilliantly staged of the three.
You will do so most easily if you imagine that I, the
one man whose approbation you have ever desired

CICERO

voluisti) tecum semper esse putabis et omnibus iis
rebus, quas dices ac facies, interesse. Reliquum est,
ut te orem, ut valetudini tuae, si me et tuos omnes
valere vis, diligentissime servias. Vale.

II

M. CICERO Q. FRATRI S.

Romae, A.U.C. 695.

1 I. Statius ad me venit a. d. VIII. Kalend. Novembr.
Eius adventus, quod ita scripsisti, direptum iri te a
tuis, dum is abesset, molestus mihi fuit. Quod autem
exspectationem tui concursumque eum, qui erat
futurus, si una tecum decederet, neque antea visus
esset, sustulit, id mihi non incommode visum est
accidisse. Exhaustus enim est sermo hominum, et
multis emissae iam eiusmodi voces, ἀλλ' αἰεί τινα
φῶτα μέγαν, quae te absente confecta esse laetor.
2 Quod autem idcirco a te missus est, mihi ut se purga-
ret, id necesse minime fuit. Primum enim numquam ille mihi fuit suspectus ; neque ego, quae ad
te de illo scripsi, scripsi meo iudicio, sed cum ratio
salusque omnium nostrum, qui ad rempublicam
accedimus, non veritate solum, sed etiam fama
niteretur, sermones ad te aliorum semper, non mea

---

a Statius was Quintus's freedman and secretary, whom
people suspected of undue influence over him.

b ἀλλ' αἰεί τινα φῶτα μέγαν καὶ καλὸν ἐδέγμην | ἐνθάδ'
ἐλεύσεσθαι Hom. *Od.* ix. 513-14, "but ever it was some
mighty man and fair to look upon, whose arrival here I
awaited." They are the words of Polyphemus, who was
disappointed in Odysseus's appearance, as people at Rome
were in Statius's.

438

above that of the whole world, am always at your side, and taking part in everything you say or do.

It only remains for me to implore you, if you wish me and all your family to keep well, to take every possible care to keep well yourself.

II

CICERO TO HIS BROTHER QUINTUS

Rome, between October 25 and December 10, 59 B.C.

I. Statius [a] reached my house on October 25th. His 1 arrival made me uneasy, because you wrote that during his absence you would be robbed in every direction by your domestics. But his balking the general expectation of seeing you and the eager crowding that would certainly have occurred if he left the province in your company, and nobody had ever seen him before,—that I thought to be a very fortunate incident; for all the gossip about it has run dry, and many have now done with uttering this sort of remark, " But ever it was some mighty man," [b] and I am right glad that it is all over and done with in your absence.

But as for his having been sent by you to clear 2 himself in my eyes, there was not the least necessity for that; in the first place I never suspected him, and again what I wrote to you about him was not the expression of my own judgment; when however the interests and safety of all those of us who take part in public affairs depended not on truth alone, but also on all the talk about us, I always wrote you a full account of what others were saying, and not what I

439

iudicia perscripsi. Qui quidem quam frequentes
essent et quam graves, adventu suo Statius ipse
cognovit. Etenim intervenit nonnullorum querellis,
quae apud me de illo ipso habebantur ; et sentire
potuit, sermones iniquorum in suum potissimum
3 nomen erumpere. Quod autem me maxime movere
solebat, cum audiebam, illum plus apud te posse,
quam gravitas illius aetatis et imperi prudentia
postularet,—quam multos enim mecum egisse putas,
ut se Statio commendarem ? quam multa autem
ipsum ἀφελῶς mecum in sermone ita protulisse—" *Id
mihi non placuit*," " *monui*," " *suasi*," " *deterrui*" ?
Quibus in rebus etiamsi fidelitas summa est, (quod
prorsus credo, quoniam tu ita iudicas,) tamen species
ipsa tam gratiosi liberti aut servi dignitatem habere
nullam potest,—atque hoc sic habeto, (nihil enim
nec temere dicere, nec astute reticere debeo,)
materiam omnem sermonum eorum, qui de te detra-
here velint, Statium dedisse ; antea tantum intellegi
potuisse, iratos tuae severitati esse nonnullos ; hoc
manumisso, iratis, quod loquerentur, non defuisse.
4 II. Nunc respondebo ad eas epistulas, quas mihi
reddidit L. Caesius,(cui, quoniam ita te velle intellego,
nullo loco deero,) quarum altera est de Blaudeno
Zeuxide, quem scribis certissimum matricidam tibi a

---

a A town in Mysia.

felt myself; and how sinister and general that talk was, Statius on his arrival discovered for himself. In fact he came in when some people were complaining at my house about that very thing, and could not but feel that the malevolent were venting their obloquy upon himself in particular.

But as to what used to aggravate me most when 3 told that he had more influence with you than was called for by the weight of your years and your wisdom in government—why, how many persons do you suppose have pleaded with me to recommend them to Statius? and again, how often do you suppose he himself in conversation with me has used with the utmost *naïveté* such expressions as " *I could not agree to that,*" " *I lectured him,*" " *I argued with him,*" " *I cautioned him* " ? And although all this only proves how perfectly honest he is (and I quite believe it, since that is what you think), still the mere appearance of a freedman or slave possessing such influence cannot fail to be utterly undignified—and indeed you may take it from me (for it is my duty neither to say anything without weighing my words, nor to keep anything back in a crafty way) that all the material for the gossip of those who would disparage you has been furnished by Statius; that previously nothing more could be gathered than that certain persons were angry with you for your strictness, but that this man's manumission gave those who were angry plenty to talk about.

II. I shall now reply to the letters delivered to me 4 by L. Caesius (a man whom I shall never in any circumstances cease to serve, since I understood that to be your wish), one of which is about Zeuxis of Blaudus,[a] whom you say I particularly recommended to you, though he had most undoubtedly murdered

me intime commendari. Qua de re, et de hoc genere toto, ne forte me in Graecos tam ambitiosum factum esse mirere, pauca cognosce. Ego cum Graecorum querellas nimium valere sentirem, propter hominum ingenia ad fallendum parata, quoscumque de te queri audivi, quacumque potui ratione placavi. Primum Dionysopolitas, qui erant inimicissimi mei, lenivi; quorum principem Hermippum non solum sermone meo, sed etiam familiaritate devinxi. Ego Apameensem Hephaestum, ego levissimum hominem, Megaristum Antandrium, ego Niciam Smyrnaeum, ego nugas maximas omni mea comitate sum complexus, Nymphontem etiam Colophonium. Quae feci omnia, non quo me aut ii homines, aut tota natio delectaret; pertaesum est levitatis, assentationis, animorum non officiis, sed temporibus servientium.

5 Sed, ut ad Zeuxim revertar, cum is de M. Cascelli sermone secum habito, quae tu scribis, ea ipsa loqueretur, obstiti eius sermoni, et hominem in familiaritatem recepi. Tua autem quae fuerit cupiditas tanta, nescio, quod scribis cupiisse te, quoniam Smyrnae duo Mysos insuisses in culeum, simile in superiore parte provinciae edere exemplum severitatis tuae, et idcirco Zeuxim elicere omni ratione voluisse; quem adductum in iudicium fortasse dimitti

---

a The conversation with Cascellius had evidently been unfavourable to Quintus.

b Parricides or matricides, for whom the regular punishment was to be tied up in a sack with a dog, a cock, a snake, and an ape, and then cast into the sea or worried by wild beasts. Quintus wished to make an example of Zeuxis (*certissimus matricida*) in the same way.

his mother. About this, and about the whole subject generally, pray listen to a few words of explanation, lest you should happen to be surprised at my having become so ready to make up to the Greeks. Because I felt that the complaints of the Greeks were carrying undue weight, since that nation has a natural aptitude for deceit, I used every means in my power to pacify whoever of them I was told were complaining about you. First I mollified the Dionysopolitans who were most hostile ; and their chief man Hermippus I made my humble servant, not only by the way I talked to him, but also by making an intimate friend of him. I welcomed with open arms and with all the courtesy I could command Hephaestus of Apamea, that weather-cock of a fellow Megaristus of Antandros, Nicias of Smyrna, yes, and that most despicable of men also, Nymphon of Colophon. And all this I did, not because either those particular individuals or the nation as a whole had any attraction for me ; no, I was heartily sick of their fickleness, their fawning, their spirit of subservience not to duty but to the advantage of the moment.

But to go back to Zeuxis. When, in describing the 5 conversation M. Cascellius had had with him, he used the very words in your letter, I put a stop to his talking,[a] and admitted the fellow into familiarity. What you meant, however, by that extraordinarily strong desire of yours I have no idea—I mean your writing that, having already sewn up in a sack two Mysians at Smyrna,[b] you desired to give a similar example of your strict discipline in the more inland part of your province, and for that purpose had been anxious to inveigle Zeuxis into the open by every means in your power. Well, if he had been brought

non oportuerat ; conquiri vero, et elici blanditiis (ut tu scribis) ad iudicium, necesse non fuit ; eum praesertim hominem, quem ego et ex suis civibus, et ex multis aliis quotidie magis cognosco nobi-
6 liorem esse prope, quam civitatem suam. At enim Graecis solis indulgeo. Quid ? L. Caecilium nonne omni ratione placavi ? quem hominem ! qua ira ! quo spiritu ! Quem denique, praeter Tuscenium, cuius causa sanari non potest, non mitigavi ? Ecce supra caput homo levis ac sordidus, sed tamen equestri censu, Catienus ; etiam is lenietur. Cuius tu in patrem quod fuisti asperior, non reprehendo ; certo enim scio, te fecisse cum causa. Sed quid opus fuit eiusmodi litteris, quas ad ipsum misisti ? illum crucem sibi ipsum constituere, ex qua tu eum ante detraxisses ; te curaturum, in furno[1] ut combureretur, plaudente tota provincia. Quid vero ad C. Fabium, nescio quem ? (nam eam quoque epistulam T. Catienus circumgestat). Renuntiari tibi Licinium plagiarium cum suo pullo milvino tributa exigere ? Deinde rogas Fabium, ut et patrem et filium vivos comburat, si possit ; sin minus, ad te mittat, uti iudicio comburantur. Hae litterae abs te per iocum missae ad C. Fabium, si modo sunt tuae, cum leguntur,

---

[1] fumo *libri* : furno *Ursinus* : in furno *Wesenberg*.

[a] *Cf.* i. 1. 19.
[b] Quintus had previously forgiven Catienus for some offence or other.

up for trial, perhaps it would not have been right that he should be let off; but that there should be a hue and cry for the man, and that he should be inveigled with wheedling words into court (as you yourself put it), all that was quite unnecessary, especially in the case of one who, as I learn more clearly every day from his own fellow-citizens and many others, is of a nobler character perhaps than any of his community.

But, you will say, it is to the Greeks alone that 6 I show indulgence. What? Did I not take every means to pacify L. Caecilius? And what a man he is! How passionate, how presumptuous! In short, with the exception of Tuscenius [a] (an incurable case), whom did I fail to mollify? And just see, we have our sword of Damocles in the shape of that shifty, disreputable rascal, who is yet assessed as a knight, Catienus; I shall appease even him. For having been somewhat harsh in your treatment of his father I do not blame you; I am quite sure you did not act without some good reason. But what need was there for the sort of a letter that you sent the man himself? "That the man was putting up for himself the cross from which you yourself had pulled him down on a previous occasion [b]; that you would take care to have him burnt up in a furnace amid the applause of the whole province." Why again that letter to C. Fabius, whoever he may be (for that letter also is being carried about by T. Catienus), "that the kidnapper Licinius, assisted by his chick of the old kite, is reported to you as collecting taxes," and you go on to ask Fabius to burn both father and son alive, if he can; if he can't, to send them to you to be burnt by order of the court. That letter you sent by way of a jest to C. Fabius (if indeed it is yours) conveys to

445

7 invidiosam atrocitatem verborum habent. Ac, si
omnium mearum litterarum praecepta repetes, in-
telleges, nihil esse a me, nisi orationis acerbitatem et
iracundiam et, si forte, raro litterarum missarum in-
diligentiam reprehensam. Quibus quidem in rebus
si apud te plus auctoritas mea, quam tua sive natura
paullo acrior, sive quaedam dulcedo iracundiae, sive
dicendi sal facetiaeque valuissent, nihil sane esset,
quod nos poeniteret. Et mediocri me dolore putas
affici, cum audiam, qua sit existimatione Vergilius,
qua tuus vicinus C. Octavius? Nam si te interioribus
vicinis tuis, Ciliciensi et Syriaco, anteponis, valde
magni facis. Atque is dolor est, quod cum ii, quos
nominavi, te innocentia non vincant, vincunt tamen
artificio benevolentiae colligendae, qui neque Cyrum
Xenophontis neque Agesilaum noverint; quorum
regum summo in imperio nemo umquam verbum
ullum asperius audivit. Sed haec a principio tibi
8 praecipiens, quantum profecerim, non ignoro. III.
Nunc tamen decedens (id quod mihi iam facere
videris) relinque, quaeso, quam iucundissimam
memoriam tui. Successorem habes perblandum;
cetera valde illius adventu tua requirentur. In
litteris mittendis (ut saepe ad te scripsi) nimium te
exorabilem praebuisti. Tolle omnes, si potes, iniquas,

---

^a Cf. Hom. Il. xviii. 109 (χόλος) ὅστε πολὺ γλυκίων μέλιτος
καταλειβομένοιο, " (anger) which is far sweeter than dripping
honey."
^b Vergilius and C. Octavius were governors, as propraetors,
of Sicily and Macedonia respectively.
^c The governor of Syria was now Lentulus Marcellinus.
Who was the governor of Cilicia is not known.
^d Perhaps C. Fabius Adrianus, but it is uncertain.
^e i.e., "requisitionary letters," of which we have an ex-
ample in § 10.

the reader an impression of brutality of language that must prejudice your reputation.

Now if you recall the injunctions in any of my 7 letters, you will find that I have found fault with nothing but your bitter and angry way of talking, and possibly once or twice a lack of due caution in the letters you write. And as regards that, had my influence with you triumphed over your somewhat hasty nature, or a sort of pleasurable thrill[a] you find in anger, or your gift of pungent and sparkling speech, I should have no reason whatever for dissatisfaction. And do you suppose I am no more than slightly saddened when I hear of the high reputation of Vergilius, and of your neighbour C. Octavius[b]? If you only think yourself better than your neighbours in the interior, in Cilicia and Syria,[c] you have a mighty high standard! And what hurts me is this—that, though the men I have mentioned do not excel you in purity of conduct, they do excel you in the art of winning friends, though they know nothing about Xenophon's Cyrus, or his Agesilaus, kings from whose lips nobody ever heard a single harsh word, supreme sovereigns though they were.

But I have been lecturing you in this way from the beginning, and what effect it has had I am perfectly well aware.

III. None the less, now that you are quitting your 8 province, I entreat you to leave behind you (as indeed I think you are doing) as pleasant a memory of yourself as possible. You have as your successor[d] a man of very seductive manners; all your other characteristics will be greatly missed when he arrives. In sending out letters[e] you have shown yourself too easily worked upon. Destroy, if possible, any that

tolle inusitatas, tolle contrarias. Statius mihi nar-
ravit, scriptas ad te solere afferri, ab se legi, et, si
iniquae sint, fieri te certiorem ; antequam vero ipse
ad te venisset, nullum delectum litterarum fuisse ;
ex eo esse volumina selectarum epistularum, quae
9 reprehendi solerent. Hoc de genere nihil te nunc
quidem moneo. Sero est enim, ac scire potes, multa
me varie diligenterque monuisse. Illud tamen, quod
Theopompo mandavi, cum essem admonitus ab ipso,
vide per homines amantes tui, quod est facile, ut
haec genera tollantur epistularum, primum iniqua-
rum, deinde contrariarum, tum absurde et inusitate
scriptarum, postremo in aliquem contumeliosarum.
Atque ego haec tam esse quam audio, non puto, et
si sunt occupationibus tuis minus animadversa, nunc
perspice et purga. Legi epistulam, quam ipse
scripsisse Sulla nomenclator dictus est, non pro-
10 bandam ; legi nonnullas iracundas. Sed tempore
ipso de epistulis. Nam cum hanc paginam tenerem,
L. Flavius, praetor designatus, ad me venit, homo
mihi valde familiaris. Is mihi, te ad procuratores
suos litteras misisse, quae mihi visae sunt iniquissimae
—ne quid de bonis, quae L. Octavi Nasonis fuissent,
cui L. Flavius heres est, deminuerent ante quam

---

^a A *nomenclator* (" name-caller ") was a slave who attended
his master, especially when canvassing, to tell him the names
of those he met in the street.
^b Probably the tribune who had proposed an agrarian law
in 60. Tyrrell.

are inequitable, eccentric, or inconsistent with others. Statius told me that they were often brought to your house ready written, and that he read them and informed you if they contained anything inequitable ; but that before he entered your service there had never been any sifting of letters, with the result that there were volumes of despatches picked out which lent themselves to adverse criticism.

In this connexion I offer you no advice now ; it is 9 too late, and you must be aware that I have often advised you already in various ways and with much particularity. Still, to repeat the message I gave to Theopompus, acting on a hint he had himself given me, pray do see to it (and it is easy enough) that, through the agency of those who are really devoted to you, all letters of that kind are destroyed—first those that are inequitable, next those that are inconsistent with others, then those that are written in bad taste, and lastly those that are insulting to anyone. At the same time I do not believe that things are as bad as I am told they are ; and if owing to pressure of work you have not given enough attention to certain things, now is the time to look into them and give them a winnowing. I have, for instance, read a letter alleged to have been written by your *nomenclator* [a] Sulla on his own authority, and I cannot say I like it ; and I have read some that show temper. Indeed this is just the 10 moment to talk about your letters ; for while this very page was under my hand, who should call upon me but L. Flavius,[b] our praetor-elect, a man on very familiar terms with me. He told me you had sent his agents a letter which struck me as most unjust, instructing them not to take anything out of the property of the late L. Octavius Naso, whom L. Flavius succeeds as

C. Fundanio pecuniam solvissent. Itemque misisse
ad Apollonidenses, ne de bonis, quae Octavi fuissent,
deminui paterentur, priusquam Fundanio debitum
solutum esset. Haec mihi verisimilia non videntur.
Sunt enim a prudentia tua remotissima. Ne de-
minuat heres ? Quid si infitiatur ? Quid si omnino
non debetur ? Quid ? praetor solet iudicare deberi ?
Quid ? ego Fundanio non cupio ? non amicus sum ?
non misericordia moveor ? Nemo magis ; sed via
iuris eiusmodi est quibusdam in rebus, ut nihil sit
loci gratiae. Atque ita mihi dicebat Flavius scriptum
in ea epistula, quam tuam esse dicebat, te aut quasi
amicis tuis gratias acturum, aut quasi inimicis in-
11 commoda laturum. Quid multa ? ferebat graviter,
id vehementer mecum querebatur, orabatque, ut ad
te quam diligentissime scriberem ; quod facio, et te
prorsus vehementer etiam atque etiam rogo, ut et
procuratoribus Flavi remittas de deminuendo, et de
Apollonidensibus, ne quid praescribas, quod contra
Flavium sit, amplius, et Flavi causa et scilicet Pompei,
facies omnia. Nolo medius fidius ex tua iniuria in
illum tibi liberalem me videri ; sed id te oro, ut tu
ipse auctoritatem et monumentum aliquod decreti

---

heir, until they had paid a certain sum of money to
C. Fundanius ; and that you had written in similar
terms to the people of Apollonis,[a] telling them not to
allow any deduction to be made from the estate of the
late L. Octavius Naso until a debt had been paid to
Fundanius. This does not seem to me to be at all
likely ; it is so utterly foreign to your usual cautious
behaviour. Not let the heir touch the property !
What if he denies the debt ? What if there is no debt
at all ? What ? Is it usual for the praetor to decide
whether there is a debt or not ? What ? Am I not
kindly disposed to Fundanius ? Am I not his friend ?
Do I not sincerely sympathize with him ? Nobody
more so. Yes, but in certain matters the path of
justice is so strait that there is no room in it for
favouritism. And moreover Flavius told me that the
letter (and he declared that it was yours) was so
written as to leave no doubt that you would either
express your gratitude to them as your friends, or else
make things unpleasant for them as your enemies.

To cut the story short, he was much annoyed ; he 11
complained of it to me in bitter terms, and implored
me to write to you as impressively as possible ; I am
doing so, and I ask you again and again in all earnestness to make a concession to Flavius's agents about
impairing the property, and, as regards the people of
Apollonis, to give them no further instructions in a
sense unfavourable to Flavius ; and you will, I am
sure, do all you can in the interests of Flavius, and of
course of Pompey. On my word of honour, I have
no desire that you should think me generous to him
at the cost of any injustice on your part ; but this I
do ask of you, that you should yourself leave behind
you some official declaration, or some record, in the

aut litterarum tuarum relinquas, quod sit ad Flavi
rem et ad causam accommodatum. Fert enim
graviter homo, et mei observantissimus et sui iuris
dignitatisque retinens, se apud te neque amicitia
neque iure valuisse ; et, ut opinor, Flavi aliquando
rem et Pompeius et Caesar tibi commendarunt, et
ipse ad te scripserat Flavius, et ego certe. Quare
si ulla res est, quam tibi me faciendam petente putes,
haec ea sit. Si me amas, cura, elabora, perfice, ut
Flavius et tibi et mihi quam maximas gratias agat.
Hoc te ita rogo, ut maiore studio rogare non possim.

12 IV. Quod ad me de Hermia scribis, mihi mehercule
valde etiam molestum fuit. Litteras ad te parum
fraterne conscripseram : quas oratione Diodoti,
Luculli liberti, commotus, de pactione statim quod
audieram, iracundius scripseram et revocare cupie-
bam. Huic tu epistulae, non fraterne scriptae,
13 fraterne debes ignoscere. De Censorino, Antonio,
Cassiis, Scaevola, te ab his diligi (ut scribis) vehementer gaudeo. Cetera fuerunt in eadem epistula
graviora quam vellem, — ὀρθὰν τὰν ναῦν, et ἅπαξ
θανεῖν. Maiora ista erunt; meae obiurgationes fuerunt amoris plenissimae ; quaerunt[1] nonnulla, sed
tamen mediocria, et parva potius. Ego te numquam

---

[1] quae sunt mss. : quaerunt (?) *Tyrrell, which I have adopted.*

---

[a] Probably a slave of M. Cicero.
[b] The details of this incident are unknown.
[c] Quintus appears to have meant " that he would keep the ship (of office) on an even keel, or on a straight course, even if he had to sink her," *i.e.*, " he would go down with colours flying." The proverb was ἴσθι ὅτι ὀρθὰν τὴν ναῦν καταδύσω.
[d] Aeschylus, *P. V.* 769, has κρεῖσσον γὰρ εἰσάπαξ θανεῖν | ἢ τὰς ἁπάσας ἡμέρας πάσχειν κακῶς.
[e] This is probably the meaning of *erunt*; *cf.* Juv. i. 126 *quiescet*, " you will find she is reposing."

form of a decree or memorandum of your own, adapted to secure the interests of Flavius in this case. For the poor fellow, who is most attentive to me, but tenacious of his due rights and position, is bitterly pained that he has had no influence with you on the score of either friendship or justice ; and, if I am not mistaken, both Pompey and Caesar have at some time or other commended to your notice the interests of Flavius, and he had written to you himself, and so certainly had I. If there is anything, therefore, which you think you ought to do at my request, let it be this. As you love me, take every care and trouble in the matter, and ensure that Flavius has reason to express his most cordial thanks both to you and to me. I could make no request with greater earnestness than I do this.

IV. What you write to me about Hermias [a] has 12 been, I do assure you, a real vexation to me. I had written you a letter not quite in a brotherly spirit, upset as I was by what Diodotus, Lucullus's freedman, had told me, directly I had heard of the compact [b] ; I had written it in a fit of temper, and was anxious to recall it. Such a letter, though written in an unbrotherly way, you ought as a brother to forgive.

As to Censorinus, Antonius, the Cassii, and 13 Scaevola, I am highly delighted that they like you as you write they do. The rest of that same letter was in stronger terms than I could have wished,—for instance your " keeping the ship on an even keel " [c] and " dying once for all." [d] Those expressions, as you will find,[e] are needlessly vehement ; my reproaches teemed with affection ; they only ask you for a few things missing, and even they are of slight and indeed negligible importance. I should never have thought

ulla in re dignum minima reprehensione putassem,
cum te sanctissime gereres, nisi inimicos multos
haberemus. Quae ad te aliqua admonitione aut
obiurgatione scripsi, scripsi propter diligentiam
cautionis meae, in qua et maneo et manebo, et, idem
14 ut facias, non desistam rogare. Attalus Hypaepenus
mecum egit, ut se ne impedires, quo minus, quod
ad Q. Publici statuam decretum est, erogaretur;
quod ego te et rogo et admoneo, ne talis viri, tamque
nostri necessari, honorem minui per te aut impediri
velis. Praeterea Aesopi tragoedi, nostri familiaris,
Licinius servus, tibi notus, aufugit. Is Athenis apud
Patronem Epicureum pro libero fuit; inde in Asiam
venit. Postea Plato quidam Sardianus, Epicureus,
qui Athenis solet esse multum, et qui tum Athenis
fuerat, cum Licinius eo venisset, cum eum fugitivum
postea esse ex Aesopi litteris cognosset, hominem
comprehendit et in custodiam Ephesi tradidit; sed
in publicam, an in pistrinum, non satis ex litteris
eius intellegere potuimus. Tu, quoquo modo potest,
quoniam Ephesi est, hominem investiges velim, summaque diligentia . . .[1] vel tecum deducas. Noli spectare, quanti homo sit; parvi enim preti est, qui tam
nihil sit[2]; sed tanto dolore Aesopus est affectus propter
servi scelus et audaciam, ut nihil ei gratius facere

---

[1] *The lacuna may be filled by some such words as* vel Romam
mittas.
[2] *Orelli:* iam nihili sit *Nobbe.*

---

[a] Hypaepa was in Lydia.
[b] Probably a Roman knight, but we know nothing more
of him.
[c] Whom Horace calls " gravis Aesopus," *Ep.* ii. 1. 82.
[d] *Cf. Fam.* xiii. 1.
[e] Where slaves were forced to grind corn.

you deserved the smallest reproof in any respect, so absolutely blameless was your conduct, were it not that we had a multitude of enemies. Whatever I have written to you in a tone of admonition and reproof, that I have written on account of my anxious watchfulness, which I maintain and ever shall maintain, and I shall never cease urging you to do so also.

Attalus of Hypaepa[a] has pleaded with me that 14 you should not stand in his way, and prevent the money decreed for the statue of Q. Publicius[b] being paid out of the public treasury ; and as regards that, I both request and strongly advise you not to allow any honour paid to a man of his standing, and one so closely attached to us, to be impaired or obstructed as far as you are concerned.

There is, moreover, the case of Licinius, the slave of Aesopus, the tragic actor,[c] and my friend ; you know the fellow ; well, he has run away. He posed as a freedman at Athens with Patro, the Epicurean,[d] and came from there into Asia. Later on one Plato of Sardis, an Epicurean, who spends much of his time at Athens, and happened to be there when Licinius arrived, on learning by a subsequent letter from Aesopus that he was a runaway slave, had the fellow arrested and handed over into custody at Ephesus ; but whether it was into a public prison or a private mill[e] I could not quite gather from his letter. In whatever way it is possible, since he is now at Ephesus, I should be glad if you would trace the man and be particularly careful [either to send him to Rome] or to bring him home with you. Don't stop to consider what the fellow is worth ; he is of no great value, seeing that he is a mere nobody ; but Aesopus is so grieved at his slave's criminal audacity

15 possis, quam si illum per te recuperarit. V. Nunc
ea cognosce, quae maxime exoptas. Rempublicam
funditus amisimus ; adeo ut Cato, adulescens nullius
consili, sed tamen civis Romanus et Cato, vix vivus
effugerit ; quod, cum Gabinium de ambitu vellet
postulare, neque praetores diebus aliquot adiri
possent vel potestatem sui facerent, in contionem
ascendit et Pompeium privatus dictatorem appellavit.
Propius nihil est factum, quam ut occideretur. Ex
hoc, qui sit status totius reipublicae, videre potes.
16 Nostrae tamen causae non videntur homines defuturi.
Mirandum in modum profitentur, offerunt se, polli
centur. Equidem cum spe sum maxima, tum maiore
etiam animo ; spe, superiores fore nos ; animo, ut
in hac republica ne casum quidem ullum pertimescam ;
sed tamen res sic se habet.[1] Si diem nobis Clodius
dixerit, tota Italia concurret, ut multiplicata gloria
discedamus ; sin autem vi agere conabitur, spero
fore, studiis non solum amicorum, sed etiam alie-
norum, ut vi resistamus. Omnes et se et suos liberos,
amicos, clientes, libertos, servos, pecunias denique
suas pollicentur. Nostra antiqua manus bonorum
ardet studio nostri atque amore. Si qui antea aut
alieniores fuerant, aut languidiores, nunc horum

---

[1] *The arrangement of the sentence from* Equidem *to* habet
is Madvig's.

---

[a] C. Porcius Cato, tribune in 56.

that you could do him no greater favour than by helping him to get the man back.

V. And now let me tell you what you most desire 15 to know. The constitution is completely lost to us, —so much so that Cato,[a] a young man of no judgment, but still a citizen of Rome and a Cato, barely escaped with his life, because, when he wished to ask for leave to prosecute Gabinius for bribery, and the praetor could not be approached for several days, and granted no opportunity for an interview, he ascended the platform at a public meeting, and, in a private capacity, called Pompey a dictator. His assassination was the nearest thing that ever was. From this you may see the condition of the Republic as a whole.

And yet it seems that people are not likely to 16 desert our cause. It amazes me how they profess their loyalty, offer their services, and make promises. Indeed, high as is my hope, my courage is even higher—hope, that we shall be victorious ; courage, in that, as public affairs now stand, I have no fear of even any accident. Be that as it may, this is how the matter stands : If Clodius gives notice of an action against me, the whole of Italy will rally round me, so that we shall leave the court with tenfold glory ; but if he attempts to carry things through by violence, the enthusiasm not of friends alone, but also of strangers, leads me to hope that I may oppose force to force. All men are promising to put at my disposal themselves and their children, their friends, clients, freedmen, slaves, and, to end up with, their purses. My old group of supporters is fired with enthusiasm and affection for me. If there are any who before were inclined to be either unfriendly or lukewarm,

regum odio se cum bonis coniungunt. Pompeius
omnia pollicetur et Caesar; quibus ego ita credo, ut
nihil de mea comparatione deminuam. Tribuni
plebis designati sunt nobis amici. Consules se
optime ostendunt. Praetores habemus amicissimos
et acerrimos cives, Domitium, Nigidium, Memmium,
Lentulum; bonos etiam alios; sed hos singulares.
Quare magnum fac animum habeas et spem bonam.
De singulis tamen rebus, quae quotidie gerantur,
faciam te crebro certiorem.

III

M. CICERO S. D. Q. FRATRI

Thessalonicae, A.U.C. 696.

1 Mi frater, mi frater, mi frater, tune id veritus
es, ne ego iracundia aliqua adductus pueros ad te
sine litteris miserim? aut etiam ne te videre noluerim? Ego tibi irascerer? tibi ego possem irasci?
Scilicet; tu enim me afflixisti: tui me inimici, tua
me invidia, ac non ego te misere perdidi. Meus ille
laudatus consulatus mihi te, liberos, patriam, fortunas, tibi velim ne quid eripuerit, praeter unum me.
Sed certe a te mihi omnia semper honesta et iucunda
ceciderunt; a me tibi luctus meae calamitatis, metus

ᵃ *i.e.*, the consuls elect, L. Piso and A. Gabinius.
ᵇ *Praetores designatos*, the praetors elect.
ᵉ F. Nigidius Figulus. See note on *Fam.* iv. 13. 1.
ᵈ See note on *Fam.* xiii. 1. 1.

their hatred of these tyrants is such that they are now joining the ranks of the loyal. Pompey makes all sorts of promises, and so does Caesar ; but my belief in them does not go so far as to make me drop any of my own preparations. The tribunes designate are friendly to me ; the consuls [a] are showing up excellently. Among the praetors [b] I have some very warm friends and fellow-citizens of energy in Domitius, Nigidius,[c] Memmius,[d] and Lentulus, and other sound men also, but these stand out by themselves. So have a good heart and high hopes. Anyhow I shall inform you at frequent intervals of any such particular events as may occur from day to day.

III

CICERO TO QUINTUS ON HIS WAY TO ROME

Thessalonica, June 13, 58 B.C.

Brother mine, brother mine, brother mine, were you 1 really afraid that some fit of anger prompted me to send my men to you without a letter ? or that I did not want to see you ? *I* be angry with *you* ? *Could* I be angry with you ? Oh yes, to be sure, it was you who brought me low ; it was your enemies, your unpopularity, that ruined me, and not I (the misery of it !) that ruined you ! Yourself, my children, my country, my fortune,—that is what that highly-lauded consulship of mine has torn away from me ; from you I could wish that it has torn away nothing more than myself. At any rate in you I have always found all that is honourable and pleasant ; in me you have found grief for my degradation, apprehen-

459

tuae, desiderium, maeror, solitudo. Ego te videre
noluerim ? Immo vero me a te videri nolui. Non
enim vidisses fratrem tuum ; non eum, quem re-
liqueras ; non eum, quem noras ; non eum, quem
flens flentem, prosequentem proficiscens dimiseras ;
ne vestigium quidem eius, nec simulacrum, sed quam-
dam effigiem spirantis mortui. Atque utinam me
mortuum prius vidisses aut audisses ! utinam te non
solum vitae, sed etiam dignitatis meae superstitem
2 reliquissem ! Sed testor omnes deos, me hac una
voce a morte esse revocatum, quod omnes in mea
vita partem aliquam tuae vitae repositam esse dicebant. Quare peccavi scelerateque feci. Nam si
occidissem, mors ipsa meam pietatem amoremque
in te facile defenderet. Nunc commisi, ut vivo me
careres, vivo me aliis indigeres ; mea vox in domesticis periculis potissimum occideret, quae saepe alie-
nissimis praesidio fuisset. Nam quod ad te pueri sine
litteris venerunt, quoniam vides non fuisse iracundiam causam, certe pigritia fuit, et quaedam infinita
3 vis lacrimarum et dolorum. Haec ipsa me quo fletu
putas scripsisse ? Eodem, quo te legere certo scio.
An ego possum aut non cogitare aliquando de te,
aut umquam sine lacrimis cogitare ? Cum enim te

sion of your own, yearning, mourning, abandonment. *I* not want to see you ? No, it was rather that I did not want to be seen by you. For it is not your brother you would have seen, not him you had left behind, not him you knew, not him you parted from with tears on either side, when he escorted you on your setting forth ; no, not a trace or likeness of *him*, but something resembling one dead, but breathing. And would that you had seen me dead, or heard of my being so, before you went ! Would that I had left you behind me to look back not upon my life alone, but upon my prestige unimpaired !

But I call all the gods to witness that the one 2 argument which called me back from death was everybody's saying that no small portion of your life was vested in mine. And so I behaved like a fool and a criminal. For had I died, my death in itself would be sufficient proof of my brotherly affection for you. As it is, I have made the mistake of depriving you of my aid while I am yet alive, and causing you, while I am yet alive, to need the aid of others, so that my voice, which had so often been the salvation of the most complete strangers, should fail of all times in the hour of domestic danger.

As for my servants having come to you without a letter, since you see that anger was not the reason, it was certainly due to the numbing of my faculties, and what I may call an overwhelming deluge of tears and sorrows.

How do you suppose I am weeping as I write these 3 very words ? Just as you are weeping, I am sure, as you read them. Can I for a moment cease from thinking about you, or ever think of you without tears ? When I miss you, is it only a brother that I

desidero, fratrem solum desidero ? Ego vero suavitate fratrem prope aequalem, obsequio filium, consilio parentem. Quid mihi sine te umquam aut tibi
sine me iucundum fuit ? Quid, quod eodem tempore desidero filiam ? qua pietate, qua modestia,
quo ingenio ? effigiem oris, sermonis, animi mei ?
Quid filium venustissimum mihique dulcissimum ?
quem ego ferus ac ferreus e complexu dimisi meo,
sapientiorem puerum quam vellem. Sentiebat enim
miser iam, quid ageretur. Quid vero tuum filium ?
quid imaginem tuam, quam meus Cicero et amabat
ut fratrem et iam ut maiorem fratrem verebatur ?
Quid, quod mulierem miserrimam, fidelissimam con-
iugem, me prosequi non sum passus, ut esset, quae
reliquias communis calamitatis, communes liberos,
4 tueretur ? Sed tamen, quoquo modo potui, scripsi,
et dedi litteras ad te Philogono, liberto tuo, quas
credo tibi postea redditas esse ; in quibus idem te
hortor et rogo, quod pueri tibi verbis meis nuntiarunt,
ut Romam protinus pergas et properes. Primum
enim te in[1] praesidio esse volui, si qui essent inimici,
quorum crudelitas nondum esset nostra calamitate
satiata. Deinde congressus nostri lamentationem
pertimui ; digressum vero non tulissem ; atque etiam
id ipsum, quod tu scribis, metuebam, ne a me
distrahi non posses. His de causis hoc maximum

---

[1] *Inserted by Madvig* : te praesidio *mss.*

miss ? No, it is one who in affection is almost a twin, in deference a son, in counsel a father. What has ever given me pleasure without your sharing it, or you without my sharing it ? And what of the fact that at the same time I miss a daughter, and how affectionate a daughter, how unassuming, how talented— the very replica of myself in face, speech, and spirit ? And, moreover, a son, the bonniest boy, and my very darling ? Harsh and hard-hearted as I was, I put him away from my embrace, a wiser boy than I could wish ; for he already sensed what was afoot. But what of my missing your son, the image of yourself, whom my Cicero loved as a brother, and was just beginning to revere as an elder brother ? What of the fact that I refused to allow that most miserable of women, my most loyal wife, to follow me into exile, so that there might be somebody to look after all that is left to us out of our common disaster, the children we have in common ?

But for all that I wrote to you as best I could, 4 and gave the letter to Philogonus, your freedman, to deliver to you, and I believe that it was so delivered later on ; in it I urge and entreat you to do exactly what my slaves repeated to you as from myself—that you should proceed on your journey to Rome, and make haste about it. In the first place I wished you to be on guard, in the event of there being any enemies, whose bloodthirstiness had not even yet been glutted by my fall. In the next place I dreaded the lamentation our meeting would cause ; indeed our parting would have been more than I could bear, and I also feared the very thing you mention in your letter— that you could not tear yourself away from me. For these reasons the crowning misfortune of my not

malum, quod te non vidi, quo nihil amantissimis et
coniunctissimis fratribus acerbius ac miserius videtur
accidere potuisse, minus acerbum, minus miserum
fuit, quam fuisset cum congressio, tum vero digressio
5 nostra. Nunc, si potes, id quod ego, qui fortis tibi
semper videbar, non possum, erige te et confirma, si
qua subeunda dimicatio erit. Spero, si quid mea
spes habet auctoritatis, tibi et integritatem tuam, et
amorem in te civitatis, et aliquid etiam miseri-
cordiam nostri praesidi laturam. Sin eris ab isto
periculo vacuus, ages scilicet, si quid agi posse de
nobis putabis. De quo scribunt ad me quidem multi
multa, et se sperare demonstrant: sed ego, quid
sperem, non dispicio, cum inimici plurimum valeant,
amici partim deseruerint me, partim etiam prodide-
rint, qui in meo reditu fortasse reprehensionem sui
sceleris pertimescant. Sed ista qualia sint, tu velim
perspicias mihique declares. Ego tamen, quamdiu
tibi opus erit, si quid periculi subeundum videbis,
vivam. Diutius in hac vita esse non possum. Neque
enim tantum virium habet ulla aut prudentia aut
6 doctrina, ut tantum dolorem possit sustinere. Scio
fuisse et honestius moriendi tempus, et utilius, sed
non hoc solum, multa alia praetermisi; quae si
queri velim praeterita, nihil agam, nisi ut augeam

---

[a] The prosecution for malversation in his province with
which he was threatened by Appius Claudius, nephew of
Clodius. Tyrrell.
464

having seen you—and it seems to me that nothing more bitter and more depressing than that could have befallen brothers so devoted to each other and so closely united—was less bitter and less depressing than would have been first our meeting, and then our parting.

And now, if you can, do what I, brave as you have 5 always thought me, cannot do—rouse yourself and show your strength, if there be any conflict you have to face. I hope, if there are any grounds for my so hoping, that your own integrity, and the love the State bears you, and to some extent even pity for me, will prove a protection to you. But if you are free from your own particular danger,[a] you will of course do whatever you think can be done in my interests. And as to that, there are many who write long letters to me and make it plain that they have their hopes ; but I cannot discern myself what I am to hope for, seeing that my enemies are exceedingly powerful, while my friends have in some cases deserted, in others actually betrayed me, perhaps because they are terribly afraid that my recall would imply a censure upon their scandalous conduct. But as to your own troubles, I should like you to get a clear idea of them, and explain them to me. Whatever happens, as long as you have need of me, or see any danger ahead, so long shall I remain alive ; longer than that I cannot brook my present life. No wisdom, no philosophy, is strong enough to bear such a weight of woe.

That there has occurred a more honourable and 6 more advantageous moment for dying, I am well aware ; but that is not my only sin of omission, it is but one of many ; and if I am going to bewail past opportunities, I shall do no more than aggravate your

dolorem tuum, indicem stultitiam meam. Illud quidem nec faciendum est, nec fieri potest, me diutius, quam aut tuum tempus aut firma spes postulabit, in tam misera tamque turpi vita commorari, ut, qui modo fratre fuerim, liberis, coniuge, copiis, genere ipso pecuniae beatissimus, dignitate, auctoritate, existimatione, gratia non inferior, quam qui umquam fuerunt amplissimi, is nunc, in hac tam afflicta perditaque fortuna, neque me neque meos lugere 7 diutius possim. Quare quid ad me scripsisti de permutatione ? quasi vero nunc me non tuae facultates sustineant. Qua in re ipsa video miser et sentio, quid sceleris admiserim, cum tu de visceribus tuis et fili tui satisfacturus sis, quibus debes, ego acceptam ex aerario pecuniam tuo nomine frustra dissiparim. Sed tamen et M. Antonio, quantum tu scripseras, et Caepioni tantumdem solutum est ; mihi ad id, quod cogito, hoc, quod habeo, satis est. Sive enim restituimur sive desperamur, nihil amplius opus est. Tu, si forte quid erit molestiae, te ad Crassum et ad 8 Calidium conferas, censeo. Quantum Hortensio credendum sit, nescio. Me summa simulatione amoris summaque assiduitate quotidiana sceleratissime insidiosissimeque tractavit, adiuncto quoque Arrio ; quorum ego consiliis, promissis, praeceptis destitutus, in hanc calamitatem incidi. Sed haec occultabis, ne

---

[a] Which chiefly consisted of large legacies left him by clients whom he had successfully defended.

[b] Which Quintus had offered to negotiate for Cicero in Rome, so that he might have the benefit of it at Thessalonica.

[c] Both were creditors of Quintus.

[d] M. Calidius, who as praetor in 57 supported Cicero's recall. *Cf. Fam.* viii. 4. 1 and Index II.

grief and divulge my own folly. But this I am not bound to do, nor can it be done—I mean my tarrying, any longer than either your needs or any trustworthy hope shall necessitate, in a life so abject and ignominious, that I who was lately so highly blessed in brother, children, wife, and wealth, yes, in the very nature of my riches,[a] and not inferior in position, influence, reputation and popularity to any who have ever stood highest in those respects,—that I, I say, should now, in this down-trodden and desperate condition of life, be any longer able to go on lamenting my own lot and that of my family.

Why, then, did you write to me about a bill of **7** exchange [b] ? As though I was not being supported as it is by your resources. And it is just there that I see and feel, alas, what a crime I have committed, seeing that you are forced to satisfy your creditors by drawing upon your own and your son's very life-blood, while I have squandered to no purpose the money I had received from the treasury on your account. Anyhow the amount you mentioned in your letter has been paid to M. Antonius, and the same amount to Caepio.[c] For myself the sum I now have in hand is sufficient for what I have in view. For whether I am restored or given up in despair, I shall need nothing more. As to yourself, if there is any trouble, you should, I think, apply to Crassus and to Calidius.[d]

How far Hortensius is to be trusted I don't know. **8** Myself, with the most misleading pretence of affection and the most assiduous daily attention, he treated most atrociously and with the basest treachery, with Arrius at his side ; and it was because I was left helpless through their advice, their promises, and their directions, that I fell into this degradation. But this

quid obsint. Illud caveto (et eo puto, per Pomponium fovendum tibi esse ipsum Hortensium), ne
ille versus, qui in te erat collatus, cum aedilitatem
petebas, de lege Aurelia, falso testimonio confirmetur.
Nihil enim tam timeo, quam ne, cum intellegant
homines, quantum misericordiae nobis tuae preces
et tua salus allatura sit, oppugnent te vehementius.
9 Messalam tui studiosum esse arbitror ; Pompeium
etiam simulatorem puto. Sed haec utinam ne ex-
periare ! quod precarer deos, nisi meas preces audire
desissent. Verumtamen precor, ut his infinitis
nostris malis contenti sint, in quibus non modo
tamen nullius inest peccati infamia, sed omnis dolor
est, quod optime factis poena est maxima constituta.
10 Filiam meam et tuam, Ciceronemque nostrum, quid
ego, mi frater, tibi commendem ? Quin illud maereo,
quod tibi non minorem dolorem illorum orbitas afferet,
quam mihi. Sed, te incolumi, orbi non erunt. Reliqua, ita mihi salus aliqua detur, potestasque in
patria moriendi, ut me lacrimae non sinunt scribere.
Etiam Terentiam velim tueare, mihique de omnibus
rebus rescribas. Sis fortis, quoad rei natura patietur.
Idibus Iuniis, Thessalonica.

<hr>

[a] Which gave the *iudicia* to the Senate, the *equites*, and
the *tribuni aerarii*. We do not know what the epigram was,
or whether Quintus really wrote it.
[b] Consul with M. Piso in 61.

you will keep dark for fear they do you some injury. You must beware particularly of this—and with that object I think you should get Pomponius to help you to make love to Hortensius himself—that your authorship of that epigram about the *Lex Aurelia* [a] which was attributed to you when you were a candidate for the quaestorship, is not established by some false testimony. There is nothing I fear so much as this, that when people realize how much compassion for me is likely to be excited by your supplications combined with your acquittal, they will attack you all the more fiercely.

I imagine that Messala [b] is devoted to you; 9 Pompey is even now, I suspect, merely affecting to be so. But may you never have to test the truth of all this! I should pray to the gods for that, had they not ceased to listen to any prayers of mine. However, I do pray that they may rest content with these endless calamities of ours—calamities in which, after all, not only is there no dishonouring taint of wrongdoing, but in which is concentrated all that there is of anguish, since what was done for the best has been visited with the heaviest penalty.

As to my daughter (who is yours), and my little 10 Cicero, why should I commend them to you, my own brother? Not but that I grieve that their bereavement will cause you no less sorrow than myself. But, as long as you are safe, they will not be bereft. As for what remains to be said, as surely as I hope for some measure of restitution, and the chance of ending my days in my fatherland, so surely am I not allowed to write it by my tears. Terentia also I would have you protect, and pray reply to me on every point. Be as brave as the nature of the case permits. Thessalonica, June 13.

CICERO

IV

M. CICERO S. D. Q. FRATRI

Thessalonicae, A.U.C. 696.

1 Amabo te, mi frater, ne, si uno meo fato et tu et omnes mei corruistis, improbitati et sceleri meo potius, quam imprudentiae miseriaeque assignes. Nullum est meum peccatum, nisi quod iis credidi, a quibus nefas putaram esse me decipi, aut etiam, quibus ne id expedire quidem arbitrabar. Intimus, proximus, familiarissimus quisque aut sibi pertimuit, aut mihi invidit. Ita mihi nihil misero praeter fidem 2 amicorum, cautum meum consilium defuit. Quod si te satis innocentia tua et misericordia hominum vindicat hoc tempore a molestia, perspicis profecto, ecquaenam nobis spes salutis relinquatur. Nam me Pomponius et Sestius et Piso noster adhuc Thessalonicae retinuerunt, cum longius discedere propter nescio quos motus vetarent. Verum ego magis exitum illorum litteris, quam spe certa exspectabam. Nam quid sperem, potentissimo inimico, dominatione obtrectatorum, infidelibus amicis, pluribus invidis? 3 De novis autem tribunis plebis est ille quidem in me

IV

CICERO TO QUINTUS

Thessalonica, early in August, 58 B.C.

I entreat you, by my love, my dear brother, do not, 1 if through my fate I alone have brought ruin upon you and all who are mine, do not attribute it to any criminality or guilt on my part, so much as to a pitiable lack of foresight. I plead guilty to nothing more than having trusted those by whom I had thought it inconceivably base that I should be deceived, and indeed imagined that it was not even to their own interest. All my most intimate, my nearest, and my dearest friends, were either panic-struck on their own account, or were jealous of me. So I lacked nothing, poor wretch, but fair dealing on the part of my friends and cautious counsel on my own.

But if your own integrity and the compassion 2 generally felt for you have delivered you from persecution at the present juncture, you are surely in a position to know whether there is left to me any hope whatever of being recalled. Pomponius and Sestius and my son-in-law Piso have so far held me back at Thessalonica, forbidding me to go further afield on account of some developments or other ; but it was their letters rather than any definite hope of my own that induced me to await the issue of those developments. For what hope have I left, with a most powerful enemy, with my detractors in supreme command, my friends faithless, and so many envious of me ?

However, of the new tribunes, Sestius, it is true, is 3 most sincerely devoted to me, and so, I hope, are

471

officiosissimus Sestius, et, spero, Curius, Milo, Fadius, Fabricius, sed valde adversante Clodio, qui etiam privatus eadem manu poterit contiones concitare; 4 deinde etiam intercessor parabitur. Haec mihi proficiscenti non proponebantur, sed saepe triduo summa cum gloria dicebar esse rediturus. Quid tu igitur? inquies. Quid? multa convenerunt, quae mentem exturbarent meam—subita defectio Pompei, alienatio consulum, etiam praetorum, timor publicanorum, arma. Lacrimae meorum me ad mortem ire prohibuerunt, quod certe et ad honestatem et ad effugiendos intolerabiles dolores fuit aptissimum. Sed de hoc scripsi ad te in ea epistula, quam Phaethonti dedi. Nunc tu, quoniam in tantum luctum et laborem detrusus es, quantum nemo umquam, si relevare potes communem casum misericordia hominum, scilicet incredibile quiddam assequeris; sin plane occidimus, (me miserum!) ego omnibus meis exitio fuero, quibus ante dedecori non 5 eram. Sed tu, ut ante ad te scripsi, perspice rem et pertenta, et ad me, ut tempora nostra, non ut amor tuus fert, vere perscribe. Ego vitam, quoad putabo tua interesse, aut ad spem servandam esse, retinebo. Tu nobis amicissimum Sestium cognosces; credo tua causa velle Lentulum, qui erit consul. Quamquam

---

^a Perhaps the M. Curius who was quaestor in 61 and tribune of the plebs in 57. See *Fam.* xiii. 49 and Index II.

^b See *Fam.* v. 18. One of the tribunes who promoted Cicero's recall.

^c Piso and Gabinius, who were at first, or seemed to be, inclined to befriend Cicero, but afterwards became hostile to him.

Curius,[a] Milo, Fadius,[b] and Fabricius; but Clodius is bitterly opposed to me, and even in his private capacity will be able to rouse the passions of public gatherings with the same old gang; and again there is this too—someone will be put up to veto the bill.

All this was not put before me as I was leaving **4** Rome, but it was repeatedly stated that I should be returning in three days' time with the greatest glory. "Why did you go, then?" you will say. Why? Well, many things occurred together to upset my mental balance—the sudden defection of Pompey, the estrangement of the consuls,[c] and of the praetors also, the timid attitude of the *publicani*, the gangs of armed roughs. The tears of my family prevented me from putting myself to death, which was certainly the course best adapted to the retention of my honour and my escape from unendurable sufferings. But I wrote to you on this point in the letter I gave Phaethon. As it is, now that you have been thrust into such a morass of grief and trouble as no man ever was before, if you, by exciting the compassion of the world, can be the means of mitigating our common misfortune, you will undoubtedly win a success of unimaginable importance; but if we are both irrevocably ruined (woe is me!), I shall prove to have brought destruction upon all my people, to whom previously I was no discredit.

But, as I wrote to you before, scrutinize and probe **5** the situation thoroughly, and report to me fully and truthfully, as our actual position and not your affection for me dictates. I shall keep my hold on life as long as I think that it is to your interest, or that it should be preserved for the possibility of hope. You will find Sestius a true friend to us, and I believe Lentulus wishes you all success, and he will be consul. And

473

sunt facta verbis difficiliora. Tu et quid opus sit, et quid sit, videbis. Omnino si tuam solitudinem communemque calamitatem nemo dispexerit, aut per te confici aliquid, aut nullo modo poterit. Sin te quoque inimici vexare coeperint, ne cessaris. Non enim gladiis tecum, sed litibus agetur. Verum haec absint velim. Te oro, ut ad me de omnibus rebus scribas, et in me animi potius aut consili putes minus esse, quam antea, amoris vero et offici non minus.

yet it is easier to talk than to act. You will see what is needful, and how things really are.

To sum up, if nobody casts a calculating eye upon your unprotected position and our common calamity, it is through you, or not at all, that something may be accomplished. But if our enemies begin to harass you as well as myself, you must be up and doing ; for their weapons against you won't be swords, but suits. However, I trust there will be none of that.

I implore you to write to me about everything, and to believe that though perhaps my courage and powers of decision are less than in the old days, there is no diminution of my love and loyalty.

M. TULLI CICERONIS
EPISTULARUM AD QUINTUM FRATREM

LIBER SECUNDUS

I

M. CICERO S. D. Q. FRATRI

Romae, a.u.c. 697.

1 Epistulam, quam legisti, mane dederam. Sed fecit
humaniter Licinius, quod ad me, misso senatu, vesperi venit, ut, si quid esset actum, ad te, si mihi
videretur, perscriberem. Senatus fuit frequentior,
quam putabamus esse posse mense Decembri sub
dies festos. Consulares nos fuimus P. Servilius, M.
Lucullus, Lepidus, Volcatius, Glabrio, duo consules
designati, praetores. Sane frequentes fuimus ;
omnino ad ducentos. Commorat exspectationem Lupus. Egit causam agri Campani sane accurate. Auditus est magno silentio. Materiam rei non ignoras.

---

a Isauricus, consul with Appius Claudius Pulcher in 79.

b M. Terentius Varro Lucullus, consul in 73.

c M. Aemilius Lepidus and L. Volcatius Tullus were
consuls in 66.

d M'. Acilius Glabrio, consul with C. Calpurnius Piso in
67.

CICERO'S LETTERS TO HIS BROTHER QUINTUS

BOOK II

I

CICERO TO QUINTUS (ON HIS WAY TO SARDINIA)

Rome, December, 57 B.C.

The letter you have just read I sent off this morn- 1 ing. But Licinius was so courteous as to visit me in the evening after the dismissal of the Senate, so that, if I thought good, I might write you a full account of anything that had been done there. The Senate was better attended than I thought possible in the month of December so near the holidays. Of us consulars there were P. Servilius,[a] M. Lucullus,[b] Lepidus,[c] Volcatius,[c] Glabrio,[d] the two consuls designate, and the praetors. We made quite a full house, being about 200 altogether. Lupus [e] had roused our expectations. He discussed the question of the Campanian land with extreme particularity, and was listened to in profound silence. You are well aware what material it offers for a speech. He omitted

[e] Publius Rutilius Lupus, who was strongly opposed to Caesar's law for the division of the Campanian land.

477

CICERO

Nihil ex nostris actionibus praetermisit. Fuerunt nonnulli aculei in C. Caesarem, contumeliae in Gellium, expostulationes cum absente Pompeio. Causa sero perorata, sententias se rogaturum negavit, ne quod onus simultatis nobis imponeret. Ex superiorum temporum conviciis, et ex praesenti silentio, quid senatus sentiret, se intellegere dixit. Ilico coepit dimittere,[2] cum Marcellinus, noli, inquit, ex taciturnitate nostra, Lupe, quid aut probemus hoc tempore aut improbemus, iudicare. Ego, quod ad me attinet, idemque arbitror ceteros, idcirco taceo, quod non existimo, cum Pompeius absit, causam agri Campani agi convenire. Tum ille se senatum negavit
2 tenere. Racilius surrexit, et de iudiciis referre coepit. Marcellinum quidem primum rogavit. Is cum graviter de Clodianis incendiis, trucidationibus, lapidationibus questus esset, sententiam dixit, ut ipse iudices praetor urbanus[1] sortiretur ; iudicum sortitione facta, comitia haberentur ; qui iudicia impedivisset, eum contra rempublicam esse facturum. Approbata valde sententia, C. Cato contra dixit, et Cassius maxima acclamatione senatus, cum comitia iudiciis
3 anteferret. Philippus assensit Lentulo. Postea

---

[1] *Manutius* : per praetorem urbanum MSS.
[2] *Orelli* : intellegere. Dixit Milo. Coepit dimittere. Tum MSS.

---

[a] Gellius Poplicola, an adherent of Clodius.
[b] Cn. Cornelius Lentulus Marcellinus, consul designate for the following year, 56.
[c] L. Racilius, a tribune and a staunch supporter of Cicero.
[d] As consul designate.
[e] *i.e.*, without the assistance of the quaestors.
[f] A tribune ; *cf. Q. Fr.* i. 2. 15.

nothing of the measures I had taken. There were some stinging references to C. Caesar, some abuse of Gellius,[a] some remonstrances with the absent Pompey. As he was late in bringing his speech to a conclusion, he said he would not ask for our votes, for fear of burdening us with a personal wrangle. He said that he clearly inferred the feelings of the Senate from the loud protests of earlier days and its present silence. He proceeds at once to dismiss the Senate, when Marcellinus[b] says, "You must not judge by our silence, Lupus, what we approve, or do not approve, at the present moment. As far as I am concerned, and I think it is the case with the rest of us, my reason for not speaking is, that I do not consider it right and proper that the question of the Campanian land should be discussed in Pompey's absence." Then Lupus said that he had no further business for the Senate.

Racilius[c] got up and began to raise the question of 2 the proposed prosecutions. Marcellinus was of course the first he called upon[d]; and he, after seriously protesting against the burnings, killings, and stonings of Clodius, proposed a resolution "that the *praetor urbanus* should himself[e] draw the lots for the jury, that the elections should not be held until after the allotment of the jurors, and that whoever obstructed the trials would be acting against the commonwealth." The proposal having met with hearty approval, C. Cato[f] spoke against it, and so did Cassius,[g] the Senate loudly protesting when he gave the elections precedence in time over the trials. Philippus agreed with Lentulus.[h]

[g] A tribune.
[h] *i.e.*, Marcellinus, the consul designate.

Racilius de privatis me primum sententiam rogavit. Multa feci verba de toto furore latrocinioque P. Clodi ; eum, tamquam reum, accusavi, multis et secundis admurmurationibus cuncti senatus. Orationem meam collaudavit satis multis verbis, non mehercule indiserte, Vetus Antistius ; isque iudiciorum causam suscepit, antiquissimamque se habiturum dixit. Ibatur in eam sententiam. Tum Clodius rogatus, diem dicendo eximere coepit. Furebat, a Racilio se contumaciter inurbaneque[1] vexatum. Deinde eius operae repente a Graecostasi et gradibus clamorem satis magnum sustulerunt, opinor, in Q. Sextilium et amicos Milonis incitatae. Eo metu iniecto, repente magna querimonia omnium, discessimus. Habes acta unius diei. Reliqua, ut arbitror, in mensem Ianuarium reicientur. De tribunis plebis longe optimum Racilium habemus. Videtur etiam Antistius amicus nobis fore. Nam Plancius totus noster est. Fac, si me amas, ut considerate diligenterque naviges de mense Decembri.

---

[1] *Müller, following ed. Rom.* : urbaneque *Tyrrell,* " *with polished insolence.*"

---

[a] A tribune.
[b] A platform near the Curia Hostilia and the *Comitium* where Greek, and afterwards other, ambassadors listened to the debates in the Senate, a sort of " strangers' gallery."

After that Racilius called upon me first of the **3**
unofficial senators for my opinion. I spoke at great
length on all the insane and murderous acts of
P. Clodius ; I arraigned him as though he were in
the dock, amid the frequent approving murmurs of
the whole Senate.   My speech was praised at quite
sufficient length and, I assure you, with no little
eloquence, by Vetus Antistius,*a* who also took upon
himself the defence of the priority of the trials—a
priority he said he would regard as being of capital
importance. The senators were crossing the floor in
favour of this opinion, when Clodius, being called
upon, set about talking out the sitting. He declared
in a frenzy of rage that Racilius had worried him in
an insulting and unmannerly way.   Thereupon his
hired ruffians on the Graecostasis *b* and the steps of
the senate-house raised quite a fierce yell, incited, I
suppose, to attack Q. Sextilius and Milo's friends.
Under the cloud of that sudden alarm, we broke up,
with strong protests on every side. So much for the
transactions of a single day. What remains to be done
will, I imagine, be put off to the month of January.
Among the tribunes of the plebs by far the best man
we have is Racilius. It seems likely that Antistius too
will be friendly to us. As for Plancius,*c* he is with
us heart and soul. As you love me, see to it that
you are deliberate and careful about taking ship now
that December is with us.

c Cn. Plancius who, as quaestor of Macedonia, showed
great kindness to Cicero during his banishment.

CICERO

II

MARCUS Q. FRATRI S.

Romae, A.U.C. 698.

1 Non occupatione, qua eram sane impeditus, sed parvula lippitudine adductus sum, ut dictarem hanc epistulam et non, ut ad te soleo, ipse scriberem. Et primum me tibi excuso in eo ipso, in quo te accuso. Me enim adhuc nemo rogavit, " num quid in Sardiniam vellem " ; te puto saepe habere, qui, " num quid Romam velis," quaerant. Quod ad me Lentuli et Sesti nomine scripsisti, locutus sum cum Cincio. Quoquo modo res se habet, non est facillima, sed habet profecto quiddam Sardinia appositum ad recordationem praeteritae memoriae. Nam, ut ille Gracchus augur, posteaquam in istam provinciam venit, recordatus est, quid sibi, in campo Martio comitia consulum habenti, contra auspicia accidisset, sic tu mihi videris in Sardinia de forma Numisiana et de nominibus Pomponianis in otio recogitasse. Sed ego adhuc emi nihil. Culleonis auctio facta est. Tusculano emptor nemo fuit. Si condicio valde bona 2 fuerit, fortasse non omittam. De aedificatione tua Cyrum urgere non cesso. Spero eum in officio fore. Sed omnia sunt tardiora, propter furiosae aedilitatis exspectationem. Nam comitia sine mora futura videntur. Edicta sunt a. d. xi. Kal. Febr. Te tamen

---

^a An agent of Atticus.
^b The father of the Gracchi ; the story is told by Cicero in *Nat. Deor.* ii. 11.
^c An architect.
^d Another architect.
^e *i.e.*, of P. Clodius.

II

Rome, January 17, 56 B.C.

It was not pressure of business (though I am sorely 1 hampered in that respect), but a slight inflammation of the eyes that induced me to dictate this letter instead of writing it, as I generally do when corresponding with you, with my own hand. And first of all I excuse myself to you on the very point on which I accuse you. For nobody so far has asked me whether I have any commands for Sardinia, while you, I fancy, often have people inquiring whether you have any commands for Rome. You wrote to me on behalf of Lentulus and Sestius ; well, I have spoken to Cincius.[a] However the matter stands, it is not of the easiest. But assuredly there is something in Sardinia peculiarly conducive to recalling past memories ; for just as the great Gracchus,[b] the augur, on his arrival in that province, recollected what had happened to him when holding the consular elections in the Campus Martius contrary to the auspices, so it seems to me that you in your moments of leisure in Sardinia have bethought yourself afresh of the house-plan of Numisius[c] and your debts to Pomponius. So far I have bought nothing. Culleo's auction is over and done with; my Tusculan property found no purchaser. If I have a very favourable offer for it, it is just possible I may not let it slip.

As regards your building, I never cease hurrying 2 on Cyrus.[d] I hope he will do his duty ; but everything hangs fire owing to the prospect of a madcap aedileship[e] ; for the elections seem likely to be held without delay. They are announced for January 20.

483

sollicitum esse nolo. Omne genus a nobis cautionis
3 adhibebitur. De rege Alexandrino factum est senatus consultum, cum multitudine eum reduci periculosum reipublicae videri. Reliqua cum esset in senatu
contentio, Lentulusne an Pompeius reduceret, obtinere causam Lentulus videbatur. In ea nos et
officio erga Lentulum mirifice, et voluntati Pompei
praeclare satisfecimus. Sed per obtrectatores Lentuli res calumnia extracta est. Consecuti sunt dies
comitiales, per quos senatus haberi non poterat.
Quid futurum sit latrocinio tribunorum, non divino ;
sed tamen suspicor per vim rogationem Caninium
perlaturum. In ea re Pompeius quid velit, non dispicio. Familiares eius quid cupiant, omnes vident.
Creditores vero regis aperte pecunias suppeditant
contra Lentulum. Sine dubio res a Lentulo remota
videtur esse, cum magno meo dolore. Quamquam
multa fecit, quare, si fas esset, iure ei succensere
possemus. Tu, si ita expedit, velim quam primum
bona et certa tempestate conscendas ad meque venias.
Innumerabiles enim res sunt, in quibus te quotidie
in omni genere desiderem. Tui nostrique valent.
xiv. Kal. Febr.

---

^a Ptolemy Auletes ; *cf. Fam.* i. 1 and 2, where the whole
story is told.
^b Cicero blamed Lentulus for his indifference, if it was
not jealousy, in the matter of fixing Cicero's indemnity.

However I do not want you to be anxious. I shall exercise every kind of caution.

In the matter of the Alexandrine king,[a] a decree **3** of the Senate has been passed to the effect that his restoration by the employment of " *a host of men* " seems fraught with danger to the commonwealth. In what remained to be discussed in the Senate—the question whether he should be restored by Lentulus or Pompey—it seemed that Lentulus was making good his case, a case in which I was amazingly successful in discharging my obligations to Lentulus, and brilliantly so in satisfying the wishes of Pompey —but Lentulus's case was protracted by the spiteful obstruction of his detractors. Then followed the comitial days, during which a meeting of the Senate could not be held. What result the ruffianly conduct of the tribunes will have, I cannot predict ; anyhow I suspect Caninius will force his bill through by violence. In all this I have no clear idea as to what Pompey wants ; what his particular friends desire, nobody can fail to see. Those who are financing the king make no secret of supplying sums of money to fight Lentulus. It is beyond doubt that the business seems to have been taken out of Lentulus's hands, and it is a great grief to me. And yet he has done many things for which I might be justly angry with him,[b] were such a thing conceivable. If it suits your interests, I should like you to take ship when the weather is fair and settled, and join me as soon as possible. For there are numberless things in which I miss you daily in all sorts of ways. Your people and mine are well. January 17.

CICERO

III

M. CICERO S. D. Q. FRATRI

Romae, A.U.C. 698.

1 Scripsi ad te antea superiora; nunc cognosce, postea quae sint acta. A Kal. Febr. legationes in Idus Febr. reiciebantur. Eo die res confecta non est. A. d. IV. Non. Febr. Milo adfuit. Ei Pompeius advocatus venit. Dixit Marcellus, a me rogatus. Honeste discessimus. Producta dies est in VIII. Id. Febr. Interim reiectis legationibus in Idus, referebatur de provinciis quaestorum et de ornandis praetoribus. Sed res, multis querellis de republica interponendis, nulla transacta est. Cato legem promulgavit de imperio Lentuli abrogando. Vestitum filius mutavit.

2 A. d. VIII. Id. Febr. Milo adfuit. Dixit Pompeius, sive voluit; nam, ut surrexit, operae Clodianae clamorem sustulerunt; idque ei perpetua oratione contigit, non modo ut acclamatione, sed ut convicio et maledictis impediretur. Qui ut peroravit (nam in eo sane fortis fuit, non est deterritus, dixit omnia; atque interdum etiam silentio cum auctoritate peregerat) sed ut peroravit, surrexit Clodius. Ei tantus

---

ᵃ *i.e.*, of Cilicia. His son assumed mourning (as was often done in such circumstances) to excite sympathy with his father.

III

CICERO TO QUINTUS IN SARDINIA

Rome, February 12 and 15, 56 B.C.

I have already told you in my letter what occurred 1
earlier ; now let me inform you of what has been
done since that. On February 1, it was proposed to
postpone the reception of foreign deputations until
February 13. The postponement was not carried on
that day. On February 2, Milo appeared to stand
his trial. Pompey came to support him. Marcellus
was called upon by me, and spoke. We came off with
the honours of war. The trial was adjourned to the
6th. Meanwhile the deputations having been put off
until the 13th, the question of assigning provinces to
the quaestors and of supplying the praetors with the
proper officers and forces was brought before the
house ; but so many complaints of the state of public
affairs were interposed, that nothing was settled. C.
Cato gave notice of a proposal to remove Lentulus
from his government,[a] and Lentulus's son put on
mourning.

On the 6th Milo again appeared for trial. Pompey 2
spoke, or rather such was his intention ; for when he
got up, Clodius's hired gangs raised a yell, and that
is what he had to endure the whole time he was
speaking, being interrupted not only with shouts,
but with insults and abuse. When he had finished his
speech (he showed great fortitude in the circumstances ; he never quailed, he said all he had to say,
and now and then amid a silence compelled by his
impressive personality), but, as I say, when he had
finished his speech, up got Clodius. He was met with

487

clamor a nostris (placuerat enim referre gratiam), ut
neque mente neque lingua neque ore consisteret. Ea
res acta est, cum hora vi. vix Pompeius perorasset,
usque ad horam viii., cum omnia maledicta, versus
etiam obscenissimi in Clodium et Clodiam dicerentur.
Ille furens et exsanguis interrogabat suos, in clamore
ipso, quis esset, qui plebem fame necaret. Respondebant operae, " Pompeius." Quis Alexandriam ire
cuperet. Respondebant, " Pompeius." Quem ire
vellent. Respondebant, " Crassum." Is aderat tum,
Miloni animo non amico. Hora fere ix., quasi signo
dato, Clodiani nostros consputare coeperunt. Exarsit dolor. Urgere illi, ut loco nos moverent. Factus
est a nostris impetus ; fuga operarum. Eiectus de
rostris Clodius ; ac nos quoque tum fugimus, ne quid
in turba. Senatus vocatus in curiam ; Pompeius
domum. Neque ego tamen in senatum, ne aut
de tantis rebus tacerem, aut in Pompeio defendendo
(nam is carpebatur a Bibulo, Curione, Favonio, Servilio filio) animos bonorum virorum offenderem. Res
in posterum dilata est. Clodius in Quirinalia produxit
3 diem. A. d. vii. Id. Febr. senatus ad Apollinis fuit,
ut Pompeius adesset. Acta res est graviter a Pompeio. Eo die nihil perfectum est. A. d. vi. Id. ad

---

^a For this rendering (from *lost* to *countenance*) I am
indebted to Tyrrell.
    ^b February 17.
    ^c He was probably afraid to enter Rome on account of
the mobs. It was not because he held *imperium*, as he had
already entered Rome to speak for Milo (§ 2).

such a deafening shout from our side (for we had determined to give him as good as he gave), that he lost all control over his faculties, his voice, and his countenance.[a] Such was the scene from the time when Pompey had barely finished his speech at noon, right up to two o'clock, when every kind of abuse, and even doggerel of the filthiest description, was vented upon Clodius and Clodia. Maddened and white with rage, he asked his partisans (and he was heard above the shouting) who the man was that starved the people to death ; his rowdies answered " Pompey." Who was bent upon going to Alexandria ? They answered " Pompey." Whom did they want to go ? They answered " Crassus." (Crassus was there at the time, but with no friendly feeling for Milo.) About three o'clock the Clodians, as if at a given signal, began to spit upon our men. We resented it in a paroxysm of rage. They tried to hustle us and get us out. Our men charged them, and the roughs took to their heels. Clodius was flung off the *rostra*, and then we too fled, for fear of something happening in the *mêlée*. The Senate was summoned to the Curia ; Pompey went home. I did not myself, however, attend the Senate, so as not, on the one hand, to keep silent on matters of such gravity, or, on the other, by defending Pompey (who was being attacked by Bibulus, Curio, Favonius, and Servilius junior) to hurt the feelings of the loyalists. The business was adjourned to the following day. Clodius got the trial postponed until the Quirinalia.[b]

On February 7 the Senate met in the temple of 3 Apollo, in order that Pompey might be present.[c] He dealt with the matter impressively, but on that day nothing was done. On the 8th in the temple of Apollo

CICERO

Apollinis senatus consultum factum est, EA, QUAE FACTA ESSENT A. D. VIII. ID. Febr. CONTRA REMPUBLICAM ESSE FACTA. Eo die Cato est vehementer in Pompeium invectus, et eum oratione perpetua tamquam reum accusavit. De me multa, me invito, cum mea summa laude dixit. Cum illius in me perfidiam increparet, auditus est magno silentio malevolorum. Respondit ei vehementer Pompeius Crassumque descripsit, dixitque aperte, se munitiorem ad custodiendam vitam suam fore, quam Africanus fuisset, 4 quem C. Carbo interemisset. Itaque magnae mihi res iam moveri videbantur. Nam Pompeius haec intellegit, nobiscumque communicat, insidias vitae suae fieri ; C. Catonem a Crasso sustentari ; Clodio pecuniam suppeditari ; utrumque et ab eo, et a Curione, Bibulo ceterisque suis obtrectatoribus confirmari ; vehementer esse providendum, ne opprimatur, contionario illo populo a se prope alienato, nobilitate inimica, non aequo senatu, iuventute improba. Itaque se comparat, homines ex agris arcessit. Operas autem suas Clodius confirmat. Manus ad Quirinalia paratur ; in eo multo sumus superiores ipsius copiis. Sed magna manus ex Piceno et Gallia exspectatur, ut etiam Catonis rogationibus de Milone

---

[a] They would not interrupt a speech likely to embroil Cicero with Pompey.

[b] C. Papirius Carbo, to whom Pompey compares Crassus, was probably innocent of the murder of Africanus. See note *b* to *Fam.* ix. 21. 3.

a decree of the Senate was carried, " that what had been done on the 6th was against the interests of the State." On that day Cato vehemently inveighed against Pompey, and throughout his speech arraigned him as though he were in the dock. He spoke a great deal about me, much against my will, though in highly laudatory terms. When he denounced Pompey's treacherous conduct to myself, he was listened to amid profound silence on the part of my ill-wishers.[a] Pompey replied to him in vehement terms, and made an obvious allusion to Crassus, openly declaring " that he himself would be better prepared to safeguard his own life than Africanus had been, who was murdered by C. Carbo." [b]

So it appears to me that issues of great importance 4 are developing. For Pompey clearly understands this, and talks to me about it—that plots are being hatched against his life ; that C. Cato is being backed up by Crassus ; that Clodius is being supplied with money, and that both of them are being encouraged, not only by Crassus, but by Curio and Bibulus and the rest of his detractors ; that he has to take strenuous measures to prevent being utterly crushed, with a speech-swallowing populace practically estranged from him, with a nobility hostile, a Senate unfairly prejudiced, and the youth of the country without principle. So he is making preparations, and calling up men from rural districts, while Clodius is strengthening his hired gangs. A regiment of them is being trained for the Quirinalia, to meet which date we are far superior in numbers, with Pompey's own forces ; besides, a large contingent is expected from Picenum and Gaul, so that we may also oppose Cato's motions about Milo and Lentulus.

5 et Lentulo resistamus. A. d. iv. Id. Febr. Sestius ab
indice Cn. Nerio, Pupinia, de ambitu est postulatus,
et eodem die a quodam P. Tullio de vi.[a] Is erat aeger.
Domum (ut debuimus) ad eum statim venimus, eique
nos totos tradidimus ; idque fecimus praeter hominum opinionem, qui nos ei iure succensere putabant ;
ut humanissimi, gratissimique et ipsi et omnibus
videremur ; itaque faciemus. Sed idem Nerius index
edidit ad allegatos Cn. Lentulum Vatiam et C.
Cornelium.[1] Eodem die senatus consultum factum
est, UT SODALITATES DECURIATIQUE DISCEDERENT ;
LEXQUE DE IIS FERRETUR, UT, QUI NON DISCESSISSENT,
6 EA POENA, QUAE EST DE VI, TENERENTUR.[b] A. d. iii. Id.
dixi pro Bestia de ambitu apud praetorem Cn. Domitium in foro medio maximo conventu, incidique
in eum locum in dicendo, cum Sestius, multis in
templo Castoris vulneribus acceptis, subsidio Bestiae
servatus esset. Hic προῳκονομησάμην quiddam
εὐκαίρως de his, quae in Sestium apparabantur
crimina, et eum ornavi veris laudibus, magno assensu
omnium. Res homini fuit vehementer grata. Quae
tibi eo scribo, quod me de retinenda Sesti gratia
7 litteris saepe monuisti. Prid. Id. Febr. haec scripsi[c]

---

[1] Cornelium : †ista ei *Tyrrell*; *Warde Fowler thinks*
ista ei *may be a corruption of* testes, *a gloss explaining*
allegatos : *Madvig suggests* instare, " *were threatening*
Sestius* " : *I follow Nobbe in omitting* ista ei *altogether* : *Prof.*
R. Ellis conjectures adalligatos, " *as being compromised as*
well."

---

[a] P. Tullius Albinovanus.
[b] Cicero was displeased with the bill Sestius drew up for
his restoration (*cf. Att.* iii. 23. 4). We know of no other
reason why Cicero should have been angry with Sestius.
[c] The text is here incurably corrupt. See critical note
above.

On February 10, Sestius was prosecuted by the 5
informer, Cn. Nerius of the Pupinian tribe, for
bribery, and on the same day by one P. Tullius[a] for
breaking the peace. He was ill. I immediately went
to see him at his house, and put myself unreservedly
at his disposal ; and what I did was more than most
people expected, for they supposed that I was justly
indignant with him,[b] with the result that both he
himself and the world in general thought me the
most kind-hearted and grateful of men ; and that is
how I mean to act. But that same informer Nerius
also gave in the names of Cn. Lentulus Vatia and
C. Cornelius as additional intermediaries.[c] On
the same day a decree of the Senate was passed
" that political clubs and caucuses should be broken
up, and that a law concerning them should be
proposed whereby all who refused to disband
should be liable to the penalty fixed for breaking
the peace."

On the 11th I defended Bestia on a charge of 6
bribery before the praetor, Cn. Domitius, in the
middle of the forum, before a vast assembly ; and in
the course of my speech, I incidentally dwelt upon the
time when Sestius, covered with wounds in the temple
of Castor, was only saved by the help of Bestia. At
this point I adroitly seized the opportunity to make a
sort of anticipatory refutation of the charges which
are being trumped up against Sestius, and I paid him
some compliments he really deserved, with the hearty
approval of all present. It gave the poor fellow the
greatest pleasure. I tell you this because you have
often advised me in your letters to keep on good
terms with Sestius.

I am writing this on the 12th, before day-break ; 7

ante lucem. Eo die apud Pomponium in eius nuptiis
eram cenaturus. Cetera sunt in rebus nostris
huiusmodi (ut tu mihi fere diffidenti praedicabas)
plena dignitatis et gratiae ; quae quidem tua, mi
frater, patientia, virtute, pietate, suavitate etiam,
tibi mihique sunt restituta. Domus tibi ad lacum[1]
Pisonis Liciniana conducta est. Sed, ut spero,
paucis mensibus post Kalend. Quint. in tuam com-
migrabis. Tuam in Carinis mundi habitatores Lamiae
conduxerunt. A te post illam Olbiensem epistulam
nullas litteras accepi. Quid agas et ut te oblectes,
scire cupio, maximeque teipsum videre quam primum.
Cura, mi frater, ut valeas ; et quamquam est hiems,
tamen Sardiniam istam esse cogites. xv. Kalend.
Mart.

IV

M. CICERO Q. FRATRI S.

Romae, A.U.C. 698.

1 Sestius noster absolutus est a. d. iv. Id. Mart. ; et,
quod vehementer interfuit reipublicae, nullam videri in eiusmodi causa dissensionem esse, omnibus
sententiis absolutus est. Illud, quod tibi saepe curae
esse intellexeram, ne cui iniquo relinqueremus vitu-
perandi locum, qui nos ingratos esse diceret, nisi il-

---

[1] *Boot*: lucum MSS., *but* luci *were generally dedicated to divinities.*

---

[a] Atticus's marriage to Pilia.

[b] The chief port of Sardinia.

[c] A notoriously unhealthy island in the summer months.

[d] Sestius had kept a band of armed men during his
tribunate in the preceding year to oppose P. Clodius and
his roughs. He had therefore been accused of *vis* (breaking
the peace), with the result here described. Cicero's speech
on the occasion is still extant.

this is the day on which I am going to dine with Pomponius to celebrate his marriage.[a]

In all other respects my position is just what you assured me it would be, though I could hardly believe it—a position of dignity and popularity ; and all this has been restored to you and me, brother mine, by your patience, courage, and brotherly devotion, and, I must also add, by your charm of manner. A house has been taken for you that belonged to Licinius, near Piso's pool, but in a few months' time, say after July 1, you will move into your own. Your house in the Carinae has been taken on lease by some genteel tenants, the Lamiae. I have received no letter from you since the one you sent from Olbia.[b] I am anxious to know how you are getting on, and how you amuse yourself, but most of all to see you in person as soon as possible. Take care of your health, my dear brother, and, although it is winter, yet bear in mind that the place you are living in is Sardinia.[c]

IV

CICERO TO QUINTUS IN SARDINIA

Rome, March, 56 B.C.

Our friend Sestius was acquitted [d] on March 11, and, moreover (and it is a matter of paramount importance to the State that there should be no appearance of difference of opinion in a case of this sort)—he was acquitted unanimously. As to what I had often gathered to be a cause of anxiety to you, that I should not leave a loophole for fault-finding to any ill-natured critic who might charge me with ingrati-

lius perversitatem ⌈quibusdam in rebus⌉ quam humanissime ferremus, scito hoc nos in eo iudicio consecutos esse, ut omnium gratissimi iudicaremur. Nam
in defendendo moroso homini cumulatissime satisfecimus, et (id quod ille maxime cupiebat) Vatinium,
a quo palam oppugnabatur, arbitratu nostro concidimus, dis hominibusque plaudentibus. Quin etiam
Paullus noster cum testis productus esset in Sestium,
confirmavit se nomen Vatini delaturum, si Macer
Licinius cunctaretur ; et Macer a Sesti subselliis
surrexit, ac se illi non defuturum affirmavit. Quid
quaeris ? homo petulans et audax, Vatinius, valde
2 perturbatus debilitatusque discessit. Quintus tuus,
puer optimus, eruditur egregie. Hoc nunc magis
animadverto, quod Tyrannio docet apud me. Domus
utriusque nostrum aedificatur strenue. Redemptori
tuo dimidium pecuniae curavi. Spero nos ante hiemem contubernales fore. De nostra Tullia, tui mehercule amantissima, spero cum Crassipede nos confecisse. Dies erant duo, qui post Latinas habentur
3 religiosi ; ceteroqui confectum Latiar erat. ⌉ Ἀμφι
λαφίαν autem illam, quam tu soles dicere, bono modo
desidero, sic prorsus, ut advenientem excipiam liben-

---

a For Vatinius see note *a* to *Fam.* i. 9. 4.
b L. Aemilius Paullus, consul in 50.
c C. Licinius Macer Calvus, orator and poet.
d The houses of the two brothers adjoined each other.
e ἀμφιλαφία (from ἀμφιλαφής, "taking in on either side,
or with both hands ") was apparently the term Quintus had
used for the "unlimited means" required for his own and his
brother's building operations. *Cf. Ep.* 15*b.* 3 of this Book.
The metaphor in *excipere* is from a hunter who stands ready
to *welcome* the game when it breaks cover. *Cf.* Hor. *Od.*
iii. 12. 12 "latitantem fruticeto excipere aprum."

tude if I failed to put up with Sestius's wrong-headedness in certain matters as good-humouredly as possible, let me assure you that in this trial I succeeded in establishing my reputation as the most grateful man alive. For in my defence not only did I give immense satisfaction to a cross-grained man, but I also (and this was his dearest wish) made mincemeat of Vatinius,[a] who was openly attacking him, just as the fancy took me, with the applause of gods and men. Furthermore, when our friend Paullus[b] was brought forward as a witness against Sestius, he declared that he would lay information against Vatinius if Macer Licinius[c] was slow about doing so; and Macer rose from the benches where sat the friends of Sestius, and declared that he would not fail to do as Paullus wished. To cut the story short, that aggressive and impudent fellow Vatinius left the court in a state of confusion and nervous collapse.

That excellent boy, your son Quintus, is being 2 admirably taught, and I notice it all the more now, because Tyrannio gives him his lessons at my house. The building of both our houses is going on vigorously. I have seen to it that your contractor has had half his money paid to him. I hope that before winter we shall be under the same roof.[d] As to our daughter Tullia, who, I positively assure you, is very much attached to you, I hope we have settled her betrothal to Crassipes. There are two days which are reckoned as holidays after the Latin festival; otherwise the festival of Jupiter Latiaris has come to an end.

Now as to that "*opulence*"[e] you so often talk about, 3 I have a longing for it, but quite in moderation—just so far as gladly to welcome my quarry, if it comes my

497

ter latentem non excitem. Etiam nunc tribus locis aedifico, reliqua reconcinno ; vivo paullo liberalius, quam solebam ; opus erat. Si te haberem, paullisper fabris locum darem. Sed et haec (ut spero) brevi 4 inter nos communicabimus. Res autem Romanae sese sic habent. Consul est egregius Lentulus, non impediente collega ; sic, inquam, bonus, ut meliorem non viderim. Dies comitiales exemit omnes. Nam etiam Latinae instaurantur ; nec tamen deerant 5 supplicationes. Sic legibus perniciosissimis obsistitur, maxime Catonis ; cui tamen egregie imposuit Milo noster. Nam ille vindex gladiatorum et bestiariorum emerat de Cosconio et Pomponio bestiarios ; nec sine his armatis umquam in publico fuerat. Hos alere non poterat. Itaque vix tenebat. Sensit Milo. Dedit cuidam non familiari negotium, qui sine suspicione emeret eam familiam a Catone ; quae simul atque abducta est, Racilius, qui unus est hoc tempore tribunus plebis, rem patefecit, eosque homines sibi emptos esse dixit (sic enim placuerat) et tabulam proscripsit, SE FAMILIAM CATONIANAM VENDITURUM. In eam tabulam magni risus consequebantur. Nunc igitur Catonem Lentulus a legibus removit, et eos, qui de Caesare monstra promulgarunt, quibus inter-

---

ᵃ Marcellinus, consul with Marcius Philippus. Acting in concert, in order to prevent C. Cato and his friends from bringing in bills to the prejudice of Lentulus Spinther and Milo, the two consuls had recourse to every possible political manœuvre to cause delay in the elections, *e.g.* the celebration of the movable festival, the *feriae Latinae*, when they might more justifiably have held the *supplicationes* that were due, and would also have had the effect of delaying the elections.

way, but not to hunt it out, if it keeps under cover. Even as it is, I am building in three different places, and refurbishing my other houses. I am living rather more generously than I used to; I have to do so. If I had you with me, I should give the masons free scope for a while. But this too we shall shortly, I hope, talk over together.

The position at Rome is as follows: Lentulus *a* is 4 an excellent consul, and his colleague does not stand in his way—so good, I repeat, that I have never seen a better. He has cancelled all the comitial days. Why, even the Latin festival is being celebrated anew; and yet he had the *supplicationes* to fall back upon.

By these means the most ruinous bills are being 5 resisted, especially that of C. Cato; but our friend Milo has played a splendid trick upon him. That champion of gladiators and beast-fighters had bought some beast-fighters from Cosconius and Pomponius, and had never appeared in public without them as an armed body-guard. He could not pay for their keep, so could hardly maintain his hold upon them. Milo got wind of it. He engaged a certain person, with whom he was not intimate, to buy the whole gang from Cato without exciting his suspicion. No sooner had they been marched off than Racilius, who just now stands alone as tribune of the plebs, divulged the whole affair, declared that the men had been bought for him (that is what they had agreed upon) and put up a notice "*that he had Cato's gang for sale.*" The result of that notice was laughter loud and long. So now Lentulus has prevented Cato, and those who promulgated outrageous proposals about Caesar, from carrying their laws, there being no

cederet nemo. Nam quod de Pompeio Caninius agit,
sanequam refrixit. Neque enim res probatur, et
Pompeius noster in amicitia P. Lentuli vituperatur,
et hercule non est idem. Nam apud illam perditis-
simam atque infimam faecem populi propter Milonem
suboffendit ; et boni multa ab eo desiderant, multa
reprehendunt. Marcellinus autem hoc uno mihi quidem non satisfacit, quod eum nimis aspere tractat ;
quamquam id senatu non invito facit ; quo ego me
libentius a curia et ab omni parte reipublicae sub-
6 traho. In iudiciis ii sumus, qui fuimus. Domus
celebratur ita, ut cum maxime. Unum accidit im-
prudentia Milonis incommode, de Sex. Clodio, quem
neque hoc tempore, neque ab imbecillis accusatoribus mihi placuit accusari. Ei tres sententiae teter-
rimo in consilio defuerunt. Itaque hominem populus
revocat et retrahatur necesse est. Non enim ferunt
homines. Et quia, cum apud suos diceret, paene
damnatus est, vident damnatum. Ea ipsa in re
Pompei offensio nobis obstitit. Senatorum enim urna
copiose absolvit, equitum adaequavit, tribuni aerarii
condemnarunt. Sed hoc incommodum consolantur
quotidianae damnationes inimicorum, in quibus me

---

^a Probably a descendant of a freedman of the *gens Claudia*,
a man of low repute, and P. Clodius's chief instrument in
carrying out his schemes of violence and outrage.

^b The *iudices* consisted of three *decuriae*, made up respec-
tively of senators, knights, and *tribuni aerarii* (probably
persons of property, representing the classes below the
knights). Each of the three *decuriae* had its separate
balloting-urn.

tribune to intervene. For as to Caninius's proposal about Pompey, it has utterly collapsed. It is not a popular proposal in itself, and our friend Pompey is censured for his breach of friendship with Lentulus, and, upon my honour, he is not the man he was. For his support of Milo is not altogether agreeable to those who constitute the worst and lowest dregs of the people, while the patriotic party regret his sins of omission and blame him for his sins of commission, and there are plenty of both. Marcellinus, however, does not quite satisfy me in one regard—he treats him too harshly ; and yet he does so with no objection on the part of the Senate, which makes me all the more wishful to withdraw myself from the House and from all participation in politics.

In the courts I hold the same position as I did. My house is as thronged as ever it was. There is one awkward incident due to Milo's lack of foresight in the matter of Sextus Clodius,[a] of whose prosecution at this particular juncture, and by a feeble lot of accusers, I did not approve. Before a most corrupt jury Milo only failed to obtain a condemnation by three votes. The populace, therefore, are for having the fellow up again, and he must be dragged back into court. People cannot tolerate it, and because he was all but condemned when pleading before a jury of his own partisans, they look upon him as already condemned. Even in this matter the feelings of dislike for Pompey stood in our way. For the votes of the senators acquitted him with a handsome margin, those of the knights were equally divided, those of the *tribuni aerarii* were against him.[b] But I am consoled for this misfortune by the daily condemnations of my enemies, among whom, to my

perlubente Servius allisus est, ceteri conciduntur.
C. Cato contionatus est, comitia haberi non siturum,
si sibi cum populo dies agendi essent exempti. Ap-
7 pius a Caesare nondum redierat. Tuas mirifice
litteras exspecto ; atque adhuc clausum mare scio
fuisse ; sed quosdam venisse tamen Ostia dicebant,
qui te unice laudarent, plurimique in provincia fieri
dicerent. Eosdem aiebant nuntiare, te prima navi-
gatione transmissurum. Id cupio ; et, quamquam
teipsum scilicet maxime, tamen etiam litteras tuas
ante exspecto. Mi frater, vale.

V

MARCUS Q. FRATRI S.

Romae, A.U.C. 698.

1 Dederam ad te litteras antea, quibus erat scriptum, Tulliam nostram Crassipedi prid. Non. April.
esse desponsatam, ceteraque de re publica privata-
que perscripseram. Postea sunt haec acta. Non.
Apr. senatus consulto Pompeio pecunia decreta est
in rem frumentariam ad HS cccc. Sed eodem die
vehementer actum de agro Campano clamore senatus

ᵃ Probably Servius Pola ; *cf. Fam.* viii. 12. 2.
ᵇ Quintus was now employed in Sardinia as Pompey's
legatus in the collection of corn-supplies.
ᶜ About £340,000.

great delight, Servius [a] has suffered shipwreck, and
all the rest are being made mince-meat of. C. Cato
announced at a public meeting that he would not
permit the elections to be held should he have been
deprived of the days for transacting business with
the people. Appius has not yet returned from visiting Caesar.

It is wonderful how eagerly I await a letter from 7
you, and yet I know that the sea is still closed to
navigation ; but for all that they tell me that certain
persons have arrived at Ostia, who praised you above
all men, and declared that you are most highly
esteemed in the province.[b] They say that it is reported by the same persons that you intend to cross
as soon as ever it is possible to sail. That is just what
I desire ; and although, of course, I look forward
to seeing you in the flesh more than anything, still
even a letter from you in the meantime is something
to look forward to. Brother mine, good-bye.

V

CICERO TO QUINTUS IN SARDINIA

Rome, April 11, 56 B.C.

I sent you a letter before in which I wrote that our 1
daughter Tullia had been betrothed to Crassipes on
April 4, and gave you a full account of everything else
concerning our public and private affairs. This is
what has happened subsequently. On April 5 by a
decree of the Senate money was voted to Pompey for
the corn-supply, amounting to 40,000 *sestertia*.[c] But
on the same day there was a heated debate on the
Campanian land, when the Senate was nearly as

prope contionali. Acriorem causam inopia pecuniae
2 faciebat et annonae caritas. Non praetermittam ne
illud quidem—M. Furium Flaccum, equitem Romanum, hominem nequam, Capitolini et Mercuriales de
collegio eiecerunt, praesentem, ad pedes unius cuius-
3 que iacentem. Exiturus a. d. viii. Id. Apr. sponsalia
Crassipedi praebui. Huic convivio puer optimus,
Quintus tuus meusque, quod perleviter commotus
fuerat, defuit; a. d. vii. Id. April. veni ad Quintum,
eumque vidi plane integrum, multumque is mecum
sermonem habuit et perhumanum de discordiis
mulierum nostrarum. Quid quaeris? nihil festivius.
Pomponia autem etiam de te questa est. Sed haec
4 coram agemus. A puero ut discessi, in aream tuam
veni. Res agebatur multis structoribus. Longilium
redemptorem cohortatus sum. Fidem mihi faciebat,
se velle nobis placere. Domus erit egregia. Magis
enim cerni iam poterat, quam quantum ex forma
iudicabamus. Itemque nostra celeriter aedificabatur.
Eo die cenavi apud Crassipedem. Cenatus in hortos
ad Pompeium lectica latus sum. Luci eum convenire
non potueram, quod abfuerat. Videre autem volebam, quod eram postridie Roma exiturus, et quod
ille in Sardiniam iter habebat. Hominem conveni
et ab eo petivi, ut quamprimum te nobis redderet.

^a A college which had charge of the Capitoline games.
^b A corporation of merchants; *cf.* Livy, ii. 27. 5.
504

noisy as a public meeting. The discussion of the
question was embittered by the scarcity of money
and the high price of provisions.

And even this is an incident I shall not omit ; the 2
Capitolini *a* and the Mercuriales *b* expelled from
their respective colleges one M. Furius Flaccus, a
Roman knight, but a rascal, he being present at the
time, prostrating himself at the feet of each member
of the college in turn.

On April 6, being about to leave Rome, I gave a 3
betrothal party to Crassipes. At that banquet that
excellent boy Quintus (he is mine too) was not present,
owing to his having been indisposed, though not at all
seriously. On the 7th I went to see him and found
him in perfect health, and he and I had a long and
very affectionate talk about the squabbles of our
women-folk ; to put it shortly, nothing could have
been merrier. Pomponia, however, grumbled about
you too ; but of this when we meet.

On leaving the boy I visited your building-site. 4
The work was being pressed on with a lot of builders.
I urged Longilius the contractor to hasten. He
convinced me that he was anxious to give every satisfaction. It will be a magnificent house ; we could
now get a clearer idea of it than we could form from
studying the plan. My own house, too, was being
rapidly built. That day I dined with Crassipes.
After dinner I rode in my litter to see Pompey at his
pleasaunce. I had not been able to have an interview
with him during the day, as he was not at home ; but
I wanted to see him, because I am leaving Rome
to-morrow, and he has to go to Sardinia. I had a talk
with him, and begged of him to let us have you back
as soon as possible. He said " without a moment's

505

5 Statim dixit.   Erat autem iturus (ut aiebat) a. d. III.
Id. Apr., ut aut Labrone, aut Pisis conscenderet.
Tu, mi frater, simul ut ille venerit, primam naviga-
tionem (dummodo idonea tempestas sit) ne omiseris.
A. d. III. Id. April. ante lucem hanc epistulam conscripseram, eramque in itinere, ut eo die apud T.
Titium in Anagnino manerem.   Postridie autem in
Laterio cogitabam ; inde, cum in Arpinati quinque
dies fuissem, ire in Pompeianum ; rediens aspicere
Cumanum, ut, quoniam in Non. Maias Miloni dies
prodita est, prid. Non. Romae essem, teque, mi carissime et suavissime frater, ad eam diem (ut sperabam)
viderem.   Aedificationem Arcani ad tuum adventum
sustentari placebat.   Fac, mi frater, ut valeas quam
primumque venias.

VIII *

M. CICERO S. D. Q. FRATRI

Romae, A.U.C. 698.

1   O litteras mihi tuas iucundissimas, exspectatas, ac
primo quidem cum desiderio, nunc vero etiam cum
timore !   Atque has scito litteras me solas accepisse

---

a Labro is unknown, but possibly we should read (as
Tyrrell suggests) Telamo, which, like Pisae, is on the coast of
Etruria.

b Titus Titius, a friend of Cicero's, who addressed to him
Fam. xiii. 75.   He had a villa at Anagnia in Latium.

c The property of Quintus in Arpinum.

d Also the property of Quintus, between Arpinum and
Aquinum.

* The numbering of the Letters from this point (VIII.,
IX., etc., instead of VI., VII., etc.) is due to the adoption of
Mommsen's admirable rearrangement of Letters IV.-VII.

delay." He intends to start (so he told me) on April 5 11, so as to take ship at Labro [a] or Pisae. See to it, my dear brother, that as soon as he arrives you do not miss the first opportunity you have of sailing, provided only that the weather be suitable. I am putting together this letter on April 11 before dawn, and am just about to start on my journey, so that I may stay to-day with T. Titius [b] at Anagnia ; but to-morrow I intend to be at Laterium,[c] and from there, after spending five days in Arpinum, to visit my Pompeian house, having a peep at my Cuman villa on my return, so that (since Milo's trial has been fixed for May 7) I may be at Rome on the 6th, and see you, my dearest and sweetest of brothers, I hope, on that day. I thought it best that the building operations at Arcanum [d] should be held up until you return. Make a point of keeping well, my dear brother, and of joining me as soon as possible.

VIII *

CICERO TO QUINTUS, ON HIS WAY TO ROME FROM SARDINIA

Rome, middle of May, 56 B.C.

Oh ! what an intense pleasure your letter was to 1 me, a letter long awaited, and at first with yearning only, but now with alarm also ! And I would have you know that it was the only letter I had received

(sadly muddled together in the MSS.), which makes them coherent and intelligible. The numbering from this point retains the commonly accepted order of the rest of the Letters in this Book.

post illas, quas tuus nauta attulit, Olbia datas. Sed cetera (ut scribis) praesenti sermoni reserventur. Hoc tamen non queo differre. Id. Maiis senatus frequens divinus fuit in supplicatione Gabinio deneganda. Adiurat Procilius hoc nemini accidisse. Foris valde plauditur. Mihi cum sua sponte iucundum, tum iucundius, quod me absente (est enim εἰλικρινὲς iudicium) sine oppugnatione, sine gratia nostra.

2 Eram Anti.[1] Quod Idibus et postridie fuerat dictum, de agro Campano actum iri, non est actum. In hac causa mihi aqua haeret. Sed plura quam constitueram. Coram enim. Vale, mi optime et optatissime frater, et advola. Idem te nostri rogant pueri; illud[2] scilicet, cenabis, cum veneris.

IX

M. CICERO S. D. Q. FRATRI

Romae, a.u.c. 699.

1 Placiturum tibi esse librum meum suspicabar; tam valde placuisse, quam scribis, valde gaudeo. Quod me admones de nostra Urania, suadesque, ut me-

---

[1] *Manutius*: gratia nostra erat. Quod ante *Mommsen*.
　　[2] pueri. Illud *Purser*.

---

a Now Governor of Syria. He had applied for a *supplicatio* either for his success in Palestine against Aristobulus and his son Alexander, or some previous victories over Arabs.

b A tribune.

c Literally "I have run dry," a metaphor from the damming of a stream, or possibly from the running down of the water allowance in the *clepsydra* (water-clock), meaning that Cicero had to stop speaking on so dangerous a subject.

d Or, as Purser takes it, "Of course there is this—you will, etc." (putting a full-stop after "request of you").

e His poem *De temporibus suis*.

since that which your sailor brought me, posted
at Olbia. But, as you write, let everything else
be kept back for personal conversation. This much,
however, I cannot put off; on May 15 a full Senate
acted gloriously in refusing a *supplicatio* to Gabinius.[a]
Procilius [b] swears that this has never happened to
anyone else. It is loudly applauded in the streets ; to
me it was not only delightful on its own account, but
even more so because it was done in my absence (it
was an unprejudiced decision) without any opposition
or favour on my part. I was at Antium.

What, it has been alleged, was to be settled 2
on the 15th and the following day in the matter of
the Campanian land, was never settled at all. In this
business I am at a deadlock.[c] But I have said more
than I had intended to say ; for we will talk it over
when we meet. Good-bye, my best and most desirable of brothers, and wing your way to me. Our two
boys make the same request of you ; of course it is
this [d]—you will dine with us when you arrive.

IX

CICERO TO QUINTUS

Rome, February, 55 B.C.

I had an idea that my book [e] would please you, 1
but that it should have pleased you as greatly as you
say in your letter is a great joy to me. As to your
reminding me of my Urania,[f] and advising me to

---

[f] The reference is obscure. Possibly it refers to a passage
in Cicero's poem *De consulatu suo*, recommending literature
and philosophy as against politics. "*And yet*," he goes on,
" in spite of what I then wrote, I went to see Pompey."

minerim Iovis orationem, quae est in extremo illo
libro, ego vero memini, et illa omnia mihi magis
2 scripsi, quam ceteris. Sed tamen postridie, quam tu
es profectus, multa nocte cum Vibullio veni ad Pompeium, cumque ego egissem de istis operibus atque
inscriptionibus, per mihi benigne respondit ; magnam
spem attulit. Cum Crasso se dixit loqui velle ;
mihique, ut idem facerem, suasit. Crassum consulem
ex senatu domum reduxi ; suscepit rem ; dixitque
esse, quod Clodius hoc tempore cuperet per se et per
Pompeium consequi ; putare se, si ego eum non im-
pedirem, posse me adipisci sine contentione, quod
vellem. Totum ei negotium permisi, meque in eius
potestate dixi fore. Interfuit huic sermoni P. Crassus,
adulescens nostri (ut scis) studiosissimus. Illud autem,
quod cupit Clodius, est legatio aliqua—si minus per
senatum, per populum—libera, aut Byzantium aut
ad Brogitarum aut utrumque. Plena res nummorum.
Quod ego non nimium laboro, etiamsi minus assequor,
quod volo. Pompeius tamen cum Crasso locutus est.
Videntur negotium suscepisse. Si perficiunt, optime ;
3 sin minus, ad nostrum Iovem revertamur. A. d. III.
Id. Febr. senatus consultum est factum de ambitu in
Afrani sententiam, quam ego dixeram, cum tu adesses ;
sed magno cum gemitu Senatus, consules non sunt

---

[a] *Libera legatio* was an unofficial embassy, enabling a
senator to travel abroad on his own private affairs at the
expense of the State. *Cf. Fam.* xi. 1. 2.

[b] Clodius, as tribune, had restored certain Byzantine
exiles, and he had made Brogitarus, a Galatian and son-in-
law of Deiotarus, priest of Cybele at Pessinus ; and he was
now going to those parts to raise the money for which he
held bonds from the exiles and Brogitarus. Tyrrell.

[c] Apparently that the praetors should be elected and enter
upon office at once, and so evade the prosecution which
Cato desired.

remember Jupiter's speech at the end of that book, I do indeed remember it, and I addressed all that to myself rather than to the rest of the world.

And yet, the day after you started, late at night, 2 taking Vibullius with me, I paid Pompey a visit ; and when I pleaded with him about the works and inscriptions in your honour, he responded with remarkable kindness, and greatly raised my hopes. He said he wanted to have a talk with Crassus, and urged me to do the same. I escorted Crassus as consul from the Senate to his house ; he took the matter up, and told me that there was something which Clodius was anxious to get just now through his own and Pompey's instrumentality ; and he thought that if I did not thwart Clodius's scheme, I could secure what I wanted without a fight. I put the whole business in his hands and assured him that I would be at his disposal. Publius Crassus, his young son, was present at this interview, and he is, as you are aware, devotedly attached to me. Now what Clodius is so anxious to get is some honorary embassy,[a] if not by decree of the Senate, then by popular vote, either to Byzantium or to Brogitarus,[b] or to both. There is a lot of money in it. I am not troubling myself unduly about the matter, even if I fail to get what I want. The fact remains that Pompey has spoken to Crassus, and it seems to me that they have taken the matter up. If they carry it through, nothing could be better ; if not, let us return to my " Jupiter."

On February 11, a decree of the Senate was passed 3 concerning bribery, on the motion of Afranius,[c] which I had explained to you when you were here with me. But, though the Senate groaned aloud at it, the consuls did not follow up the proposals of those

F

persecuti eorum sententias qui, Afranio cum essent
assensi, addiderunt, ut praetores ita crearentur, ut
dies LX. privati essent. Eo die Catonem plane repudia-
runt. Quid multa? tenent omnia, idque ita omnes
intellegere volunt.

<h1 style="text-align:center">X</h1>

MARCUS Q. FRATRI S.

Cumani, A.U.C. 699.

1 Tu metuis, ne me interpelles? Primo, si in isto
essem, tu scis, quid sit interpellare? An te Ateius?
Mehercule mihi docere videbaris istius generis
humanitatem, qua quidem ego nihil utor abs te. Tu
vero, ut me et appelles et interpelles et obloquare et
colloquare, velim. Quid enim mihi suavius? Non
mehercule quisquam μουσοπάτακτος libentius sua re-
centia poemata legit, quam ego te audio quacumque
de re, publica, privata, rustica, urbana. Sed mea factum est insulsa verecundia, ut te proficiscens non
tollerem. Opposuisti semel ἀναντίλεκτον causam,
Ciceronis nostri valetudinem; conticui: iterum Ci-
2 cerones; quievi. Nunc mihi iucunditatis plena
epistula hoc aspersit molestiae, quod videris, ne mihi

---

^a This would have suited Cato, since, as private citizens,
they could be proceeded against. But the consuls would have
none of it, and they were, as Cicero adds, " omnipotent."

^b Or "has Ateius been interrupting you?" Ateius being
some notorious bore.

who, when they agreed to Afranius's motion, added a rider that the praetors should only be appointed with the proviso that they should remain private citizens for sixty days.[a] On that day the consuls' repudiation of Cato was uncompromising. Why should I waste words? They have everything in their hands, and they want everybody to know it.

X

CICERO TO QUINTUS

Cumanum, April or May, 55 B.C.

You afraid that you will interrupt *me* ? In the first 1 place, supposing I were as busy as you think, do you know what is meant by the term " *to interrupt* " ? Is Ateius [b] your informant ? Upon my word, it would seem that you are teaching me a form of courtesy peculiarly your own for which I have no use at all— coming as it does from *you*. Why, I should like to have you attract as well as distract my attention, talk *at* me as well as talk *to* me. What could delight me more ? I solemnly aver that no muse-smitten poetaster ever recites his latest effusions with greater pleasure than I listen to you holding forth on any topic, be it public or private, rural or urban. But it was all the fault of my stupid reserve that I did not take you with me when I set out. Once you put me off with an unanswerable excuse—the health of my boy Cicero ; I held my tongue ; the second time it was both the young Ciceros ; I raised no objection.

And now I have a letter as pleasant as could be, 2 with just this touch of annoyance—that you seem to

513

CICERO

molestus esses, veritus esse atque etiam nunc vereri. Litigarem tecum, fas si esset ; sed mehercule istuc si umquam suspicatus ero, nihil dicam aliud, nisi verebor, ne quando ego tibi, cum sum una, molestus sim. Marium autem nostrum in lecticam mehercule coniecissem, non illam regis Ptolemaei Asicianam. Memini enim, cum hominem portarem ad Baias, Neapoli, octophoro Asiciano, machaerophoris centum sequentibus, miros risus nos edere, cum ille, ignarus sui comitatus, repente aperuit lecticam, et paene ille timore, ego risu corrui. Tunc, ut dico, certe sustulissem, ut aliquando subtilitatem veteris urbanitatis et humanissimi sermonis attingerem. Sed hominem infirmum in villam apertam, ac ne rudem quidem
3 etiam nunc, invitare nolui. Hoc vero mihi peculiare fuerit, hic etiam isto frui. Nam illorum praediorum scito mihi vicinum Marium lumen esse. Apud Anicium videbimus ut paratum sit. Nos enim ita philologi sumus, ut vel cum fabris habitare possimus. Habemus hanc philosophiam non ab Hymetto, sed ab arce Ψυρίᾳ.[1] Marius et valetudine est et natura im-
4 becillior. De interpellatione tantum sumam a vobis temporis ad scribendum, quantum dabitis. Utinam nihil detis, ut potius vestrā iniuriā, quam ignaviā meā

---

[1] *Tunstall* : Abdera *or* Gargetto *Dr. Reid* : ab arce *or* arcula Cyrea *Tyrrell*.

---

[a] For Marius see note *a* on *Fam.* vii. 1. 1.

[b] Asicius seems to have been a close friend of Ptolemy Auletes, who either gave or sold him his capacious litter with its regular body-guard of a hundred swordsmen, the sight of whom frightened the nervous valetudinarian Marius.

[c] Cicero elsewhere (*Att.* xvi. 13*a*. 2) refers to Arpinum as νῆσος Ψυρίη. Psyria is an island in the Aegean sea mentioned by Homer (*Od.* iii. 171). He means that he is no effeminate valetudinarian, but a hardy hillman.

have been, and even now to be, afraid of being an annoyance to me. I should go to law with you, if such a thing were conceivable ; but I swear that if ever I suspect your harbouring such a thought—I'll say no more than this, that at any moment when I am in your company I shall be afraid of being a nuisance to you. As for our friend Marius,[a] I declare I should have bundled him into my litter—not the one that Asicius [b] got from King Ptolemy. For I remember how when I was giving the fellow a lift from Naples to Baiae in Asicius's eight-man litter, with a hundred swordsmen in our train, I can't tell you how I laughed when Marius, all unconscious of his escort, suddenly opened the litter and nearly collapsed with fright, and I with laughter. Well, as I say, I should certainly have picked him up then, so as to get into touch (better late than never) with that subtle charm of old-world courtesy and exquisitely refined conversation. But to invite a man in feeble health to a villa exposed to the weather and, up to the present, not even roughly finished—I simply hadn't the heart.

It would of course be a special treat to me to **3** enjoy his company here also ; for I would have you know that to have him for my neighbour is as the very light of the sun on that country seat of mine. I will see about his being put up at the house of Anicius. As for myself I am the sort of book-worm that can get along with workmen in the house. For that philosophy I have to thank, not Hymettus, but the heights of Arpinum.[c] Marius is somewhat feeble both in health and character.

As for my being interrupted, I shall take from you **4** just so much time for writing as you allow me. I pray that you may allow me none, so that my doing no

cessem ! De republica nimium te laborare doleo ;
(video te ingemuisse ; sic fit εἰ δ᾽ ἐν αἴᾳ ἔζησας ; nunquam enim dicam ἔα πάσας[1]) et meliorem civem
esse, quam Philoctetam, qui, accepta iniuria, illa
spectacula quaerebat, quae tibi acerba esse video.
Amabo te, advola ; consolabor te et omnem abstergebo dolorem ; et adduc, si me amas, Marium.
Sed adproperate. Hortus domi est.

XI

M. CICERO S. D. Q. FRATRI

Romae, A.U.C. 700.

1 Epistulam hanc convicio efflagitarunt codicilli tui.
Nam res quidem ipsa et is dies, quo tu es profectus,
nihil mihi ad scribendum argumenti sane dabat. Sed
quemadmodum, coram cum sumus, sermo nobis
deesse non solet, sic epistulae nostrae debent inter
2 dum alucinari. Tenediorum igitur libertas securi
Tenedia praecisa est, cum eos praeter me et Bibulum
3 et Calidium et Favonium nemo defenderet. De te a

---

[1] sc. μελεδώνας *Lambinus* : τὰς μεληδόνας *Ed. Crat.*

---

[a] The source of this quotation is unknown, but the
meaning seems to be " What would you have done, had
you been on the spot ? And indeed there is much to be
anxious about."

[b] No such passage appears in Sophocles' play.

[c] *Codicilli* were tablets made of thin pieces of wood and
covered with wax, used in cases of urgency and haste.

[d] The inhabitants of Tenedos had petitioned the Senate
for some measure of independence, which the Senate refused.

[e] A proverbial expression for summary execution ; Tenes,

work may be due to your wrong treatment of me rather than to my own indolence.

As to politics, I grieve that you are distressing yourself unduly (I notice you have groaned; well, there's no getting out of it, " Yet hadst thou but lived in the land "—I shall never add the words, " away with all sorrow and care "),[a] and that you are a better citizen than Philoctetes,[b] who, having suffered wrong, desired to see such sights as, I perceive, are painful to you.

I entreat you, wing your way here : I shall comfort you and wipe all sorrow from your eyes ; and, as you love me, bring Marius with you. But hurry up, both of you. There is a garden attached to my house.

XI

CICERO TO QUINTUS IN SOME SUBURBAN RESIDENCE

Rome, February 10 or 11, 54 B.C.

This letter has been elicited by the strong and importunate language of your note.[c] As to the actual business, and what occurred the day you set out, it affords no material at all to write about. But just as when we are together it is not often that we are at a loss for something to talk about, so our letters ought occasionally to ramble at random.

Well, then, the liberty of the Tenedians [d] has been cut short with a Tenedian axe,[e] since there was nobody to defend them except myself, Bibulus, Calidius, and Favonius.

" the fabled eponym " of the island, had established there an ultra-Draconian penal code.

517

Magnetibus ab Sipylo mentio est honorifica facta,
cum te unum dicerent postulationi L. Sextii Pansae
4 restituisse. Reliquis diebus, si quid erit, quod te scire
opus sit, aut etiamsi nihil erit, tamen scribam quotidie
aliquid. Prid. Id. neque tibi, neque Pomponio deero.
5 Lucreti poemata, ut scribis, ita sunt,—multis luminibus ingeni, multae tamen artis.[1] Sed cum veneris . . .
Virum te putabo, si Sallusti *Empedoclea* legeris, hominem non putabo. Vale.

XII

MARCUS Q. FRATRI S.

Romae, a.u.c. 700.

1 Gaudeo tibi iucundas esse meas litteras, nec tamen
habuissem scribendi nunc quidem ullum argumen-
tum, nisi tuas accepissem. Nam prid. Id., cum Ap-

---

[1] *M*: multae etiam *Orelli*: multae tamen artis cum
inveneris virum te putabo; si Sallusti *etc. H. A. J. Munro*:
non multae tamen artis. Sed si ad umbilicum veneris, virum
te putabo. Si Sallusti *etc. Bergk.*

---

[a] Probably a *publicanus* against whose demands an appeal
had been made by the Magnesians of Lydia (*ab Sipylo*).

[b] Lucretius's *De Rerum Natura* had just been published,
a few months after the poet's death. That the text (that of
M) of this solitary and casual allusion by Cicero to Lucretius
is probably corrupt would appear from the use of *poemata*
for the singular, and the sudden change from the abl.
luminibus to the gen. *artis.*
   The text as it stands probably means that Lucretius shows
the *genius* of the old school (*e.g.* Ennius, "ingenio maximus,
arte rudis," and Attius), surprisingly combined (*tamen*)
with much of the *ars*, the more polished craftsmanship, of the
New, or Alexandrine, School (*e.g.* Catullus). But is there
much of such *ars* in the *De Rerum Natura*?

The Magnesians from Sipylus made a compli- **3** mentary reference to you, to the effect that you were the only man to stand up against the demand of L. Sextius Pansa.[a] During the days that remain, if any- **4** thing occurs which it is necessary for you to know, or even if nothing occurs, I shall nevertheless write something to you every day. On February 12, I shall not fail either you or Pomponius.

The poems of Lucretius are just as you write— **5** with frequent flashes of genius, and yet exceedingly artistic.[b] But when you come . . . [c] If you get through Sallust's *Empedoclea*, I shall think you a fine fellow, but no ordinary mortal.

XII

CICERO TO QUINTUS IN THE COUNTRY

Rome, February 13, 54 B.C.

I am delighted that you were pleased with my **1** letter ; and yet I should not have had any material for a letter even then, had I not received yours. For,

Munro suggests another reading, which may be rendered " as for any great artistry, however, if you discover the poems to possess it, I shall think you a hero"; and Bergk yet another, meaning "They do *not*, however, show much artistry. But if you read them to the last page, I shall think you a hero." (See critical note.)

It is after all possible that the *ars* in our text may not mean "artistic finish" at all, but simply "the scientific treatment of a subject"—here *ars physica* (natural science), as we have *ars metrica, grammatica, rhetorica*. In that case the passage would mean "The poems contain 'purple patches' of genius in plenty, but for all that they are extremely *technical*,"—which is no unfair description of the *De Rerum Natura*.

[c] Supply some such words as " we can discuss the matter."

pius senatum infrequentem coegisset, tantum fuit
2 frigus, ut pipulo[1] coactus sit nos dimittere. De Com-
mageno, quod rem totam discusseram, mirifice mihi
et per se et per Pomponium blanditur Appius. Videt
enim, hoc genere dicendi si utar in ceteris, Februa-
rium sterilem futurum ; eumque lusi iocose satis,
neque solum illud extorsi oppidulum, quod erat
positum in Euphrati Zeugmate, sed praeterea togam
sum eius praetextam, quam erat adeptus Caesare
3 consule, magno hominum risu cavillatus. " Quod nos
vult," inquam, " renovare honores eosdem, quo minus
togam praetextam quotannis interpolet, decernen-
dum nihil censeo. Vos autem homines nobiles, qui
Bostrenum praetextatum non ferebatis, Commage-
num feretis ? " Genus vides et locum iocandi. Multa
dixi in ignobilem regem ; quibus totus est explosus.
Quo genere commotus (ut dixi) Appius totum me
amplexatur. Nihil est enim facilius, quam reliqua
discutere. Sed non faciam, ut illum offendam, ne

---

[1] *An emendation (for* populi convicio *MSS.) adopted by
Prof. Housman, who rejects* convicio *as a gloss on* pipulo.
Tyrrell reads pipulo, convicio *asyndetically.*

---

[a] Lit. " chirping of chickens," then used of demonstrations
of restlessness at public meetings.

[b] Antiochus, King of Commagene in Syria. He had
received the little kingdom from Pompey at the end of the
Mithridatic war.

[c] Which Antiochus had impudently claimed.

[d] Cicero's meaning is somewhat obscure, but, assuming
the text to be right, it seems to be this : " As far as I am
concerned, Antiochus is at liberty to have a clean *toga prae-*

on the 12th, after Appius had got together a sparsely attended Senate, the proceedings were so frosty, that he was forced by our whimperings [a] to dismiss us.

As to the Commagenian,[b] because I had exploded 2 the whole affair, it is amazing how Appius fawns upon me, both personally and through Pomponius ; for he sees that if I adopt the same style of speaking in all the other cases, February will be a barren month for him. And I made fun of Antiochus in quite a merry way, and not only made him take his hands off that tiny town situated in the territory of Zeugma on the Euphrates,[c] but I moreover excited much general laughter by jeering at the fellow's *toga praetexta* which he had obtained in the consulship of Caesar. " As to his wishing us (I said) to renew those same 3 honours, it is my opinion that no decree at all is needed to forbid his furbishing up his *toga praetexta* every year. But will you, my noble friends, who did not tolerate the wearing of the *toga praetexta* by the Bostran, tolerate it in the case of this Commagenian ? "[d] You see the style I adopted, and the opportunity I had for a bit of fun. I spoke a lot in condemnation of his scurvy majesty, with the result that he was hissed off the stage neck-and-crop. But that same style of mine greatly agitated Appius, and he embraces me like a mother. The rest of his proposals it is the easiest thing in the world to scatter to the winds. But I am not going so far as to offend him, for fear he implores the protection of Jupiter

texta as often as he pleases, but as for his wearing it in public you will not allow him to do so any more than you allowed the Bostran to do so." Bostra (the Bozrah of Isaiah) was in Arabia Petraea. The reference is to some unknown tetrarch of that district.

imploret fidem Iovis Hospitalis, Graios omnes con-
4 vocet, per quos mecum in gratiam rediit. Theopompo satisfaciemus. De Caesare fugerat me ad te
scribere. Video enim, quas tu litteras exspectaris.
Sed ille scripsit ad Balbum, fasciculum illum epistularum, in quo fuerat et mea et Balbi, totum sibi aqua
madidum redditum esse, ut ne illud quidem sciat,
meam fuisse aliquam epistulam. Sed ex Balbi epistola pauca verba intellexerat, ad quae rescripsit his
verbis : " De Cicerone video te quiddam scripsisse,
quod ego non intellexi ; quantum autem coniectura
consequebar, id erat eiusmodi, ut magis optandum,
5 quam sperandum putarem." Itaque postea misi ad
Caesarem eodem illo exemplo litteras. Iocum autem
illius de sua egestate ne sis aspernatus. Ad quem ego
rescripsi, nihil esse, quod posthac arcae nostrae fiducia
conturbaret ; lusique in eo genere et familiariter et
cum dignitate. Amor autem eius erga nos perfertur
omnium nuntiis singularis. Litterae quidem ad id,
quod exspectas, fere cum tuo reditu iungentur ;
reliqua singulorum dierum scribemus ad te, si modo
tabellarios tu praebebis. Quamquam eiusmodi frigus
impendebat, ut summum periculum esset, ne Appio
suae aedes urerentur.

---

[a] *i.e.*, Ζεὺς Ξένιος. We can only conjecture that certain
Greeks helped to effect a reconciliation between Cicero and
Appius.

[b] *i.e.*, Quintus. What Caesar gathered from Balbus's
letter was probably that Quintus was prepared to desert
Pompey and come over to him. Caesar thought the news
was " too good to be true."

[c] This sentence may be paraphrased thus : " And yet
(there will be little to tell you because) Appius's proposals
are so *coldly* received that there may be a *hot* reaction
against him "—a pretty instance of παρὰ προσδοκίαν.

Hospitalis,[a] and rouses a rally of all the Greeks, for it was through them that we became reconciled.

I shall satisfy Theopompus. I forgot to write to 4 you about Caesar ; for I see what sort of a letter you have been expecting. But he wrote to Balbus and told him that the whole packet of letters, in which were mine and Balbus's, was so soaked with water when he received it that he did not even know there was any letter from me. He had, however, made out a few words in Balbus's letter, to which he replied in the following words : " I see that you have written something about Cicero,[b] which I could not understand, but as far as I could conjecture, it was the sort of thing that I thought more to be desired than hoped for." So later on I sent Caesar an exact duplicate of 5 my letter.

You must not be put off with that little joke of Caesar's about his lack of means. My reply to it was that there was no reason why he should in future make a mess of his affairs by relying on my money-chest ; and I kept up the joke with him in that sort of way, familiarly but without loss of dignity. His devotion to us, however, as reported by messages from all sides, is quite extraordinary. The letter bearing upon what you are waiting for will practically coincide with your return. Anything more that happens day by day I will let you know by letter, provided only that you furnish me with letter-carriers. And yet the political barometer is so near freezing-point that Appius is in extreme danger of having his house burnt about his ears.[c]

Tyrrell takes *suae aedes urerentur* as meaning " his house may be *frost-bitten*," *i.e.*, utterly deserted by *salutatores*, etc.

CICERO

XIII

M. CICERO S. D. Q. FRATRI

Romae, a.u.c. 700.

1 Risi " nivem atram," teque hilari animo esse et
prompto ad iocandum valde me iuvat. De Pompeio
assentior tibi, vel tu potius mihi. Nam, ut scis,
iampridem istum canto Caesarem. Mihi crede, in
2 sinu est, neque ego discingor. Cognosce nunc Idus.
Decimus erat Caelio dies. Domitius ad numerum
iudices non habuit. Vereor, ne homo teter et ferus,
Pola Servius, ad accusationem veniat. Nam noster
Caelius valde oppugnatur a gente Clodia. Certi nihil
est adhuc ; sed veremur. Eodem igitur die Syriis[1]
est senatus datus frequens ; frequentes contra Syriaci
publicani. Vehementer vexatus Gabinius ; exagitati
tamen a Domitio publicani, quod eum essent cum
equis prosecuti. L. noster Lamia paullo ferocius,
cum Domitius dixisset, Vestra culpa haec acciderunt,
equites Romani ; dissolute enim iudicatis, Nos iudi-
camus, vos laudatis, inquit. Actum est eo die nihil ;

---

[1] M^2: Tyriis MSS.

---

a The tenth day after his arraignment, ten days having,
according to custom, to intervene between the arraignment
and the trial of a person accused, here M. Caelius Rufus,
Cicero's correspondent. This trial is referred to in *Fam.* viii.
12. 2.

b L. Domitius Ahenobarbus, the consul for the year (54).

c A sort of professional prosecutor. *Cf. Fam.* viii. 12. 2.

d Governor, as proconsul, of Syria ; but he had quitted
his province in order to restore Ptolemy Auletes to the
throne of Egypt, with the result that Syria was harassed
by pirates.

XIII

CICERO TO QUINTUS IN THE COUNTRY

Rome, February 14, 54 B.C.

Your " black snow " tickled me, and I am highly 1
delighted that you are in a merry mood which
prompts you to joke. As to Pompey, I quite agree
with you, or rather you agree with me. For, as you
are aware, I have long been singing the praises of
your friend Caesar. Believe me, he is my bosom
friend, and I never try to unbind " the hoops of
steel."

Now let me tell you about the Ides. It was 2
Caelius's tenth day.[a] Domitius [b] failed to get the
requisite number of jurors. I am afraid that abomin-
able and ruffianly fellow, Pola Servius,[c] will turn up
for the prosecution. For our friend Caelius is being
bitterly attacked by the Clodian family. There is
nothing certain so far; but I am apprehensive. On the
same day then the Syrians were granted a full Senate;
on the other side the *publicani* of Syria appeared in full
force. Gabinius[d] was fiercely abused; but the *publicani*
on the other hand were denounced by Domitius for
having (as he said) honoured Gabinius with an escort
of cavalry. When Domitius said: " It is all your
fault, Knights of Rome, that this happened, since
your verdicts are lax," our friend L. Lamia [e] rather
too impetuously rejoined: " Yes, they are our verdicts, but it is you senators who vouch for a man's
character." On that day nothing was done, and
night broke off the discussion.

[e] An *eques* who had befriended Cicero during his exile.
Cf. Fam. xi. 16. 2 and xii. 29. 1.

3 nox diremit. Comitialibus diebus, qui Quirinalia se-
quuntur, Appius interpretatur, non impediri se lege
Pupia, quo minus habeat senatum, et quod Gabinia
sanctum sit, etiam cogi, ex Kal. Febr. usque ad Kal.
Mart. legatis senatum quotidie dare. Ita putantur
detrudi comitia in mensem Martium. Sed tamen his
comitialibus tribuni plebis de Gabinio se acturos esse
dicunt. Omnia colligo, ut novi scribam aliquid ad te.

4 Sed, ut vides, res me ipsa deficit. Itaque ad Calli-
sthenem et ad Philistum redeo, in quibus te video vo-
lutatum. Callisthenes quidem vulgare et notum negotium, quemadmodum Graeci aliquot locuti sunt.
Siculus ille capitalis, creber, acutus, brevis, paene
pusillus Thucydides, sed utros eius habueris libros
(duo enim sunt corpora), an utrosque, nescio. Me
magis de Dionysio delectat. Ipse est enim veterator
magnus, et perfamiliaris Philisto Dionysius. Sed quod
ascribis, aggrederisne ad historiam ? me auctore
potes. Et, quoniam tabellarios subministras, hodierni
diei res gestas Lupercalibus habebis. Oblecta te
cum Cicerone nostro quam bellissime.

---

^a For this and the Gabinian law see note *c* on *Fam.* i. 4. 1.

^b *i.e.*, the legality of Gabinius's restoration of Ptolemy
Auletes.

^c A native of Olynthus, who wrote a history of the Phocian
War, and the campaigns of Alexander the Great, whom he
accompanied to Asia. *Cf. Fam.* v. 12. 2. Callisthenes lived
387–327 B.C.

^d A Syracusan, born about 435 B.C., a great favourite of
Dionysius the elder.

Appius takes the view that he is not prevented **3**
by the Pupian law *a* from holding a Senate on the
comitial days which follow the Quirinalia, and that
by the provisions of the Gabinian law he is even
compelled to grant a Senate to the emissaries every
day from February 1 to March 1. So it is thought that
the elections are being postponed till the month of
March. For all that the tribunes of the plebs declare
that they will settle the affair of Gabinius *b* in the
course of these comitial days. I am collecting every
scrap of news so that I may have something fresh
to tell you. But, as you see, it is just material that
fails me.

So I return to Callisthenes *c* and Philistus,*d* in both **4**
of whom I see you have been wallowing. Callisthenes
is a hackneyed and commonplace piece of goods, as
several Greeks have remarked. The Sicilian is a
first-class writer, pithy, pointed, and concise, almost
a pocket-edition of Thucydides ; but which of his
books you have had in your hands (for there are two
compilations), or whether you have had both, I don't
know. The one on Dionysius gives me most pleasure ;
for Dionysius is a big rogue, and Philistus knows him
thoroughly. But about your postscript—do you
really intend taking up history ? If I may say so,
you have the ability. And now that you are supplying me with letter-carriers, you will hear to-day's
achievements on the Lupercalia. Amuse yourself
with our dear Cicero as agreeably as you can.

CICERO

XIV

Cumis aut Pompeiis, a.u.c. 700.

1 Duas adhuc a te accepi epistulas ; earum alteram in
ipso discessu nostro, alteram Arimino datam. Plures,
quas scribis te dedisse, non acceperam. Ego me in
Cumano et Pompeiano, praeterquam quod sine te,
ceterum satis commode oblectabam ; et eram in iisdem locis usque ad Kal. Iun. futurus. Scribebam illa,
quae dixeram, πολιτικά ; spissum sane opus et
operosum ; sed si ex sententia successerit, bene erit
opera posita ; sin minus, in illud ipsum mare deicie-
mus, quod spectantes scribimus. Aggrediemur alia,
2 quoniam quiescere non possumus. Tua mandata per-
sequar diligenter et adiungendis hominibus et quibusdam non alienandis. Maximae mihi vero curae
erit, ut Ciceronem tuum nostrumque videam, si licet[1],
quotidie ; sed inspiciam, quid discat, quam saepissime ; et, nisi ille contemnet, etiam magistrum me ei
profitebor ; cuius rei nonnullam consuetudinem nactus sum in hoc horum dierum otio, Cicerone nostro
3 minore producendo.[2] Tu, quemadmodum scribis, quod
etiamsi non scriberes, facere te diligentissime tamen
sciebam, facies scilicet, ut mea mandata digeras,

---

[1] *Tyrrell*: scilicet *edd.*, *which Purser thinks is right,*
" *of course* ; *but* (*more than that I shall, etc.*)."
[2] *Boot* : perdocendo *Nobbe.*

XIV

CICERO TO QUINTUS IN GAUL

Cumae or Pompeii, middle of May, 54 B.C.

I have so far received two letters from you, one 1
of them at the very moment of my departure, the
other posted at Ariminum ; the additional letters you
write that you have sent me I have not received. I am
enjoying myself quite comfortably, except that you
are not with me, at my Cuman and Pompeian resid-
ences, and I intend being in these same spots till
June 1. I am engaged upon the treatise I told you
about, on the *Republic*—a very stiff and toilsome
piece of work ; but if it succeeds to my satisfaction,
the labour will have been well laid out ; if not, I
shall hurl it down into that very sea I am gazing upon
as I write. I shall apply myself to something else,
since inactivity is more than I can stand.

I shall carry out your instructions to the letter, 2
both as regards conciliating certain people, and not
estranging certain others. My chief anxiety, however, will be to see your Cicero (he belongs to both
of us), if I may, every day, but I shall test his progress
as often as possible, and, unless he disdains me, I shall
even offer him my services as a teacher—a capacity
in which I have acquired some amount of experience
during these days of leisure in bringing on my own,
I mean the younger, Cicero.

You will, of course, do as you write you will (and 3
even if you did not put it down on paper, I am none
the less assured that you are most conscientious in
doing so), I mean that you will arrange, follow out,

persequare, conficias. Ego, cum Romam venero,
nullum praetermittam Caesaris tabellarium, cui
litteras ad te non dem. His diebus (ignosces) cui darem, fuit nemo ante hunc M. Orfium, equitem Romanum, nostrum et pernecessarium, et quod est ex mu-
nicipio Atellano, quod scis esse in fide nostra. Itaque eum tibi commendo in maiorem modum, hominem domi splendidum, gratiosum etiam extra domum ; quem fac ut tua liberalitate tibi obliges. Est
tribunus militum in exercitu nostro. Gratum hominem observantemque cognosces. Trebatium ut valde
ames, vehementer te rogo.

XV<small>A</small>

M. CICERO S. D. Q. FRATRI

Romae, A.U.C. 700.

1   A. d. IV. Non. Iun., quo die Romam veni, accepi
tuas litteras, datas Placentiae : deinde alteras postridie, datas Blandenone, cum Caesaris litteris, re-
fertis omni officio, diligentia, suavitate. Sunt ista
quidem magna, vel potius maxima. Habent enim
vim magnam ad gloriam et ad summam dignitatem.

<small>a</small> See *Fam.* xiii. 7. 1.
<small>b</small> C. Trebatius Testa, Cicero's lawyer friend, to whom
he wrote *Fam.* vii. 6-22, who was now serving with Quintus,
under Caesar, in Gaul.
<small>c</small> A town near Placentia in Cisalpine Gaul.

and execute my instructions. For myself, when I arrive in Rome, I shall allow no letter-carrier of Caesar's to pass by without giving him a letter for you. During these last days (pray forgive me) there has been no one to whom I might entrust a letter, until the present bearer turned up—M. Orfius, a knight of Rome, one who is my friend, not only on account of his very close connexion with me, but also because he comes from the municipality of Atella, which, as you are aware, is under my patronage.[a] I accordingly commend him to you with more than ordinary warmth as a man of exalted position in his own town, and popular outside it too. Pray make a point of laying him under an obligation to you by treating him handsomely. He is a military tribune in your army. You will find him a grateful fellow, who will show you every attention. I earnestly beg of you to be a good friend to Trebatius.[b]

XVa

CICERO TO QUINTUS IN GAUL

Rome, early in June, 54 b.c.

I received your letter posted at Placentia on June 1, the day I arrived in Rome; then, on the following day, I got another posted at Blandeno,[c] together with a letter from Caesar, brimming over with every sort of kindness, assiduous attention, and charm. These expressions of goodwill on his part are significant or rather *most* significant; for they have a powerful influence in the direction of our honour and glory and exaltation in the State. But believe me (you know

531

Sed mihi crede, quem nosti, quod in istis rebus ego plurimi aestimo, id iam habeo, te scilicet primum tam inservientem communi dignitati ; deinde Caesaris tantum in me amorem, quem omnibus his honoribus, quos me a se exspectare vult, antepono. Litterae vero eius una datae cum tuis (quarum initium est quam suavis ei tuus adventus fuerit, et recordatio veteris amoris, deinde, se effecturum, ut ego in medio dolore ac desiderio tui te, cum a me abesses, potissimum secum esse laetarer) incredibiliter delectarunt

2 Quare facis tu quidem fraterne, quod me hortaris, sed mehercule currentem nunc quidem, ut omnia mea studia in istum unum conferam. Ego vero ardenti quidem studio hoc fortasse efficiam, quod saepe viatoribus, cum properant, evenit, ut, si serius, quam voluerunt, forte surrexerint, properando etiam citius quam si de multa nocte vigilassent, perveniant, quo velint, sic ego, quoniam in isto homine colendo tam indormivi diu, te mehercule saepe excitante, cursu corrigam tarditatem, tum equis, tum vero (quoniam scribis poema ab eo nostrum probari) quadrigis poeticis. Modo mihi date Britanniam, quam pingam coloribus tuis penicillo meo. Sed quid ago ? quod mihi

---

me by this time) when I say that I already possess what I value most of all in the whole situation—I mean, first of all, your own efficient service in support of our common position, and, secondly, Caesar's extraordinary affection for me, which I set above all those honours he wishes me to anticipate at his hands. In fact, his letter, delivered simultaneously with yours (which begins with his saying how delighted he was with your arrival and the renewal of the memory of your old affection, and he goes on to say that he will so manage matters that in the midst of my sorrow and yearning for you, I should be cheered by your being, though away from me, in *his* company more than any other), that letter, I say, gave me more pleasure than you could possibly believe.

You are therefore acting, indeed, like a brother in urging me (though at the present moment, upon my honour, you are but spurring a willing horse) to concentrate all my energies upon him alone. Yes, verily, so hot is my zeal that I shall perhaps succeed in doing what often occurs in the case of travellers, when they are in a hurry—I mean that, if they happen to get up later than they intended, by making extra haste they arrive at their destination even sooner than if they had woke up at dead of night; so I, since I have been asleep so long over the matter of paying court to your friend (though you, heaven knows, repeatedly tried to rouse me), shall make up for my slowness by galloping, not only on a relay of horses, but also (since you write that my poem *a* meets with his approval) by driving a four-horsed chariot of poesy. Only you people must give me Britain for a subject, so that I may paint it in your colours, but with my own brush. But what am I about? What

CICERO

tempus, Romae praesertim, ut iste me rogat, manenti, vacuum ostenditur ? Sed videro. Fortasse enim (ut 3 fit) vincet tuus amor omnes difficultates. Trebatium quod ad se miserim, persalse et humaniter etiam gratias mihi agit. Negat enim, in tanta multitudine eorum, qui una essent, quemquam fuisse, qui vadimonium concipere posset. M. Curtio tribunatum ab eo petivi (nam Domitius se derideri putasset, si esset a me rogatus ; hoc enim est eius quotidianum, se ne tribunum militum quidem facere ; etiam in senatu lusit Appium collegam, propterea isse ad Caesarem, ut aliquem tribunatum auferret), sed in alterum 4 annum. Id et Curtius ita volebat. Tu, quemadmodum me censes oportere esse in republica et in nostris inimicitiis, ita et esse et fore auricula infima 5 scito molliorem. Res Romanae se sic habebant. Erat nonnulla spes comitiorum, sed incerta ; erat aliqua suspicio dictaturae, ne ea quidem certa ; summum otium forense, sed senescentis magis civitatis, quam acquiescentis. Sententia autem nostra in senatu eiusmodi, magis ut alii nobis assentiantur, quam nosmetipsi.

Τοιαῦθ' ὁ τλήμων πόλεμος ἐξεργάζεται.

<hr>

[a] M. Curtius Postumus ; Cicero calls himself his *patronus* in *Att.* ix. 6. 2.

[b] Ahenobarbus, consul with Appius Claudius Pulcher for 54.

[c] Possibly borrowed from Catullus (*mollior imula oricilla*, 25. 2), but as Cicero never once mentions Catullus (*cf.* 9. 2 above), it may only be, as Tyrrell suggests, an ordinary

prospect have I of a moment's leisure, especially if I stay, as he asks me to, in Rome ? But I shall bear it in mind. Very likely, as usual, my love for you will surmount all difficulties.

For having sent him Trebatius he expresses his 3 gratitude to me very wittily and courteously too. He declares that in all that crowd who were on his staff there was not a single man who could draw up so much as a form of recognizance. I applied to him for a tribuneship for M. Curtius [a] (as for Domitius,[b] he would have suspected me of making fun of him had I asked him for it ; indeed his daily joke is that he has not even the appointment of a military tribune ; even in the Senate he twitted his colleague Appius with having gone to Caesar for the sole purpose of getting a tribuneship out of him), but for next year ; and that is just what Curtius wanted.

As to what you think my behaviour should be in 4 politics and in dealing with my enemies, I would have you know that I am, and always will be, " softer than the lobe of your ear." [c]

The position of affairs in Rome is as follows : there 5 is some hope of the elections being held, but it is a vague one ; there is also some suspicion of a dictator-ship, but even that has no certain foundation ; the forum is profoundly tranquil, but that indicates senile decay, rather than acquiescence, on the part of the State, while the opinions I express in the Senate are such that others agree with them more than I do myself. " *Such is the havoc wrought by wretched war.*" [d]

proverb. For *oricilla* = *auricilla* *cf.* *plostrum* = *plaustrum.* *Polla* = *Paulla* and *Clodius* = *Claudius.*

[d] Eur. *Suppl.* 119.

CICERO

XV_B

M. CICERO S. D. Q. FRATRI

Romae, a.u.c. 700.

1 Calamo bono et atramento temperato, charta etiam
dentata res agetur.ᵃ Scribis enim, te meas litteras
superiores vix legere potuisse ; in quo nihil eorum,
mi frater, fuit, quae putas. Neque enim occupatus
eram, neque perturbatus nec iratus alicui ; sed hoc
facio semper, ut, quicumque calamus in manus meas
2 venerit, eo sic utar, tamquam bono. Verum attende
nunc, mi optime et suavissime frater, ad ea dum re-
scribo, quae tu in hac eadem brevi epistula πραγμα-
τικῶς valde scripsisti. De quo petis, ut ad te, nihil
occultans, nihil dissimulans, nihil tibi indulgens, ger-
mane fraterneque rescribam, id est, utrum advoles,
ut dixerimus, an ad expediendum te, si causa sit,
commorere—si, mi Quinte, parva aliqua res esset, in
qua sciscitarere, quid vellem, tamen, cum tibi per-
missurus essem, ut faceres, quod velles, ego ipse, quid
vellem, ostenderem. In hac vero re hoc profecto
quaeris, cuiusmodi illum annum, qui sequitur, exspectem ; plane aut tranquillum nobis, aut certe
munitissimum ; quod quotidie domus, quod forum,

ᵃ Polished or smoothed with the *dens* (tusk) of the
elephant.

XV_B

Rome, July 27, 54 B.C.

For this letter I shall use a good pen, well-mixed 1
ink, and ivory-polished *ᵃ* paper too. For you write
that you could hardly read my last, but for that
there were none of those reasons which you suspect,
my dear brother. I was not busy, nor upset, nor
angry with someone, but it is always my practice to
use whatever pen I find in my hand as if it were a
good one.

But now, my best and dearest of brothers, let me 2
have your attention while I reply to what you have
written in such a very business-like manner in this
short letter I have before me. As to the matter about
which you beg of me to write back to you, concealing
nothing, withholding nothing, not sparing your feelings, but frankly, and as a brother should—I mean
whether you are to wing your way home as we had
arranged, or to stay on to clear yourself of liabilities,
if there be any reason to do so—well, my dear
Quintus, if the matter in regard to which you in-
quired what I wished were a small one, yet, though
I should have allowed you to do what you wished, I
should have shown you what I myself wished. In this
matter, however, the real meaning of your inquiry is
—what sort of a year do I expect next year to be?
I expect it to be either an entirely tranquil one for us
or, at any rate, an impregnable one in respect of my
position; and this is clearly proved every day at my
house, in the forum, and by manifestations of feeling

537

CICERO

quod theatri significationes declarant, nec laboramus
mea conscientia copiarum nostrarum, quod Caesaris,
quod Pompei gratiam tenemus. Haec me, ut con-
fidam, faciunt. Sin aliquis erumpet amentis hominis
furor, omnia sunt ad eum frangendum expedita.
3 Haec ita sentio, iudico, ad te explorate scribo. Dubitare te, non assentatorie, sed fraterne veto. Quare
suavitatis equidem nostrae fruendae causa cuperem
te ad id tempus venire, quod dixeras ; sed illud malo
tamen, quod putas magis e re tua ; nam illa etiam
magni aestimo—ἀμφιλαφίαν illam tuam, et explica-
tionem debitorum tuorum. Illud quidem sic habeto,
nihil nobis expeditis, si valebimus, fore fortunatius.
Parva sunt, quae desunt, pro nostris quidem moribus,
et ea sunt ad explicandum expeditissima, modo valea-
4 mus. Ambitus redit immanis. Numquam fuit par.
Idib. Quint. fenus fuit bessibus ex triente, coitione
Memmi et consulum cum Domitio ; hanc Scaurus
utinam vinceret ! Messalla flaccet. Non dico
ὑπερβολικῶς ; vel HS centies constituunt in praero-

ᵃ P. Clodius.
ᵇ *Cf. Ep.* 4. 3.
ᶜ It must be remembered that the consuls for this year
(54) were L. Domitius Ahenobarbus and Appius Claudius
Pulcher. The candidates for the consulship in the ensuing
year (53) were C. Memmius (for whom *cf. Fam.* xiii. 1), Cn.
Domitius Calvinus, M. Valerius Messalla, and M. Aemilius
Scaurus. Memmius was favoured by Caesar, Scaurus at
first, but not subsequently, by Pompey. To secure the
existing consuls' influence in the coming election, Memmius
and Domitius Calvinus made a disgraceful compact with
them, pledging themselves to produce false testimony in the
interests of the out-going consuls, giving them provinces
with *imperium*, etc. Memmius, however, at Pompey's
instigation, divulged the whole matter to the Senate, and

in the theatre ; and I am in no anxiety, conscious as I am of my resources, seeing that I retain the favour of Caesar and that of Pompey. This gives me confidence. If, on the other hand, there is any outburst of frenzy on the part of our demented friend,[a] all preparations have been made to crush him.

These are my sentiments and my considered 3 opinions, and I send them to you with full assurance. I forbid you to have any doubt about it, not because I would tickle your ears, but because I am your brother. I should therefore desire you for my part to come at the time you mentioned, so that we may enjoy the pleasure of each other's society ; on the other hand, I prefer that other course even more— the course you consider more to your interest ; for I attach much importance to those other things also— the " *opulence* "[b] you talk about, and getting rid of your liabilities. You may take my word for it that, once we are free of debt, if only we keep well, we shall be better off than anybody in the world. Our wants are trifling, considering the way we live, and those wants we are perfectly free to get rid of, if only we keep our health.

There is a horrible recrudescence of bribery and 4 corruption. Never has there been anything equal to it. On July 15, interest rose from 4 to 8 per cent, in consequence of the coalition arranged by Memmius and the consuls with Domitius : [c] would that Scaurus could defeat it. Messalla has no backbone. I am not indulging in exaggerations ; they are contracting to distribute as much as 10,000 *sestertia* [d] among the

gained nothing thereby ; while Domitius Calvinus and the " flabby " Messalla were elected consuls for 53.
  [d] About £88,000.

gativa pronuntiare. Res ardet invidia. Tribunicii
candidati compromiserunt, HS quingenis in singulos
apud M. Catonem depositis, petere eius arbitratu,
ut, qui contra fecisset, ab eo condemnaretur. Quae
quidem comitia gratuita si fuerint, ut putantur, plus
unus Cato fuerit, quam omnes leges omnesque iudices.

XVI

M. CICERO S. D. Q. FRATRI

Romae, a.u.c. 700.

1 Cum a me litteras librari manu acceperis, ne
paullum quidem oti me habuisse iudicato, cum autem
mea, paullum. Sic enim habeto, numquam me a
causis et iudiciis districtiorem fuisse, atque id anni
tempore gravissimo et caloribus maximis. Sed haec
(quoniam tu ita praescribis) ferenda sunt; neque com-
mittendum, ut aut spei aut cogitationi vestrae ego
videar defuisse; praesertim cum, tametsi id difficilius
fuerit, tamen ex hoc labore magnam gratiam mag-
namque dignitatem sim collecturus. Itaque, ut tibi
placet, damus operam, ne cuius animum offendamus,
atque ut etiam ab his ipsis, qui nos cum Caesare tam
coniunctos dolent, diligamur, ab aequis vero, aut
etiam a propensis in hanc partem, vehementer et

---

a The century voting first at the *comitia centuriata* was
called *centuria praerogativa*, and its vote would have a
great moral effect on the voting of the other centuries.
b More than £4000 each.
c This was a great compliment to Cato's integrity. He
was now praetor.

540

first century.*a* The business is a blaze of scandal.
The candidates for the tribuneship, having agreed
to abide by arbitration, have deposited 500 *sestertia*^b
apiece in the hands of M. Cato *c*—they to canvass
according to his instructions, and any of them failing
to do so to be condemned by him.   And if that election proves free from all corruption, as it is supposed
it will, Cato will have proved himself more powerful
than all the laws and jurors put together.

XVI

CICERO TO QUINTUS IN GAUL

Rome, end of August, 54 b.c.

When you receive a letter from me in my secre- 1
tary's hand, you may be sure that I have not had even
a moment's leisure ; if in my own, that I have had
just a little. For you may take it from me that I
have never been more distracted by cases and trials,
and that in the most unhealthy season of the year, and
when the heat is most oppressive.   But, since it is you
who so instruct me, I must put up with it all, and
never make the mistake of seeming to have disappointed either the expectations or the ideas you
and Caesar have of me, especially since, however
difficult it may have proved, it is nevertheless likely
that the result of my effort will be no little gain in
popularity and prestige.   And so, as you would have
me do, I shall take every care not to hurt anyone's feelings, but to win the esteem of even those
who resent my having become so closely attached to
Caesar, and the sincere respect and affection of those
who are impartial, or even inclined to our side.

2 colamur et amemur. De ambitu cum atrocissime
agereter in senatu multos dies, quod ita erant pro-
gressi candidati consulares, ut non esset ferendum,
in senatu non fui. Statui ad nullam medicinam rei-
3 publicae sine magno praesidio accedere. Quo die
haec scripsi, Drusus erat de praevaricatione a tribunis
aerariis absolutus, in summa, quattuor sententiis,
cum senatores et equites damnassent. Ego eodem
die post meridiem Vatinium eram defensurus. Ea
res facilis est. Comitia in mensem Sept. reiecta sunt.
Scauri iudicium statim exercebitur, cui nos non
deerimus. Συνδείπνους Σοφοκλέους, quamquam a te
actam fabellam video esse festive, nullo modo probavi.
4 Venio nunc ad id, quod nescio an primum esse debuerit. O iucundas mihi tuas de Britannia litteras !
Timebam Oceanum, timebam litus insulae. Reliqua non equidem contemno, sed plus habent tamen
spei, quam timoris, magisque sum sollicitus exspecta-
tione ea, quam metu. Te vero ὑπόθεσιν scribendi
egregiam habere video. Quos tu situs, quas naturas
rerum et locorum, quos mores, quas gentes, quas pug-
nas, quem vero ipsum imperatorem habes ! Ego te
libenter, ut rogas, quibus rebus vis, adiuvabo et tibi

---

^a See the preceding letter.
^b Probably Livius Drusus Claudianus, father of Livia,
mother of the emperor Tiberius.
^c *Praevaricatio*, a fraudulent mismanagement of the case
by collusion of the parties. *Cf. Fam.* viii. 8. 2.
^d See note *b* on 4. 6 above.
^e At Caesar's pressing request. For the whole story see
Fam. i. 9. 19.
^f Sophocles wrote a satyric drama, entitled Σύνδειπνοι,
the theme being the anger of Achilles at being excluded
from a banquet in Tenedos. Some *contretemps* of the kind
had occurred in Caesar's camp in Gaul, and Cicero was

There were very heated discussions for several 2
days in the Senate on the question of bribery and
corruption, the candidates for the consulship having
gone to such lengths as could no longer be tolerated ; [a]
but I was not in the House. I have made up my mind
to make no move in the direction of remedying the
ills of the State without a powerful backing.

On the day I am writing this, Drusus [b] has been 3
acquitted on a charge of *praevaricatio* [c] by the *tribuni
aerarii* [d] by four votes in the final count, though the
senators and knights had condemned him. This
same afternoon I am going to defend Vatinius. [e] That
will be an easy matter. The *comitia* have been postponed to the month of September. Scaurus's trial will
be brought on forthwith, and I shall not fail to support him. Your *Sophoclean Banqueters* [f] I don't at all
like, though I see that you played your part with
éclat.

I now come to a topic which I should perhaps have 4
taken first. Oh ! what a delightful letter was yours
to me about Britain ! I dreaded the ocean, I dreaded
the coast of that island. What remains of your
enterprise I do not underrate, but it is more hopeful
than alarming, and it is just the eager anticipation of
it rather than apprehension that makes me restless.
I can see, however, that you have glorious subject
matter for your pen. What encampments, what
natural characteristics of things and places, what
manners and customs, what tribes, and what battles
you have to write about, and, finally, what a man in
your commander-in-chief himself ! I shall willingly
assist you, as you ask me, in any way you wish, and
perturbed at the incident, in which Quintus appears to have
been involved.

versus, quos rogas, γλαῦκ' εἰς 'Αθήνας[1] mittam.
5 Sed heus tu, celari videor a te. Quomodonam, mi
frater, de nostris versibus Caesar? nam primum
librum se legisse scripsit ad me ante, et prima sic,
ut neget, se ne Graeca quidem meliora legisse. Reliqua ad quemdam locum ῥαθυμότερα. Hoc enim
utitur verbo. Dic mihi verum, num aut res eum, aut
χαρακτήρ non delectat ? Nihil est, quod vereare. Ego
enim ne pilo quidem minus me amabo. Hac de re
φιλαλήθως et, ut soles, scribe fraterne.

[1] *Cratander* : Athenas noctuam *M*.

---

[a] Literally " an owl to Athens," where the owl, as the bird
sacred to Pallas Athene, was bred and protected.
[b] Or " easy-going," " lacking in elaboration."

shall send you the verses for which you ask—" coals to Newcastle." [a]

But look you here, it seems to me that you are [5] keeping something back from me. What, oh what, my dear brother, did Caesar think of my verses? He wrote to me some time ago that he had read my first book; and of the first part he declared that he had never read anything better, even in Greek; the rest of it, as far as a certain passage, was rather " happy-go-lucky " [b]—that is the term he uses. Tell me the truth—is it the subject or the style that does not please him? You needn't be afraid; I shall fancy myself not a whit the less. Write about this like a lover of truth and, as you always do, like a brother.

M. TULLI CICERONIS
EPISTULARUM AD QUINTUM FRATREM

LIBER TERTIUS

I

M. CICERO S. D. Q. FRATRI

Romae, A.U.C. 700.

1 I. Ego ex magnis caloribus (non enim meminimus maiores) in Arpinati summa cum amoenitate fluminisᵃ me refeci ludorumᵇ diebus, Philotimo tribulibus commendatis.ᶜ In Arcano a. d. IV. Idus Sept. fui. Ibi Mescidium cum Philoxeno,ᵈ aquamque, quam ii ducebant non longe a villa, belle sane fluentem vidi, praesertim maxima siccitate, uberioremque aliquanto sese collecturos esse dicebant. Apud Herumᵉ recte erat. In Manilianoᶠ offendi Diphilum Diphiloᵍ tardiorem. Sed tamen nihil ei restabat praeter balnearia et ambulationem et aviarium. Villa mihi valde

---

ᵃ The Fibrenus.
ᵇ The *Ludi Romani*, held from 4th to 19th September.
ᶜ So that he might secure accommodation for them at the games.
ᵈ Probably contractors. ᵉ A steward at Arcanum.
ᶠ Probably the estate of a neighbour. ᵍ An architect.

546

CICERO'S LETTERS TO HIS BROTHER QUINTUS

BOOK III

I

CICERO TO QUINTUS IN GAUL

Partly from Arpinum, and partly from Rome, September, 54 B.C.

I. After the great heat—indeed, I cannot remem- **1** ber greater—I have been recuperating at Arpinum, and enjoying the lovely scenery of the river *a* while the games *b* are on, having left my fellow-tribesmen under the charge of Philotimus.*c* On September 10 I was at Arcanum. There I saw Mescidius along with Philoxenus *d* and the water, which they were bringing by a canal not far from your villa, flowing quite beautifully, especially considering the intense drought ; and they told me that they were going to collect a much more abundant supply of it. Everything is all right with Herus.*e* On your Manilian estate *f* I found Diphilus *g* out-doing himself in dilatoriness ; and yet he had nothing left to do but the baths and a promenade and an aviary. I was extremely pleased with the villa, because the paved

placuit, propterea quod summam dignitatem pavimentata porticus habebat, quod mihi nunc denique apparuit, posteaquam et ipsa tota patet et columnae politae sunt. Totum in eo est (quod mihi erit curae), tectorium ut concinnum sit. Pavimenta recte fieri videbantur. Cameras quasdam non probavi, mutari- 2 que iussi. Quo loco in porticu te scribere aiunt ut atriolum fiat, mihi, ut est, magis placebat. Neque enim satis loci esse videbatur atriolo ; neque fere solet nisi in his aedificiis fieri, in quibus est atrium maius ; nec habere poterat adiuncta cubicula et eiusmodi membra. Nunc hoc vel honestate testudinis, valde bonum aestivum locum obtinebit. Tu tamen si aliter sentis, rescribe quam primum. In balneariis assa in alterum apodyteri angulum promovi, propterea quod ita erant posita, ut eorum vaporarium, ex quo ignis erumpit, esset subiectum cubiculis. Subgrande cubiculum autem et hibernum altum valde probavi, quod et ampla erant et loco posita ambulationis uno latere, eo, quod est proximum balneariis. Columnas neque rectas, neque e regione Diphilus collocarat. Eas scilicet demolietur. Aliquando perpendiculo et linea discet uti. Omnino spero paucis mensibus opus Diphili perfectum fore. Curat enim diligentissime 3 Caesius, qui tum mecum fuit. II. Ex eo loco recta

colonnade gives it a dignity that cannot be surpassed, and that has only just struck me since the whole colonnade itself has come into view, and the columns have been polished. All depends upon the stuccoing being neatly done, and that I shall see to. It seemed to me that the pavements were being properly laid. There were some arched roofs which I did not care for, and I ordered them to be altered.

As regards the place in which they tell me that, 2 according to your written instructions, the ante-chamber should be built, that is, in the colonnade, I liked it better as it is. For there did not seem to be room enough for the antechamber, nor is one usually built, except in those edifices which have a larger court, nor could it have bedrooms and apartments of that sort built in it. As it is, the handsome curve of its ceiling will of itself make it serve as an excellent summer-room. However, if you think otherwise, write back as soon as possible. In the bathroom I removed the stove to the other corner of the dressing-room, because it was so placed that its steam-pipe, from which flames break out, was exactly under the bed-rooms. There was a fairly spacious bedroom and another lofty one for winter use, of which I heartily approved, because they were not only roomy, but situated in the right place, on one side of the prom-enade, that next the bathroom. The columns Diphilus had placed were neither perpendicular nor opposite each other. He will, of course, have to pull them down. Some day or other he will learn the use of the plumb-line and the tape. On the whole, I hope Diphilus's job will be completed in a few months, for Caesius, who was with me at the time, is keeping a very careful eye upon him.

Vitularia via profecti sumus in Fufidianum fundum, quem tibi proximis nundinis Arpini de Fufidio HS cccɔɔ. emeramus. Ego locum aestate umbrosiorem vidi numquam, permultis locis aquam profluentem, et eam uberem. Quid quaeris ? Iugera L. prati Caesius irrigaturum facile te arbitrabatur. Equidem hoc, quod melius intellego, affirmo, mirifica suavitate te villam habiturum, piscina et salientibus additis, palaestra, et silva vitium ridicata.[1] Fundum audio te hunc Bovillanum velle retinere. De eo quid videatur, ipse constitues. Cascellius[2] aiebat, aqua dempta, et eius aquae iure constituto, et servitute fundo illi imposita, tamen nos pretium servare posse, si vendere vellemus. Mescidium mecum habui. Is se ternis nummis in pedem tecum transegisse dicebat ; sese autem mensum pedibus aiebat passuum ɪɪɪcɪɔ. Mihi plus visum est. Sed praestabo, sumptum nusquam melius posse poni. Cillonem arcessieram Venafro. Sed eo ipso die quattuor eius conservos et 4 discipulos Venafri cuniculus oppresserat. Idibus Sept. in Laterio fui. Viam perspexi, quae mihi ita

---

[1] *Kayser* : †viridicata *MSS.* : viridicata *Nobbe.*
[2] *Reid* (cf. Att. xv. 26. 4) : Caesius *Manutius.*

---

[a] Along which cattle were driven to the Greek cities on the coast.

[b] About £850.

[c] A *iugerum* was rather more than half an acre.

[d] It is not known where this was ; certainly not at Bovillae in Latium.

[e] " As owner of the two estates (at Arpinum and Bovillae) Quintus could deal with the water as he liked. But if he sold the estate whence he took the water, he would have to declare in the conveyance that he sold subject to this right. That would be establishing for the dominant estate (where

II. From that spot I proceeded straight along the *via* 3
*Vitularia*ᵃ to your Fufidian estate, which we purchased
for you in the last few weeks from Fufidius for 100,000
sestercesᵇ at Arpinum. A more shady spot in summer
I never saw, water also gushing out in lots of places,
and a plentiful supply of it too. To put it shortly,
Caesius thought that you would have no difficulty in
irrigating fifty *jugera* ᶜ of meadow land. For my
part, I can assure you of this, and it is a matter I
know more about, that you will have a marvellously
charming villa to live in, with the addition of a fish-
pond with *jets d'eau*, an exercising-ground, and a
plantation of vines ready staked. I am told that
you wish to retain this Bovillan estate.ᵈ You will
yourself decide to do what you think best about
it. Cascellius often told me that even if the water
were taken away, and the right of drawing it were
established, and a servitude imposed on that estate,
we could still keep our price, if we desired to sell it.ᵉ
I have had Mescidius with me. He said that he had
agreed with you to do the work for three sesterces a
foot, and that he had paced the ground and found
it to be 3000 paces. I should have thought it more.
But I will guarantee that nowhere would the money
be spent more profitably. I had summoned Cillo
from Venafrum ; but on that very day four of his
fellow-workmen and pupils had been crushed by the
falling in of a tunnel at Venafrum.

On September 13 I was at Laterium.ᶠ I thorough- 4
ly examined the road, which pleased me so much

he used the water) a *ius aquae ducendae*, and imposing on
the servient estate the obligation to allow the water to be so
taken." Roby, *Classical Review*, i. 67, quoted by Tyrrell.
    ᶠ Another property of Quintus at Arpinum.

placuit, ut opus publicum videretur esse, praeter CL.
pass. Sum enim ipse mensus ab eo ponticulo, qui est
ad Furinae, Satricum versus. Eo loco pulvis, non
glarea iniecta est (id mutabitur), et ea viae pars valde
acclivis est, sed intellexi aliter duci non potuisse,
praesertim cum tu neque per Locustae, neque per
Varronis velles ducere. Varro ante suum fundum
prope munierat. Locusta non attigerat ; quem ego
Romae aggrediar et, ut arbitror, commovebo, et simul
M. Taurum, quem tibi audio promisisse, qui nunc
Romae erat, de aqua per fundum eius ducenda rogabo.
5 Nicephorum, villicum tuum, sane probavi ; quaesivi-
que ex eo, ecquid ei de illa aedificatiuncula Lateri, de
qua mecum locutus es, mandavisses. Tum is mihi
respondit, se ipsum eius operis HS xvi. conductorem
fuisse, sed te postea multa addidisse ad opus, nihil
ad pretium ; itaque id se omisisse. Mihi hercule
valde placet, te illa, ut constituebas, addere ; quamquam ea villa, quae nunc est, tamquam philosopha
videtur esse, quae obiurget ceterarum villarum in-
saniam. Verumtamen illud additum delectabit.
Topiarium laudavi ; ita omnia convestit hedera,
qua basim villae, qua intercolumnia ambulationis, ut

---

^a Nothing much is known of this goddess.
^b A village in the neighbourhood of Arpinum.
^c " Quintus seems to have drawn the road in such a way
as not to trench on their property, and in return he expected
each proprietor to keep the road in repair where it skirted
his estate." Tyrrell.
^d About £140.

I thought it might have been a public highway, except for 150 paces,—for I measured it myself from the little bridge near the temple of Furina,[a] walking towards Satricum.[b] Just there it had a surface of dry clay instead of gravel (that will have to be altered), and that section of the road is a very steep incline, but I understand that it could not be taken in any other direction, especially as you yourself objected to taking it through either Locusta's property or Varro's. Varro had properly paved the road in front of his own estate ; Locusta had not touched it,[c] but I shall approach him in Rome, and I fancy I shall make an impression upon him, and at the same time I shall ask M. Taurus, who, I am told, has made you a promise to that effect, and is now in Rome, about bringing the water through his property.

I highly approved of your steward Nicephorus, 5 and I asked him if you had given him any instructions as to that little house which is being built at Laterium, about which you spoke to me. Then he told me in reply that he himself had contracted to do the work for sixteen *sestertia*,[d] but that you had subsequently made many additions to the work, but nothing to the payment, in consequence of which he had thrown it up. That you are making those additions as you had resolved, is, I positively assure you, most gratifying to me ; and yet that villa, just as it stands, strikes one as having such a philosophic air as to reprove the craziness of all the other villas. And yet after all the proposed addition will be charming. Your landscape - gardener won my praise ; he has so enveloped everything with ivy, not only the foundation wall of the villa, but also the spaces between the

553

denique illi palliati topiariam facere videantur et
hederam vendere. Iam ἀποδυτηρίῳ nihil alsius, nihil
6 muscosius. Habes fere de rebus rusticis. Urbanam
expolitionem urget ille quidem et Philotimus et
Cincius ; sed etiam ipse crebro interviso ; quod est
facile factu. Quamobrem ea te cura liberatum volo.
7 III. De Cicerone quod me semper rogas, ignosco
equidem tibi, sed tu quoque mihi velim ignoscas.
Non enim concedo tibi, plus ut illum ames, quam ipse
amo. Atque utinam his diebus in Arpinati, quod et
ipse cupierat, et ego non minus, mecum fuisset. Quod
ad Pomponiam, si tibi videtur, scribas velim, cum
aliquo exibimus, eat nobiscum, puerumque ducat.
Clamores efficiam, si eum mecum habuero otiosus.
Nam Romae respirandi non est locus. Id me scis
antea gratis tibi esse pollicitum ; quid nunc putas,
8 tanta abs te mihi mercede proposita ? Venio nunc
ad tuas litteras ; quas pluribus epistulis accepi, dum
sum in Arpinati. Nam mihi uno die tres sunt
redditae, et quidem, ut videbantur, eodem abs te
datae tempore ; una pluribus verbis, in qua primum
erat, quod antiquior dies in tuis fuisset ascripta litteris, quam in Caesaris. Id facit Oppius nonnumquam

---

a We should say, " bring down the house," by his success
as a teacher.
b In your gratitude and affection.

columns of the promenade, that I declare the Greek statues seem to be in business as landscape-gardeners, and to be advertising their ivy. As it now is, the dressing-room is the coolest and mossiest retreat in the world.

That is about all as far as country matters are 6 concerned. It is true that the gardener and Philotimus, and Cincius also, are pressing forward the elaborate adornment of your town house, but I often drop in and I see them myself, too, and it is no trouble to me. I would therefore have you freed from any anxiety on that account.

III. You are always asking me about your son 7 Cicero ; well, I pardon your solicitude, of course, but I should be glad if you, too, would pardon me. For that you love him more than I do myself is a point on which I refuse to yield to you. And I only wish that he had been with me these last few days at Arpinum, as he had himself desired, and I no less ! As to Pomponia, I should like you, if you please, to write and tell her to come with me, whenever I go out of town anywhere, and bring the boy. If I have him with me when I am at leisure, I shall win loud applause ; [a] at Rome I have no time to breathe. You know I promised you this for nothing before : what do you expect now that you have offered me so great a reward [b] ?

I come now to your letters, which I received in 8 several packets when I was at Arpinum. In fact, three were delivered to me in one day, and indeed apparently despatched by you at the same time, one of them of considerable length, in which the first thing you noticed was that my letter to you bore an earlier date than that to Caesar. That is

necessario, ut, cum tabellarios constituerit mittere,
litterasque a nobis acceperit, aliqua re nova impedia-
tur, et necessario serius, quam constituerat, mittat,
neque nos datis iam epistulis diem commutari cure-
9 mus. Scribis de Caesaris summo in nos amore.
Hunc et tu fovebis et nos, quibuscumque poterimus
rebus, augebimus. De Pompeio et facio diligenter et
faciam quod mones. Quod tibi mea permissio man-
sionis tuae grata est, id ego, summo meo dolore et desiderio, tamen ex parte gaudeo. In Hippodamis et
nonnullis aliis arcessendis quid cogites, non intellego.
Nemo istorum est, quin abs te munus, fundi suburbani
instar, exspectet. Trebatium vero meum quod isto
admisceas, nihil est. Ego illum ad Caesarem misi,
qui mihi iam satisfecit ; si ipsi minus, praestare nihil
debeo, teque item ab eo vindico et libero. Quod
scribis te a Caesare quotidie plus diligi, immortaliter
gaudeo. Balbum vero, qui est istius rei (quemadmodum scribis) adiutor, in oculis fero. Trebonium meum
10 a te amari, teque ab illo, pergaudeo. De tribunatu
quod scribis, ego vero nominatim petivi Curtio, et
mihi ipse Caesar nominatim Curtio paratum esse

---

^a Oppius and Balbus were Caesar's agents at Rome.
^b *Cf.* § 21 of this letter.
^c For C. Trebatius Testa, the lawyer, see *Fam.* vii. 6,
note *e*.
^d See note *a* on *Fam.* x. 28.
^e *Cf. Q.F.* ii. 15*a*. 2.

what Oppius [a] occasionally cannot help doing—I mean that, when he has decided to send letter-carriers and has received a letter from me, something unexpected occurs to hinder him, and he is unavoidably later than he intended in sending the carriers ; while I, when once the letter has been handed to him, do not trouble about having the date altered.

You write of Caesar's extraordinary affection for 9 us. That affection not only will you encourage, but I, too, shall foster it in every possible way. As to Pompey, I am, and shall be, careful to do what you advise. That you are pleased with my permission to prolong your stay, though I shall grieve and miss you greatly, I am to some extent glad. What your intention is in sending for your Hippodamuses [b] and some others passes my comprehension. There is not one of that gang who does not expect something equivalent to a suburban estate as a *douceur* from you. But that you should lump up my friend Trebatius [c] with that lot is sheer nonsense. I have sent him to Caesar, and Caesar has already done quite enough for me ; if he has not done so much for Trebatius, it is no business of mine to guarantee him anything, and you, too, I deliver and release from all obligation to him. Your writing that Caesar's esteem for you increases daily is an undying joy to me. Balbus, indeed, who, as you write, is helping on that state of affairs, is the very apple of my eye. It is a great joy to me that you love my friend Trebonius,[d] and he you.

You write about the military tribuneship ; well, 10 I really did canvass for it in specific terms for Curtius,[e] and Caesar himself wrote back to me in specific terms that there was one ready for Curtius, and twitted

557

rescripsit, meamque in rogando verecundiam obiurgavit. Si cui praeterea petiero (id quod etiam Oppio dixi, ut ad illum scriberet), facile patiar mihi negari, quoniam illi, qui mihi molesti sunt, sibi negari a me non facile patiuntur. Ego Curtium (id quod ipsi dixi) non modo rogatione, sed etiam testimonio tuo diligo, quod litteris tuis studium illius in salutem nostram facile perspexi. De Britannicis rebus, cognovi ex tuis litteris, nihil esse, nec quod metuamus, nec quod gaudeamus. De publicis negotiis, quae vis ad te Tironem scribere, neglegentius ad te ante scribebam, quod omnia, minima maxima, ad Caesarem mitti 11 sciebam. IV. Rescripsi epistulae maximae. Audi nunc de minuscula; in qua primum est de Clodi ad Caesarem litteris; in quo Caesaris consilium probo, quod tibi, amantissime petenti, veniam non dedit, uti ullum ad illam Furiam verbum rescriberet. Alterum est de Calventi Mari oratione. Quod scribis, miror, tibi placere, me ad eum rescribere, praesertim cum illam nemo lecturus sit, si ego nihil rescripsero, meam in illum pueri omnes, tamquam dictata, per-

---

ᵃ He means that, though he is obliged to grant such requests, the ultimate success of such canvassing is a matter of no concern to him; " I canvass for them under pressure; if the canvass is of no avail, serve them right for pestering me."

ᵇ Calventius (so called after his maternal grandfather) is L. Calpurnius Piso Caesoninus, whom Cicero had attacked the year before (55) for his misdeeds as governor of Macedonia in 57 and 56. (That is the speech mentioned just below.) Cicero here calls him *Marius*, because Piso was now to him what Marius had once been to Metellus. The story is as follows: In 100 B.C. Q. Metellus Numidicus refused to take the oath of obedience to the agrarian laws of Saturninus, the adherent of C. Marius. Metellus was

me with the shy way I made the request. If I canvass for anybody besides (as I told Oppius to write to Caesar) I shall have little objection to a refusal, since those who pester me with requests decidedly object to my refusing them.[a] I esteem Curtius (as I told him himself) not only because you ask me to do so, but also because of your testimony in his favour, since your letter enabled me easily to appreciate his enthusiasm for my restoration. As to the situation in Britain, your letter gives me to understand that we have no reason either for apprehension or for exultation. As to public affairs, about which you wish Tiro to write to you, I have hitherto been writing to you less minutely because I was aware that everything as of the least, so of the greatest, importance was being reported to Caesar.

IV. I have answered your longest letter; now 11 hear what I have to say about your very little one, which begins about Clodius's letter to Caesar; in regard to that incident, I think Caesar was quite right in not acceding to your request, prompted though it was by the friendliest feeling, that he should send a single word of reply to that arch-fiend. Your second point is about the speech of Calventius Marius.[b] I am surprised at your writing that my replying to him would give you pleasure, especially as nobody is likely to read his speech, if I make no reply to it, whereas every schoolboy learns mine

expelled from the Senate, and threatened with exile by Marius. He might have resisted Marius with success, but, to avoid civil dissension, he retired from Rome. Cicero here implies that he could have defied Piso, had he chosen to do so, as Metellus could have defied Marius, but decided to treat him with silent contempt. *Cf. Fam.* i. 9. 16, where Cicero again compares himself to Metellus.

discant. Libros meos, quos exspectas, inchoavi sed
conficere non possum his diebus. Orationes efflagi-
tatas pro Scauro et pro Plancio absolvi. Poema ad
Caesarem, quod composueram, incidi. Tibi quod
rogas, quoniam ipsi fontes iam sitiunt, si quid habebo
12 spati, scribam. Venio ad tertiam. Balbum quod ais
mature Romam bene comitatum esse venturum mecumque assidue usque ad Id. Maias futurum, id mihi
pergratum perque iucundum erit. Quod me in eadem
epistula, sicut saepe antea, cohortaris ad ambitionem
et ad laborem, faciam equidem ; sed quando vive-
13 mus ? Quarta epistula mihi reddita est Id. Sept.,
quam a d. IV. Id. Sext. ex Britannia dederas. In ea
nihil sane erat novi, praeter *Erigonam* ; quam si ab
Oppio accepero, scribam ad te, quid sentiam ; nec
dubito, quin mihi placitura sit. Et, quod praeterii,
de eo, quem scripsisti de Milonis plausu scripsisse ad
Caesarem, ego vero facile patior ita Caesarem existimare, illum quam maximum fuisse plausum. Et
prorsus ita fuit ; et tamen ille plausus, qui illi
14 datur, quodammodo nobis videtur dari. Reddita est
etiam mihi pervetus epistula, sed sero allata, in qua
de aede Telluris et de porticu Catuli me admones.
Fit utrumque diligenter. Ad Telluris quidem etiam

---

[a] His treatise, *De Republica*, of which only portions have
come down to us.

[b] *Cf. Ep.* 4. 4.

[c] Some commentators take this as meaning " with plenty
of money in his purse." But it probably means " with a
large escort of Caesar's troops," to take part in the elections.

[d] Adjoining Cicero's house in Rome, destroyed with the
house when he went into exile, but afterwards restored by
order of the Senate.

against him by rote as an exercise. My books,[a] all of which you are eagerly awaiting, I have begun, but cannot finish for the next few days. The speeches in defence of Scaurus and Plancius, which you so insistently demand, I have accomplished. The poem to Caesar, which I had put together for final arrangement, I have broken off. For *you*, since your own wells of poesy are now running dry,[b] if I have any spare time, I shall write what you request.

I come to your third letter. You say that Balbus 12 will come to Rome at an early date, handsomely attended,[c] and that he will be with me without a break till May 15 ; that will be very gratifying to me, and will give me much pleasure. In the same letter you urge me, as you often have before, to be ambitious and strenuous ; well, I certainly shall be so ; but when shall we begin to enjoy life ?

Your fourth letter I received on September 13 ; 13 you had posted it in Britain on August 10. There was nothing new in it except about your *Erigona* ; if I get it from Oppius, I'll write and tell you what I think of it ; but I have no doubt that I shall find it charming. And there is that bit, too (I forgot to mention it), about the man who, according to your letter, wrote to Caesar about the applause given to Milo ; well, I have not the least objection to Caesar's getting the impression that nothing could have been heartier; and such was undoubtedly the case. And yet the applause given to Milo seems in a sense to be given to me.

I have also received a very old letter, but late in 14 its delivery, in which you remind me of the temple of Tellus and the colonnade of Catulus.[d] Both works are being carefully executed. Indeed, I have even had a statue of you set up near the temple of Tellus.

tuam statuam locavi. Item de hortis quod me admones, nec fui umquam valde cupidus, et nunc domus
suppeditat mihi hortorum amoenitatem. Romam
cum venissem a. d. XIII. Kal. Octob., absolutum offendi
in aedibus tuis tectum ; quod supra conclavia non
placuerat tibi esse multorum fastigiorum, id nunc
honeste vergit in tectum inferioris porticus. Cicero
noster, dum ego absum, non cessavit apud rhetorem.
De eius eruditione quod labores, nihil est, quoniam
ingenium eius nosti ; studium ego video. Cetera
15 eius suscipio, ut me puto praestare debere. V. Gabinium tres adhuc factiones postulant ; L. Lentulus,
flaminis filius, qui iam de maiestate postulavit ; Ti.
Nero cum bonis subscriptoribus; C. Memmius tribunus plebis cum L. Capitone. Ad Urbem accessit
a. d. XII. Kal. Octobr. Nihil turpius, nec desertius.
Sed his iudiciis nihil audeo confidere. Quod Cato
non valebat, adhuc de pecuniis repetundis non erat
postulatus. Pompeius a me valde contendit de reditu
in gratiam ; sed adhuc nihil profecit ; nec, si ullam
partem libertatis tenebo, proficiet. Tuas litteras
16 vehementer exspecto. Quod scribis te audisse in
candidatorum consularium coitione me interfuisse, id
falsum est. Eiusmodi enim pactiones in ea coitione

---

a *Maiestas* (in full *laesa* or *minuta maiestas*) was any act
derogatory to the dignity or prejudicial to the interests of
the Roman people. In this case it was Gabinius's un-
authorized intervention (for the handsome fee of 10,000
talents) in the restoration of Ptolemy Auletes to the neglect
of his duties as Governor of Syria.

b Father of the emperor Tiberius.

c Not to be confused with C. Memmius Gemellus, one of
the candidates for the consulship.

d M. Cato, now praetor.

e For a fuller account of this see the next letter.

Also you remind me about the pleasure-gardens; well, I was never very keen on them, and, as it is, my town house supplies me with all the amenities of a pleasure-garden. When I arrived at Rome on September 18, I found the roof on your house completely finished; that part above the day-rooms, which you had not cared to be too heavily gabled, has now a noble slope down to the roof of the colonnade below.

Our boy Cicero had no holiday with his rhetoric-master while I was away. There is no reason why you should be anxious about his education, since you know his ability, and I see to his application. All else connected with him I take on my shoulders, as I think it my duty to make myself responsible.

V. So far Gabinius is being prosecuted by three 15 parties—by L. Lentulus, son of the *flamen*, who has now indicted him for *maiestas* [a]; Ti. Nero,[b] with sound men backing his indictment; and C. Memmius,[c] tribune of the plebs, in conjunction with L. Capito. He approached the walls of the city on September 19, the picture of disrepute and desolation. But with the present law-courts, I dare not be confident of anything. On account of Cato's [d] ill-health he has not yet been indicted for extortion. Pompey is making a strong effort to become reconciled with me, but as yet has met with no success, and, if I retain a particle of independence, he will never succeed. I await your letter with intense eagerness.

You write that you have been told that I took 16 part in the coalition of the candidates for the consulship; [e] well, that is not true. The compacts made in that coalition—compacts subsequently divulged by

factae sunt, quas postea Memmius patefecit, ut nemo
bonus interesse debuerit ; et simul mihi committen-
dum non fuit, ut his coitionibus interessem, quibus
Messalla excluderetur ; cui quidem vehementer satis-
facio rebus omnibus ; ut arbitror, etiam Memmio.
Domitio ipsi multa iam feci, quae voluit, quaeque **a**
me petivit. Scaurum beneficio defensionis valde
obligavi. Adhuc erat valde incertum, et quando
17 comitia, et qui consules futuri essent. Cum hanc iam
epistulam complicarem, tabellarii a vobis venerunt
a. d. XI. Kal. Oct. Septimo vicesimo die. O me sollicitum ! quantum ego dolui in Caesaris suavissimis
litteris ! sed quo erant suaviores, eo maiorem dolorem
illius ille casus afferebat. Sed ad tuas venio litteras.
Primum tuam remansionem etiam atque etiam probo,
praesertim cum, ut scribis, cum Caesare communi-
caris. Oppium miror quidquam cum Publio ; mihi
18 enim non placuerat. Quod interiore epistula scribis,
me Idib. Sept. Pompeio legatum iri, id ego non audivi,
scripsique ad Caesarem, neque Vibullium Caesaris
mandata de mea mansione ad Pompeium pertulisse,
neque Oppium. Quo consilio ? Quamquam Oppium ego tenui, quod priores partes Bibuli erant.
Cum eo enim coram Caesare egerat, ad Oppium

---

a About the death of his daughter Julia.
b P. Clodius.

Memmius—were of such a kind that no honest man ought to have been party to them ; and, at the same time, it was not for me to make the mistake of being party to those coalitions from which Messalla was shut out. To him I am giving complete satisfaction in every respect, and also, I believe, to Memmius. To Domitius himself I have rendered many services, which he desired and requested of me. Scaurus I have laid under a great obligation by my kindness in defending him. So far it is extremely uncertain both when the elections will be held and who will be consuls.

Just as I was in the act of folding this letter, there 17 came letter-carriers from you and Caesar on September 20; they had been twenty-seven days on the road. How distressed I was ! And how I grieved over Caesar's most charming letter [a] ! But the more charming it was, the greater the grief it caused me for his affliction. But I come to your letter. In the first place, I reiterate my approval of your staying on, especially after having had, as you write, an interview with Caesar. I am surprised at Oppius having anything to do with Publius [b] ; it was not what I advised.

As to what you say in the middle of your letter— 18 that I am going to be appointed *legatus* to Pompey on September 13—I have heard nothing about it, and I wrote to Caesar saying that neither Vibullius nor Oppius had conveyed his message to Pompey about my staying on in Rome. What their object was I don't know. And yet, in the case of Oppius, it was I who held him back, because it was Bibulus who had a prior claim ; for it was with him that Caesar had had an interview, while he had only

565

scripserat. Ego vero nullas δευτέρας φροντίδας habere
possum in Caesaris rebus. Ille mihi secundum te et
liberos nostros ita est, ut sit paene par. Videor id
iudicio facere. Iam enim debeo, sed tamen amore
sum incensus.

19 VI. Cum scripsissem haec infima, quae sunt mea
manu, venit ad nos Cicero tuus ad cenam, cum Pomponia foris cenaret. Dedit mihi epistulam legendam
tuam, quam paullo ante acceperat, Aristophanec
modo valde mehercule et suavem et gravem ; qua
sum admodum delectatus. Dedit etiam alteram
illam mihi, qua iubes eum mihi esse affixum, tamquam magistro. Quam illum epistulae illae delectarunt ! quam me ! Nihil puero illo suavius, nihil nostr
amantius. Hoc inter cenam Tironi dictavi, ne mirere

20 alia manu esse. Annali litterae tuae pergratae
fuerunt, quod et curares de se diligenter, et tamen
consilio se verissimo iuvares. P. Servilius pater ex
litteris, quas sibi a Caesare missas esse dicebat, significat valde te sibi gratum fecisse, quod de sua
voluntate erga Caesarem humanissime diligentissime-

21 que locutus esses. Cum Romam ex Arpinati rever-
tissem, dictum mihi est, Hippodamum ad te profectum
esse. Non possum scribere, me miratum esse, illum
tam inhumaniter fecisse, ut sine meis litteris ad te

---

[a] It is doubtful whether he means the great comic poet or
Aristophanes of Byzantium, the critic; *suavem* would rather
indicate the former.

[b] L. Villius Annalis, a senator. *Cf. Fam.* viii. 8. 3.

[c] P. Servilius Isauricus, father of Cicero's correspondent,
the proconsul of Asia (*Fam.* xiii. 68, and 66-72).

written to Oppius. I assure you that, as for " second thoughts," I could have none in my relations with Caesar. He comes next to you and my children with me, and so closely next that he is almost on a par with them. It seems to me that such is my deliberate conviction (and it ought to be so by this time), and yet a strong predilection has its influence upon me.

VI. After I had written these last words, which 19 are in my own hand, your son Cicero came in and had dinner with me, as Pomponia was dining out. He gave me your letter to read, which he had only just received—and, upon my word, it was a clever mixture of grave and gay in the style of Aristophanes,[a] and I was highly delighted with it. He also gave me that other letter of yours in which you bid him cling to me as to a tutor. How delighted he was with those letters, and so was I ! He is the most charming boy in the world, and most devoted to me. I dictated this to Tiro during dinner, so do not be surprised at its being written in a different hand.

Annalis [b] was much pleased with your letter, 20 because, as he said, you took such pains about him, and at the same time helped him with your very frank advice. P. Servilius [c] senior, in consequence of a letter which he said Caesar had sent him, expresses his extreme gratitude to you for having spoken so very courteously and impressively of his kindly feeling for Caesar.

After my return to Rome from Arpinum I was 21 told that Hippodamus [d] had set out to join you. I cannot say that I was surprised at his having acted so unkindly as to have set out without any letter to

---

[a] *Cf.* § 9 of this letter.

proficisceretur ; illud scribo, mihi molestum fuisse. Iam enim diu cogitaveram, ex eo, quod tu ad me scripseras, ut, si quid esset, quod ad te diligentius perferri vellem, illi darem ; quod mehercule hisce litteris, quas vulgo ad te mitto, nihil fere scribo, quod si in alicuius manus inciderit, moleste ferendum sit. Minucio me et Salvio et Labeoni reservabam. Labeo aut tarde proficiscetur aut hic manebit. Hippodamus

22 ne numquid vellem quidem rogavit. T. Pinarius amabiles ad me de te litteras mittit ; se maxime litteris, sermonibus, cenis denique tuis delectari. Is homo semper me delectavit, fraterque eius mecum est multum. Quare, ut instituisti, complectere adu-

23 lescentem. VII. Quod multos dies epistulam in manibus habui, propter commorationem tabellariorum, ideo multa coniecta sunt, aliud alio tempore, velut hoc : T. Anicius mihi saepe iam dixit, sese tibi, suburbanum si quod invenisset, non dubitaturum esse emere. In eius sermone ego utrumque soleo admirari, et te de suburbano emendo, cum ad illum scribas, non modo ad me non scribere, sed etiam aliam in sententiam scribere, et, cum ad illum scribas, nihil te recordari de se, de epistulis illis, quas in Tusculano eius tu mihi ostendisti, nihil de praeceptis Epicharmi, γνῶθι πῶς ἄλλῳ κέχρηται ; totum

---

[a] Cicero's friend, whom he recommends to Cornificius in *Fam.* xii. 24. 3.

[b] We know no more of him than that Cicero did not think him a man to be trusted.

you from me; I simply remark that I was annoyed. For I had long since resolved, after what you wrote to me, to entrust to him whatever there might be which I should like to be conveyed to you with particular care; because I assure you that in these letters, which I send you in an ordinary way, I hardly write anything which would cause me annoyance if it fell into anybody else's hands. I reserve myself for Minucius and Salvius and Labeo. Labeo will either be late in setting out, or will not set out at all. Hippodamus never so much as asked me whether I had any commission.

T. Pinarius [a] sends me an amiable letter about 22 you; he says he is highly delighted with your literary taste, your conversation, and, last but not least, with your dinners. I have always found pleasure in his society, and I see a great deal of his brother. For that reason you will, I am sure, continue, as you have begun, to show the young man marked attention.

Because I have had a letter on my hands for 23 many days on account of delay on the part of the letter-carriers, many things have been jumbled up in it, written at various times, as, for instance, this: T. Anicius [b] has repeatedly told me that if he found a suburban property he would not hesitate to buy it for you. In my conversations with him, I am surprised at two things—that when you write to him about buying a suburban property, not only do you fail to write to me about it, but even write as if you had other intentions; and again, that when you write to him, you recall nothing about himself, about those letters of his which you showed me at Tusculum, nothing about the precept of Epicharmus, " Find out how he has treated another," in short, as far as I

denique vultum, animum, sermonem eius, quemadmodum conicio, quasi dedidicisse[1]; sed haec tu videris.
24 De suburbano, cura, ut sciam, quid velis ; et simul, ne quid ille turbet, vide. Quid praeterea ? Quid ? Etiam. Gabinius a. d. IV. Kal. Octobr. noctu in Urbem introivit ; et hodie h. VIII., cum edicto C. Alfi de maiestate eum adesse oporteret, concursu magno et odio universi populi paene afflictus est. Nihil illo turpius. Proximus est tamen Piso. Itaque mirificum ἐμβόλιον cogito in secundum librorum meorum includere, dicentem Apollinem in concilio deorum, qualis reditus duorum imperatorum futurus esset ; quorum alter exercitum perdidisset, alter
25 vendidisset. Ex Britannia Caesar ad me Kal. Sept. dedit litteras, quas ego accepi a. d. IV. Kalend. Octobr. satis commodas de Britannicis rebus ; quibus, ne admirer, quod a te nullas acceperim, scribit, se sine te fuisse, quum ad mare accesserit. Ad eas ego ei litteras nihil rescripsi, ne gratulandi quidem causa, propter eius luctum. Te oro etiam atque etiam, mi frater, ut valeas.

[1] *Added by Wesenberg.*

---

[a] C. Alfius was tribune of the plebs in 59. He was *quaesitor* in the trial of Gabinius for *maiestas*.
[b] Piso had wasted his army in petty warfare with the tribes on the borders of Macedonia, and Gabinius had practically sold his by employing it to restore Ptolemy Auletes for a bribe.

can make out, that you have entirely unlearnt, as it were, what you must have gathered from his looks, his disposition, and his conversation ; but all this is for you to see to.

Take care to let me know your wishes as to the 24 suburban estate, and, incidentally, see that Anicius doesn't cause you any trouble. What else is there ? What ? Oh yes, Gabinius entered the city by night on September 27, and to-day, at two o'clock, when according to C. Alfius's [a] edict, he ought to have appeared to face the charge of *maiestas*, he was almost crushed to the ground by the enormous throng that proved the hatred of the whole people. He was the most ignominious sight in the world. Piso, however, is a good second. So I am thinking of inserting in the second of my books an amazing paragraph—Apollo holding forth at a council of the gods on what sort of a home-coming there would be in the case of two commanders, one of whom had lost, and the other sold, his army.[b]

Caesar posted me a letter from Britain on Septem- 25 ber 1, which I received on the 27th—a satisfactory letter enough as far as regards the situation in Britain ; and in it, to prevent my being surprised at not getting a letter from you, he writes that you were not with him when he got down to the coast. To that letter I made no reply, not even by way of congratulation, because of his mourning.

I implore you again and again, my dear brother, to keep well.

571

CICERO

II

M. CICERO S. D. Q. FRATRI

Romae, a.u.c. 700.

1 A. d. vi. Id. Octob. Salvius Ostiam vesperi navi profectus erat cum his rebus, quas tibi domo mitti volueras. Eodem die Gabinium ad populum luculente calefecerat Memmius, sic, ut Calidio verbum facere pro eo non licuerit. Postridie autem eius diei, qui erat tum futurus, cum haec scribebam ante lucem, apud Catonem erat divinatio in Gabinium futura inter Memmium et Ti. Neronem et C. et L. Antonios, M. F. Putabamus fore, ut Memmio daretur, etsi erat Neronis mira contentio. Quid quaeris ? Probe premitur, nisi noster Pompeius, dis hominibusque 2 invitis, negotium everterit. Cognosce nunc hominis audaciam, et aliquid in republica perdita delectare. Cum Gabinius, quacumque veniebat, triumphum se postulare dixisset, subitoque, bonus imperator, noctu in Urbem (hostium plane[1]) invasisset, in senatum se non committebat. Interim ipso decimo die, quo ipsum oportebat hostium caesorum numerum et militum renuntiare, inrepsit, summa infrequentia.

---

[1] hostium plenam *Koch* : hostilem in modum *Wesenberg*.

[a] C. Memmius, the tribune.

[b] Counsel for Gabinius. There is no doubt a play in the Latin on *calefecerat* and *Calidius* (*calidus*).

[c] *Divinatio* was the technical term for a formal inquiry as to which of several accusers presenting themselves was the proper person to conduct the prosecution.

[d] *i.e.*, the combination against Gabinius.

[e] It would seem that all governors on returning from their provinces were called up to report to the Senate any losses

II

On October 10 in the evening, Salvius took ship 1
and started for Ostia, taking the things you wanted
sent to you from home. On the same day Memmius [a] gave Gabinius such a blazing hot time of it
before the people, that Calidius [b] hadn't a chance of
saying a word for him. To-morrow (that is the day
after to-morrow, since I am writing before daybreak)
there is to be a trial [c] before Cato to decide who is to
conduct his prosecution, among Memmius, Tiberius
Nero, and C. and L. Antonius, the sons of Marcus.
I think it likely that Memmius will be appointed,
though Nero is making a wonderful effort. In short,
Gabinius is in a very tight corner, unless our friend
Pompey, to the disgust of gods and men, contrives
to upset the apple-cart.[d]

Now mark the fellow's impudence, and find 2
something to amuse you amid the ruins of the
Republic. Gabinius, having declared wherever he
came, that he was demanding a triumph, and having suddenly changed his plans, and—consummate
commander that he is—entered the city (he knew
it was his enemies' city) by night, did not, however, trust himself to enter the Senate. Meantime,
exactly on the tenth day, on which it was his duty in
person to report the number of the slain among the
enemy and his own men,[e] he crept into the Senate
when it was very thinly attended. When he wished

sustained by the Romans and the enemy in any actions
fought during the governorships.

573

Cum vellet exire, a consulibus retentus est ; intro-
ducti publicani. Homo undique saucius[1] cum a me
maxime vulneraretur, non tulit, et me trementi voce
exsulem appellavit. Hic (o di ! nihil umquam honorificentius nobis accidit) consurrexit senatus cum
clamore ad unum, sic ut ad corpus eius accederet ;
pari clamore atque impetu publicani. Quid quaeris ?
omnes, tamquam si tu esses, ita fuerunt. Nihil
hominum sermone foris clarius. Ego tamen me teneo
ab accusando, vix mehercule ; sed tamen teneo,
vel quod nolo cum Pompeio pugnare (satis est, quod
instat de Milone), vel quod iudices nullos habemus.
Ἀπότευγμα formido ; addo etiam malevolentiam hominum, et timeo, ne illi, me accusante, aliquid ac-
cedat ; nec despero rem et sine me et nonnihil per
3 me confici posse. De ambitu postulati sunt omnes,
qui consulatum petunt ; a Memmio Domitius, a Q.
Acutio, bono et erudito adulescente, Memmius, a
Q. Pompeio Messalla, a Triario Scaurus. Magna in
motu res est, propterea quod aut hominum aut legum
interitus ostenditur. Opera datur, ut iudicia ne fiant.
Res videtur spectare ad interregnum. Consules comitia habere cupiunt ; rei nolunt, et maxime Mem-

---

[1] *Tyrrell* : actus *Manutius* : saeptus *Boot*.

---

[a] *sc*. of Syria, who had suffered from the depredations
of pirates while Gabinius was otherwise engaged—restoring
Ptolemy in Egypt.
[b] Cicero's enemies might support Gabinius to spite him.
[c] The tribune.
[d] The candidate for the consulship.

to leave, he was detained by the consuls, and the *publicani* [a] were brought in. Wounded on every side, and being most bitterly assailed by myself, the fellow could stand it no longer, and, in a voice trembling with rage, he called me an *exile*. Upon that (and, O ye gods, never was I paid a higher compliment) the Senate rose with a shout, every man of them, and even made a move to attack him, as did the *publicani*, shouting and making for him in like manner. To cut the story short, they all behaved exactly as you would have done yourself. Nothing can be more unmistakable than the general talk outside the House. Yet I refrain from prosecuting him ; it is difficult, upon my word ; but, still, I do refrain, whether because I do not wish to be at feud with Pompey (the near approach of Milo's affair is sufficient reason for that) or because we have no proper jurors. I am afraid of a *fiasco*; and, besides, I have to consider the ill-will of certain folk, and fear that *my* being his prosecutor will be of some advantage to him ; [b] and I am not without hope that the business may be settled without me, and at the same time to some extent through my instrumentality.

All who are candidates for the consulship have 3 been indicted for bribery—Domitius by Memmius,[c] Memmius [d] by Q. Acutius, an excellent and learned young man, Messalla by Q. Pompeius, Scaurus by Triarius. There is great excitement over the affair, because it obviously means the destruction either of certain persons or of the laws. Every effort is being made to prevent the trials taking place. The situation seems to point to an interregnum. The consuls are anxious to hold the elections, but the defendants

mius, quod Caesaris adventu sperat se futurum consulem. Sed mirum in modum iacet. Domitius cum Messalla certus esse videbatur. Scaurus refrixerat. Appius sine lege curiata confirmat se Lentulo nostro successurum : qui quidem mirificus illo die (quod paene praeterii) fuit in Gabinium ; accusavit maiestatis ; nomina data, quum ille verbum nullum. Habes forensia. Domi recte, et ipsa domus a redemptoribus tractatur non indiligenter. Vale.

III

M. CICERO S. D. Q. FRATRI

Romae, A.U.C. 700.

1 Occupationum mearum tibi signum sit librari manus. Diem scito esse nullum, quo die non dicam pro reo. Ita, quidquid conficio aut cogito, in ambulationis fere tempus confero. Negotia nostra sic se habent ; domestica vero, ut volumus. Valent pueri, studiose discunt, diligenter docentur ; et nos et inter se amant. Expolitiones utriusque nostrum sunt in manibus ; sed tua ad perfectum iam res rustica Arcani et Lateri. Praeterea de aqua et via nihil praetermisi quadam epistula, quin enucleate ad te

---

^a Because as long as they were under an accusation, they could not stand for the consulship.

^b See *Fam.* i. 9. 25, where the whole situation is explained.

don't want it,[a] and least of all Memmius, who hopes
that on Caesar's arrival he will be consul. But he is
" down and out "—surprisingly so. Domitius, with
Messalla as colleague, seems to be a certainty.
Scaurus is stale fish. Appius declares that he will
step into our friend Lentulus's shoes, even without
a *lex curiata*;[b] and on the great day (I nearly forgot
to mention it) he astonished everybody by his attack
on Gabinius; he accused him of *maiestas*, and gave
the names of his witnesses, while Gabinius spoke not
a word. Now you have all the news of the forum.
At home all is right, and your house itself is being
dealt with by the contractors with considerable
assiduity.

III

CICERO TO QUINTUS

Rome, October 21, 54 B.C.

The handwriting of my secretary should indicate 1
to you the pressure of my engagements. I assure
you that there is never a day on which I don't speak
on behalf of some defendant, with the result that
whatever I compose or think out, I generally pile on to
the time for my walks. So it stands with my business;
affairs at home, however, are just as I would have them
be. Our boys are well, they apply themselves to
their lessons, they are being carefully taught, and
they are devoted to us and to each other. The
elaborate finishing off of each of our houses is still
in hand; but your rural operations at Arcanum and
Laterium are now approaching completion. Again,
as to the water and the road, in a certain letter of
mine I omitted no single detail, so as not to fail to

perscriberem. Sed me illa cura sollicitat angitque vehementer, quod dierum iam amplius L. intervallo nihil a te, nihil a Caesare, nihil ex istis locis, non modo litterarum, sed ne rumoris quidem affluxit. Me autem iam et mare istuc et terra sollicitat; neque desino (ut fit in amore) ea, quae minime volo, cogitare. Quare non equidem iam te rogo, ut ad me de te, de rebus istis scribas (numquam enim, cum potes, praetermittis), sed hoc te scire volo, nihil fere umquam me sic exspectasse, ut, cum haec scribebam, litteras 2 tuas. Nunc cognosce ea, quae sunt in republica. Comitiorum quotidie singuli dies tolluntur obnuntiationibus, magna voluntate bonorum omnium; tanta invidia sunt consules propter suspicionem pactorum a candidatis praemiorum. Candidati consulares quattuor, omnes rei; causae sunt difficiles; sed enitemur, ut Messalla noster salvus sit, quod est etiam cum reliquorum salute coniunctum. Gabinium de ambitu reum fecit P. Sulla, subscribente privigno Memmio, fratre Caecilio, Sulla filio. Contra dixit L. Torquatus; omnibusque libentibus non obtinuit. 3 Quaeris, quid fiat de Gabinio? Sciemus de maiestate triduo; quo quidem in iudicio odio premitur omnium

---

^a Who had prosecuted Sulla on a charge of " breaking the peace " (*de vi*) in 62, when Sulla was defended by Cicero.

write fully and explicitly. But the anxiety that so
seriously disturbs and tortures me is that, for a period
of now over fifty days, nothing in the shape of a letter
or even of a rumour has trickled its way to me from you
or from Caesar, or from those parts where you are.
And now both the sea and the land, where you are,
cause me anxiety, and, as always happens when one's
affections are engaged, I never cease imagining what
I least desire to imagine. And for that reason I am
not now asking you to write to me about yourself
and all that concerns you (which you never omit to do
when you can), but I should like you to know this,
that I have hardly ever looked forward with such
eagerness to anything as I do to a letter from you
as I write these words.

Now let me tell you about the political situation. 2
One date after another for the holding of the elections is being daily cancelled by the announcement
of adverse omens, to the great satisfaction of all
sound citizens; so utterly unpopular are the consuls,
because they are suspected of having bargained for
a bribe from the candidates. All the four candidates
for the consulship are on their trial; their cases are
difficult to defend, but I shall make a strenuous effort
to secure the acquittal of our friend Messalla, and
that is closely bound up with the acquittal of the
rest. Gabinius has been accused of bribery by
P. Sulla, and the backers of Sulla's indictment are
his stepson Memmius, his cousin Caecilius, and his
son Sulla. L. Torquatus [a] opposed him, but, to
everybody's satisfaction, failed to establish his claim.

You ask what is being done about Gabinius. Well, 3
in three days' time we shall know about the charge
of *maiestas*; and in that trial he is handicapped by

generum, maxime testibus laeditur[1]; accusatoribus frigidissimis utitur; consilium varium; quaesitor gravis et firmus Alfius; Pompeius vehemens in iudicibus rogandis. Quid futurum sit, nescio; locum tamen illi in civitate non video. Animum praebeo ad illius perniciem moderatum, ad rerum eventum 4 lenissimum. Habes fere de omnibus rebus. Unum illud addam. Cicero tuus nosterque summo studio est Paeoni sui rhetoris, hominis, opinor, valde exercitati et boni. Sed nostrum instituendi genus esse paullo eruditius et θετικώτερον, non ignoras. Quare neque ego impediri Ciceronis iter atque illam disciplinam volo, et ipse puer magis illo declamatorio genere duci et delectari videtur. In quo quoniam ipsi quoque fuimus, patiamur illum ire nostris itineribus; eodem enim perventurum esse confidimus. Sed tamen, si nobiscum eum rus aliquo eduxerimus, in hanc nostram rationem consuetudinemque inducemus. Magna enim nobis a te proposita merces est, quam certe nostra culpa numquam minus assequemur. Quibus in locis et qua spe hiematurus sis, ad me quam diligentissime scribas velim. Vale.

[1] *Madvig*: caeditur *M*.

---

[a] See *Q.F.* iii. 1. 24.

[b] θετικώτερον, belonging rather to the province of θέσις, which Cicero defines (*Top.* 79) as a discussion of a general or abstract principle, as opposed to ὑπόθεσις, the discussion of a particular case.

[c] *i.e.*, Quintus's gratitude and enhanced affection.

the hatred all classes entertain for him ; he is damaged most of all by witnesses ; he has the most ineffective accusers ; the panel of jurors is of a promiscuous kind ; the presiding praetor, Alfius,[a] is a man of strong and sterling character ; Pompey is very active in soliciting the jurors. What will happen I don't know, but I cannot see that there is any room for him in the State. My own feelings as regards his condemnation are under control, as regards the issue of events perfectly placid.

I have now told you about almost everything. 4 There is one thing I must add ; your Cicero (and indeed he is our Cicero) is deeply devoted to his rhetoric master Paeonius, in my opinion, an exceedingly well-trained and excellent fellow. But, as you are well aware, my own system of instruction is somewhat more scholarly and argumentative.[b] I do not therefore desire that your Cicero's educational course should be interfered with, and the boy himself appears to be more attracted and charmed by that declamatory style ; and since I myself once followed that line, let us allow him to proceed along the same paths as I did ; for I feel sure that he will arrive at the same goal. But, all the same, if I take him with me into the country anywhere, I shall bring him over to this system and practice of my own. For the reward [c] you have set before me is a magnificent one, and it will certainly not be through any fault of mine that I shall forfeit it. I should like you to write and tell me as exactly as possible, where, and with what prospects in view, you are going to spend the winter. Good-bye.

CICERO

IV

M. CICERO S. D. Q. FRATRI

Romae, a.u.c. 700.

1 Gabinius absolutus est. Omnino nihil accusatore
Lentulo subscriptoribusque eius infantius, nihil illo
consilio sordidius. Sed tamen nisi incredibilis contentio et preces Pompei, dictaturae etiam rumor
plenus timoris fuisset, ipsi Lentulo non respondisset,
qui tamen illo accusatore, illoque consilio sententiis
condemnatus sit xxxii., cum lxx. tulissent. Est
omnino tam gravi fama hoc iudicium, ut videatur
reliquis iudiciis periturus, et maxime de pecuniis repetundis. Sed vides nullam esse rempublicam,
nullum senatum, nulla iudicia, nullam in ullo nostrum
dignitatem. Quid plura de iudicibus ? Duo prae-
torii sederunt, Domitius Calvinus,—is aperte absolvit,
ut omnes viderent, et Cato,—is, diribitis tabellis,
de circulo se subduxit et Pompeio primus nuntiavit.
2 Aiunt nonnulli, Sallustius item, me oportuisse accusare. Iis ego iudicibus committerem ? Quid
essem, si me agente esset elapsus ? Sed me alia
moverunt. Non putasset sibi Pompeius de illius

---

a Cn. Sallustius, to whom Cicero addressed *Fam.* ii. 17.
He was quaestor to Bibulus in Syria ; Cicero seems to have
thought highly of him.
582

IV

CICERO TO QUINTUS IN GAUL

Rome, October 24, 54 B.C.

Gabinius has been acquitted ! Nothing on earth 1
could have been more puerile than his accuser
Lentulus, and those who endorsed his indictment ;
nothing more corrupt than that panel of jurors.
But still, had it not been for the strenuous efforts and
supplications of Pompey, and an alarming rumour
also of a dictatorship, even Lentulus would have
been more than a match for him, seeing that even
with such an accuser and such a jury he was condemned by no less than 32 votes out of 70 recorded.
This trial is so utterly discredited that it seems
likely that he will be convicted in the other trials,
and most of all in that for extortion. But you can
see that there is really no Republic in existence,
no Senate, no law-courts, no position of authority
held by any one of us. What more can I tell you
about the jurors ? Two praetorians took their seats,
Domitius Calvinus—he voted for acquittal quite
openly, for all to see—and Cato—he, as soon as the
voting-tablets had been counted, withdrew from the
surrounding throng and was the first to tell Pompey
the news.

There are some, Sallustius [a] among them, who say 2
that I ought to have undertaken the prosecution.
Was I to entrust myself to such jurors as that ?
What would have become of me, had I conducted
the case, and he had escaped ? But I was influenced
by other considerations. Pompey would not have

583

salute, sed de sua dignitate mecum esse certamen;
in Urbem introisset: ad inimicitias res venisset;
cum Aesernino Samnite Pacideianus comparatus
viderer; auriculam fortasse mordicus abstulisset.
Cum Clodio quidem certe rediisset in gratiam. Ego
vero meum consilium (si praesertim tu non improbas)
vehementer approbo. Ille, cum a me singularibus
meis studiis ornatus esset, cumque ego illi nihil de-
berem, ille mihi omnia, tamen in republica me a se
dissentientem non tulit (nihil dicam gravius), et minus
potens eo tempore, quid in me florentem posset,
ostendit. Nunc, cum ego ne curem quidem multum
posse, res quidem publica certe nihil possit, unus
ille omnia possit, cum illo ipso contenderem? Sic
enim faciendum fuisset. Non existimo te putare id
3 mihi suscipiendum fuisse. Alterutrum, inquit idem
Sallustius, defendisses idque Pompeio contendenti
dedisses. Etenim vehementer orabat. Lepidum
amicum Sallustium, qui mihi inimicitias putet peri-
culosas subeundas fuisse aut infamiam sempiternam! Ego vero hac mediocritate delector; ac mihi
illud iucundum est, quod, cum testimonium secundum
fidem et religionem gravissime dixissem, reus dixit,

---

a Pacideianus (*cf.* Hor. *Sat.* ii. 7. 97) was the most skilful
gladiator of the time, but Aeserninus was his superior in
courage and brute force.

b "Or else you should have prosecuted him" is obviously
understood.

584

thought he was having a struggle with me for
Gabinius's salvation, but for his own position ; he
would have entered the city ; it would have ended
in our becoming enemies ; I should have looked
like some Pacideianus pitted against the Samnite
Aeserninus,[a] and quite possibly he would have bitten
my ear off. He would certainly have effected a
reconciliation with Clodius. For my part, I warmly
approve (especially if you do not disapprove) of my
own decision. Although it was my unique oratorical
efforts on his behalf that had brought him distinction,
and although I owed him nothing, while he owed
me everything, for all that, my not agreeing with
him in politics was more than he could stand (I shall
use no stronger expression), and, though less powerful
than myself at the time, he showed me what power
he could wield against me, in the heyday of my
career. As things now are, when I don't even care
for much power, and the State has certainly no
power at all, while he stands alone in his omnipotence,
was I to enter upon a personal conflict with him ?
For that is what would have had to be done. I don't
believe you think I should have taken up the cudgels
in such a matter.

"One thing or the other," says that same Sallustius, 3
" you should have defended him, and made that
concession to Pompey's prayers ; he implored you
earnestly enough."[b] A pretty sort of friend Sallustius,
to think that I should have incurred either dangerous
enmities, or everlasting infamy. For my part, I rub
my hands over this middle course I have adopted,
and I am delighted that when, in accordance with
my honour and my oath I had given my evidence in
the most impressive manner, the defendant declared,

si in civitate licuisset sibi esse, mihi se satisfacturum,
4 neque me quidquam interrogavit. De versibus, quos
tibi a me scribi vis, deest mihi quidem opera, quae
non modo tempus, sed etiam animum vacuum ab
omni cura desiderat; sed abest etiam ἐνθουσιασμός;
non enim sumus omnino sine cura venientis anni,
etsi sumus sine timore. Simul et illud (sine ulla mehercule ironia loquor): tibi istius generis in scribendo
5 priores partes tribuo, quam mihi. De bibliotheca
tua Graeca supplenda, libris commutandis, Latinis
comparandis, valde velim ista confici, praesertim cum
ad meum quoque usum spectent. Sed ego, mihi ipsi
ista per quem agam, non habeo. Neque enim venalia
sunt, quae quidem placeant, et confici, nisi per
hominem et peritum et diligentem, non possunt.
Chrysippo tamen imperabo, et cum Tyrannione
loquar. De fisco quid egerit Scipio, quaeram.
Quod videbitur rectum esse, curabo. De Ascanione,
tu vero, quod voles, facies; me nihil interpono. De
suburbano, quod non properas, laudo; ut tu habeas,
6 hortor. Haec scripsi a. d. ix. Kalend. Novemb.
quo die ludi committebantur, in Tusculanum proficiscens, ducensque mecum Ciceronem meum in
ludum discendi, non lusionis; ea re non longius

ᵃ Cf. Juv. Sat. vii. 53-58, " sed vatem egregium . . . |
anxietate carens animus facit, omnis acerbi | impatiens."
ᵇ Nothing is known of this transaction, but cf. Q.F. iii. 5. 6.
ᶜ Probably one of Quintus's slaves.

that if he were permitted to remain a member of the
State, he would satisfy my claims to his gratitude ;
and he refrained from cross-examining me at all.

About the verses you wish me to write for you, as **4**
a matter of fact, I lack the necessary energy, which
requires not only leisure, but a mind free from all
anxiety ;^a but the divine *afflatus* is also wanting ; for
I am not altogether without anxiety as regards the
coming year, although I do not fear it. At the same
time there is also the fact (and, on my oath, I am
speaking without a touch of irony) that in this style
of composition I assign a higher rank to you than
I do to myself.

As to the replenishing of your Greek library, the **5**
exchange of books, and the collection of Latin books,
I should be very glad to see all that done, especially
as it tends to my own advantage as well. But I have
nobody whom I could employ as my own agent in
the business. For such books as are really desirable
are not for sale, and cannot be got together except
through an agent who is both an expert and a man
who takes pains. I shall send orders to Chrysippus,
however, and have a talk with Tyrannio. I shall
find out what Scipio has done as regards the treasury.^b
I shall see to it that what seems right is done. As to
Ascanio ^c you will do as you please ; I have no finger
in the pie. As to a suburban property, I approve
your being in no hurry, but I urge you to secure one.

I am writing this on October 24, the day on **6**
which the games begin, just as I am starting for my
Tusculan villa, taking my dear Cicero with me to a
school for learning, not a school of gladiators, no
farther away from Rome than I wished to be, the
reason being that I wanted to be there on Novem-

quam vellem, quod Pomptino ad triumphum a. d. III.
Non. Novemb. volebam adesse. Etenim erit nescio
quid negotioli. Nam Cato et Servilius praetores pro-
hibituros se minantur ; nec, quid possint, scio. Ille
enim et Appium consulem secum habebit, et praetores,
et tribunos plebis. Sed minantur tamen, in primisque Ἄρη πνέων Q. Scaevola. Cura, mi suavissime et
carissime frater, ut valeas.

V AND VI

M. CICERO S. D. Q. FRATRI

Tusculani, A.U.C. 700.

1 Quod quaeris, quid de illis libris egerim, quos,
cum essem in Cumano, scribere institui, non cessavi
neque cesso ; sed saepe iam scribendi totum consilium rationemque mutavi. Nam iam duobus factis
libris, in quibus, novendialibus iis feriis, quae fuerunt
Tuditano et Aquilio consulibus, sermo est a me in-
stitutus Africani, paullo ante mortem, et Laeli,
Phili, Manili, P. Rutili, Q. Tuberonis et Laeli genero-
rum, Fanni et Scaevolae ; sermo autem in novem et
dies et libros distributus de optimo statu civitatis
et de optimo cive ; sane texebatur opus luculenter,

---

^a He was one of Cicero's *legati* in Cilicia. He claimed a
triumph for his successful campaign against the Allobroges
in 61.

^b *De Republica.*

^c In 129 B.C. the Novendialia were a nine days' festival
held on the occasion of some inauspicious portent.

^d For Scipio Africanus's supposed murder see note *b* on
Fam. ix. 21. **3.**

ber 3 to support Pomptinus's[a] application for a triumph. As a matter of fact, there is going to be some little trouble about it. Cato and Servilius, the praetors, threaten to forbid it, and yet I don't know what they can do. He will have with him Appius the consul, the praetors, and the tribunes of the plebs. And yet they do threaten him, and in particular Q. Scaevola, "*breathing battle.*" My most charming and dearest of brothers, take care of your health.

V AND VI

CICERO TO QUINTUS IN GAUL

Tusculanum, late in October, 54 b.c.

You ask me what I have done about those books [b] I began to write at my Cuman villa ; well, I have not been, and am not, idle, but I have often remodelled the whole plan and scheme of the composition. I had already completed two books, in which I had set going a conversation held during the festival of the Novendialia, which took place in the consulship of Tuditanus and Aquilius [c] between Africanus (shortly before his death [d]) and Laelius, Philus, Manilius, P. Rutilius, Q. Tubero,[e] and Laelius's sons-in-law, Fannius and Scaevola. Now that conversation, spread over nine days and taking nine books, was on " The ideal constitution of the State " and " The ideal citizen." The work was being composed excellently well, and the

---

[e] L. Furius Philus was consul in 136 ; Manilius was consul in 146 ; Q. Tubero was a nephew of Africanus and a strong opponent of the Gracchi.

hominumque dignitas aliquantum orationi ponderis
afferebat. Hi libri cum in Tusculano mihi legerentur
audiente Sallustio, admonitus sum ab illo, multo
maiore auctoritate illis de rebus dici posse, si ipse
loquerer de republica, praesertim cum essem non
Heraclides Ponticus, sed consularis et is, qui in
maximis versatus in republica rebus essem. Quae
tam antiquis hominibus attribuerem, ea visum iri
ficta esse ; oratorum sermonem in illis nostris libris,
qui essent[1] de ratione dicendi, belle a me removisse ;
ad eos tamen rettulisse, quos ipse vidissem ; Aristo-
telem denique, quae de republica et praestante viro
2 scribat, ipsum loqui. Commovit me, et eo magis,
quod maximos motus nostrae civitatis attingere non
poteram, quod erant inferiores, quam illorum aetas,
qui loquebantur. Ego autem id ipsum tum eram
secutus, ne, in nostra tempora incurrens, offenderem
quempiam. Nunc et id vitabo, et loquar ipse tecum,
et tamen illa, quae institueram, ad te, si Romam
venero, mittam. Puto enim te existimaturum a me
libros illos non sine aliquo meo stomacho esse relictos.
3 Caesaris amore, quem ad me perscripsti,[2] unice delector ; promissis his, quae ostendit, non valde
pendeo ; nec honores sitio nec desidero gloriam ;
magisque eius voluntatis perpetuitatem, quam pro-

---

[1] *Wesenberg* : quod esset MSS.
[2] *Bücheler, followed by Tyrrell* : perscripsit M.

---

[a] Who was no more than a theorist on politics.
[b] The three books *De oratore*.
[c] *i.e.*, in his *Politics* and *Ethics*.

speeches were given considerable weight by the high rank of the interlocutors. But when these books were being read out to me at my Tusculan villa, in the hearing of Sallustius, it was suggested to me by him that these subjects could be discussed with far greater authority if the speaker on the Republic were myself, especially as I was not a mere Heraclides Ponticus,[a] but a consular, and one who had been engaged in the most critical State affairs; that the words I attributed to men of such antiquity would surely be regarded as so much fiction; that in those books of mine, which dealt with the science of rhetoric,[b] I had shown good taste in dissociating myself from the conversation of the orators, and yet had assigned the speeches to men whom I had personally met; and, finally, that Aristotle speaks in the first person when he writes on " The Republic " and " The eminently good man." [c]

He impressed me, and all the more because of my 2 inability to touch upon the most important disturbances in our State, since they were of a later date than the age of my speakers. But that is the very plan I had adopted at the time, so as not to hurt somebody's feelings by encroaching upon our own days. As it is, I shall avoid doing that, and shall myself be the man speaking with you, and, all the same, when I come to Rome, I shall send you the original draft; for I am sure you will believe that I did not abandon the first draft of those books without something of a pang.

Caesar's affection for me, of which you write so 3 fully, gives me exceptional pleasure; I do not depend to any great extent upon the offers he holds out; I do not thirst for public offices, nor do I pine for glory; and I look forward more to the continu-

missorum exitum exspecto. Vivo tamen in ea ambitione et labore, tamquam id, quod non postulo,
4 exspectem. Quod me de faciendis versibus rogas,
incredibile est, mi frater, quam egeam tempore ; nec
sane satis commoveor animo ad ea, quae vis, canenda.
Ὑποθέσεις[1] vero ad ea, quae ipse ego ne cogitando
quidem consequor, tu, qui omnes isto eloquendi et
exprimendi genere superasti, a me petis ? Facerem
tamen, ut possem ; sed (quod te minime fugit) opus
est ad poema quadam animi alacritate, quam plane
mihi tempora eripiunt. Abduco equidem me ab
omni reipublicae cura, dedoque litteris ; sed tamen
indicabo tibi, quod mehercule in primis te celatum
volebam. Angor, mi suavissime frater, angor, nullam
esse rempublicam, nulla iudicia ; nostrumque hoc
tempus aetatis, quod in illa auctoritate senatoria
florere debebat, aut forensi labore iactari, aut domesticis litteris sustentari ; illud vero, quod a puero
adamaram,

πολλὸν[2] ἀριστεύειν καὶ ὑπείροχον ἔμμεναι ἄλλων,

totum occidisse ; inimicos a me partim non oppugna-
tos, partim etiam esse defensos ; meum non modo
animum, sed ne odium quidem esse liberum ; unum-
que ex omnibus Caesarem esse inventum, qui me
tantum, quantum ego vellem, amaret, aut etiam (sicut

----

[1] *most edd.*: διατυπώσεις *Bücheler*; *possibly. as Tyrrell
suggests,* ἐμπνεύσεις, "*inspirations.*"
[2] *MSS.*: *but Homer has* αἰὲν *in* Il. vi. 208 *and* xi. 784.

ance of his goodwill, than to the fulfilment of his
promises. Yet my life is spent in such a laborious
effort to please him, as if I were looking forward to
what I do not ask for.

As to your asking me about writing some verses, 4
you couldn't believe, my dear brother, how pressed
I am for time, and I really lack the necessary inclination to write the poetry you want. But come now,
is it you who seek suggestions for what I myself do
not succeed in attaining, even in imagination—you
who have surpassed everybody in that kind of fluent
and graphic expression? I would do your bidding
to the best of my ability, but (as you are the last man
to forget) the composition of a poem demands a
certain sprightliness of mind, of which I have been
completely robbed by the times we live in. I withdraw
myself, it is true, from all public cares, and devote
myself to literature ; and yet, I will divulge to you
what, on my oath, I especially wished to keep hidden
from you. It is agony to me, my dearest brother,
sheer agony, to think that there is no constitution,
no administration of justice, and that during the
period of my life when my proper influence in the
Senate should have been at its zenith, I am either
distracted by my forensic labours, or fortified only
by my literary pursuits at home, while that aspiration
to which I had been passionately devoted from my
very boyhood, " *Far to excel, and alone to be leader
of others,*" has completely vanished; that my foes,
in some cases, I have left unattacked, in others I
have even defended ; that not only my inclinations,
but my very dislikes are not free; and that in all
the world I have found in Caesar the one man to
love me as I could wish, or even (as others think) the

alii putant) hunc unum esse, qui vellet. Quorum
tamen nihil est eiusmodi, ut ego me non multa consolatione quotidie leniam ; sed illa erit consolatio
maxima, si una erimus ; nunc ad illa vel gravissimum
5 accedit tui desiderium. Gabinium si, ut Pansa putat
oportuisse, defendissem, concidissem ; qui illum
oderunt (hi sunt toti ordines), propter quem oderunt,[1]
meipsum odisse coepissent. Tenui me, ut puto, egregie, tantum ut facerem, quantum omnes viderent.[a]
Et in omni summa, ut mones, valde me ad otium
6 pacemque converto. De libris Tyrannio est cessator. Chrysippo dicam. Sed res operosa est et
hominis perdiligentis. Sentio ipse, qui in summo
studio nihil assequor. De Latinis vero, quo vertam
me, nescio, ita mendose et scribuntur et veneunt;
sed tamen, quod fieri poterit, non neglegam. Crebrius, ut ante ad te scripsi, Romae est ; et qui omnia
se adiurat debere tibi, valde renuntiat.[2] De aerario
puto confectum esse, dum absum.

7 Quattuor tragoedias xvi. diebus absolvisse cum
scribas, tu quidquam ab alio mutuaris ? et πλείους[3]

---

[1] *The extraordinary construction of the phrase* propter
quem oderunt, *in which* quem *is apparently governed by
both the preposition and the verb, has escaped the notice of
commentators. We must either suppose that* eum *has dropped
out after* propter, *or accuse Cicero of a solecism.*

[2] valde te nunc iactat (*abuses you*) Boot.

[3] *Prof. Robinson Ellis :* †πλέος *MSS. :* κλέος *Nobbe :* πάθος
Usener.

---

[a] I agree with Prichard and Bernard that some such words
as " mihi faciendum esse " are understood after *viderent.*

one man who had any wish to do so. Still there is nothing in all this so bad but that I daily soothe myself with many a consolation; but the greatest consolation of all will be our being together; as it is, to my other sorrows is added my yearning for you, and that is the hardest to bear of all.

Had I defended Gabinius, as Pansa thinks I ought **5** to have done, I should have brought utter ruin upon myself; those who hate him (and that means the orders in their entirety) would have begun to hate me personally, because of him they hate. I have, I think, kept an admirable course, in confining myself to doing what the world saw I had to do.[a] And, to sum up the whole situation, I am taking your advice, and resolutely turning my face in the direction of tranquillity and peace.

In the matter of the books, Tyrannio is a sluggard. **6** I shall have a word with Chrysippus, but it is a laborious business, and one that needs a very energetic man. My own experience tells me that, for however strenuously I work, I have nothing to show for it. As for the Latin books, I don't know which way to turn; they are copied out and sold so full of mistakes. However I shall not omit to do all that can be done. Crebrius, as I wrote to you before, is at Rome, and, while he swears that he owes you everything, he stoutly refuses repayment. I fancy that business of the treasury was settled in my absence.[b]

Though you write that you had finished off four **7** tragedies in sixteen days, are you sure that you are not borrowing anything from someone else? And

[b] *Cf.* § 5 in *Ep.* 4 of this Book.

quaeris, cum *Electram* et *Troada*[1] scripseris ? Cessator esse noli ; et illud γνῶθι σεαυτόν noli putare ad arrogantiam minuendam solum esse dictum, verum etiam ut bona nostra norimus. Sed et istas et *Erigonam* mihi velim mittas. Habes ad duas epistulas proximas.

VII

M. CICERO S. D. Q. FRATRI

Tusculani, A.U.C. 700.

1 Romae, et maxime Appia ad Martis, mira proluvies. Crassipedis ambulatio ablata, horti, tabernae plurimae ; magna vis aquae usque ad piscinam publicam. Viget illud Homeri :

ἤματ' ὀπωρινῷ, ὅτε λαβρότατον χέει ὕδωρ
Ζεύς, ὅτε δή γ' ἄνδρεσσι κοτεσσάμενος χαλεπαίνῃ,

cadit enim in absolutionem Gabini

οἳ βίῃ εἰν ἀγορῇ σκολιὰς κρίνωσι θέμιστας,
ἐκ δὲ δίκην ἐλάσωσι, θεῶν ὄπιν οὐκ ἀλέγοντες.

2 Sed haec non curare decrevi. Romam cum venero,

---

[1] *Prof. Robinson Ellis* : †Troadem MSS.

---

[a] Reading πλείους with Prof. Robinson Ellis, I append an epitome of his ingenious explanation of this obscure passage. " I believe this," he says, " to be a learned mythological allusion to the *varying number of the Pleiades*, which, according as Electra was visible or not, were reckoned as six or seven alternately." And he takes Cicero to mean, " Are you not content with the six tragedies you have written, but still look for the seventh, or missing, Pleiad, after showing such familiarity with Electra and her conduct as a Trojan woman ? " *Hermathena*, xiii. (1887), p. 139, quoted by Tyrrell.

[b] Hom. *Il.* xvi. 385-388.

596

after writing the *Electra* and the *Trojan Woman*, are you searching for one Pleiad more ?[a] You must not rest on your oars, and you must not be under the idea that the well-known *nosce teipsum* was only meant to apply to the abatement of arrogance, but also means that we should recognize our own gifts. But I should like you to send me those tragedies and the *Erigona* also. You now have an answer to your last two letters.

VII

CICERO TO QUINTUS

Tusculanum, late in October or early in November, 54 B.C.

At Rome, and especially on the Appian Way, up 1 to the Temple of Mars, there is a tremendous flood. Crassipes' promenade has been carried away, pleasure-grounds too, and quite a number of shops. There is an immense quantity of water right up to the public fish-pond. That passage in Homer still holds true :

As on a day in late autumn when down in a torrent resistless
Zeus pours the rain, in resentment and wrath at the misdeeds of mortals

(for it exactly fits in with the acquittal of Gabinius)

Who in the place of assembly distort without mercy their
judgments,
Banishing justice from earth, and the voice of the gods never
heeding.[b]

But I am determined not to let these things trouble me.

When I return to Rome, I shall write and tell you 2

597

CICERO

quae perspexero, scribam ad te, et maxime de dic
tatura, et ad Labienum et ad Ligurium litteras dabo
Hanc scripsi ante lucem, ad lychnuchum ligneolum
qui mihi erat periucundus, quod eum te aiebant
cum esses Sami, curasse faciendum. Vale, mi sua
vissime et optime frater.

VIII

M. CICERO S. D. Q. FRATRI

Romae, a.u.c. 700.

1   Superiori epistulae quod respondeam, nihil est
quae plena stomachi et querellarum est ; quo in
genere alteram quoque te scribis pridie Labien
dedisse ; qui adhuc non venerat. Delevit enim mih
omnem molestiam recentior epistula. Tantum te e
moneo et rogo, ut in istis molestiis et laboribus e
desideriis recordere, consilium nostrum quod fueri
profectionis tuae. Non enim commoda quaedam
sequebamur parva ac mediocria. Quid enim erat
quod discessu nostro emendum putaremus ? Prae
sidium firmissimum petebamus et optimi et poten
tissimi viri benevolentia ad omnem statum nostra
dignitatis. Plura ponuntur in spe, quam in pecuniis
reliqua ad iacturam struantur.[1] Quare si crebr

[1] *Nobbe* : struentur *M* : reservantur *Cratander*.

---

[a] To join Caesar in Gaul.
[b] Just as in a storm it was usual to throw part of the carg
overboard to lighten and save the ship, so now they mus
sacrifice all prospect of immediate gain to secure this hop
for the future. For *iactura cf.* Acts, xxvii. 38.

the result of my observations, and send a letter to
Labienus and to Ligurius also.

I am writing this before daybreak, by the light of
a little wooden torch-stand, which has always been
a great delight to me, because they told me that you
had seen to its construction when you were in Samos.

Good-bye, my dearest and best of brothers.

VIII

CICERO TO QUINTUS

Rome, late in November, 54 B.C.

I have nothing to say in answer to your earlier 1
letter, which teems with resentment and dissatisfaction, and you write that on the preceding day you
entrusted another letter also of the same sort to
Labienus, who has not yet arrived. I do not answer
your earlier letter, because all feeling of annoyance
has been obliterated from my mind by your letter of
more recent date. This much only I advise you, and
indeed beg of you to do—in the midst of your troubles
and toils and longings, to recall to mind the purpose
we had in view when you left Rome.[a] It was not
petty or paltry advantages that we were aiming at.
What was it then, for which we thought that even
our separation was a proper price to pay ? Well,
what we sought was the strongest possible reinforce-
ment of our whole political position by enlisting
the goodwill of a man of irreproachable character,
and at the same time of unquestioned ascendancy.
The investment is in hope rather than in cash ; let
all else be got ready for throwing overboard.[b] So

599

referes animum tuum ad rationem et veteris consili nostri, et spei, facilius istos militiae labores ceteraque, quae te offendunt, feres ; et tamen, cum voles, depones. Sed eius rei maturitas nequedum venit,
2 et tamen iam appropinquat. Etiam illud te admoneo, ne quid ullis litteris committas, quod, si prolatum sit, moleste feramus. Multa sunt, quae ego nescire malo, quam cum aliquo periculo fieri certior. Plura ad te vacuo animo scribam, cum (ut spero) se Cicero meus belle habebit. Tu velim cures, ut sciam, quibus nos dare oporteat eas, quas ad te deinde litteras mittemus ;—Caesarisne tabellariis, ut is ad te protinus mittat, an Labieni. Ubi enim isti
3 sint Nervii, et quam longe absint, nescio. De virtute et gravitate Caesaris, quam in summo dolore adhibuisset, magnam ex epistula tua accepi voluptatem. Quod me institutum ad illum poema iubes perficere, etsi distentus cum opera, tum animo sum multo magis, quoniam tamen ex epistula, quam ad te miseram, cognovit Caesar, me aliquid esse exorsum, revertar ad institutum, idque perficiam his supplicationum otiosis diebus ; quibus Messallam iam nostrum reliquosque molestia levatos, vehementer gaudeo; eumque quod certum consulem cum Domitio nume-

---

[a] It was in the winter of this year that Quintus so gallantly defended his camp against an overwhelming force of Nervii. Their territory in Gallia Belgica extended from the river Sabis (*Sambre*) to the sea, and was partly covered by the forest of Arduenna (*Ardennes*).

[b] For the loss of his daughter Julia (*cf. Ep.* 1. 25 above).

if you constantly throw your thoughts back to the purpose of our original policy, and what we then had in view, you will find less difficulty in enduring your military labours, and anything else that is obnoxious to you ; and, after all, you can give up those duties whenever you please ; but the hour for that has not arrived, though it is already approaching.

I give you this piece of advice also—not to commit 2 to any form of writing anything the publication of which may cause us annoyance. There are many things I would rather not know than be told of them at some considerable risk. I shall write to you at greater length with a mind free from care when my Cicero, as I hope he will be, is in comfortable health. Please be careful to let me know to whom I ought to entrust the letter I shall send you later on —to Caesar's letter-carriers, so that he may send them straight to you, or to Labienus's ; for I have no idea where those Nervii[a] of yours are, and how far off they are.

Your letter about the courage and dignity of 3 Caesar, which, as you tell me, he displayed in the midst of his intense sorrow,[b] was a source of great pleasure to me. You bid me finish the poem addressed to him which I have begun ; well, in spite of the distractions of work, and far more of my thoughts, still, now that Caesar has got to know from a letter which I sent you that I have something on the stocks, I shall return to what I have begun, and shall finish it during these leisure days of the *supplicationes* ; and I am greatly delighted that during those days our friend Messalla and the rest have at last been relieved from annoyance ; and in reckoning upon him as certain to be consul together with Domitius, you

601

ratis, nihil a nostra opinione dissentitis. Ego Messallam Caesari praestabo. Sed Memmius in adventu
Caesaris habet spem ; in quo illum puto errare ; hic
quidem friget. Scaurum autem iampridem Pompeius
4 abiecit. Res prolatae. Ad interregnum comitia
adducta. Rumor dictatoris iniucundus bonis ; mihi
etiam magis, quae loquuntur. Sed tota res et
timetur et refrigescit. Pompeius plane se negat
velle ; antea ipse mihi non negabat. Hirrus auctor
fore videtur. O di, quam ineptus ! quam se ipse
amans sine rivali ! Caelium Vinicianum, hominem
mihi deditum, per me deterruit. Velit, nolit, scire
difficile est. Hirro tamen agente, nolle se non pro-
babit. Aliud hoc tempore de republica nihil loque-
5 bantur. Agebatur quidem certe nihil. Serrani
Domestici fili funus perluctuosum fuit a. d. VIII.
6 Kalend. Decemb. Laudavit pater scripto meo. Nunc
de Milone. Pompeius ei nihil tribuit, et omnia
Cottae, dicitque se perfecturum, ut illo Caesar in-
cumbat. Hoc horret Milo, nec iniuria, et, si ille
dictator factus sit, paene diffidit. Intercessorem dic-

---

a Strictly speaking, the *interregnum* would only become
necessary when the consuls left office at the end of the year.
. . . But Cicero was right, and the *interregnum* lasted till
July 53. W. W. How.

b Probably he means Pompey, and not Hirrus.

c *Cf. Fam.* viii. 4. 3, where he is mentioned as having
urged the dictatorship of Pompey with disastrous results
to himself.

d Nothing more is known of him.

e M. Aurelius Cotta held Sardinia for Pompey in 49.

are all of you in strict agreement with what I think myself. I will go bail to Caesar for Messalla's conduct. But Memmius pins his hopes on Caesar's arrival in Italy ; in which I think he is mistaken ; here there is no doubt that he is a back number. Scaurus has long since been thrown over by Pompey.

All business has been postponed, and the elections 4 so long deferred that there must be an interregnum.[a] The rumour of a dictatorship is not to the liking of the loyalists ; still less to my liking is what people say. But the whole proposal is regarded with alarm, and falling into the background. Pompey flatly denies that he has any wish for it ; previously he used to make no such denial in talking to me himself. It seems likely that Hirrus will be the proposer. Ye gods, what a fool he is ![b] What a lover of himself, without a rival in the field ! As for Caelius Vinicianus,[c] a man devoted to me, it was through me that Pompey managed to frighten him off. It is hard to be sure whether he does or does not desire it. If it is Hirrus, however, who proposes it, he will not convince people that he does not desire it. There is no other topic of political conversation at the present moment ; nothing at any rate is being done.

The funeral of Serranus Domesticus's[d] son on 5 November 23 was a very sad incident. His father delivered a funeral oration over him which I had written.

And now about Milo. Pompey gives him no 6 encouragement, and gives it all to Cotta,[e] and says he will contrive that Caesar shall throw his weight on that side. Milo is alarmed at this, and rightly so, and if Pompey is made dictator, he almost gives up hope. If he helps anyone who vetoes the dictator-

taturae si iuverit manu et praesidio suo, Pompeium
metuit inimicum ; si non iuverit, timet, ne per vim
perferatur. Ludos apparat magnificentissimos : sic,
inquam, ut nemo sumptuosiores ; stulte bis terque,
non postulatus, vel quia munus magnificum dederat,
vel quia facultates non erant, vel quia potuerat magistrum se, non aedilem putare. Omnia fere scripsi.
Cura, mi carissime frater, ut valeas.

IX

M. CICERO S. D. Q. FRATRI

Romae, A.U.C. 700.

1 De Gabinio nihil fuit faciendum istorum, quae
amantissime cogitata sunt. Τότε μοι χάνοι. Feci
summa cum gravitate, ut omnes sentiunt, et summa
cum lenitate, quae feci. Illum neque ursi neque le-
vavi. Testis vehemens fui, praeterea quievi. Exitum iudici foedum et perniciosum levissime tuli.
Quod quidem bonum mihi nunc denique redundat,
ut his malis reipublicae licentiaque audacium, qua

ᵃ The death of a wealthy friend had given Milo, as his
executor, the opportunity of giving games on a lavish scale
in his honour. Such "funeral" games were not uncommon.
ᵇ Hom. *Il*. iv. 182, the end of the line being εὐρεῖα χθών.
Virgil has a similar expression in *Aen*. iv. 24 "sed mihi
vel tellus optem prius ima dehiscat."

ship with his bands and bodyguard, he fears he will make Pompey his enemy ; if he does not do so, he is afraid that the measure will be carried by force. He is preparing to give the most magnificent games, at a cost, I assure you, that has never been exceeded by anyone.[a] Considering that they are not demanded of him, he is acting like a fool for these two or three reasons at least—because he has already given a magnificent gladiatorial show, or because he has not the means, or because he might have remembered that he was only an executor, and no aedile. That is about all I have to write.

My dearest brother, be careful of your health.

IX

CICERO TO QUINTUS IN GAUL

Rome, December, 54 B.C.

In the matter of Gabinius, I was not obliged to 1 adopt any of the measures, you, in the kindness of your heart, proposed. No, rather than that, " *may earth gape and swallow me.*" [b] In all I did, I acted with the utmost dignity, as everybody feels, and with the utmost tenderness too. I neither jumped upon him nor picked him up. I was a forcible witness, but beyond that I did and said nothing. The result of the trial, disgraceful and pernicious as it was, I bore with unruffled equanimity. And that was a blessing, which now, when all is done, redounds to my advantage, in that I am not in the least disturbed by these evils of the Republic, and the unbridled excesses of shameless men, which used previously

ante rumpebar, nunc ne movear quidem. Nihil est
2 enim perditius his hominibus, his temporibus. Itaque, ex republica quoniam nihil iam voluptatis capi
potest, cur stomacher, nescio. Litterae me, et studia
nostra et otium villaeque delectant, maximeque pueri
nostri. Angit unus Milo. Sed velim finem afferat
consulatus; in quo enitar non minus, quam sum
enisus in nostro; tuque istinc, quod facis, adiuvabis.
De quo cetera (nisi plane vis eripuerit) recte sunt;
de re familiari timeo. Ὁ δὲ μαίνεται οὐκ ἔτ᾽ ἀνεκτῶς,
qui ludos HS. ccccɔɔɔɔ. comparet. Cuius in hoc uno
inconsiderantiam et ego sustinebo, ut potero, et, tu
3 ut possis, est tuorum nervorum. De motu temporum venientis anni, nihil te intellegere volueram
domestici timoris, sed de communi reipublicae statu;
in quo etiamsi nihil procuro, tamen nihil curare vix
possum. Quam autem te velim cautum esse in
scribendo, ex hoc conicito, quod ego ad te ne haec
quidem scribo, quae palam in republica turbantur, ne
cuiusquam animum meae litterae interceptae offen-
dant. Quare domestica cura te levatum volo. In republica scio quam sollicitus esse soleas. Video Messallam nostrum consulem, si per interregem, sine

---

ᵃ Hom. *Il.* viii. 355.
ᵇ Or, as Schütz suggests, "I shall cover by aiding him
with money," or again, "I shall restrain."

to break my heart. For anything more corrupt than the men and the times of to-day cannot be conceived.

And so, since no pleasure can be got out of politics, 2 I don't see why I should fret myself; I find a joy in literature and my favourite pursuits, in the leisure of my country houses, but most of all in our boys. My one and only trouble is Milo. But I hope his being made consul will put an end to all that ; in that matter I shall exert myself as much as I did in the case of my own consulship, and you will help, as indeed you do, from where you are. In his case everything else is in good train, unless all is lost by absolute violence ; but it is his private estate that I am afraid of. " *And now is he beyond endurance mad,*" [a] since the games he is going to give will cost a million sesterces. His thoughtlessness in this one particular I shall bear [b] as well as I can, and it will require all your strength of mind to enable you to do so.

As regards the vicissitudes of fortune in the coming 3 year, I did not intend you to take me as implying any alarm concerning our domestic affairs, but only referring to the general political situation ; and in that, though I have no official charge of anything, still I can scarcely have no charge at all upon me. But how cautious I should like you to be in writing, you must infer from the fact that I, in writing to you, avoid mentioning even those political irregularities which all may see, for fear my letter should be intercepted and hurt anybody's feelings. For that reason I would have you be relieved of all domestic anxiety. I know how deeply concerned you always are in public affairs. I foresee that our friend Messalla will be consul, if appointed by the *interrex*, without

I

iudicio ; si per dictatorem, tamen sine periculo.
Odi nihil habet. Hortensi calor multum valebit.
Gabini absolutio lex impunitatis putatur. Ἐν
παρέργῳ—de dictatore tamen actum adhuc nihil est.
Pompeius abest ; Appius miscet ; Hirrus parat ;
multi intercessores numerantur ; populus non curat ;
4 principes nolunt ; ego quiesco. De mancipiis quod
mihi polliceris, valde te amo ; et sum equidem, ut
scribis, et Romae et in praediis infrequens. Sed cave,
amabo, quidquam, quod ad meum commodum attineat, nisi maximo tuo commodo et maxima tua
5 facultate, mi frater, cogitaris. De epistula Vatini
risi. Sed me ab eo ita observari scio, ut eius ista odia
6 non sorbeam solum, sed etiam concoquam. Quod me
hortaris, ut absolvam, habeo absolutum suave, mihi
quidem uti videtur, ἔπος ad Caesarem ; sed quaero
locupletem tabellarium, ne accidat, quod *Erigonae*
tuae, cui soli, Caesare imperatore, iter ex Gallia
7 tutum non fuit. Quid ? si caementum¹ bonum non
haberem, deturbarem aedificium ? quod quidem
quotidie mihi magis placet, in primisque inferior
porticus et eius conclavia fiunt recte. De Arcano,

---

¹ *Editio Jensoniana*: canem tam *M, which Prof. Robinson
Ellis supports with an ingenious explanation which, however,
hardly tallies with what follows.*

ᵃ Because, in the former case, he would take up his office
at once, and so escape trial ; in the latter, even if brought
to trial (for which there would be time) he would certainly
be acquitted. Tyrrell.

ᵇ Or " keeps such a watchful eye upon me." It appears
that Vatinius (for an account of whom see *Fam.* i. 19. 4,
7, 19, 20 and v. 9. 1) had written a letter to Caesar about
Cicero which Quintus had seen.

ᶜ Quintus's tragedy, the *Erigona*, had been lost in transit
to Rome.

any trial at all,[a] if by a dictator, even then without risk of condemnation. There is no hatred of him, and Hortensius's warm defence will greatly strengthen his case. The acquittal of Gabinius is regarded as an Act of General Amnesty. *En passant,*—after all, nothing has yet been done about a dictator. Pompey is away ; Appius is making mischief ; Hirrus is on the warpath ; many tribunes are reckoned upon as ready to veto ; the people are apathetic ; the leading men object to it, and as for myself, I lie low.

For your promise about the slaves, I heartily bless 4 you ; and it is true that both at Rome and on my estates I am short-handed. But be sure, my dear brother, that you do not contemplate doing anything with a view to my convenience, unless it is entirely convenient to yourself, and quite within your means.

I laughed over Vatinius's letter. But I know he 5 has such a respect for me [b] that I swallow his bitter animosities without suffering indigestion.

As to your urging me to finish my job, I have now 6 finished my " epic " to Caesar, and a charming one it is, in my opinion ; but I am in search of a trustworthy letter-carrier, so that it may not meet with the same mishap as your *Erigona* ; she is the only traveller who did not find the journey from Gaul a safe one since Caesar has been in chief command.[c]

What do you mean ? If the quarry-stone I had 7 was not good, was I to pull down the whole building ? and a building that pleases me more every day, and the lower arcade in particular and the chambers connected with it are being properly constructed. As for Arcanum,[d] it is an edifice worthy of Caesar,

[d] One of Quintus's two estates near Arpinum, the other being Laterium.

609

CICERO

Caesaris[1] opus est vel mehercule etiam elegantioris
alicuius. Imagines enim istae, et palaestra, et piscina, et nilus, multorum Philotimorum est, non Diphi-
lorum. Sed et ipsi ea adibimus, et mittemus et
8 mandabimus. De Felicis testamento tum magis
querare, si scias. Quas enim tabulas se putavit ob-
signare, in quibus in unciis firmissimum locum
tenemus[2] (lapsus est per errorem et suum et Sicurae
servi), non obsignavit; quas noluit, eas obsignavit.
9 Ἀλλ᾿ οἰμωζέτω! nos modo valeamus. Ciceronem, et
ut rogas, amo, et ut meretur, et ut debeo. Dimitto
aut ι a me, et ut a magistris ne abducam, et quod
mater a Porcia[3] non discedit, sine qua edacitatem
pueri pertimesco. Sed sumus una tamen valde
multum. Rescripsi ad omnia, mi suavissime et
optime frater. Vale.

[1] *Tyrrell is inclined to substitute* Caesi; *for Caesius see*
iii. 1. 2 (ad fin.).
[2] *Wesenberg*: firmissimum tenes MSS.
[3] *Prof. R. Ellis*: in Porcianam (sc. domum) discedit, "*is
going to stay with Porcia," Wesenberg.*

---

[a] Philotimus was a satisfactory architect; Diphilus, the
cessator ("lazy dog"), was not.

or, upon my word, of even some more fastidious connoisseur. For your statues, exercising-ground, fish-pond, and conduit are worthy of ever so many Philotimuses (not Diphiluses).[a] But I shall visit them myself, and send men there, and give them instructions.

About Felix's[b] will, you would complain still more 8 bitterly, if you only knew the facts. The document he thought he was sealing, in which we most certainly have a place as heirs to a twelfth of his estate (his slip was due to a mistake on his own part as much as on that of his slave Sicura), he did not seal; the document he didn't want to seal, he sealed! But let him go hang, so long as we keep our health.

I love your Cicero as you ask me to, and as he 9 deserves, and as I am bound to do. But I am letting him leave me for two reasons ;—so as not to take him away from his teachers, and because his mother never leaves Porcia's side, and when she is away the boy's voracity appals me. But for all that we have a great deal of each other's company. I have now answered all your inquiries, my dearest and best of brothers. Good-bye.

[b] We know no more than appears here of this Felix.

CICERO'S
LETTERS TO BRUTUS

WITH AN ENGLISH TRANSLATION BY
M. CARY, D.Litt.

FORMERLY PROFESSOR OF ANCIENT HISTORY
AT THE UNIVERSITY OF LONDON

PREFACE

THE letters written by Cicero to Brutus and by Brutus to Cicero were not included in the first issue of volume III of Cicero's correspondence in 1929. These letters have now been added with a translation by M. Cary.

26 *June* 1953

E. H. WARMINGTON
Editor

INTRODUCTION

I. The Text of the Letters to Brutus

The 26 letters of which the text and translation are
given below constituted in ancient times the IXth
book of the published correspondence between Cicero
and Marcus Brutus, falling within the last few months
of Cicero's life (March or April to July, 43 B.C.).
Four other letters of earlier date survive in the collection of Cicero's "Letters to his Friends" (xiii. 10-14);
they will be found in the translation of that series by
Mr. Glynn Williams.

Of the 26 letters that compose the present volume
21 (nos. VI-XXVI, forming Bk. I according to the
traditional classification) are preserved in a number of
MSS., mostly of the fourteenth and fifteenth centuries,
of which the Codex Mediceus (M) is generally regarded as the most authoritative ; one main branch
of this family also contains the letters to Atticus and
to Quintus Cicero. The remaining five letters (nos.
I-V, constituting Bk. II) remained unknown until
1528, when a scholar named Cratander transcribed
them from a family of MSS. which has since disappeared.

In all the MSS. the letters are arranged out of their
proper chronological order ; and certain small portions of the text are plainly not in their correct place
—an error due to the transposition of several sheets

in the archetype. In three cases (Bk. I. 2, 2a ; 3, 3a ; 4, 4a) two distinct letters have been amalgamated into one composite piece. Minor errors in the MSS. are neither numerous nor important.

The most recent editions by modern scholars are those of L. C. Purser (Clarendon Press, 1903) ; of H. Sjögren (Teubner, 1914) ; and of W. Y. Tyrrell and L. C. Purser (*The Correspondence of Cicero*, 2nd edition, vol. vi. : Dublin University Press and Longmans, Green ; 1933).

The text of Tyrrell and Purser, which closely follows that of Sjögren, has been adopted in the present volume, with a few alterations which are indicated in the footnotes. The letters are printed in the chronological order established by Tyrrell and Purser. Like all students of Cicero's correspondence, the present translator has derived much assistance from the introduction and notes to Tyrrell and Purser's edition.

Further details about the MS. tradition will be found in the Introduction to Sjögren's text and in an article by H. Sternkopf (*Hermes*, 1911, pp. 355-375).

II. THE AUTHORSHIP OF THE LETTERS TO BRUTUS

The genuineness of the correspondence between Cicero and Brutus was not called into question until 1741, when a Cambridge scholar, Dr. James Tunstall,[a] declared it to be a forgery and thus gave rise to a controversy which lasted until the later years of the nineteenth century. The main reasons advanced against the genuineness of the letters were : (1) that

---

[a] The earliest defender of the letters was another Cambridge man, Dr. Conyers Middleton.

their language contained specimens of Silver Age latinity ; (2) that they perpetrated errors of fact, relating to the situation of 43 B.C., such as would have been impossible to Cicero and Brutus ; (3) that they were not in keeping with the characters and accomplishments of Cicero and of Brutus, as revealed to us in the other works of Cicero and in Plutarch's " Life of Brutus."

A closer examination of the " Letters to Brutus " has shown to the general satisfaction of modern scholars that most if not all of them are genuine. For some of the alleged specimens of Silver Age latinity parallels have been adduced from undoubtedly genuine works of Cicero ; and most of the apparent historical errors have been disposed of by re-arranging the pieces in their correct chronological order. The only letters whose authenticity is not generally accepted are nos. XVII and XXV (I. 17 and 16), addressed by Brutus to Atticus and to Cicero respectively.[a] These arouse suspicion by the poverty of their argument and the abruptness, not to say incoherence of their style, which would seem unworthy of a well-educated man like Brutus. But the argument of these letters turned on highly controversial questions of public policy in which Brutus had a difficult case to uphold ; and if we bear in mind that behind his Stoic pose there lurked a hot and stubborn temper,[b] we need not be surprised that he should in these two

---

[a] One of the chief defenders of the authenticity of the letters, L. Gurlitt, maintains that no. XXIV (I. 15) is made up of two authentic letters (§§ 1-2 and 12-13) and an interpolated middle piece (§§ 3-11).

[b] See the excellent appreciation in Tyrrell and Purser, vol. vi. pp. cix-cxxiv.

instances have lapsed into the sputtering and at times downright rude style which has shocked modern critics. In the absence of more compelling adverse evidence, letters XVII and XXV have been recognized as genuine in the present volume.

III. Summary of Events, January–July, 43 b.c.

The period covered by the " Letters to Brutus " was one of renewed civil war after the uneasy truce which followed upon the murder of Caesar. The issues on which this war was fought were complex, and the various contending parties did not at first aline themselves on a common front.

The main seat of war was in North Italy, where Mark Antony claimed for himself the province of Gallia Cisalpina and sought to evict the governor in possession, Decimus Brutus. With the authorization of the Senate, which had rallied round Cicero against Antony, Decimus Brutus refused to quit his province and stood a siege in the town of Mutina (December, 44 b.c.). By April, 43 b.c., Brutus was being hard pressed ; but meanwhile the Senate had mobilized new armies under the command of the consuls A. Hirtius and C. Vibius Pansa (two old officers of Caesar), and at the instigation of Cicero it had enlisted in its service a force of Caesarian veterans which Caesar's adoptive son, C. Iulius Caesar Octavianus, had raised on his own responsibility, and had conferred upon him the rank of an independent commander. On April 14 the combined armies of the consuls and of Octavian beat off an attack by Antony at Forum Gallorum, and on the 21st they inflicted a severe defeat upon him near Mutina. The siege of

the town was now raised, and Antony made a hasty
retreat from Italy to Gallia Narbonensis (S.E.
France).

At Rome it was at first assumed that the victorious
armies would pursue Antony and make short work of
him. But the deaths of Hirtius and Pansa, of whom
the former was killed in the action of Mutina, and the
latter died shortly afterwards of wounds, deprived
the coalition forces of their best leaders; and
Octavian, the son of Caesar, refused to co-operate
with Decimus Brutus, his father's murderer. Antony
was thus able to extricate himself and to put pressure upon the governor of Gallia Narbonensis, M.
Aemilius Lepidus, to join hands with him. Lepidus,
who had previously assured the Senate of his loyalty,
consented to put his powerful army at Antony's disposal; and it was an insufficient offset to this success
of Antony that L. Munatius Plancus, governor of
Gallia Comata (Central and Northern France), remained loyal to the Republic for the time being (till
July or August). Meanwhile Octavian showed signs
of breaking with the Senate and coming to terms with
Antony. By midsummer, 43 B.C., therefore, the
situation had become critical for the senatorial forces
in Italy, and the Senate's only chance now lay in the
timely arrival of reinforcements from Marcus Brutus.

In August, 44 B.C., M. Brutus and C. Cassius
ended a period of indecision, during which they had
wandered somewhat aimlessly about Italy, by betak-
ing themselves to the eastern provinces and raising
armies there on their own authority. By March,
43 B.C., Cassius had rendered himself master of
Syria; but he still had to reckon with opposition
from P. Cornelius Dolabella, Antony's colleague in

the consulship of 44 B.C., who claimed Syria as his province and had gained possession of the province of Asia (W. Asia Minor) by a treacherous attack on its governor, C. Trebonius. Though Cassius eventually overcame Dolabella, he was not in a position to bring timely succour to the senatorial forces in Italy.

Meanwhile Brutus had gained possession of Macedonia and Illyria and had captured Antony's brother C. Antonius, who had sought to occupy this province for himself. During the spring and summer of 43 B.C., therefore, he was free to send an expeditionary force to Italy. In March or early April, while Decimus Brutus lay in great straits at Mutina, Cicero called for M. Brutus' intervention. After the battle of Mutina he offered M. Brutus a free hand and suggested his opening a campaign against Dolabella in Asia Minor. In June and July, when Antony was making his recovery, Cicero repeatedly summoned Brutus to Italy, but Brutus refused to budge. Though he, like Cicero, had quarrelled with Antony, he was less determined to resist Antony *à l'outrance*; he was allied with Lepidus by a marriage connexion; above all, he differed profoundly from Cicero in his estimate of Octavian. While Cicero had his suspicions about Octavian, he hoped against hope to retain him in the service of the Senate; Brutus could see nothing in Octavian but another usurper of monarchy, like his adoptive father. On long views Brutus was probably right; yet it may be debated whether in 43 B.C. he did not make a " great refusal " and throw away the last chance of a Republican victory, or at least of a peace by compromise.

M. TULLI CICERONIS EPISTULARUM AD BRUTUM

I (II. 1)

M. CICERO S. D. M. BRUTO

Romae, A.U.C. 711

1 Cum haec scribebam, res existimabatur in extremum adducta discrimen : tristes enim de Bruto nostro litterae nuntiique afferebantur : me quidem non maxime conturbabant : his enim exercitibus ducibusque, quos habemus, nullo modo poteram diffidere : neque assentiebar maiori parti hominum : fidem enim consulum non condemnabam, quae suspecta vehementer erat. Desiderabam non nullis in rebus prudentiam et celeritatem, qua si essent usi, iam pridem rem publicam recuperassemus. Non enim ignoras quanta momenta sint in re publica temporum et quid intersit idem illud utrum ante an post decernatur, suscipiatur, agatur. Omnia, quae severe decreta sunt hoc tumultu, si aut, quo die dixi senten-

---

a Decimus Brutus, who was being besieged by Mark Antony in Mutina.

622

THE CORRESPONDENCE OF CICERO
AND BRUTUS

I (II. 1)

CICERO TO BRUTUS

Rome, end of March or beginning of April, 43 B.C.

As I write this letter, the war is considered to have 1
reached a highly critical stage. The news brought in
by letters and by couriers about our friend Brutus [a]
is discouraging. Yet for my part I am not greatly
disturbed ; for I simply cannot lose confidence in the
armies and the generals now at our disposal, nor can
I fall in with the prevailing opinion. For I have
nothing to say against the loyalty of the consuls,
which has come under sharp suspicion ; what I find
lacking is good judgement and promptitude in several
matters : had they shown this, we should have regained a free state long ago. For you do not need
to be told how much turns on time in politics, and
what a difference it makes to the selfsame policy,
whether one is beforehand or belated in laying it
down, taking it in hand, and carrying it into effect.
Take all the drastic resolutions which have been
voted in this emergency—if these had been imple-
mented on the date when I spoke to the motion,

tiam, perfecta essent et non in diem ex die dilata
aut, quo ex tempore suscepta sunt ut agerentur, non
tardata et procrastinata, bellum iam nullum habe-
2 remus. Omnia, Brute, praestiti rei publicae, quae
praestare debuit is, qui esset in eo, in quo ego sum,
gradu senatus populique iudicio collocatus, nec illa
modo, quae nimirum sola ab homine sunt postulanda,
fidem, vigilantiam, patriae caritatem : ea sunt enim,
quae nemo est qui non praestare debeat : ego autem
ei, qui sententiam dicat in principibus de re publica,
puto etiam prudentiam esse praestandam, nec me,
cum mihi tantum sumpserim, ut gubernacula rei
publicae prenderem, minus putarim reprehendendum, si inutiliter aliquid senatui suaserim quam si
3 infideliter. Acta quae sint quaeque agantur scio
perscribi ad te diligenter. Ex me autem illud est
quod te velim habere cognitum, meum quidem animum in acie esse neque respectum ullum quaerere,
nisi me utilitas civitatis forte converterit. Maioris
autem partis animi te Cassiumque respiciunt. Quam
ob rem ita te para, Brute, ut intellegas aut, si hoc
tempore bene res gesta sit, tibi meliorem rem publicam esse faciendam aut, si quid offensum sit, per te
esse eamdem recuperandam.

instead of being put off from day to day, or if they had not been held back and postponed ever since they were adopted for translation into action, we should by now have the war off our hands.

Brutus, I have displayed in the service of the state **2** all those qualities which should be shown by one who stands as I do in senatorial rank and popular estimation, and not merely those which should be demanded in a man as a matter of course, loyalty, watchfulness, love of country—for those are what no man may withhold. Now my view is that he who takes the lead in stating an opinion on public affairs should display sagacity into the bargain ; and seeing that I have taken so much upon myself as to grasp the helm of state, I should consider myself no less worthy of censure if my advice to the Senate were unpractical than if it were disloyal.

I know that you receive full and accurate accounts **3** of past and present doings ; but coming from me, this is what I would have you understand, that I for one am in spirit in the fighting line and am not looking for any line of retreat, unless by any chance the interest of the community should make me change my front. But most men regard you and Cassius as their standby. Therefore, Brutus, get yourself to realize that if the present campaign goes in our favour, the reform of the state will be incumbent upon you ; or else, if we have a set-back, it will be for you to retrieve the state.

CICERO

II (II. 3)

M. BRUTUS S. D. M. CICERONI

Dyrrhachii, A.U.C. 711

1 Litteras tuas valde exspecto, quas scripsisti post
nuntios nostrarum rerum, et de morte Trebonii :
non enim dubito quin mihi consilium tuum explices.
Indigno scelere et civem optimum amisimus et provinciae possessione pulsi sumus, quam recuperari
facile est : neque minus turpe aut flagitiosum erit
2 post recuperari. Antonius adhuc est nobiscum, sed
me dius fidius et moveor hominis precibus et timeo
ne illum aliquorum furor excipiat. Plane aestuo.
Quod si scirem quid tibi placeret, sine sollicitudine
essem. Id enim optimum esse persuasum esset
mihi. Qua re quam primum fac me certiorem quid
3 tibi placeat. Cassius noster Syriam, legiones Syria-
cas habet, ultro quidem a Murco et a Marcio et
ab exercitu ipso arcessitus. Ego scripsi ad Tertiam
sororem et matrem, ne prius ederent hoc, quod
optime ac felicissime gessit Cassius, quam cum con-
4 silium cognovissent tibique visum esset. Legi orationes duas tuas, quarum altera Kal. Ian. usus es,
altera de litteris meis, quae habita est abs te contra

ᵃ C. Trebonius, one of Caesar's assassins, and governor
of the province of Asia. He was treacherously attacked and
killed by Dolabella.

ᵇ Gaius Antonius, brother of Mark Antony. Appointed
governor of Macedonia, he was defeated and captured by
Brutus.

ᶜ L. Statius Murcus and Q. Marcius Crispus were two
officers of Caesar whom he sent to quell disorders in Syria.

ᵈ A. Fufius Calenus, consul in 47 B.C. Antony's chief

626

II (II. 3)

I anxiously await the letter which you wrote on 1
receipt of the news of our campaign and of the death
of Trebonius.[a] I feel sure it contains for me an orderly
statement of your policy. A foul crime has taken
from us an excellent citizen and has wrested from us
the control of a province. To retrieve it is no
trouble ; but it will be none the less a humiliation
and a scandal that we should be retrieving the loss
instead of preventing it.

Antonius [b] is still with me. But I'll take my oath 2
upon it, I am being impressed by the man's entreaties,
and I am afraid that the passionate pleadings of
several persons may snatch him away. I am in a
downright fever. If I but knew what you would
have me do, I should be free from worry, for I should
be convinced that you know best. Therefore let me
know as soon as possible what you think right.

Our friend Cassius holds Syria and the Syrian 3
legions : Murcus and Marcius [c] and the troops themselves actually called him in before he made a move.
I have written to my sister Tertia and my mother not
to publish the report of this splendid and most fortunate exploit of Cassius before ascertaining what you
would advise, and what you think of it.

I have read your two speeches, the one which you 4
delivered on January 1, and the other on my dispatches, when you spoke in opposition to Calenus.[d]

spokesman in the Senate. The two *Philippics* to which
Cicero refers here are the fifth and the seventh.

Calenum. Nunc scilicet hoc exspectas, dum eas
laudem. Nescio animi an ingenii tui maior in his
libellis laus contineatur. Iam concedo ut vel Philip-
pici vocentur, quod tu quadam epistula iocans scrip-
5 sisti. Duabus rebus egemus, Cicero, pecunia et
supplemento : quarum altera potest abs te expediri,
ut aliqua pars militum istinc mittatur nobis, vel
secreto consilio adversus Pansam vel actione in
senatu, ab ipso senatu altera, quae magis est necessaria neque meo exercitui magis quam reliquorum.
Hoc magis doleo Asiam nos amisisse : quam sic vexari
a Dolabella audio, ut iam non videatur crudelissimum
eius facinus interfectio Trebonii. Vetus Antistius
6 me tamen pecunia sublevavit. Cicero, filius tuus,
sic mihi se probat industria, patientia, labore, animi
magnitudine, omni denique officio, ut prorsus numquam dimittere videatur cogitationem cuius sit filius.
Qua re quoniam efficere non possum, ut pluris facias
eum, qui tibi est carissimus, illud tribue iudicio meo,
ut tibi persuadeas non fore illi abutendum gloria tua,
ut adipiscatur honores paternos. Kalend. April.
Dyrrhachio.

ᵃ C. Vibius Pansa, consul in 43 B.C. One of the commanders of the senatorial forces in the campaign of Mutina.
ᵇ The Roman province of Asia (W. Asia Minor).
ᶜ P. Cornelius Dolabella, son-in-law of Cicero, and consul
in 44 B.C. Appointed governor of Syria, he invaded Asia
without orders.
ᵈ See Letter XVI.
ᵉ M. Tullius Cicero, junior. He interrupted his studies at
Athens in order to join Brutus' army.

Now I'll warrant you are waiting for me to pay you compliments on them. I cannot say whether these pamphlets are a higher testimonial to your fine spirit or to your wealth of genius. I readily grant you that they should be dubbed " Philippics," if you like : that is the title you jestingly gave them in one of your letters.

We stand in want of two things, Cicero, money and 5 fresh drafts. The latter it is in your power to make available : you can send us a contingent from where you are, either by a private understanding with Pansa,[a] or by proceedings in the Senate ; the former could come from the Senate directly. The need for the former, which is just as great in the armies of the other generals as in mine, makes me regret so much the more the loss of Asia.[b] I hear that Dolabella [c] is harrying it to such effect that his murder of Trebonius no longer strikes me as his most fiendish atrocity. All the same, Vetus Antistius [d] has met part of my needs with a money contribution.

Your son Cicero [e] gives me such a good account of 6 himself in respect of his energy, power of endurance, application, high spirits, in a word, in every helpful quality, that he seems never for a moment to lose out of mind whose son he is. Therefore, seeing that I cannot contrive to make you hold him in still higher affection (for he is the apple of your eyes), I ask you, in deference to my considered opinion, to assure yourself that he will not need to poach on your renown in order to attain his father's high rank. Dyrrhachium, April 1.

CICERO

III (II. 2)

Romae, A.U.C. 711

1 Planci animum in rem publicam egregium, legiones,[a] auxilia, copias ex litteris eius, quarum exemplum tibi missum arbitror, perspicere potuisti. Lepidi,[b] tui necessarii, qui secundum fratrem affines habet quos oderit proximos, levitatem et inconstantiam animumque semper inimicum rei publicae iam credo **2** tibi ex tuorum litteris esse perspectum. Nos exspectatio sollicitat, quae est omnis iam in extremum adducta discrimen. Est enim spes omnis in Bruto[c] **3** expediendo, de quo vehementer timebamus. Ego hic cum homine furioso satis habeo negotii, Servilio,[d] quem tuli diutius quam dignitas mea patiebatur, sed tuli rei publicae causa, ne darem perditis civibus[e] hominem, parum sanum illum quidem, sed tamen nobilem, quo concurrerent, quod faciunt nihilo minus, sed eum alienandum a re publica non putabam. Finem feci eius ferendi. Coeperat enim esse tanta insolentia, ut neminem liberum duceret. In Planci vero causa exarsit incredibili dolore, mecumque per biduum ita contendit et a me ita fractus est, ut eum in perpetuum modestiorem sperem fore. Atque in

---

[a] L. Munatius Plancus, governor of Gallia Comata. For his relations to Cicero see *Epp. ad Fam.* x. 1-24.

[b] M. Aemilius Lepidus, the future triumvir. At this time he was governor of Gallia Comata, and the husband of Brutus' sister. He subsequently consented to his brother being placed on the proscription lists.   [c] Decimus Brutus.

[d] P. Servilius Vatia Isauricus, consul 48 B.C. He advocated negotiation with Mark Antony.

[e] Antony's adherents.

III (II. 2)

Rome, April 11, 43 B.C.

Of Plancus' [a] splendid loyalty to the state, of his 1 legions, auxiliary forces and equipment, you have been able to get a clear idea from his letter, of which I think you received a copy. As for your bosom friend Lepidus,[b] who hates his connexions by marriage only one degree less than he hates his brother, I believe you will by now have realized from the letters of your own family that he is lacking in principle and consistency, and is chronically ill-disposed to the free state.

We are haunted by a feeling of suspense, which is 2 now wholly centred on our extremely critical position; for all our hopes are set on the relief of Brutus,[c] about whom we are exceedingly anxious.

Here I am having trouble enough with that mad-3 man Servilius.[d] I have put up with him longer than my self-respect would allow ; yet I did put up with him for the state's sake, for fear I should present him to the desperadoes [e] as a rallying-point—a man, you know, who is lacking in sense, but to offset that has blue blood in his veins. Even so, they are rallying round him ; but I think I ought not to provoke him to disaffection.—I have done with my complaisance to him, for he is becoming so rude as to treat us like so many slaves. In the matter of Plancus, to be sure, he blazed up with extraordinary bitterness, and for two whole days he battled with me so fiercely and received such a mauling from me, that I hope he will mend his manners for once and all. Oh, and in the

hac contentione ipsa, cum maxime res ageretur, a. d.
v. Idus Apriles litterae mihi in senatu redditae sunt
a Lentulo nostro de Cassio, de legionibus, de Syria :
quas statim cum recitavissem, cecidit Servilius, complures praeterea : sunt enim insignes aliquot, qui
improbissime sentiunt, sed acerbissime tulit Servilius
assensum esse mihi de Planco.   Magnum illud mon-
strum in re publica est ; sed quomodo nunc est, mihi
crede, non erit, III. Id. April.[1]

IV (II. 4)

M. CICERO S. D. M. BRUTO

Romae, A.U.C. 711

1   Datis mane a. d. III. Id. April. Scaptio litteris,
eodem die tuas accepi Kal. April. Dyrrhachio datas
vesperi.   Itaque mane prid. Id. Apr. cum a Scaptio
certior factus essem non esse eos profectos, quibus
pridie dederam, et statim ire, hoc paullulum exaravi
2 ipsa in turba matutinae salutationis.   De Cassio
laetor et rei publicae gratulor, mihi etiam, qui re-
pugnante et irascente Pansa sententiam dixerim, ut
Dolabellam bello Cassius persequeretur.   Et quidem
audacter dicebam sine nostro senatus consulto iam

---

[1] *See Tyrrell and Purser.*

---

[a] P. Cornelius Lentulus Spinther, deputy-governor of
Asia after the death of Trebonius.   See *Epp. ad Fam.* xii.
14-15.
  [b] See Introduction.
  [c] Letter III (II. 2).   Scaptius was an agent of Brutus
(perhaps to be identified with his bailiff in Cilicia—*Epp. ad
Att.* v. 21, vi. 2).

very middle of the duel, just while we were having it out, a letter dated April 9 was handed to me in the Senate ; it was from our friend Lentulus [a] and brought news of Cassius,[b] the legions, and of Syria. I had hardly finished reading it out, than Servilius collapsed, and a number of others with him ; for there are several persons of note whose attitude is quite unscrupulous. But what exasperated Servilius most of all was that I carried the House in the matter of Plancus. That is an impressive indication of the trend of politics. But take my word for it, the present mood won't last. April 11.

IV (II. 4)

CICERO TO BRUTUS

Rome, April 12, 43 B.C.

Early on April 11 I handed a letter [c] to Scaptius, 1 and on the same day received the note dispatched by you on the evening of April 1. On the morning of April 12, accordingly, having ascertained from Scaptius that the messengers to whom I had given my note on the previous day were not yet on the way, and were now on the point of starting out, I am jotting down this short postscript even while my morning callers are thronging round me.

I am glad about Cassius ; and my congratulations 2 go to the state, and also to myself, seeing that it was I who proposed in opposition to Pansa and in disregard of his anger, that Cassius should be charged with the operations against Dolabella. Yes, and I defiantly announced that he was already engaged on

633

illud eum bellum gerere. De te etiam dixi tum quae
dicenda putavi. Haec ad te oratio perferetur, quo-
3 niam te video delectari Philippicis nostris. Quod
me de Antonio consulis, quoad Bruti exitum cog-
norimus, custodiendum puto. Ex iis litteris, quas
mihi misisti, Dolabella Asiam vexare videtur et in
ea se gerere taeterrime. Compluribus autem scripsisti Dolabellam a Rhodiis esse exclusum : qui si ad
Rhodum accessit, videtur mihi Asiam reliquisse. Id
si ita est, istic tibi censeo commorandum : sin eam
semel cepit, mihi crede, statim[1] in Asiam censeo per-
sequendum : nihil mihi videris hoc tempore melius
acturus.

4   Quod egere te duabus necessariis rebus scribis,
supplemento et pecunia, difficile consilium est. Non
enim mihi occurrunt facultates, quibus uti te posse
videam praeter illas, quas senatus decrevit, ut pecunias a civitatibus mutuas sumeres. De supplemento autem non video quid fieri possit. Tantum
enim abest ut Pansa de exercitu suo aut dilectu tibi
aliquid tribuat, ut etiam moleste ferat tam multos
ad te ire voluntarios, quo modo equidem credo, quod
iis rebus, quae in Italia decernuntur, nullas copias
nimis magnas esse arbitretur, quo modo autem multi
suspicantur, quod ne te quidem nimis firmum esse
velit, quod ego non suspicor.

---

[1] statim *conj. by Tyrrell and Purser* : at.

[a] Gaius Antonius.
[b] See Letter II § 5.

that campaign without waiting for our commission from the Senate. In the same session I made such reference to you as seemed appropriate. My speech shall be communicated to you, for I observe that you take a delight in our " Philippics."

In answer to your inquiry about Antonius,[a] my 3 view is that he ought to be kept in detention until we know the result of Brutus' campaign. I gather from the letter which you sent me that Dolabella is harrying Asia and is behaving atrociously in it. And yet you have written to quite a number of people that Dolabella had been shut out from Rhodes ; but if he went as far as Rhodes, it looks to me as if he had left Asia. If that is a fact, I recommend that you should stay where you are ; but once he has captured Rhodes—if that happens, believe me, you must pursue him into Asia at once. It seems to me you could do nothing better at this time.

Touching upon your remark that you are short of 4 two necessaries, fresh drafts and money,[b] I am puzzled what to propose to you. I cannot think of any expedients to which in my view you could have recourse, except the resolutions which the Senate carried, that you should raise a loan among the free communities. But I do not see what can be done about reinforcements ; for Pansa is so little disposed to let you have any part of his army or of his new levies, that he even takes offence at the numbers which are joining you as volunteers. According to my own belief, he estimates that no force can be too large for the operations which are being decided on in Italy ; but the reason which many people surmise is that he wants no one, not even you, to make too firm a stand. This suspicion I do not share.

5 Quod scribis te ad Tertiam sororem et matrem scripsisse, ut ne prius ederent ea, quae gesta a Cassio essent, quam mihi visum esset, video te veritum esse id, quod verendum fuit, ne animi partium Caesaris, quomodo etiam nunc partes appellantur, vehementer commoverentur. Sed ante quam tuas litteras accepimus, audita res erat et pervulgata, tui etiam tabellarii ad multos familiares tuos litteras attulerant. Qua re neque supprimenda res erat, praesertim cum id fieri non posset, neque, si posset, non divulgandam 6 potius quam occultandam putaremus. De Cicerone meo et, si tantum est in eo, quantum scribis, tantum scilicet, quantum debeo, gaudeo, et si, quod amas eum, eo maiora facis, id ipsum incredibiliter gaudeo, a te eum diligi.

V (II. 5)

M. CICERO S. D. M. BRUTO

Romae, a.u.c. 711

1 Quae litterae tuo nomine recitatae sint Id. April. in senatu eodemque tempore Antonii, credo ad te scripsisse tuos, quorum ego nemini concedo; sed nihil necesse erat eadem omnes, illud necesse me ad te scribere, quid sentirem tota de constitutione huius belli et quo iudicio essem quaque sententia. Volun-

You say that you wrote to your sister and your **5** mother, not to make known the successes of Cassius before I thought proper. I see you were afraid, as you had a right to be, lest the Caesarian party, which is the name still being given to that body, should be badly upset. But before we received your note the story was out and had become common property ; your own couriers too had delivered correspondence to many acquaintances of yours. To suppress the news was therefore false policy, especially as that was not practicable ; and we thought that, supposing it were possible, we should all the same publish it rather than keep it dark.

As for my son Cicero, if there is as much in him as **6** you tell me, I am of course as glad as I should be ; or again, if your fondness for him makes you exaggerate, your very excess gives me immense pleasure at the thought that you are his good friend.

V (II. 5)

CICERO TO BRUTUS

Rome, April 14, 43 B.C.

I believe you have heard from your family which **1** of your letters was read out in the Senate on April 13, and of Antony's letter being read at the same time. I yield to none of your folk in my concern for you ; but there is no need for all of us to tell the same story. My special duty is to inform you of my impressions about the general condition of this war, of my considered opinion and my personal feeling on it. My ideals on the main political issue

tas mea, Brute, de summa re publica semper eadem
fuit, quae tua, ratio quibusdam in rebus—non enim
omnibus—paullo fortasse vehementior. Scis mihi
semper placuisse non rege solum, sed regno liberari
rem publicam : tu lenius, immortali omnino cum tua
laude, sed, quid melius fuerit, magno dolore sensimus,
magno periculo sentimus. Recenti illo tempore tu
omnia ad pacem, quae oratione confici non poterat,
ego omnia ad libertatem, quae sine pace nulla est,
pacem ipsam bello atque armis effici posse arbitrabar :
studio non deerant arma poscentium, quorum re-
2 pressimus impetum ardoremque restinximus. Itaque
res in eum locum venerat, ut, nisi Caesari Octaviano
deus quidam illam mentem dedisset, in potestatem
perditissimi hominis et turpissimi M. Antonii venien-
dum fuerit, quocum vides hoc tempore ipso quod sit
quantumque certamen : id profecto nullum esset,
nisi tum conservatus esset Antonius. Sed haec
omitto : res enim a te gesta memorabilis et paene
caelestis repellit omnes reprehensiones, quippe quae
ne laude quidem satis idonea affici possit. Exstitisti
nuper vultu severo ; exercitum, copias, legiones
idoneas per te brevi tempore comparasti : di im-
mortales ! qui ille nuntius, quae illae litterae, quae
laetitia senatus, quae alacritas civitatis erat ! nihil
umquam vidi tam omnium consensione laudatum.

---

[a] This refers to the seduction of Antony's troops by
Octavian in November 44 B.C., which in Cicero's opinion
prevented a military dictatorship by Antony.

[b] Brutus had vetoed a suggestion by his fellow-conspira-
tors, that Antony too should be killed on the Ides of March.

have always been the same as yours, Brutus ; my way of thinking in certain matters (I do not say in all) was perhaps a little more drastic. You know that it was always my resolve that the state should be freed not merely of a monarch but of monarchy. You took a more lenient view, and this was altogether to your undying credit ; but which was the better policy we have been made to feel to our bitter sorrow, and are experiencing at our great peril. At that time, not so long ago, your supreme goal was peace, which could not be won by oratory ; mine was liberty, which without peace is an illusion. I considered that peace as well as liberty could be secured by force of arms. The party that called for arms was thoroughly in earnest ; yet we stifled their enthusiasm and damped down their ardour.

Consequently things came to such a pass, that but for that divine inspiration which came to Caesar Octavianus,[a] we should have had to fall under the power of that utter desperado, that foul wretch, Marcus Antonius, and you can see what a struggle, and how hard-fought, we have even now with him. This conflict of course would be non-existent, if Antony's life had not then been spared.[b] But I say nothing of this, for your unforgettable and almost superhuman exploit disarms all criticism, indeed I cannot even match it with really adequate words of praise. In these last days you have asserted yourself with a grim visage ; by your own effort you have in a short time raised sufficient troops, supplies and legions. Heavens, what a piece of news that was, what a bulletin ! How gladdened was the Senate, and how elated the citizens ! I never saw such an unanimous expression of praise for anything.

K

CICERO

Erat exspectatio reliquiarum Antonii, quem equitatu
legionibusque magna ex parte spoliaras : ea quoque
habuit exitum optabilem ; nam tuae litterae, quae
recitatae in senatu sunt, et imperatoris et militum
virtutem et industriam tuorum, in quibus Ciceronis
mei, declarant. Quod si tuis placuisset de his litteris
referri et nisi in tempus turbulentissimum post discessum Pansae consulis incidissent, honos quoque
iustus et debitus dis immortalibus decretus esset.
3 Ecce tibi Idib. April. advolat mane Celer Pilius, qui
vir, di boni, quam gravis, quam constans, quam
bonarum in re publica partium ! hic epistulas affert
duas, unam tuo nomine, alteram Antonii ; dat Servilio tribuno plebis, ille Cornuto : recitantur in
senatu. ANTONIUS PROCOS. : magna admiratio, ut si
esset recitatum DOLABELLA IMPERATOR, a quo quidem
venerant tabellarii, sed nemo Pili similis, qui proferre
litteras auderet aut magistratibus reddere. Tuae
recitantur, breves illae quidem, sed in Antonium
admodum lenes : vehementer admiratus senatus ;
mihi autem non erat explicatum, quid agerem :
falsas dicerem ? quid, si tu eas approbasses ? con-
4 firmarem ? non erat dignitatis tuae. Itaque ille dies
silentio ; postridie autem, cum sermo increbruisset

---

^a Probably to be identified with an obscure partisan of
Caesar.
^b M. Caecilius Cornutus, praetor urbanus. In the absence
of the consuls, he presided over the Senate.

Curiosity was rife concerning Antonius' remnant, after you had taken most of his cavalry and legions from him. In this case too it heard the result for which it had hoped ; for your dispatch, which was read out in the Senate, proclaims the gallantry of commander and soldiers alike, and the good work of your staff, including my son Cicero. If only your kinsfolk had agreed to a motion on this dispatch and had not been caught in a period of great disorder after the departure of the consul Pansa, a vote of homage to the immortal gods would also have been passed, as is usual and proper.

Now just imagine ! On the morning of April 13 **3** Celer Pilius [a] came scurrying in. Good lord, what a man ! What dignified bearing ! What aplomb ! What a fine figure he cuts on the political scene ! This fellow brings two dispatches, one from you, the other from Antony ; he hands them to Servilius the tribune of the plebs, who passes them on to Cornutus.[b] They are read out in the Senate : " Antonius, proconsul." We were quite taken aback, as if we had heard the words " Dolabella, imperator." He too, to be sure, had sent couriers, but there was nobody of Pilius' kidney who had the face to exhibit them or hand them over to the magistrates. Your letter was read out—that note which had little indeed to say but was decidedly lenient to Antony. The Senate was greatly astonished. For my part, I had no idea what course I should take. Was I to denounce the note as a forgery ? But suppose you had guaranteed your authorship ! Was I to certify it ? But that would have let you down !

So this day passed with nothing said. But next **4** day, when everybody was talking about it, and the

CICERO

Piliusque oculos vehementius hominum offendisset,
natum omnino est principium a me : de proconsule
Antonio multa ; Sestius causae non defuit : post
mecum, quanto suum filium, quanto meum in periculo futurum duceret, si contra proconsulem arma
tulissent ; nosti hominem : causae tamen non defuit.
Dixerunt etiam alii ; Labeo vero noster nec signum
tuum in epistula nec diem appositum nec te scripsisse
ad tuos, ut soleres : hoc cogere volebat, falsas litteras
5 esse et, si quaeris, probabat. Nunc tuum est consilium, Brute, de toto genere belli. Video te lenitate
delectari et eum putare fructum esse maximum,
praeclare quidem, sed aliis rebus, aliis temporibus
locus esse solet debetque clementiae : nunc quid
agitur, Brute ? Templis deorum immortalium im-
minet hominum egentium et perditorum spes nec
quidquam aliud decernitur hoc bello, nisi utrum simus
necne. Cui parcimus aut quid agimus ? His ergo
consulimus, quibus victoribus vestigium nostrum
nullum relinquetur ? Nam quid interest inter Dolabellam et quemvis Antoniorum trium ? Quorum si
cui parcimus, duri fuimus in Dolabella. Haec ut ita
sentiret senatus populusque Romanus, etsi res ipsa
cogebat, tamen maxima ex parte nostro consilio

a P. Sestius, a former supporter of Cicero whom the
orator defended in the speech *Pro Sestio*.
b Pacuvius Antistius Labeo, one of the tyrannicides.
c The three brothers Marcus, Gaius and Lucius Antonius.
642

sight of Pilius gave people a bad shock, it was on my
initiative that a discussion took place at all. I let
myself go about the " proconsul Antonius." Sestius,[a]
who came after me, backed up my case. He had a
word with me afterwards and warned me in what
danger his son and mine, he thought, would stand, if
they had borne arms against a " proconsul." You
know the man : he *did* back me up. Others spoke
besides. But our friend Labeo[b] pointed out that the
letter contained neither your signature nor a date-
mark, and that you had not written as usual to your
family. He offered this as certain evidence that the
letter was a forgery and, if you care to know, he was
carrying his point.

Now, Brutus, it is for you to advise me about the **5**
general conduct of the war. I observe that you
glory in leniency and think that it carries the richest
reward. An excellent principle, no doubt ! But it
is not conditions and times like these that give the
usual and proper scope for a policy of pardon. At
present, Brutus, what is afoot ? The hopes of down-
at-heels and desperadoes are grimly set on the
temples of the immortal gods, and the issue at stake
in this war is nothing else than whether we are to
exist or not. To whom are we showing mercy ? Or
what are we about ? Are we then in this crisis
having regard for men who, if theirs is the victory,
will not leave a trace of us ? For what is the difference between Dolabella and any one of the Antonius
trio ? [c] If we show indulgence to any of these, our
treatment of Dolabella was harsh. Though the logic
of facts compelled the Senate and people of Rome to
adopt this view, yet it was mainly at my prompting
and by the weight of my support that this result was

atque auctoritate perfectum est. Tu si hanc rationem non probas, tuam sententiam defendam, non
relinquam meam : neque dissolutum a te quidquam
homines exspectant nec crudele ; huius rei moderatio
facilis est, ut in duces vehemens sis, in milites liberalis.
6 Ciceronem meum, mi Brute, velim quam plurimum
tecum habeas : virtutis disciplinam meliorem reperiet nullam quam contemplationem atque imitationem tui. xviii. Kalend. Maias.

VI (I. 2 §§ 3-6)

M. CICERO S. D. M. BRUTO

Romae, a.u.c. 711

3 . . . Te benevolentiam exercitus equitumque
4 expertum vehementer gaudeo. De Dolabella, ut
scribis, si quid habebis novi, facies me certiorem, in
quo delector me ante providisse, ut tuum iudicium
liberum esset cum Dolabella belli gerendi : id valde
pertinuit, ut ego tum intellegebam, ad rem publicam,
5 ut nunc iudico, ad dignitatem tuam. Quod scribis
me maximo otio egisse, ut insectarer Antonios, idque
laudas, credo ita videri tibi, sed illam distinctionem
tuam nullo pacto probo : scribis enim acrius prohibenda bella civilia esse quam in superatos iracundiam exercendam. Vehementer a te, Brute, dissentio,
nec clementiae tuae concedo, sed salutaris severi-

achieved. If you reject this way of thinking I shall speak up for your view, but without abandoning mine. Men do not look for any behaviour on your part that is either lax or vindictive. You may easily strike a balance in this case by dealing drastically with the leaders and showing generosity to the troops.

I would like you, my dear Brutus, to have my son 6 Cicero at your side as much as possible. He will never obtain a better training in the manly arts than by studying and imitating you. April 14.

VI (I. 2 §§ 3-6)

CICERO TO BRUTUS

Rome, April 17, 43 B.C.

. . . I am delighted to hear that you found the 3 army and the mounted troops well disposed. If, as 4 you say, you have news of Dolabella, you will let me know. I rejoice that in his case I made timely provision, so that you should be free to decide whether to make war on Dolabella. As I perceived at the time, my action closely touched the interests of the state; as I now judge matters, it touches your honour.

You remark that I took plenty of time before I 5 opened my attack on the Antonii, and you commend me for this. Well, I do believe that this is your point of view. But nothing could induce me to accept that distinction which you draw. You say that we should display more zeal in banning civil wars than in wreaking vengeance on the vanquished. I heartily disagree with you, Brutus, and I cannot defer to your leniency. No, a wholesome sternness carries the day

tas vincit inanem speciem clementiae ; quod si
clementes esse volumus, numquam deerunt bella
civilia.   Sed de hoc tu videris : de me possum idem,
quod Plautinus pater in Trinummo :

Mihi quidem aetas acta ferme est: tua istuc refert maxime.

6 Opprimemini, mihi crede, Brute, nisi provideritis ;
neque enim populum semper eundem habebitis neque
senatum neque senati ducem.   Haec ex oraculo
Apollinis Pythii edita tibi puta : nihil potest esse
verius.   xv. Kal. Maias.

VII (I. 3 §§ 1-3)

M. CICERO S. D. M. BRUTO

Romae, a.u.c. 711

1   Nostrae res meliore loco videbantur ; scripta enim
ad te certo scio, quae gesta sunt.   Quales tibi saepe
scripsi consules esse tales exstiterunt.   Caesaris vero
pueri mirifica indoles virtutis : utinam tam facile eum
florentem et honoribus et gratia regere ac tenere
possimus, quam facile adhuc tenuimus ! est omnino
illud difficilius, sed tamen non diffidimus ; persuasum
est enim adulescenti, et maxime per me, eius opera

---

^a L. 219.
^b The battle of Forum Gallorum.
^c Octavian (C. Iulius Caesar Octavianus).

against the vain show of leniency !   Why, if we choose
to be lenient, there will never be a lack of civil wars !
But this is for you to look into.   To myself I can
apply the same words as the father uses in Plautus'
" Trinummus " [a] :

> My life is all but over; but for you
> This matter is of close concern.

Take my word for it, Brutus, you will all be over- 6
whelmed, if you will not look ahead ; for you will not
find the people ever unchanging, nor the Senate, nor
the leaders of the Senate.   Take this utterance as
voiced from the oracle of the Pythian Apollo ; nothing could be more true.   April 17.

VII (I. 3 §§ 1-3)

CICERO TO BRUTUS

Rome, about April 21, 43 b.c.

Our cause seems in better circumstance ; for I 1
know for sure that you have been posted up about
our achievements.[b]   The consuls have shown up true
to their character, as I have often described it to you.
But the boy Caesar [c] is marvellously well endowed
with manly character.   If only I could direct and
hold him, now that he is gathering strength from his
official position and patronage, as easily as I have
held him hitherto !   That is altogether a harder task,
though I am not losing confidence for all that ; for the
young man has made up his mind—and it was I who
chiefly impressed it upon him—that we owe our safety

647

nos esse salvos, et certe, nisi is Antonium **ab urbe**
2 avertisset, perissent omnia. Triduo vero aut qua-
triduo ante hanc rem pulcherrimam timore quodam
perculsa civitas tota ad te se cum coniugibus et
liberis effundebat; eadem recreata a. d. xii. Kal.
Maias te huc venire quam se ad te ire malebat : quo
quidem die magnorum meorum laborum multarum-
que vigiliarum fructum cepi maximum—si modo est
aliquis fructus ex solida veraque gloria ;—nam tantae
multitudinis, quantam capit urbs nostra, concursus
est ad me factus, a qua usque in Capitolium deductus
maximo clamore atque plausu in rostris collocatus
sum : nihil est in me inane—neque enim debet,—sed
tamen omnium ordinum consensus, gratiarum actio
gratulatioque me commovet propterea, quod popularem me esse in populi salute praeclarum est. Sed
3 haec te malo ab aliis. Me velim de tuis rebus con-
siliisque facias diligentissime certiorem illudque
consideres, ne tua liberalitas dissolutior videatur : sic
sentit senatus, sic populus Romanus, nullos umquam
hostes digniores omni supplicio fuisse quam eos cives,
qui hoc bello contra patriam arma ceperunt, quos
quidem ego omnibus sententiis ulciscor et persequor
omnibus bonis approbantibus. Tu quid de hac **re**
sentias, tui iudicii est : ego sic sentio, trium fratrum
unam et eandem esse causam.

---

^a The speaker's platform in the Forum.

to his efforts ; and to be sure, if he had not drawn
Antony away from the city, all would have been lost.

And yet, three or four days before this glorious 2
event the entire citizen body, as if unnerved with
fear, was fain to stream out to you with family and
all ; yet on April 20 they had recovered their nerve
and would rather that you should come here than
that they should go to you. That was the day on
which I gathered the full harvest of my hard toil
and frequent vigils, if any substantial harvest can
indeed accrue from a well-founded and genuine renown ; for the crowd that flocked round me was as
vast as our city could contain. I was escorted by it
right up to the Capitol and then was made to take my
stand on the Rostra *a* amid huge acclamation and
applause. I am not at all being vain ; there is no
justification for that. But all the same, I am deeply
impressed by the unanimity of all classes, by their
thanksgivings and felicitations, and for this reason,
that it is glorious to achieve popularity in the cause
of the people's safety. But I would sooner you heard
about this from others.

Please spare no pains to keep me informed of your 3
position and your policy, and bear in mind that your
generosity must not give an impression of a loss of
firm purpose. This is the Senate's, this is the people's
conviction, that no enemy ever deserved more richly
the utmost rigour of punishment than those citizens
who took up arms against their country in this war.
These are the men whom I castigate and pursue in all
my pronouncements, with the approval of all loyal
men. You must judge for yourself how you feel
about this ; my feeling is that the three brothers are
one and all in the same case.

CICERO

VIII (I. 3 § 4)

M. CICERO S. D. M. BRUTO

Romae, a.u.c. 711

4   Consules duos, bonos quidem, sed dumtaxat bonos
consules, amisimus : Hirtius quidem in ipsa victoria
occidit, cum paucis diebus ante magno proelio vicisset ; nam Pansa fugerat vulneribus acceptis, quae
ferre non potuit.   Reliquias hostium Brutus persequi-
tur et Caesar ; hostes autem omnes iudicati, qui
M. Antoni sectam secuti sunt, idque senatus consultum plerique interpretantur etiam ad tuos sive
captivos sive dediticios pertinere.   Equidem nihil
disserui durius, cum nominatim de C. Antonio de-
cernerem, quod ita statueram, a te cognoscere causam
eius senatum oportere.   v. Kal. Maias.

IX (I. 5)

M. CICERO S. D. M. BRUTO

Romae, a.u.c. 711

1   A. d. v. K. Maias, cum de iis, qui hostes iudicati
sunt, bello persequendis sententiae dicerentur, dixit
Servilius etiam de Ventidio et ut Cassius persequere-

---

    a The consul A. Hirtius won successive victories over
Antony's forces at Forum Gallorum (April 14th) and Mutina
(April 21st).
    b Decimus Brutus and Octavian.

VIII (I. 3 § 4)

Rome, April 27, 43 b.c.

We have lost two consuls, loyal men both, but 4 nothing more than loyal. Hirtius to be sure met his death in the hour of victory, after he had won another victory in a great battle a few days earlier.[a] They were his victories, for Pansa had taken to flight with wounds which he could not endure. The remnants of the enemy are being pursued by Brutus and Caesar.[b] Now all those who have attached themselves to Marcus Antonius' following have been declared public enemies, and according to the general construction put upon it this resolution of the Senate applies also to your captives or capitulants. For my part I used no specially harsh language when I pronounced on Gaius Antonius in person, because I had decided that the Senate must obtain the facts of the case from you. April 27.

IX (I. 5)

Rome, May 5, 43 b.c.

On April 27, when the debate was on concerning 1 measures of war against those who have been declared public enemies, Servilius went on to speak about Ventidius,[c] and proposed that Cassius should take

[c] P. Ventidius Bassus, an officer of Antony who brought him reinforcements after the battle of Mutina.

tur Dolabellam. Cui cum essem assensus, decrevi hoc
amplius, ut tu, si arbitrarere utile exque re publica
esse, persequerere bello Dolabellam, si minus id commodo rei publicae facere posses sive non existimares
ex re publica esse, ut in iisdem locis exercitum con-
tineres. Nihil honorificentius potuit facere senatus,
quam ut tuum esset iudicium, quid maxime conducere
rei publicae tibi videretur. Equidem sic sentio, si
manum habet, si castra, si ubi consistat uspiam Dolabella, ad fidem et ad dignitatem tuam pertinere eum
2 persequi. De Cassii nostri copiis nihil sciebamus—
neque enim ab ipso ullae litterae neque nuntiabatur
quidquam, quod pro certo haberemus— ; quanto
opere autem intersit opprimi Dollabellam, profecto
intellegis, cum ut sceleris poenas persolvat, tum ne
sit, quo se latronum duces ex Mutinensi fuga confe-
rant. Atque hoc mihi iam ante placuisse potes ex
superioribus meis litteris recordari : quamquam tum
et fugae portus erat in tuis castris et subsidium salutis
in tuo exercitu. Quo magis nunc liberati, ut spero,
periculis in Dolabella opprimendo occupati esse debemus. Sed hoc cogitabis diligentius, statues sapienter : facies nos, quid constitueris et quid agas, si tibi
3 videbitur, certiores. Ciceronem nostrum in vestrum
collegium cooptari volo. Existimo omnino absentium

---

a By a Lex Domitia of 104 B.C. the election of pontifices
was vested in a special electoral assembly of 17 tribes. The
collegium pontificum had the right of nomination and of a
formal *congé d'élire.*

652

the field against Dolabella. I gave him my support
and added this rider, that *you* should take the field
against Dolabella, if you should decide that this was
expedient and in the interests of the state ; but that
if you were not in a position to do so with advantage
to the state, or if you reckoned it bad policy, you
should keep your army in its present position. The
Senate could not have paid you a greater compliment
than to leave it to your discretion what you considered to be most in the public interest. My own
opinion is that if Dolabella has an armed band, a fortified position, any place where he can make a stand,
your cause and your high position demand that you
should go after him.

I know nothing about the forces of our friend Cas- **2**
sius, for I have no letter from him in person, and no
news in which I could have assurance has come in.
But you understand of course how important it is
that Dolabella should be overcome, partly that he may
pay the full penalty of his crime, but also to deprive
the robber-chiefs who have fled from Mutina of a
rallying-point. And indeed you may recall from my
previous correspondence that I favoured this course
for some time back, although your camp was then our
haven of refuge and your army the last guarantee of
our safety. Now that, as I hope, we are free from
danger, we ought all the more to be taken up with
the overthrow of Dolabella. But you will ponder
over this with particular care, and you will summon
wisdom to your resolve. You will, if you think fit,
let us know what decision you have reached, and
what measures you are taking.

I want my son Cicero to be co-opted into your **3**
college.[a] I reckon that it is quite possible to take

rationem sacerdotum comitiis posse haberi ; nam
etiam factum est antea : Gaius enim Marius, cum in
Cappadocia esset, lege Domitia factus est augur, nec
quo minus id postea liceret, ulla lex sanxit ; est etiam
lege Iulia, quae lex est de sacerdotiis proxima, his
verbis, QVI PETET CVIVSVE RATIO HABEBITVR. Aperte
indicatum posse rationem haberi non petentis. Hac
de re scripsi ad eum, ut tuo iudicio uteretur, sicut in
rebus omnibus, tibi autem statuendum est de Domitio, de Catone nostro ; sed quamvis licet absentis
rationem haberi, tamen omnia sunt praesentibus fa-
ciliora. Quod si statueris in Asiam tibi eundum, nulla
4 erit ad comitia nostros arcessendi facultas. Omnino[1]
Pansa vivo celeriora omnia putabamus ; statim enim
collegam sibi subrogavisset, deinde ante praetoria
sacerdotum comitia fuissent : nunc per auspicia
longam moram video ; dum enim unus erit patricius
magistratus, auspicia ad patres redire non possunt :
magna sane perturbatio. Tu, tota de re quid sentias,
velim me facias certiorem. iii. Nonas Maias.

[1] facultas. Omnino Pansa *Purser*. facultas omnino.
Pansa *Tyrrell and Purser*.

---

[a] A law of Caesar, not otherwise known.
[b] Cn. Domitius Ahenobarbus, consul in 32 B.C.
[c] M. Porcius Cato, son of Cato of Utica, and brother-in-
law of Brutus.
[d] If this had happened, the corporate patricians would
at once have nominated an interrex, who would have con-
vened the electoral assembly in place of the deceased consul.

absent persons into consideration at the elections of priests. In fact, this has been done before now, for when Gaius Marius was in Cappadocia, he was made augur under the Domitian law, and no statute has ruled out this procedure for the future. There is also a phrase in the Julian law,[a] the latest measure to regulate the priesthoods : " whosoever shall make application or be taken into consideration." This plainly implies that a person not applying may also be taken into consideration. I have written to him, so that he may avail himself of your advice on this as on all other matters ; but it is for you to settle the case of Domitius [b] and our friend Cato.[c] And yet, although it may be lawful to take an absent person into consideration, everything is made easier all the same for those who are present ; and if you decide that you must go to Asia, there will be no opportunity of summoning our candidates to the polls.

If Pansa were still alive, I believe that everything 4 all round would have moved faster, for he would have held the by-election for his new colleague without loss of time, and then the elections for the priesthoods would have preceded those for the praetorships. Now I can see that the auspices will cause a long delay ; for so long as an individual patrician remains in the magistracy, the auspices cannot revert to the patriciate.[d] Quite an imbroglio, I do declare ! I wish you would let me know your opinion on the whole question. May 5.

CICERO

X (I. 4 §§ 1-3)

M. BRUTUS S. D. M. CICERONI

Dyrrhachii, A.U.C. 711

1 Quanta sim laetitia affectus cognitis rebus Bruti
nostri et consulum,[a] facilius est tibi existimare quam
mihi scribere : cum alia laudo et gaudeo accidisse,
tum quod Bruti[b] eruptio non solum ipsi salutaris fuit,
2 sed etiam maximo ad victoriam adiumento. Quod
scribis mihi trium Antoniorum unam atque eandem
causam esse, quid ego sentiam mei iudicii esse, statuo
nihil nisi hoc, senatus aut populi Romani iudicium esse
de iis civibus, qui pugnantes non interierint. "At hoc
ipsum," inquies " inique facis, qui hostilis animi in
rem publicam homines cives appelles." Immo iustis-
sime ; quod enim nondum senatus censuit nec populus Romanus iussit, id arroganter non praeiudico
neque revoco ad arbitrium meum : illud quidem non
muto, quod ei, quem me occidere res non coegit,[c]
neque crudeliter quidquam eripui neque dissolute
quidquam remisi habuique in mea potestate, quoad
bellum fuit. Multo equidem honestius iudico magisque quod concedere possit res publica miserorum
fortunam non insectari quam infinite tribuere po-

---

[a] In answer to Letter VII.
[b] Decimus Brutus, who had broken out of Mutina.
[c] Gaius Antonius.

656

X (I. 4 §§ 1–3)

It is easier for you to imagine than for me to ex- 1
press in writing how delighted I was to be informed
of the doings of our friend Brutus [b] and of the consuls.
Of all the events, that which earns my highest praise
and gives me most satisfaction is that Brutus' sortie
not only secured his own safety, but contributed more
than anything to the victory.

You tell me that the case of the three Antonii is 2
one and the same, and that it is for me to form my
own conclusions. I have only this one rule to lay
down, that judgement on those citizens who escaped
death in battle belongs to the Senate and people of
Rome. " Ah," you will exclaim, " you are wrong in
what you just said, in that you give the name of
citizens to men who are enemies of the state in intention ! " No, no, I am absolutely right ! For I
will not presume to pass a premature judgement on
a case on which the Senate has not yet formulated
an opinion nor the people expressed its will, nor will
I call away the case for my private decision. In this
I stand firm : in dealing with a man [c] whom the force
of circumstances did not oblige me to kill, I have
not robbed him of anything in a spirit of vindictiveness, nor have I carelessly given anything away to
him, but I have retained him in my power for the
war's duration. Nay, I consider it far more honourable and more permissible under the state's authority
to refrain from pressing hard on the plight of the
stricken than to lavish without stint upon the power-

657

tentibus, quae cupiditatem et arrogantiam incendere
3 possint. Qua in re, Cicero, vir optime atque fortissime mihique merito et meo nomine et rei publicae
carissime, nimis credere videris spei tuae statimque,
ut quisque aliquid recte fecerit, omnia dare ac per-
mittere, quasi non liceat traduci ad mala consilia
corruptum largitionibus animum. Quae tua est
humanitas, aequo animo te moneri patieris, praesertim de communi salute : facies tamen, quod tibi
visum fuerit ; etiam ego, cum me docueris . . .

XI (I. 4 §§ 3-6)

M. BRUTUS S. D. M. CICERONI

In castris, A.U.C. 711

3 . . . Nunc, Cicero, nunc agendum est, ne frustra
oppressum esse Antonium gavisi simus neu semper
primi cuiusque mali excidendi causa sit, ut aliud re-
4 nascatur illo peius. Nihil iam neque opinantibus aut
patientibus nobis adversi evenire potest, in quo non
cum omnium culpa, tum praecipue tua futura sit,
cuius tantam auctoritatem senatus ac populus Romanus non solum esse patitur, sed etiam cupit, quanta
maxime in libera civitate unius esse potest : quam
tu non solum bene sentiendo, sed etiam prudenter

ful such gifts as may inflame their greed and insolence.

In this matter, Cicero, you best and bravest of 3
men, and deservedly dearest to me both on my own
and on the public account, I think your hopes colour
your beliefs overmuch, and as soon as any man has
taken some right step, you are over-hasty in granting
him everything and putting all at his disposal, as
though it were against the laws of Nature that a
man should have his head turned by immoderate
favours and be perverted to wicked purposes. A
man of your high culture will take my warning good-
humouredly, the more so as it touches on our common safety. All the same, you will act on your own
discretion. I too, when you have informed me, . . .

XI (I. 4 §§ 3-6)

BRUTUS TO CICERO

In camp, May 15, 43 B.C.

Now, Cicero, now we must so act, that our rejoicings 3
over the crushing of Antony shall not prove delusive,
and that the agency by which we seek to remove each
evil as it presents itself shall not always be the means
of producing a worse evil in its stead. For no di- 4
saster which may befall us through lack of foresight
or through supineness can fail to bring discredit on all
of us, but especially on you, whom the Senate and
people of Rome allow, nay desire to wield such a
measure of plenary authority as a free state can
commit to one man. This authority you must protect, not by your loyal sentiment alone, but by your

tueri debes. Prudentia porro, quae tibi superest, nulla
abs te desideratur nisi modus in tribuendis honoribus.
Alia omnia sic adsunt, ut cum quolibet antiquorum
comparari possint tuae virtutes : unum hoc a grato
animo liberalique profectum, cautiorem ac modera-
tiorem liberalitatem, desiderant ; nihil enim senatus
cuiquam dare debet, quod male cogitantibus exemplum aut praesidio sit. Itaque timeo de consulatu,
ne Caesar tuus altius se ascendisse putet decretis tuis,
5 quam inde, si consul factus sit, sit descensurum. Quod
si Antonius ab alio relictum regni instrumentum
occasionem regnandi habuit, quonam animo fore putas, si quis auctore non tyranno interfecto, sed ipso
senatu putet se imperia quaelibet concupiscere
posse ? quare tum et facilitatem et providentiam lau-
dabo tuam, cum exploratum habere coepero Caesarem honoribus, quos acceperit, extraordinariis fore
contentum. "Alienae igitur," inquies, "culpae me
reum subiicies ?" Prorsus alienae, si provideri potuit,
ne exsisteret : quod utinam inspectare possis timorem
de illo meum !

6   His litteris scriptis consulem te factum audivimus :
vero incipiam proponere mihi rem publicam iustam

sagacity. Moreover, your sagacity, of which you have enough and to spare, is all that we ask for—save for some moderation in the bestowal of high office.

You have everything else in such abundance, that your merits would bear comparison with any of the ancient worthies ; they lack but one thing as the outcome of a grateful and generous disposition, that its generosity should be tempered by greater prudence and a keener sense of proportion. For the Senate should not bestow upon anyone such gifts as may provide a precedent or position of vantage to men with evil designs. That is why I feel alarmed about the consulship, lest your Caesar should think that your decrees had raised him to such a pinnacle that, once elected to a consulship, he should refuse to climb down from it.

Why, if Antony found in the equipment of mon- 5 archy left by another man an opportunity of making himself a monarch, how do you think it will affect a man if he should imagine himself free to covet any sort of sovereign power, and this at the prompting, not of a slain tyrant, but of the Senate itself ? Therefore I shall extol your readiness and your foresight on the day when I begin to feel convinced that Caesar will be content with such extraordinary honours as he may receive. " Then you will hold me to account for the failings of others ? " you will say. Yes, for others' faults, no less, if they could have been prevented by a display of foresight ! I say this, because I wish you could gain insight into my apprehensions about that man !

After writing this note I heard that you had been 6 made consul. If I see that come true, then indeed I shall begin to visualize a free state true to its name

CICERO

et iam suis nitentem viribus, si istuc videro. Filius
valet et in Macedoniam cum equitatu praemissus
est. Idibus Maiis, ex castris.

XII (I. 6)

M. BRUTUS S. D. M. CICERONI

Candaviae, A.U.C. 711

1 Noli exspectare, dum tibi gratias agam : iampridem hoc ex nostra necessitudine, quae ad summam
benevolentiam pervenit, sublatum esse debet. Filius
tuus a me abest, in Macedonia congrediemur ; iussus
est enim Ambracia ducere equites per Thessaliam et
scripsi ad eum, ut mihi Heracleam occurreret : cum
eum videro, quoniam nobis permittis, communiter
constituemus de reditu eius ad petitionem aut com-
2 mendationem honoris. Tibi Glycona, medicum
Pansae, qui sororem Achilleos nostri in matrimonio
habet, diligentissime commendo. Audimus eum venisse in suspicionem Torquato de morte Pansae cus-
todirique ut parricidam. Nihil minus credendum
est; quis enim maiorem calamitatem morte Pansae
accepit ? praeterea est modestus homo et frugi,
quem ne utilitas quidem videatur impulsura fuisse ad
facinus. Rogo te, et quidem valde rogo—nam Achil-
leus noster non minus, quam aequum est, laborat—,
eripias eum ex custodia conservesque : hoc ego ad

---

a In answer to Letter IX.
b A. Manlius Torquatus, Pansa's quaestor.

and standing firmly once more on its own feet. Your son is well, and I have sent him in advance to Macedonia with a troop of horse. May 15, in camp.

XII (I. 6)

BRUTUS TO CICERO [a]

Candavia (in Epirus), May 19, 43 b.c.

Don't wait for me to express my thanks to you. 1
In view of our intimacy, which has risen to the highest degree of friendliness, we ought long ago to have dispensed with this formality. Your son has parted company with me ; we are to meet again in Macedonia. He is under orders to conduct a troop of horse from Ambracia by way of Thessaly. I have written to him to rejoin me at Heraclea. When I see him, we shall confer and come to an arrangement—since you are leaving the matter in our hands—for him to return for his suit or to obtain a recommendation.

To you I most earnestly recommend Glycon, the 2
physician of Pansa, who has the sister of our man Achilles for his wife. I hear he has fallen under Torquatus' [b] suspicion in connexion with the death of Pansa, and is being kept in custody as a parricide. Nothing could deserve less credence, for to whom has Pansa's death dealt a worse disaster ? Besides, he is steady and a worthy fellow who, you would think, could not even be driven to crime by the prospect of gain. I beg you, yes, I beg you insistently (for our man Achilles is as much perturbed as the occasion demands), rescue him from detention and

meum officium privatarum rerum aeque atque ullam
3 aliam rem pertinere arbitror. Cum has ad te scriberem litteras, a Satrio, legato C. Trebonii, reddita
est epistula mihi, a Tillio et Deiotaro Dolabellam
caesum fugatumque esse : Graecam epistulam tibi
4 misi Cicerei cuiusdam ad Satrium missam. Flavius
noster de controversia, quam habet cum Dyrrhachi-
nis hereditariam, sumpsit te iudicem : rogo te, Cicero,
et Flavius rogat, rem conficias. Quin ei, qui Flavium
fecit heredem, pecuniam debuerit civitas, non est
dubium, neque Dyrrhachini infitiantur, sed sibi dona-
tum aes alienum a Caesare dicunt : noli pati a
necessariis tuis necessario meo iniuriam fieri. xiiii.
K. Iunias ex castris ad imam Candaviam.

XIII (I. 1)

M. CICERO S. D. M. BRUTO

Romae, a.u.c. 711

1 L. Clodius, tribunus plebis designatus, valde me
diligit vel, ut ἐμφατικώτερον dicam, valde me amat :
quod cum mihi ita persuasum sit, non dubito—bene
enim me nosti—, quin illum quoque iudices a me
amari ; nihil enim mihi minus hominis videtur quam
non respondere in amore eis, a quibus provocere. Is
mihi visus est suspicari, nec sine magno quidem

---

* L. Tillius Cimber, a tyrannicide ; governor of Bithynia.
ᵇ King of the Galatians.
ᶜ C. Flavius, Brutus' praefectus fabrum.
664

keep him safe. I consider that this is as clear a case as any of a call to duty in a private affair.

While I was writing this note, I was handed a 3 dispatch from Satrius, the legate of Trebonius, that Dolabella had been cut up and routed by Tillius *a* and Deiotarus.*b* I have sent you a letter in Greek from a certain Cicereius to Satrius.

Our friend Flavius *c* has chosen you umpire in a 4 dispute about a legacy which he has on hand with the people of Dyrrhachium. I beg you, Cicero, and Flavius begs you, to settle the matter. It is not in doubt that the person who appointed Flavius as his heir had the money owing to him by the city, and the people of Dyrrhachium do not deny it ; but they allege that the debt was remitted in their favour by Caesar. Do not suffer a wrong to be done to my close friend by yours. May 19, in camp, at the base of the Candavia valley.

XIII (I. 1)

Rome, about May 20, 43 b.c.

L. Clodius, a tribune of the plebs elect, has a great 1 fondness or, to express myself with more verve, a great love for me. Having satisfied myself of this, I have no doubt you will conclude (for you can read me like a book) that I requite his love. For it seems to me that nothing less becomes a man than to make no response to those who would draw you out in mutual love. I have had the impression that he suspects (and does so indeed to his own great distress)

dolore, aliquid a suis vel per suos potius iniquos ad te esse delatum, quo tuus animus a se esset alienior. Non soleo, mi Brute, quod tibi notum esse arbitror, temere affirmare de altero, est enim periculosum propter occultas hominum voluntates multiplicesque naturas : Clodi animum perspectum habeo, cognitum, iudicatum ; multa eius indicia, sed ad scribendum non necessaria, volo enim testimonium hoc tibi videri potius quam epistulam. Auctus Antonii beneficio est—eius ipsius beneficii magna pars a te est— :

2 itaque eum salvis nobis vellet salvum. In eum autem locum rem adductam intellegit—est enim, ut scis, minime stultus—, ut utrique salvi esse non possint : itaque nos mavult ; de te vero amicissime et loquitur et sentit. Quare, si quis secus ad te de eo scripsit aut si coram locutus est, peto a te etiam atque etiam, mihi ut potius credas, qui et facilius iudicare possum quam ille nescio quis et te plus diligo. Clodium tibi amicissimum existima civemque talem, qualis et prudentissimus et fortuna optima esse debet.

that his personal enemies have originated or rather transmitted to you some piece of news, so as to make you less well-disposed to him. It is not my habit, my dear Brutus—and I think you need not be told so—to make haphazard assertions about another man : the hidden motives of men and their complex natures make that a rash proceeding ; but Clodius' mind I have probed and tried and weighed up judicially. There are many revelations of it, but these need not be set down on paper, for I want you to take this as a formal deposition rather than a letter of recommendation. He has obtained promotion by favour of Antony, and Antony's favour was actually inspired in large measure by you. So he would like Antony to come to no harm, provided that we suffer none.

But he realizes (for he is, as you know, anything but 2 dull-witted) that it has come to this, that *both* parties cannot be secure. For this reason he prefers us to be so, indeed his remarks and his feelings in regard to you are most friendly. Therefore if anyone has represented him otherwise to you in a letter or in conversation, I beg you insistently to take my word in preference, seeing that I have better means of judging than his traducer (whoever he may be), and I have a greater affection for you. Let Clodius rank in your esteem as a very good friend and as a citizen of such worth as his ample good sense and his abundant fortune ought to make him.

CICERO

XIV (I. 2)

M. CICERO S. D. M. BRUTO

Romae, A.U.C. 711

1 Scripta et obsignata iam epistula litterae mihi redditae sunt a te plenae rerum novarum, maximeque
mirabile Dolabellam quinque cohortes misisse in
Chersonesum. Adeone copiis abundat, ut is, qui ex
Asia fugere dicebatur, Europam appetere conetur ?
quinque autem cohortibus quidnam se facturum arbitratus est, cum tu eo loco quinque legiones, optimum
equitatum, maxima auxilia haberes ? quas quidem
cohortes spero iam tuas esse, quoniam latro ille tam
2 fuit demens. Tuum consilium vehementer laudo,
quod non prius exercitum Apollonia Dyrrhachioque
movisti, quam de Antonii fuga audisti, Bruti eruptione, populi Romani victoria. Itaque, quod scribis
postea statuisse te ducere exercitum in Chersonesum
nec pati sceleratissimo hosti ludibrio esse imperium
populi Romani, facis ex tua dignitate et ex re publica.
3 Quod scribis de seditione, quae facta est in legione
quarta decima fraude C. Antonii—in bonam partem
accipies—magis mihi probatur militum severitas
quam tua clementia. . . .

ᵃ The Gallipoli peninsula.

XIV (I. 2)

My note had already been written and sealed up 1
when your letter came to hand with its big budget
of news, and most astonishing of all, that Dolabella
had sent five cohorts to the Chersonese.[a] Is he so
over-provided with troops, that when reported in
flight from Asia he should make a dash at Europe ?
But five cohorts !   Whatever did he expect to achieve
with those, when you had five legions in the same
quarter, an excellent cavalry and very strong auxiliary forces ?   Indeed, seeing that the bandit has
committed such a mad act, I hope that by now those
cohorts are in your possession.

I heartily commend your strategy, in that you did 2
not move your army from Apollonia and Dyrrhachium until you had heard of the flight of Antony,
of Brutus' sortie, of the Roman people's victory.
Therefore when you decided (as you inform me) to
conduct your army to the Chersonese and not to
suffer that utter scoundrel of an enemy to insult the
sovereignty of Rome, your action is in keeping with
your high position and in the interests of the state.

As for the mutiny which was caused, so you say, by 3
the intrigues of C. Antonius among the fourteenth
legion, you will take it in good part—I think better
of the strong measures taken by the troops than of
your leniency. . . .

CICERO

XV (I. 8)

M. CICERO S. D. M. BRUTO

Romae, A.U.C. 711

1 Multos tibi commendabo et commendem necesse
est—optimus enim quisque vir et civis maxime sequitur tuum iudicium tibique omnes fortes viri navare
operam et studium volunt nec quisquam est, quin
ita existimet, meam apud te et auctoritatem et
2 gratiam valere plurimum—sed C. Nasennium, muni-
cipem Suessanum, tibi ita commendo, ut neminem
diligentius. Cretensi bello Metello imperatore oc-
tavum principem duxit ; postea in re familiari occupatus fuit : hoc tempore cum rei publicae partibus,
tum tua excellenti dignitate commotus vult per te
aliquid auctoritatis assumere. Fortem virum, Brute,
tibi commendo, frugi hominem et, si quid ad rem
pertinet, etiam locupletem : pergratum mihi erit, si
eum ita tractaris, ut merito tuo mihi gratias agere
possit.

XVI (I. 11)

M. BRUTUS S. D. M. CICERONI

In castris, A.U.C. 711

1 Veteris Antistii talis animus in rem publicam, ut
non dubitem, quin et in Caesare et in Antonio se

---

^a 69–67 B.C., against the Cretan pirates.
^b Q. Caecilius Metellus Creticus, consul 69 B.C.
^c C. Antistius Vetus, a former officer of Caesar ; perhaps
to be identified with the consul suffectus of 30 B.C.

XV (I. 8)

Rome, end of May or early June, 43 B.C.

I shall recommend large numbers of men to you, 1
and recommend them I must needs. For all the
worthiest men and citizens pay the highest regard to
your judgement, and all stout-hearted men want
to work heart and soul for you, and there is none but
holds the view that my claim to your deference and
gratitude carry great weight with you.

But C. Nasennius, from the borough of Suessa, I 2
recommend to you with special earnestness. In the
Cretan war,[a] under the command of Metellus,[b] he was
first centurion of the eighth cohort. In the years
to follow he attended to his family affairs. At
the present time, under the compelling influence of
party loyalty and of your pre-eminent high rank,
he wants to obtain through you some position of
authority. I recommend him to you, Brutus, as a
gallant man, a man of distinction and, if this is
relevant to the case, of ample means. I shall be
deeply obliged, if you give him such treatment that
he may be able to thank me on the strength of your
good deed.

XVI (I. 11)

In camp, first half of June, 43 B.C.

Vetus Antistius [c] is so good a patriot that he would, 1
I doubt not, have stood forth as an enthusiastic

L

praestaturus fuerit acerrimum propugnatorem communis liberatis, si occasioni potuisset occurrere ; nam,
qui in Achaia congressus cum P. Dolabella milites
atque equites habente quodvis adire periculum ex
insidiis paratissimi ad omnia latronis maluerit quam
videri aut coactus esse pecuniam dare aut libenter
dedisse homini nequissimo atque improbissimo, is no-
bis ultro et pollicitus est et dedit HS. |$\overline{\mathrm{XX}}$| ex sua pe-
cunia et, quod multo carius est, se ipsum obtulit et
2 coniunxit. Huic persuadere cupiimus, ut imperator
in castris remaneret remque publicam defenderet :
sed[1] statuit id sibi non licere,[2] quoniam exercitum
dimisisset ; statim vero rediturum ad nos confirmavit
legatione suscepta, nisi praetorum comitia habituri
essent consules—nam illi ita sentienti de re publica
magno opere auctor fui, ne differret tempus petitionis
suae— : cuius factum omnibus gratum esse debet,
qui modo iudicant hunc exercitum esse utilem[3] rei
publicae, tibi tanto gratius, quanto maiore et animo
gloriaque libertatem nostram defendis et dignitate, si
contigerit nostris consiliis exitus, quem optamus,
perfuncturus es. Ego etiam, mi Cicero, proprie fa-
miliariterque te rogo, ut Veterem ames velisque esse
quam amplissimum, qui etsi nulla re deterreri a
proposito potest, tamen excitari tuis laudibus indul-

---

[1] sed *added by Tyrrell and Purser.*
[2] non licere *added by Gurlitt.*
[3] utilem *A*[3] *Crat.* : debet *or* debere.

champion of the common liberty in the face of Caesar
and Antony, if he had been able to meet the emergency. When he came across Dolabella with in-
fantry and mounted troops in Achaia, he preferred
to brave any danger from a covert attack by a bandit
who is quite prepared for any trick, than to offer the
appearance of having given money, whether under
duress or of his own free will, to an utterly villainous
and unscrupulous fellow ; and the same man has
offered and actually made us a free gift of 2,000,000
sesterces out of his funds and has presented himself
in person and come to my side—a service which I
prize far more highly.

We were anxious to induce him to stay with the **2**
colours as an independent commander and defend the
free state. He has decided that this course is not
open to him, seeing that he has disbanded his forces.
But he assured us that he would return to me with
a legate's commission, were it not that the consuls
were about to hold elections for the praetorships. I
mention this, for since this was what he felt about
his political career, I strongly urged him not to put
off the time of his candidature. What he has done
should earn the gratitude of all men, if they but
recognize that this army of mine is of service to the
state ; but you should feel all the more obliged to
him, as you have shown more spirit and won more
renown in defence of our liberty, and will crown your
career with a higher honour, if our policy should be
favoured with the result for which we hope. I too,
my dear Cicero, beg you particularly and as a close
friend to be kind to Vetus and to wish him all possible distinction. Though nothing could deter him
from his resolve, yet encouragement and generous

gentiaque poterit, quo magis amplexetur ac tueatur
iudicium suum : et mihi gratissimum erit.

XVII (I. 17)

M. BRUTUS S. D. ATTICO

In castris, A.U.C. 711

1 Scribis mihi mirari Ciceronem, quod nihil significem
umquam de suis actis : quoniam me flagitas, coactu
tuo scribam, quae sentio. Omnia fecisse Ciceronem
optimo animo scio ; quid enim mihi exploratius esse
potest quam illius animus in rem publicam ? sed
quaedam mihi videtur, quid dicam ? " imperite," vir
omnium prudentissimus, an " ambitiose " fecisse, qui
valentissimum Antonium suscipere pro re publica
non dubitarit inimicum ? Nescio, quid scribam tibi,
nisi unum : pueri et cupiditatem et licentiam potius
esse irritatam quam repressam a Cicerone, tantumque
eum tribuere huic indulgentiae, ut se maledictis non
abstineat, iis quidem, quae in ipsum dupliciter reci-
dunt, quod et plures occidit uno seque prius oportet
fateatur sicarium, quam obiiciat Cascae quod obiicit,
et imitatur in Casca Bestiam. An, quia non omnibus horis iactamus Idus Martias similiter atque ille
Nonas Decembres suas in ore habet, eo meliore con-

---

^a Octavian.
^b P. Servilius Casca, one of the leading tyrannicides.
^c L. Calpurnius Bestia, one of Cicero's principal opponents
at the time of the Catilinarian conspiracy.
^d December 5th, 63 B.C., was the date on which Cicero
executed Catiline's accomplices, after a debate in the Senate.

treatment from you may stimulate him to adhere
to his decision and persist in it all the more firmly.
And you will do me a great favour.

XVII (I. 17)

BRUTUS TO ATTICUS

In camp, early June, 43 B.C.

You write to me that Cicero is surprised that 1
I never refer to any of his activities. In view of
your insistence, I shall record my opinions under
duress from you. I know that Cicero has always
acted with the best intentions ; for what could be
better approved in my eyes than his high spirit in
matters of politics ? But I have the impression that
this most sagacious of men has acted on some
occasions—how shall I put it ?—unskilfully, or in his
personal interest, seeing that he has not hesitated,
" for the state's sake," to incur a feud with Antony
when at the height of his power. I know not what to
write to you, save just this, that Cicero has inflamed
rather than checked the boy's [a] greed and lawlessness
and is lavishing upon him so many signs of obsequi-
ousness, that he cannot refrain from making malicious
remarks, which recoil upon him in a double sense, in
that he has more than one man's blood on his hands
and so must own up to murder on his own part,
before he can reproach Casca [b] as he does ; and again,
when he attacks Casca he follows in Bestia's [c] wake.
Granted that we do not boast at all hours of the Ides
of March, in the same way as he carries the Nones
of December on his tongue,[d] does that give Cicero a

675

dicione Cicero pulcherrimum factum vituperabit, quam Bestia et Clodius reprehendere illius consula-
2 tum soliti sunt? Sustinuisse mihi gloriatur bellum Antoni togatus Cicero noster: quid hoc mihi prodest, si merces Antoni oppressi poscitur in Antoni locum successio et si vindex illius mali auctor exstitit alterius fundamentum et radices habituri altiores. Sic patiamur, ut iam ista, quae facit, dominationem an dominum an Antonium timentis sint? Ego autem gratiam non habeo, si quis, dum ne irato serviat, rem ipsam non deprecatur. Immo triumphus et stipendium et omnibus decretis hortatio, ne eius pudeat concupiscere fortunam, cuius nomen susceperit: consu-
3 laris hoc aut Ciceronis est? Quoniam mihi tacere non licuit, leges, quae tibi necesse est molesta esse; etenim ipse sentio, quanto cum dolore haec ad te scripserim, noc ignoro, quid sentias in re publica et quam desperatum quoque sanari putes posse, nec mehercule te, Attice, reprehendo, aetas enim, mores, liberi segnem efficiunt, quod quidem etiam ex Flavio
4 nostro perspexi. Sed redeo ad Ciceronem: quid inter Salvidienum et eum interest? quid autem amplius ille decerneret? "Timet," inquies, "etiam nunc reliquias belli civilis." Quisquam ergo ita timet

---

* Q. Salvidienus Rufus, a man of obscure origin who had bound up his fortune with that of Octavian.

better warrant to cast abuse on our magnificent deed than Bestia and Clodius possessed when they made a habit of carping at his consulship ?

Our Cicero boasts to me, that in civilian garb he 2 bore the brunt of Antony's armed assault. Of what benefit is this to me, if the reward claimed for the overthrow of Antony is to be the reversion to Antony's position, and if he who championed us against that evil has taken the lead in raising up another evil which will be more firmly based and more deeply rooted ? Are we to humour him, on the theory that his present doings are inspired by fear of despotism, or of a despot—or of Antony in person ? I for my part can feel no obligation to a man who draws the line at serving an *angry* despot, but does not protest against despotism as such. Nay more, a triumph, pay for the army, an incitation in every decree to brazen it out and scramble for the position of the man whose name he has assumed—is that what one expects of a consular or of Cicero ?

Since you would not let me remain silent, you will 3 read things which are bound to annoy you. To be sure I also can feel how much it hurts me to write to you in this strain, and I am well aware what are your views about the state, and how desperate too, though not incurable, you consider its condition. And I swear, Atticus, I do not blame you ! Your age, your habits, your family dull your spirit ; yes, and our friend Flavius too made me realize this !

But to return to Cicero. What is the difference 4 between Salvidienus [a] and him ? Why, what more fullsome honours could the former propose ? You say, " he fears even now the aftermath of the civil war." Does anyone hold a war that is as good as

profligatum, ut neque potentiam eius, qui exercitum
victorem habet, neque temeritatem pueri putet ex-
timescendam esse ? an hoc ipsum ea re facit, quod
illi propter amplitudinem omnia iam ultroque de-
ferenda putat ? O magnam stultitiam timoris, id
ipsum, quod verearis, ita cavere, ut, cum vitare fortasse potueris, ultro arcessas et attrahas ! Nimium
timemus mortem et exsilium et paupertatem : haec
nimirum[1] videntur Ciceroni ultima esse in malis, et
dum habeat a quibus impetret, quae velit, et a quibus
colatur ac laudetur, servitutem, honorificam modo,
non aspernatur—si quidquam in extrema ac miser-
5 rima contumelia potest honorificum esse. Licet ergo
patrem appellet Octavius Ciceronem, referat omnia,
laudet, gratias agat, tamen illud apparebit, verba
rebus esse contraria : quid enim tam alienum ab
humanis sensibus est quam eum patris habere loco,
qui ne liberi quidem hominis numero sit ? atqui eo
tendit, id agit, ad eum exitum properat vir optimus,
ut sit illi Octavius propitius. Ego vero iam iis artibus
nihil tribuo, quibus Ciceronem scio instructissimum
esse ; quid enim illi prosunt, quae pro libertate
patriae, quae de dignitate, quae de morte, exsilio,
paupertate scripsit copiosissime ? quanto autem magis

[1] *Stangl* : mihi.

won in such dread, as not to give a thought to the
power of the man who disposes of the victorious army,
nor for the adventurousness of the boy, that these
give occasion for the utmost alarm ? Is this the
reason for his particular line of action, that he thinks
that everything should be laid at that man's feet, in
anticipation of his demands, as a tribute to his great-
ness ? What fools fear makes of men, that your precautions against the object of your dread should
actually have the effect of drawing it on and bringing
it over you, when there was a chance of steering clear
of it ! We carry our fear of death and exile and
poverty too far. These of course appear to Cicero
as the extremes of misfortune, and so long as he can
find people who will give him what he wants and will
cultivate and compliment him, he does not disdain
servitude, so long as it is servitude with honour—if
there can be any honour in suffering the deepest and
most ignominious affronts.

Let Octavius then call Cicero " father," submit 5
everything to him, compliment him, and express his
gratitude, all the same the fact will show through,
that his words are belied by his deeds. For what
can be so inconsistent with decent human feeling as to
treat like a parent a person who does not even count
as a free man ? Yet this is the object and proceeding
of that worthy fellow, this the goal to which he is
driving, that Octavius may be gracious to him. For
my part I no longer pay any homage to those arts in
which I know that Cicero is a virtuoso. For of what
use to him are those extremely voluminous writings
of his *In Defence of our Country's Freedom*, *On
Dignified Conduct*, *On Death*, *On Exile*, *On Poverty* ?
Aye, how much surer a touch in those matters has

illa callere videtur Philippus, qui privigno minus
tribuerit, quam Cicero, qui alieno tribuat ! Desinat
igitur gloriando etiam insectari dolores nostros : quid
enim nostra victum esse Antonium, si victus est, ut
6 alii vacaret, quod ille obtinuit ? Tametsi tuae litterae
dubia etiam nunc significant. Vivat hercule Cicero,
qui potest, supplex et obnoxius, si neque aetatis
neque honorum neque rerum gestarum pudet : ego
certe, quin cum ipsa re bellum geram, hoc est cum
regno et imperiis extraordinariis et dominatione et
potentia, quae supra leges se esse velit, nulla erit tam
bona condicio serviendi, qua deterrear, quamvis sit
vir bonus, ut scribis, Octavius,[1] quod ego numquam
existimavi ; sed dominum ne parentem quidem maiores nostri voluerunt. Te nisi tantum amarem, quantum Ciceroni persuasum est diligi se ab Octavio, haec
ad te non scripsissem : dolet mihi, quod tu nunc
stomacharis amantissimus cum tuorum omnium, tum
Ciceronis ; sed persuade tibi de voluntate propria mea
nihil esse remissum, de iudicio largiter, neque enim
impetrari potest, quin, quale quidque videatur ei, ta-
7 lem quisque de illo opinionem habeat. Vellem mihi
scripsisses, quae condiciones essent Atticae nostrae :
potuissem aliquid tibi de meo sensu perscribere.
Valetudinem Porciae meae tibi curae esse non miror.
Denique, quod petis, faciam libenter, nam etiam

[1] *Tunstall* : Antonius.

---

[a] L. Marcius Philippus, consul in 56 B.C., and stepfather
of Octavian. He favoured a compromise between Antony
and the Senate.

[b] The daughter of Atticus, eventually betrothed to
M. Vipsanius Agrippa. (She was only seven years old at
the time.)

[c] Brutus' wife, daughter of Cato of Utica.

Philippus,[a] seeing that he has given away less to his stepson than Cicero gives away to a stranger. So let him cease positively to pursue us with his boastings and inflame our sores ! For what advantage is it to us that Antony has suffered defeat, if his defeat merely serves to put the place which he held at another's disposal ?

And yet your letter implies a doubt even now. **6** Very well then ! Let Cicero live on as a suppliant and an underling, since he is capable of such things, if he has no respect for his age or high rank or his achievements. For me, I am sure, no terms of servitude will ever be so attractive, but I shall wage war against the real enemy, that is, with monarchy and irregular commands and despotism and a power that presumes to set itself above the laws, no matter how good a man (as you say) Octavius is, though I never took him for that. Nay, our ancestors would not tolerate despotism even in a parent.

If my affection for you were not as great as is Octavius' fondness for Cicero in Cicero's own conviction, I should not have written to you in this tone. I am sorry that your abundant love for your own folk, aye, and for Cicero, is causing you vexation ; but assure yourself of this, that my personal goodwill is unabated, though my judgement of him is greatly impaired : for you cannot prevent a man from seeing things in that particular light in which they present themselves to him.

I wish you had informed me of the terms for our **7** dear Attica's [b] betrothal ; I should then have been able to give you something of my views. I am not surprised that Porcia's [c] health is causing you anxiety. Finally, I shall be glad to do what you ask me, for

sorores me rogant : et hominem noro et quid sibi voluerit.

XVIII (I. 10)

M. CICERO S. D. M. BRUTO

Romae, A.U.C. 711

1 Nullas adhuc a te litteras habebamus, ne famam quidem, quae declararet te cognita senatus auctoritate in Italiam adducere exercitum ; quod ut faceres idque maturares, magno opere desiderabat res publica, ingravescit enim in dies intestinum malum nec externis hostibus magis quam domesticis laboramus, qui erant omnino ab initio belli, sed facilius frangebantur : erectior senatus erat non sententiis solum nostris, sed etiam cohortationibus excitatus : erat in senatu satis vehemens et acer Pansa cum in ceteros huius generis, tum maxime in socerum, cui consuli non animus ab initio, non fides ad extremum defuit.

2 Bellum ad Mutinam ita gerebatur, nihil ut in Caesare reprehenderes, nonnulla in Hirtio ; huius belli fortuna,

ut in secundis, fluxa, ut in adversis, bona:

erat victrix res publica caesis Antonii copiis, ipso

---

[a] Fufius Calenus (Letter II § 4).

your sisters are making the same request. I shall get to know the man and find out his intentions.

XVIII (I. 10)

CICERO TO BRUTUS

Rome, middle of June, 43 b.c.

I have so far received no letter from you, no, nor 1 even a rumour to notify me that you were acquainted with the Senate's resolution and were bringing an army to Italy. The free state is most anxious that you should do so, and that quickly, for our home troubles are growing more serious every day, and our difficulties with our enemies in the field are no greater than with those inside the gate. These enemies were present since the very beginning of the war, but it used to be easier to suppress them. The Senate had been encouraged, not only by our formal statements of opinion, but also by our calls to action, to take up a stiffer attitude. In the Senate Pansa displayed sufficient energy and zeal in dealing with the others of this sort and especially with his father-in-law *a*; in his consulship he showed no lack of spirit from the outset, and no lack of loyalty at the end.

The operations at Mutina were being conducted 2 in such a manner that no fault could be found with Caesar, albeit a certain amount with Hirtius. The luck of this war was

Frail for prosperous times, but good for times of woe.

Victory was the free state's when Antony's forces

683

expulso. Bruti deinde ita multa peccata, ut quodam modo victoria excideret e manibus : perterritos, inermes, saucios non sunt nostri duces persecuti datumque Lepido tempus est, in quo levitatem eius saepe perspectam maioribus in malis experiremur. Sunt exercitus boni, sed rudes Bruti et Planci, sunt fide-3 lissma et maxima auxilia Gallorum. Sed Caesarem meis consiliis adhuc gubernatum, praeclara ipsum indole admirabilique constantia improbissimis litteris quidam fallacibusque interpretibus ac nuntiis impulerunt in spem certissimam consulatus : quod simul atque sensi, neque ego illum absentem litteris monere destiti nec accusare praesentes eius necessarios, qui eius cupiditati suffragari videbantur. Nec in senatu sceleratissimorum consiliorum fontes aperire dubitavi, nec vero ulla in re memini aut senatum meliorem aut magistratus ; numquam enim in honore extraordinario potentis hominis vel potentissimi potius—quandoquidem potentia iam in vi posita est et armis—accidit ut nemo tribunus plebis, nemo alio in magistratu, nemo privatus auctor exsisteret. Sed in hac constantia atque virtute erat tamen sollicita civitas : illudimur enim, Brute, tum militum deliciis, tum imperatoris insolentia : tantum quisque

---

[a] Antony. See the eighth *Philippic.*

were cut up and himself driven off. After that Brutus committed so many blunders that victory, as it were, slipped out of his grasp. Our leaders failed to pursue a demoralized, disarmed and badly mauled army, and time was given to Lepidus to exhibit that fickleness of his, which has often shown through in worse disasters. The troops of Brutus and Plancus are sound, but lacking in experience ; the Gallic auxiliaries are entirely loyal, and strong in numbers.

But Caesar, who had hitherto been guided by my 3 advice, and is a man of splendid natural endowment and remarkable firmness of character, has been instigated by some utterly unscrupulous letters from certain quarters, and by deceitful agents and messengers, to reckon with complete certainty on a consulship. As soon as I became aware of this, I neither ceased to send him warning letters in his absence, nor to upbraid to their face his intimates who appeared to be pandering to his greed, and in the Senate I never hesitated to disclose the sources of those most criminal suggestions. And yet, to be sure, I cannot remember on any occasion a more patriotic Senate or boards of magistrates ; for it has never yet happened that when an irregular office was being claimed by a powerful, or rather by an overwhelmingly strong personage [a] (for to be sure power now rests on physical force and armed might), that not a tribune of the plebs, not a magistrate of any other rank, not a private member came forward with a motion to that effect. But in the face of this firmness and manly bearing the citizens felt none the less uneasy ; for, Brutus, the troops with their fastidious attitude and the general with his brazen demands, both of them are making play with us. Every man

se in re publica posse postulat, quantum habet virium;
non ratio, non modus, non lex, non mos, non officium
valet, non iudicium, non existimatio civium, non
4 posteritatis verecundia. Haec ego multo ante pro-
spiciens fugiebam ex Italia tum, cum me vestrorum
edictorum fama revocavit; incitavisti vero tu me,
Brute, Veliae. Quamquam enim dolebam in eam me
urbem ire, quam tu fugeres, qui eam liberavisses,
quod mihi quoque quondam acciderat periculo simili,
casu tristiore, perrexi tamen Romamque perveni nul-
loque praesidio quatefeci Antonium contraque eius
arma nefanda praesidia, quae oblata sunt Caesaris,
consilio et auctoritate firmavi: qui si steterit fide
mihique paruerit, satis videmur habituri praesidii;
sin autem impiorum consilia plus valuerint quam
nostra aut imbecillitas aetatis non potuerit gravita-
tem rerum sustinere, spes omnis est in te. Quam
ob rem advola, obsecro, atque eam rem publicam,
quam virtute atque animi magnitudine magis quam
eventis rerum liberavisti, exitu libera: omnis om-
5 nium concursus ad te futurus est. Hortare idem per
litteras Cassium: spes libertatis nusquam nisi in
vestrorum castrorum principiis est. Firmos omnino
et duces habemus ab occidente et exercitus; hoc

claims for himself a power in the state proportionate to his military strength; reason, moderation, legality, tradition, loyalty carry no weight; trained judgement, public opinion, respect for posterity go for nothing.

Foreseeing this a long time in advance, I was 4 making my escape from Italy at the moment when the stir which was caused by your proclamations called me back; but it was you at Velia, Brutus, that roused me to action. For although I was loth to set foot in a city from which you were fleeing after you had set it free—an experience which had once befallen me under similar conditions of danger, but by a more distressing turn of events—I held my course all the same and made my way to Rome and without any military protection I shook up Antony, and in defiance of his armed ruffians, by my guidance and influence I strengthened the forces of defence that offered themselves under Caesar. If he will stand immutable and follow my lead, I believe that we can count on adequate protection; but if the promptings of those villains carry more weight with him than my advice, or if the infirmity of my old age falters under the weight of my commitments, all our hopes reside in you. Therefore come flying, I implore you, and definitely set free the state which hitherto you have freed by your manly bearing and highmindedness rather than by the actual outcome of events. All the world is ready to cast itself upon you.

Write to Cassius to urge him to the same course. 5 Our hope of freedom dwells nowhere but in the headquarters of your camp. In the West our generals and our troops are absolutely steadfast. I feel con-

adulescentis praesidium equidem adhuc firmum esse
confido, sed ita multi labefactant, ut, ne moveatur,
interdum extimescam. Habes totum rei publicae
statum, qui quidem tum erat, cum has litteras
dabam. Velim deinceps meliora sint: sin aliter fuerit
—quod di omen avertant!—rei publicae vicem dolebo,
quae immortalis esse debebat, mihi quidem quantu-
lum reliqui est ?

XIX (I. 9)

M. CICERO S. D. M. BRUTO

Romae, A.U.C. 711

1 Fungerer officio, quo tu functus es in meo luctu,
teque per litteras consolarer, nisi scirem iis remediis,
quibus meum dolorem tu levasses, te in tuo non egere,
ac velim facilius, quam tunc mihi, nunc tibi tute
medeare. Est autem alienum tanto viro, quantus es
tu, quod alteri praeceperit, id ipsum facere non posse.
Me quidem cum rationes, quas collegeras, tum auctoritas tua a nimio maerore deterruit ; cum enim
mollius tibi ferre viderer, quam deceret virum, praesertim eum, qui alios consolari soleret, accusasti me

---

a By the death of his wife Porcia. See Letter XVII § 7.

fident indeed that the defence which the young man provides here stands firm ; but so many hands are causing it to reel that I am sometimes filled with alarm lest it should give ground.

You have the whole political situation, just as it is at the time of my sending off this letter. I could wish that it should improve with the march of events. But should it be otherwise (may heaven forfend what this betokens !), my sorrow will go to the free state, for this by rights should be immune from death. As for myself, how little have I left to me !

XIX (I. 9)

CICERO TO BRUTUS

Rome, about the 18th of June, 43 b.c.

I should discharge the friendly duty which you 1 performed on the occasion of my bereavement, and should send you a letter of condolence, did I not know that you do not require for your bereavement [a] those solaces with which you mitigated my grief, and I hope you will now effect an easier cure in your own case than you did then in mine. A man of your strength of character would indeed be untrue to himself, if he were not able to accomplish in his own case what he had enjoined upon some other person. For my part, the arguments which you had mustered, and also your moral influence, deterred me from extravagant mourning ; for when I appeared to you to bear up with less resoluteness than befitted a man, especially one who was in the habit of consoling others,

per litteras gravioribus verbis quam tua consuetudo
2 ferebat. Itaque iudicium tuum magni aestimans
idque veritus me ipse collegi et ea, quae didiceram,
legeram, acceperam, graviora duxi tua auctoritate
addita. Ac mihi tum, Brute, officio solum erat et
naturae, tibi nunc populo et scenae, ut dicitur, serviendum est ; nam, cum in te non solum exercitus tui,
sed omnium civium ac paene gentium coniecti oculi
sint, minime decet, propter quem fortiores ceteri
sumus, eum ipsum animo debilitatum videri. Quam
ob rem accepisti tu quidem dolorem—id enim ami-
sisti, cui simile in terris nihil fuit,—et est dolendum
in tam gravi vulnere, ne id ipsum, carere omni sensu
doloris, sit miserius quam dolere ; sed, ut modice, ce-
3 teris utile est, tibi necesse est. Scriberem plura, nisi
ad te haec ipsa nimis multa essent. Nos te tuum-
que exercitum exspectamus, sine quo, ut reliqua
ex sententia succedant, vix satis liberi videmur fore.
De tota re publica plura scribam et fortasse iam
certiora iis litteris, quas Veteri nostro cogitabam
dare.

you wrote me a reproving letter in terms more severe than your usual style would admit.

Therefore, as I attached great value to your judge- **2** ment and feared your reproof, I pulled myself together and took the lessons which I had taught and studied and assimilated the more to heart, when you reinforced them with your moral weight. Yes, and I, Brutus, was at that time under no obligation save to the social code and the law of Nature ; but *you* must now play up to the public and the stage you hold, as the saying goes. For when the gaze of your soldiers, and not only of them, but of all citizens and of almost the entire world is centred upon you, it would be scandalous for a man who inspires the rest of us with greater courage to exhibit in his own case an enfeebled spirit. For this reason you opened your heart to your sorrow (for what you lost never had its like on earth), and under such a heavy blow you must needs sorrow, lest your very anodyne, complete imperviousness to pain, should afflict you worse than the sense of pain ; but whereas moderation in grief is expedient in others, it is indispensable for you.

I should write more, were it not that what I *have* **3** written is too long, when addressed to you. We are waiting for you and your army ; without it we think we shall scarcely attain sufficient freedom, even though all else should fall out as we have planned. I shall write more about the general political situation and perhaps shall give you more certain news in the letter which I propose to give to our friend Vetus.

CICERO

XX (I. 7)

M. BRUTUS S. D. M. CICERONI

In castris, A.U.C. 711

1 L. Bibulus quam carus mihi esse debeat, nemo
melius iudicare potest quam tu, cuius tantae pro re
publica contentiones sollicitudinesque fuerunt: itaque
vel ipsius virtus vel nostra necessitudo debet conciliare
te illi ; quo minus multa mihi scribenda esse arbitror,
voluntas enim te movere debet nostra, si modo iusta
est aut pro officio necessario suscipitur. Is in Pansae
locum petere constituit ; eam nominationem a te
petimus : neque coniunctiori dare beneficium, quam
nos tibi sumus, neque digniorem nominare potes
2 quam Bibulum. De Domitio et Apuleio quid attinet
me scribere, cum ipsi per se tibi commendatissimi
sint ? Apuleium vero tu tua auctoritate sustinere
debes ; sed Apuleius in sua epistula celebrabitur,
Bibulum noli dimittere e sinu tuo, tantum iam virum,
ex quanto, crede mihi, potest evadere, qui vestris
paucorum respondeat laudibus.

---

^a L. Calpurnius Bibulus, son of Caesar's old opponent,
and stepson of Brutus. He was an officer in Brutus' army.
   ^b In the collegium pontificum.
   ^c See Letter IX § 3.
   ^d M. Apuleius, quaestor in 43 B.C., and one of Brutus'
paymasters.

XX (I. 7)

In camp, about June 22, 43 B.C.

You have been such a stout champion of the state, 1
and have shown such anxious care for it, that no one
can appraise better than you how fond I ought to be
of L. Bibulus.[a] In view of this, either consideration
ought to win your interest in him, his own merits or
my intimacy with him. That is all the more reason,
I think, for my not writing at length ; for my wish
ought to carry weight with you, granted that it is
reasonable, and that I am seeking to realize it as in
duty bound to oblige a friend. He has decided to
sue for Pansa's place[b] ; we beg you to nominate him
for it. You could not bestow a favour on a closer
friend than I am to you, nor nominate a more worthy
candidate than Bibulus.

As for Domitius[c] and Apuleius,[d] what concern of 2
mine is it to write, since they stand high in your
favour by virtue of their own personalities ? Apuleius,
you know, has a claim to be supported by your influence. But Apuleius will receive a testimonial in his
own letter. Do not deprive Bibulus of your fostering
care : he is already a man of such calibre that,
believe me, he may in the course of his development
rise equal to the eulogies of your élite.

XXI (I. 13)

M. BRUTUS S. D. M. CICERONI

In castris, a.u.c. 711

1 De M. Lepido vereri me cogit reliquorum timor :
qui si eripuerit se nobis, quod velim temere atque
iniuriose de illo suspicati sint homines, oro atque obsecro te, Cicero, necessitudinem nostram tuamque
in me benevolentiam obtestans, sororis meae liberos
obliviscaris esse Lepidi filios meque eis in patris locum
successisse existimes : hoc si a te impetro, nihil profecto dubitabis pro eis suscipere. Aliter alii cum suis
vivunt, nihil ego possum in sororis meae liberis facere,
quo possit expleri voluntas mea aut officium. Quid
vero aut mihi tribuere boni possunt—si modo digni
sumus, quibus aliquid tribuatur—aut ego matri ac
sorori puerisque illis praestaturus sum, si nihil valuerit
apud te reliquumque senatum contra patrem Lepi-
2 dum Brutus avunculus ? Scribere multa ad te neque
possum prae sollicitudine ac stomacho neque debeo ;
nam, si in tanta re tamque necessaria verbis mihi
opus est ad te excitandum et confirmandum, nulla spes
est facturum te, quod volo et quod oportet : quare
noli exspectare longas preces ; intuere me ipsum,
qui hoc a te, vel a Cicerone, coniunctissimo homine,
privatim, vel a consulari tali viro remota necessitudine

XXI (I. 13)

My fear of what is to follow makes me feel alarmed 1
about M. Lepidus. If he has bolted from us—and I
would fain hope that people's suspicions about him
are unfounded and do him injustice—I beg and
entreat you, Cicero, in the name of our close friendship and your kindly feelings towards me, forget that
the children of my sister are the sons of Lepidus, and
imagine that I now stand in the position of father to
them. If I can obtain this request of you, there is
nothing, I am sure, that you will hesitate to undertake on their behalf. Each man orders his family
life differently ; in the case of my sister's children
nothing that I can do could give full expression to my
goodwill and sense of duty towards them. What gift
indeed can I accept from loyal citizens—supposing
that I am worthy of any gifts—or what assistance
am I to offer to my mother or sister or those boys,
if in your eyes and those of the Senate their uncle
Brutus carries no weight against their father Lepidus?

I am too much worried and chagrined to write to 2
you at length, nor is that my duty. For if in such
an important and intimate matter I must expend
words in order to rouse your interest and make up
your mind, there is no hope of your doing what I
wish and what duty bids. Therefore don't expect
a long supplication. Look into my heart : it is I
who have a right to this favour from you, either on
private considerations, because you are Cicero, my
intimate friend, or, personal ties apart, because of your

privata, debeo impetrare. Quid sis facturus, velim
mihi quam primum rescribas. Kal. Quinctilibus ex
castris.

XXII (I. 12)

M. CICERO S. D. M. BRUTO

Romae, A.U.C. 711

1   Etsi daturus eram Messallae Corvino[a] continuo litteras, tamen Veterem nostrum ad te sine litteris meis
venire nolui. Maximo in discrimine res publica,
Brute, versatur victoresque rursus decertare cogimur :
id accidit M. Lepidi scelere et amentia. Quo tempore
cum multa propter eam curam, quam pro re publica
suscepi, graviter ferrem, tum nihil tuli gravius quam
me non posse matris tuae precibus cedere, non sororis,
nam tibi, quod mihi plurimi est, facile me satisfacturum arbitrabar. Nullo enim modo poterat causa
Lepidi distingui ab Antonio omniumque iudicio etiam
durior erat, quod, cum honoribus amplissimis a senatu
esset Lepidus ornatus, tum etiam paucis ante diebus praeclaras litteras ad senatum misisset, repente
non solum recepit reliquias hostium, sed bellum
acerrime terra marique gerit, cuius exitus qui futurus sit, incertum est : ita, cum rogamur, ut miseri-

---

[a] M. Valerius Messalla Corvinus, a former associate of
Brutus at Athens. Subsequently one of Augustus' right-
hand men.

consular rank and record. Please inform me as soon as possible in a return letter what you intend to do. July 1, in camp.

XXII (I. 12)

CICERO TO BRUTUS

Rome, early July, 43 B.C.

Although I shall be handing a letter to Messalla **1** Corvinus [a] directly, all the same I do not want our friend Vetus to come to you without a note from me. Brutus, the state is in a highly dangerous situation, and we who won the day are obliged to stake our whole fortunes once more. This has befallen us through the wickedness and sheer folly of Lepidus. In a time like this the task which I have shouldered on the state's behalf is causing me much vexation, but nothing vexes me more than that I cannot yield to the entreaties of your mother and your sister; as for yourself, I believe it will be an easy matter to meet your wishes, and that is what matters most. The case of Lepidus cannot possibly be considered apart from that of Antony; indeed the general opinion is that he was the more hardened villain, in that Lepidus had been honoured by the Senate with the highest marks of distinction, yes, and a few days before he had sent to the Senate an admirable dispatch; yet all of a sudden he has not only given refuge to the remnant of the enemy, but is conducting a campaign by land and sea with the utmost vigour; and how the issue of this campaign will fall out cannot be foreseen. Therefore when we are asked to show

697

cordiam liberis eius impertiamus, nihil affertur, quo
minus summa supplicia, si—quod Iuppiter omen aver-
tat !—pater puerorum vicerit, subeunda nobis sint.
2 Nec vero me fugit, quam sit acerbum parentum
scelera filiorum poenis lui, sed hoc praeclare legibus
comparatum est, ut caritas liberorum amiciores par-
entes rei publicae redderet ; itaque Lepidus crudelis
in liberos, non is, qui Lepidum hostem iudicat. Atque
ille si armis positis de vi damnatus esset, quo in iudicio
certe defensionem non haberet, eandem calamitatem
subirent liberi bonis publicatis. Quamquam, quod
tua mater et soror deprecatur pro pueris, id ipsum et
multa alia crudeliora nobis omnibus Lepidus, Antonius et reliqui hostes denuntiant ; itaque maximam
spem hoc tempore habemus in te atque exercitu tuo :
cum ad rei publicae summam, tum ad gloriam et
dignitatem tuam vehementer pertinet te, ut ante
scripsi, in Italiam venire quam primum : eget enim
vehementer cum viribus tuis, tum etiam consilio res
3 publica. Veterem pro eius erga te benevolentia sin-
gularique officio libenter ex tuis litteris complexus
sum eumque cum tui, tum rei publicae studiosissimum amantissimumque cognovi. Ciceronem meum
propediem, ut spero, videbo ; tecum enim illum

some measure of pity for his children, there is no
effective guarantee that we may not have to endure
the most cruel punishment, if the father of the boys
should be the winner (and I pray to Heaven that my
foreboding may not come true).

Of course I am well aware how harsh it is that the **2**
sins of the parents should be expiated by punishment
of the sons ; but this is an excellent provision of our
laws, so that affection for their children should make
parents hold the state more dear.   Thus it is Lepidus
who is cruel towards his children, not the man who
pronounces Lepidus a public enemy.   And again,
suppose that after laying down his arms he had been
sentenced by court on a charge of breaking the peace
—and on such a count he certainly could not offer a
defence—his children would suffer the same injury
through the confiscation of their estate.   And yet
the very treatment which your mother and sister wish
to spare the boys, Lepidus, Antonius and the other
public enemies proclaim that this and many other and
harsher penalties shall be inflicted on us.   Therefore
in this crisis our chief hope resides in you and your
army.   It is of the most urgent importance for the
whole future of the state, aye, and for your reputation
and prestige, that you should come to Italy without
losing a moment, as I have told you before ; for the
state urgently needs both your strong forces, and
your advice as well.

In consideration of his goodwill and his outstand- **3**
ing sense of duty towards you, I have given Vetus
a hearty welcome, as you asked me in your letter ;
and I recognized that he had a great enthusiasm
and affection for you and for the free state.   I
hope to see my son Cicero before long ; for I am

et te in Italiam celeriter esse venturum confido.

XXIII (I. 14)

M. CICERO S. D. M. BRUTO

Romae, A.U.C. 711

1 Breves litterae tuae, breves dico ? immo nullae : tri-
busne versiculis his temporibus Brutus ad me ? nihil
scripsissem potius.   Et requiris meas : quis umquam
ad te tuorum sine meis venit ? quae autem epistula
non pondus habuit ? quae si ad te perlatae non
sunt, ne domesticas quidem tuas perlatas arbitror.
Ciceroni scribis te longiorem daturum epistolam : recte id quidem, sed haec quoque debuit esse plenior.
Ego autem, cum ad me de Ciceronis abs te discessu
scripsisses, statim extrusi tabellarios litterasque ad
Ciceronem, ut, etiamsi in Italiam venisset, ad te re-
diret ; nihil enim mihi iucundius, nihil illi honestius.
Quamquam aliquoties ei scripseram sacerdotum
comitia mea summa contentione in alterum annum
esse reiecta—quod ego cum Ciceronis causa elabo-
ravi, tum Domitii, Catonis, Lentuli, Bibulorum,
quod ad te etiam scripseram— : sed videlicet, cum
illam pusillam epistulam tuam ad me dabas, nondum

---

a See Letters III § 3, IX § 3, XX.

confident that he will be coming with you to Italy, and coming quickly.

XXIII (I. 14)

CICERO TO BRUTUS

Rome, July 14, 43 B.C.

That is a brief note of yours ; brief, I say : nay 1 rather, it amounts to nothing. Can Brutus address me in days like these in three short lines ? Had I been in your place, I should rather not have written at all. And you ask for a note from me ! What courier of yours ever reached you without a letter of mine ? And which letter did not contain a heavy budget ? If these haven't been delivered to you, I conclude that not even your home correspondence has come to hand. You say you will give a longer letter to my son Cicero. Good so far, but this one too should be more substantial. For my part, as soon as you informed me that Cicero had parted company with you, I at once bundled off a courier and a note to Cicero, bidding him return to you, even if he had arrived in Italy ; for nothing could give me more satisfaction or give him more credit. And yet I had told him in several letters that the election for the priesthoods had been postponed to another year— a result for which I fought tooth and nail. I went to these pains both for the sake of Cicero and of Domitius, Cato, Lentulus, and the Bibuli [a] ; this I notified to you also. But obviously you had not yet received word of it when you sent off that tiny note of yours to me.

701

2 erat tibi id notum. Quare omni studio a te, mi
Brute, contendo, ut Ciceronem meum ne dimittas
tecumque deducas, quod ipsum, si rem publicam, cui
susceptus es, respicis, tibi iam iamque faciendum est.
Renatum enim bellum est, idque non parvum scelere
Lepidi ; exercitus autem Caesaris, qui erat optimus,
non modo nihil prodest, sed etiam cogit exercitum
tuum flagitari, qui si Italiam attigerit, erit civis nemo,
quem quidem civem appellari fas sit, qui se non in
tua castra conferat.   Etsi Brutum praeclare cum
Planco coniunctum habemus, sed non ignoras, quam
sint incerti et animi hominum infecti partibus et exitus proeliorum.   Quin etiam, si, ut spero, vicerimus,
tamen magnam gubernationem tui consilii tuae-
que auctoritatis res desiderabit : subveni igitur, per
deos, idque quam primum, tibique persuade non te
Idibus Martiis, quibus servitutem a tuis civibus de-
pulisti, plus profuisse patriae quam, si mature veneris, profuturum. ii. Idus Quinctiles.

XXIV (I. 15)

M. CICERO S. D. M. BRUTO

Romae, A.U.C. 711

1   Messallam habes : quibus igitur litteris tam accurate scriptis assequi possum, subtilius ut explicem,
quae gerantur quaeque sint in re publica, quam tibi

ª These two commanders temporarily joined hands near
Grenoble.

Therefore, dear Brutus, I urge you most emphati- 2
cally not to let my son Cicero leave you, but to bring
him back with you ; and your own return, if you have
any regard for the free state to which you are dedicated, must take place now and at once.   For the
war has re-started, and this on a large scale, thanks
to the criminal act of Lepidus.   And the forces of
Caesar, which were excellent, are not merely of no
use but even compel me to clamour for your army.   If
this is landed in Italy, no citizen worth the name will
fail to betake himself to your camp.   We have in our
favour, it is true, the junction of Brutus with Plancus ^a
—a splendid achievement ; but you know well how
uncertain are the minds of men when corrupted by
party intrigue, and the issues of battles.   Moreover
if, as I hope, victory is ours, even so the situation will
require the strong guidance of your counsel and your
moral influence.   In Heaven's name, then, come to
our rescue, and that with all possible speed, and be
convinced that you did your country no greater service on the Ides of March, when you struck away the
chains of servitude from your fellow-citizens, than you
will yet render it, if you arrive betimes.   July 14.

XXIV (I. 15)

CICERO TO BRUTUS

Rome, between July 11 and 27, 43 b.c.

You have Messalla at your side.   No matter how 1
carefully I indite my letters, how can I contrive to
explain with greater finesse what is happening and
how the state stands, than he will report it ?   He is

is exponet, qui et optime omnia novit et elegantissime
expedire et deferre ad te potest ? cave enim existimes, Brute—quamquam non necesse est ea me ad
te, quae tibi nota sunt, scribere, sed tamen tantam omnium laudum excellentiam non queo silentio
praeterire—, cave putes probitate constantia, cura
studio rei publicae quidquam illi esse simile, ut elo-
quentia qua mirabiliter excellit, vix in eo locum ad
laudandum habere videatur, quamquam in hac ipsa
sapientia plus apparet : ita gravi iudicio multaque arte
se exercuit in verissimo genere dicendi. Tanta autem
industria est tantumque evigilat in studio, ut non
maxima ingenio, quod in eo summum est, gratia ha-
2 benda videatur.   Sed provehor amore : non enim id
propositum est huic epistulae, Messallam ut laudem,
praesertim ad Brutum, cui et virtus illius non minus
quam mihi nota est et haec ipsa studia, quae laudo,
notiora ; quem cum a me dimittens graviter ferrem,
hoc levabar uno, quod ad te tamquam ad alterum
me proficiscens et officio fungebatur et laudem maxi-
3 mam sequebatur.   Sed haec hactenus.   Venio nunc
longo sane intervallo ad quandam epistulam, qua
mihi multa tribuens unum reprehendebas, quod in
honoribus decernendis essem nimius et tamquam pro-
digus.   Tu hoc : alius fortasse, quod in animadver-
sione poenaque durior, nisi forte utrumque tu ; quod

---

excellently posted up about everything and can explain and convey it to you in the most accomplished style. You must not suppose, Brutus—though I need not tell you what you know already ; yet for all that I cannot pass over in silence his high pre-eminence in all noble pursuits—you must not imagine that in the matter of good character, firmness of purpose, conscientiousness, and zeal for the free state there is anything to approach him ; so much so that methinks the art of oratory, in which he holds a wonderful supremacy, scarcely finds scope for eulogy in such a man ! And yet his merit stands out all the more in this very expertness of knowledge : so severe was the judgement, so exacting the technique, with which he has trained himself in the soundest style of oratory. And his application is so great, he spends so many hours of the night in study, that most of the credit does not go to his natural endowment, which in his case is consummate !

But my affection is carrying me away ; for it is not 2 the purpose of this letter to sing Messalla's praises, especially not to Brutus, who knows his merits as well as I, and knows even better these particular accomplishments which I am extolling. As I was bidding him a sorrowful good-bye, I had this one consolation, that in passing over to you—to my second self, as it were—he was performing a friendly duty and treading the path of high distinction. But enough of this !

I now come, at long last, to a certain letter,[a] in 3 which amid a mass of compliments you find one fault, that I am immoderate and as it were a spendthrift in votes of honour. That is what you say ; some one else perhaps will say that I am too harsh in the matter of censure and punishment—but maybe *you* say this

si ita est, utriusque rei meum iudicium studeo tibi
esse notissimum, neque solum, ut Solonis dictum
usurpem, qui et sapiens unus fuit ex septem et
legum scriptor solus ex septem : is rem publicam
contineri duabus rebus dixit, praemio et poena. Est
scilicet utriusque modus, sicut reliquarum, et quae-
4 dam in utroque genere mediocritas. Sed non tanta
de re propositum est hoc loco disputare. Quid ego
autem secutus hoc bello sim in sententiis dicendis,
aperire non alienum puto. Post interitum Caesaris
et vestras memorabiles Idus Mart., Brute, quid ego
praetermissum a vobis quantamque impendere rei
publicae tempestatem dixerim, non es oblitus : magna pestis erat depulsa per vos, magna populi Romani
macula deleta, vobis vero parta divina gloria, sed
instrumentum regni delatum ad Lepidum et Antonium, quorum alter inconstantior, alter impurior, uterque pacem metuens, inimicus otio. His ardentibus
perturbandae rei publicae cupiditate quod opponi
posset praesidium, non habebamus—erexerat enim
se civitas in retinenda libertate consentiens, nos tum
nimis acres, vos fortasse sapientius excessistis urbe
ea, quam liberaratis, Italiae sua vobis studia profi-
5 tenti remisistis. Itaque, cum teneri urbem a parrici-
dis viderem nec te in ea nec Cassium tuto esse posse

as well. If that is the case, I am anxious to make
quite clear to you my opinion on either point, and
this not only that I may appropriate a saying of Solon,
who was the sage *par excellence* among the Seven, and
the only legislator of their number. He said that two
things held a state together, reward and punishment.
In either case of course a certain adherence to the
mean is involved, as in all other things, and a certain
moderation should be observed under both heads.

But this is not the place for a dissertation on so 4
large a subject. Yet I do not think it amiss to set
forth what principles I followed during this war in
my formal statements of opinion.

You have not forgotten, Brutus, what I said after
the death of Caesar and your memorable Ides of
March, about your lost opportunities and the storm
which was about to break over the state. A great
pestilence had been driven off, thanks to you, a great
stain on the Roman people had been wiped out, aye,
and for yourselves you had achieved undying fame ;
but the apparatus of monarchy had been transferred
to Lepidus and Antony ; one of these was more of
a turncoat, the other more of a ruffian, either of them
dreaded peace and disliked tranquillity. While these
men were burning with eagerness to plunge the state
into chaos, we had no means of defence to set against
them ; for while the citizens braced themselves up in
a united resolve to retain their freedom, and I at that
time showed an excess of zeal, you quitted the city
which you had set free and dispensed with the devoted service which Italy was offering—and this was
perhaps the more discreet course.

So when I saw that the city was in the power of 5
cutthroats, and that neither you nor Cassius could

eamque armis oppressam ab Antonio, mihi quoque
ipsi esse excedendum putavi—tetrum enim spectacu-
lum oppressa ab impiis civitas opitulandi potestate
praecisa— ; sed animus idem, qui semper infixus in
patriae caritate, discessum ab eius periculis ferre non
potuit. Itaque in medio Achaico cursu, cum etesia-
rum diebus Auster me in Italiam quasi dissuasor mei
consilii rettulisset, te vidi Veliae doluique vehementer ; cedebas enim, Brute, cedebas—quoniam Stoici
6 nostri negant fugere sapientes. Romam ut veni,
statim me obtuli Antonii sceleri atque dementiae,
quem cum in me incitavissem, consilia inire coepi Bru-
tina plane—vestri enim haec sunt propria sanguinis—
rei publicae liberandae. Longa sunt, quae restant,
et praetereunda, sunt enim de me : tantum dico,
Caesarem hunc adulescentem, per quem adhuc sumus,
si verum fateri volumus, fluxisse ex fonte consiliorum
7 meorum. Huic habiti a me honores, nulli quidem,
Brute, nisi debiti, nulli nisi necessarii ; ut enim primum
libertatem revocare coepimus, cum se nondum ne
Decimi quidem Bruti divina virtus ita commovisset, ut
iam id scire possemus, atque omne praesidium esset in
puero, qui a cervicibus nostris avertisset Antonium,
quis honos ei non fuit decernendus ? quamquam ego
illi tum verborum laudem tribui, eamque modicam ;

live there in safety while it was being held down by
Antony with armed force, I decided that I also ought
to leave it ; for a community under the heel of
scoundrels, with all possibility of relief cut off, was a
shocking sight. But my spirit, which is immutably
and for ever rooted in my country, could not endure
that I should leave it in its hour of peril. Thus it
was that midway on my course to Achaia, when a
south wind in the season of the trades bore me back
to Italy, as if in protest against my plan, I saw you at
Velia, to my deep distress : for you were backing out,
Brutus,—I say " backing out," since our Stoic teachers
declare that the sage never " takes to flight."

On my arrival in Rome I at once took a stand **6**
against Antony's lawlessness and insanity. When I
had drawn his anger upon me, I began to entertain
plans in Brutus' own vein (for these plans are inbred
in your family's blood) for the liberation of the state.
What followed is a long story and need not be retold,
for it is about me. I merely mention that this young
Caesar, to whom we owe our survival (if we are willing to admit the truth), derived from the headspring
of my mentorship.

I obtained for him marks of honour, Brutus, but **7**
none that were unearned or superfluous. For as we
made a first beginning of recovering our liberty at
a time when not even the heroic courage of Decimus
Brutus had yet been roused to action so far as to give
us an assurance of freedom regained, and our entire
defence rested in the hands of the boy who had
removed Antony off our necks, what honour should
have been withheld from him ? Though the compliments which *I* then bestowed upon him were votes
of thanks couched in moderate terms, I also had a

decrevi etiam imperium, quod quamquam videbatur
illi aetati honorificum, tamen erat exercitum habenti
necessarium, quid enim est sine imperio exercitus ?
Statuam Philippus decrevit, celeritatem petitionis
primo Servius, post maiorem etiam Servilius : nihil
8 tum nimium videbatur. Sed nescio quo modo homines facilius in timore benigni quam in victoria grati
reperiuntur : ego enim, D. Bruto liberato cum lae-
tissimus ille civitati dies illuxisset idemque casu Bruti natalis esset, decrevi, ut in fastis ad eum diem
Bruti nomen ascriberetur, in eoque sum maiorum exemplum secutus, qui hunc honorem mulieri Larentiae
tribuerunt, cuius vos pontifices ad aram in Velabro
sacrificium facere soletis : quod ego cum dabam Bruto,
notam esse in fastis gratissimae victoriae sempiternam volebam ; atqui illo die cognovi paullo plures in
senatu malevolos esse quam gratos. Eos per ipsos
dies effudi—si ita vis—honores in mortuos, Hirtium
et Pansam, Aquilam etiam ; quod quis reprehendit,
nisi qui deposito metu praeteriti periculi fuerit ob-
9 litus ? Accedebat ad beneficii memoriam gratam
ratio illa, quae etiam posteris esset salutaris : exstare
enim volebam in crudelissimos hostes monumenta

---

* For Servius Sulpicus Rufus see *Epp. ad Fam.* iv. 1-6.
Like Philippus and Servilius, he was prepared to negotiate
with Antony.

b Acca Larentia, a mysterious personage of early Roman
legend.

c L. Pontius Aquila, a tyrannicide. He was killed in the
action at Mutina.

high command conferred upon him ; though this might appear honour indeed for a man of his age, it was none the less indispensable for one at the head of an army—for what is an army without a high command ? Philippus carried a motion for a statue, Servius [a] made a first proposal for earlier acceptance as a candidate, Servilius followed this up with still higher priority. Nothing at that time appeared excessive.

But for some strange reason you will sooner find **8** benevolence in the hour of fear than gratitude in the hour of victory. For after the relief of Brutus, when that most joyful day had dawned upon the community, and by a coincidence that day too was Brutus' anniversary, I carried a motion that the name of Brutus be entered under date in the state calendar, and therein I followed the example of our forefathers, who bestowed this honour upon the lady Larentia,[b] at whose altar in the Velabrum you pontiffs are wont to make sacrifice. In paying this tribute to Brutus I wanted to insert in the calendar a permanent record of a most welcome victory. Yes, on that day I discovered that in the Senate ill-will commanded somewhat larger numbers than gratitude. At that particular time I showered honours—if you like to put it so—on dead men, Hirtius and Pansa, and even on Aquila.[c] Who will find fault with this, except a man who has forgotten his past peril now that his fear is no longer on him ?

My grateful recollection of a service rendered was **9** reinforced by a consideration which posterity too might do well to bear in mind ; for it was my wish that everlasting monuments of the public loathing for a most brutal enemy should be raised up in the

711

odii publici sempiterna. Suspicor illud tibi minus
probari, quod a tuis familiaribus, optimis illis quidem
viris, sed in re publica rudibus, non probabatur, quod
ut ovanti introire Caesari liceret decreverim ; ego
autem—sed erro fortasse, nec tamen is sum, ut mea
me maxime delectent—nihil mihi videor hoc bello
sensisse prudentius ; cur autem ita sit, aperiendum
non est, ne magis videar providus fuisse quam gratus.
Hoc ipsum nimium, quare alia videamus.   D. Bruto
decrevi honores, decrevi L. Planco : praeclara illa
quidem ingenia, quae gloria invitantur, sed senatus
etiam sapiens, qui, qua quemque re putat, modo honesta, ad rem publicam iuvandam posse adduci, hac
utitur.   At in Lepido reprehendimur, cui cum statuam in rostris statuissemus, iidem illam evertimus :
nos illum honore studuimus a furore revocare ; vicit
amentia levissimi hominis nostram prudentiam, nec
tamen tantum in statuenda Lepidi statua factum est
10 mali, quantum in evertenda boni.   Satis multa de
honoribus : nunc de poena pauca dicenda sunt ; intellexi enim ex tuis saepe litteris te in eis, quos bello
devicisti, clementiam tuam velle laudari.   Existimo
equidem nihil a te nisi sapienter ; sed sceleris poe-
nam praetermittere—id enim est, quod vocatur ignoscere—, etiamsi in ceteris rebus tolerabile est, in hoc
bello perniciosum puto : nullum enim bellum civile

ᵃ An *ovatio* was a triumphal procession on a smaller
scale.

sight of all. I suspect that you did not altogether approve what was disapproved by your intimates (excellent men, I admit, but unversed in politics), that I carried a resolution conferring upon Caesar the right of a Joyous Entry.[a] For myself—but perhaps I am at fault, only I am not the man to take the highest pleasure in my own achievements—I do not think that in this war I ever had a sounder idea ; the reason for this I must not disclose, lest I should make an impression of foresight rather than of gratitude.—I am labouring this point too much ; so let us turn to something else. I had honours conferred upon D. Brutus and upon L. Plancus. Theirs are indeed noble natures that heed the call of glory ; but the Senate too shows discretion, in that it offers whatever inducement (consistent with honour) it thinks will serve in each particular case to win a man to the service of the state. But you take me to task about Lepidus : we first set up a statue in his honour on the Speakers' Platform, then we cast it down. We made an effort to recall him from his madness by honouring him. The infatuation of that fluffiest of fellows proved too strong for our precautions ; even so, less harm was done in setting up Lepidus' statue than good in casting it down.

Enough has been said about honours. Now I must make a few remarks about punishment ; for I have often discerned from your letters that you wish to be given credit for leniency in regard to those whom you have overmastered in war. I consider indeed that your wisdom is unfailing ; yet I believe that to remit punishment for crime (for that is what " pardoning " amounts to), however passable it may be on another occasion, is utterly ruinous in this war.

713

fuit in nostra re publica omnium, quae memoria mea
fuerunt, in quo bello non, utracumque pars vicisset, tamen aliqua forma esset futura rei publicae ;
hoc bello victores quam rem publicam simus habituri,
non facile affirmarim, victis certe nulla umquam erit.
Dixi igitur sententias in Antonium, dixi in Lepidum severas, neque tam ulciscendi causa, quam ut
et in praesens sceleratos cives timore ab impugnanda
patria deterrerem et in posterum documentum statu-
11 erem, ne quis talem amentiam vellet imitari. Quamquam haec quidem sententia non magis mea fuit
quam omnium : in qua videtur illud esse crudele, quod
ad liberos, qui nihil meruerunt, poena pervenit ; sed
id et antiquum est et omnium civitatum, si quidem
etiam Themistocli liberi eguerunt, et, si iudicio
damnatos eadam poena sequitur cives, qui potuimus
leniores esse in hostes ? quid autem queri quisquam
potest de me, qui, si vicisset, acerbiorem se in me
futurum fuisse confiteatur necesse est ? Habes rationem mearum sententiarum de hoc genere dumtaxat honoris et poenae ; nam, de ceteris rebus quid
senserim quidque censuerim, audisse te arbitror.
12 Sed haec quidem non ita necessaria : illud valde necessarium, Brute, te in Italiam cum exercitu venire
quam primum. Summa est exspectatio tui ; quod si
Italiam attigeris, ad te concursus fiet omnium. Sive
enim vicerimus—qui quidem pulcherrime viceramus

For of all the civil wars in our state which I can recall, none were waged on such terms but that whichever side won, at all events some form of free state would have survived. In the present war I should not find it easy to lay down what manner of free state we shall have, if we are to be the winners ; if we lose, the free state will certainly disappear for ever. I therefore advocated severe measures against Antony and against Lepidus, not so much for retribution's sake, as to discourage and deter evil-minded citizens from attacking their country at the present time, and to set up a warning example for the future, so that none should feel inclined to repeat such acts of madness.

And yet this particular measure did not reflect 11 mine any more than the universal opinion. You see vindictiveness in this, that the penalty extends to the innocent children. But that is an ancient usage and common to all states, if it be true that even Thermistocles' children were left destitute ; and if the same punishment falls upon citizens condemned by a court, how could we be more lenient towards public enemies ? And what complaint can any man make about me, if he cannot help confessing that if victory had been his he would have treated me more harshly ? You have the reasoned statement of my views on this particular subject of honour and punishment ; I believe you have heard my opinions and pronouncements on other matters.

But of course this is not so urgent ; what *is* highly 12 urgent, Brutus, is that you should come to Italy with your army at the earliest possible moment. We are awaiting you most anxiously. Why, if you land in Italy there will be a general rush to meet you ! For suppose we win, and a very handsome victory

nisi Lepidus perdere omnia et perire ipse cum
suis concupivisset—, tua nobis auctoritate opus est
ad collocandum aliquem civitatis statum ; sive etiam
nunc certamen reliquum est, maxima spes est cum
in auctoritate tua, tum in exercitus tui viribus. Sed
propera, per deos ! scis, quantum sit in temporibus,
13 quantum in celeritate. Sororis tuae filiis quam diligenter consulam, spero te ex matris et ex sororis
litteris cogniturum : qua in causa maiorem habeo
rationem tuae voluntatis, quae mihi carissima est,
quam, ut quibusdam videor, constantiae meae ; sed
ego nulla in re malo quam in te amando constans
et esse et videri.

XXV (I. 16)

M. BRUTUS S. D. M. CICERONI

In castris, a.u.c. 711

1 Particulam litterarum tuarum, quas misisti Octavio,
legi missam ab Attico mihi. Studium tuum curaque
de salute mea nulla me nova voluptate affecit ; non
solum enim usitatum, sed etiam cotidianum est aliquid
audire de te, quod pro nostra dignitate fideliter atque
honorifice dixeris aut feceris. At dolore, quantum
maximum capere animo possum, eadem illa pars epistulae scripta ad Octavium de nobis affecit. Sic enim
illi gratias agis de re publica, tam suppliciter ac

was ours, had not Lepidus insisted on undoing every-thing and undoing himself with his own associates, we need your moral influence in order to effect some sort of political settlement ; but if we have even now a stiff fight before us, our chief hope rests both in your influence and especially in the might of your army. But make haste, for Heaven's sake ! You know how much depends on correct timing and on speed.

I hope you will perceive from your mother's and 13 sister's letters what an earnest interest I take in your nephews. In their case my chief consideration is to fulfil your desire, which I hold most dear, rather than to be consistent with myself, as some people imagine. But there is nothing in which I would rather be consistent, and show it, than in my affec-tion for you.

XXV (I. 16)

BRUTUS TO CICERO

In camp, mid July, 43 B.C.

I have read the short extract from the note which 1 you sent to Octavius : Atticus sent it to me. Your devotion and concern about my safety brought no fresh pleasure to me, for it is not only a usual but a daily experience for me to hear about you, of some loyal or complimentary words or deeds with which you protected my honour. But that part of the letter in which you wrote to Octavius about me brought upon me the most acute distress that I could possibly endure in my mind. For this is how you offer him thanks in matters of state, in such a

demisse—quid scribam ? pudet condicionis ac fortunae, sed tamen scribendum est—commendas nostram salutem illi—quae morte qua non perniciosior ?
—, ut prorsus prae te feras non sublatam dominationem, sed dominum commutatum esse. Verba tua
recognosce et aude negare servientis adversus regem
istas esse preces. Unum ais esse, quod ab eo postu-
letur et exspectetur, ut eos cives, de quibus viri boni
populusque Romanus bene existimet, salvos velit :
quid ? si nolit, non erimus ? atqui non esse quam
2 esse per illum praestat. Ego medius fidius non existimo tam omnes deos aversos esse a salute populi
Romani, ut Octavius orandus sit pro salute cuiusquam
civis, non dicam pro liberatoribus orbis terrarum—
iuvat enim magnifice loqui et certe decet adversus
ignorantes, quid pro quoque timendum aut a quoque
petendum sit—. Hoc tu, Cicero, posse fateris Octavium et illi amicus es ? aut, si me carum habes, vis
Romae videri, cum, ut ibi esse possem, commen-
dandus puero illi fuerim ? cui quid agis gratias, si, ut
nos salvos esse velit et patiatur, rogandum putas ?
an hoc pro beneficio habendum est, quod se quam
718

suppliant and humble tone! What am I to write?
I'm ashamed at being in such a position—I'm ashamed
of my lot—and yet, write I must. You entrust him
with our protection : is that not more disastrous than
no matter what sort of death? Just in order that you
may plume yourself, not on the overthrow of autocracy but on a change of autocrat! Consider your
own words, and dare to deny that those are the entreaties of a person of servile estate in the presence
of a king! There is, so you affirm, one demand and
one claim to be made upon him, that he should agree
to the safety of those citizens of whom good patriots
and the Roman people have a high opinion. Well!
Suppose he refuses : will that put an end to our existence? Ah, but I would rather not exist than owe my
existence to him!

I'll take an oath upon it, I cannot believe that all 2
Heaven has so little regard for the safety of the
Roman people that we must beg Octavius for the
safety of any citizen whatsoever—I shall not say for
the liberators of the whole world. You see, I take
pleasure in high flown language, and this is clearly
appropriate in the face of men who do not know what
fears we should harbour, what requests we should
make in this case and that. Can you, Cicero, admit
that Octavius holds such power, and give him
your friendship? Or, if you have any affection for
me, do you want me to show myself in Rome, on the
condition that this boy's favour must first be obtained
for me, so that I can have my existence there? Why
do you offer thanks to him, if you think that application must be made to him, so that our safety shall
depend on his consent and sufferance? Or is this
to count as a favour, that he chose to be the person,

719

Antonium esse maluerit, a quo ista petenda essent?
Vindici quidem alienae dominationis, non vicario, ec-
quis supplicat, ut optime meritis de re publica liceat
3 esse salvis? Ista vero imbecillitas et desperatio,
cuius culpa non magis in te residet quam in omnibus
aliis, et Caesarem in cupiditatem regni impulit et
Antonio post interitum illius persuasit, ut interfecti
locum occupare conaretur, et nunc puerum istum ita
extulit, ut tu iudicares precibus esse impetrandam
salutem talibus viris misericordiaque unius vix etiam
nunc viri tutos fore nos, haud ulla[1] alia re. Quod si
Romanos nos esse meminissemus, non audacius dominari cuperent postremi homines, quam id nos pro-
hiberemus, neque magis irritatus esset Antonius
regno Caesaris quam ob eiusdem mortem deterritus.
4 Tu quidem, consularis et tantorum scelerum vindex—
quibus oppressis vereor ne in breve tempus dilata
sit abs te pernicies—, qui potes intueri, quae gesseris,
simul et ista vel probare vel ita demisse ac facile pati,
ut probantis specimen habeas? quod autem tibi cum
Antonio privatim odium? nempe, quia postulabat
haec, salutem ab se peti, precariam nos incolumita-
tem habere, a quibus ipse libertatem accepisset, esse

---

[1] *Var. lect.* aut nulla.

rather than Antony, from whom those favours would have to be begged ? Given a true champion against a despotism imposed from outside, not a substitute despot, does any man make humble request to him, that he should permit those who have deserved nobly of the state to live in safety ?

It was your faint-heartedness, your abandonment of **3** hope (the blame for which rests no more upon you than upon everyone else), that prompted Caesar to aspire to kingship, and induced Antony after his death to try to usurp the place of him who was slain ; and now it has exalted that boy of yours, leading you to the conclusion that men with a record like ours must obtain security by supplication, and that our safety should even now depend precariously on the merciful-ness of one person hardly yet a man, not on anything else. Yet if we had borne in mind that we were Romans, the dregs of mankind would not be more forward in their scramble for despotism than we in making a stand against it, nor would Caesar's monarchy have been more of an incitement to Antony than his death has proved a deterrent.

As for you, who have been consul and have avenged **4** crimes of such magnitude—yet I fear that by their suppression you have merely gained a short respite from ruin—how can you contemplate your past achievements and at the same time approve of your friend's actions, or acquiesce in them in such a humble and pliant spirit as to offer a semblance of approval ? And what means this privately conducted feud of yours with Antony ? Why, because he made these demands, that our lives should be in his gift, that we should hold our position by his leave, though he had received his freedom at our hands, that he

721

arbitrium suum de re publica, quaerenda esse arma
putasti, quibus dominari prohiberetur: scilicet, ut illo
prohibito rogaremus alterum, qui se in eius locum
reponi pateretur, an ut esset sui iuris ac mancipii
res publica ? nisi forte non de servitute, sed de con-
dicione serviendi recusatum est a nobis. Atqui non
solum bono domino potuimus Antonio tolerare nostram fortunam, sed etiam beneficiis atque honoribus ut participes frui, quantis vellemus ; quid enim
negaret eis, quorum patientiam videret maximum
dominationis suae praesidium esse ? Sed nihil tanti
fuit, quo venderemus fidem nostram et libertatem.
5 Hic ipse puer, quem Caesaris nomen incitare videtur
in Caesaris interfectores, quanti aestimet, si sit com-
mercio locus, posse nobis auctoribus tantum, quantum
profecto poterit, quoniam vivere per se et pecunias
habere et dici consulares volumus ! Ceterum ne
nequidquam perierit ille (cuius interitu quid gavisi
sumus, si mortuo eo nihilo minus servituri eramus ?),
nulla cura adhibetur ? Sed mihi prius omnia di deae-
que eripuerint quam illud iudicium, quo non modo
heredi eius, quem occidi, id non concesserim, quod
in illo non tuli, sed ne patri quidem meo, si reviviscat,
ut patiente me plus legibus ac senatu possit : an hoc
722

should have the last word in the state, was it for this that you thought we should have recourse to arms as a means of beating off despotism—with this result, mark you!, that after beating off one despot we should solicit another to let himself be installed in the former man's place, or that he should be vested with a full title of property in the state ? Unless maybe we made our protest, not against slavery, but against the particular terms of our bondage. And yet under Antony's benevolent tyranny we could not only have endured our own lot, but we could have enjoyed the greatest preferments and high positions of state that we might have asked for, on a basis of partnership ; for what would he deny to the men in whose passivity he could see a bulwark of his own autocracy ? But no favour carried so high a price as to induce us to sell our loyalty and liberty.

This boy in particular, whom the name of Caesar **5** seems to spur on against Caesar's slayers, what price would he offer (suppose this were a matter of haggling), that we should procure him such power as he will of course obtain, seeing that by his goodwill we want to remain alive, and to keep our estates, and to be styled consulars ! Besides, are we taking no precautions lest our old enemy should have perished to no purpose ? How could we rejoice at his death, if now that he is gone we were to remain none the less in bondage ? But may the host of heaven strip me of all else rather than of my settled resolve not to give away, I shall not say to the heir of the man whom I slew, but not even to my own father, should he come to life again, what I could not brook in the slain man, a power superior to the Laws and Senate, with my connivance ! Do you really believe that the rest of

tibi persuasum est, fore ceteros ab eo liberos, quo
invito nobis in ista civitate locus non sit ? Qui porro
id, quod petis, fieri potest ut impetres ? Rogas enim,
velit nos salvos esse : videmur ergo tibi salutem ac-
cepturi, cum vitam acceperimus ? quam, si prius
dimittimus dignitatem et libertatem, qui possumus
6 accipere ? An tu Romae habitare, id putas incolu-
mem esse ? res, non locus oportet praestet istuc
mihi : neque incolumis Caesare vivo fui, nisi posteaquam illud conscivi facinus, neque usquam exsul esse
possum, dum servire et pati contumelias peius odero
malis omnibus aliis. Nonne hoc est in easdem tene-
bras recidisse, si ab eo, qui tyranni nomen ascivit
sibi,—cum in Graecis civitatibus liberi tyrannorum
oppressis illis eodem supplicio afficiantur,—petitur,
ut vindices atque oppressores dominationis salvi sint ?
Hanc ego civitatem videre velim aut putem ullam,
quae ne traditam quidem atque inculcatam libertatem recipere possit plusque timeat in puero nomen
sublati regis, quam confidat sibi, cum illum ipsum,
qui maximas opes habuerit, paucorum virtute sublatum videat ? Me vero posthac ne commendaveris
Caesari tuo, ne te quidem ipsum, si me audies : valde
care aestimas tot annos, quot ista aetas recipit, si prop-
7 ter eam causam puero isti supplicaturus es. Deinde,

the people will be free from the man whose favour we must win before we can hold a place within that citizen body ? Moreover, how can you possibly obtain what you are after ? You ask that he should consent to our security. Do you think, then, that when we have been given our lives we shall be given our security ? How can we be in receipt of this, if to begin with we divest ourselves of our high rank and liberty ?

To have your residence in Rome, is that your idea 6 of civic security ? The facts, not the place, must be my guarantee. Neither could I enjoy my full civic rights in Caesar's lifetime, until after I had resolved upon my great deed, nor can I be an exile in any place, so long as I hold slavery and the suffering of indignities in deeper loathing than all other misfortunes. Is this not a relapse into our former Dark Age, if I must beg the man who took for himself the name of tyrant, that those who avenged and overthrew a despotism should come to no harm, whereas in the Greek states the children of tyrants suffer the same punishment when the tyranny is overthrown ? Could I wish to set eyes on a state, or regard it as a state at all, if it cannot even recover the freedom handed down to it and driven home into it, and feels more alarm at the name of a fallen king, when assumed by a boy, than confidence in itself, though it can see that the monarch himself in the plenitude of his power owed his fall to the firm action of a mere handful ? No, don't you hereafter commend me to your Caesar, do not commend yourself either, if you will listen to me ! You must attach a rare value to those years of life which your present age allows you, if for that reason you are going to fall on your knees before that boy !

quod pulcherrime fecisti ac facis in Antonio, vide
ne convertatur a laude maximi animi ad opinionem
formidinis ; nam, si Octavius tibi placet, a quo de
nostra salute petendum sit, non dominum fugisse,
sed amiciorem dominum quaesisse videberis.   Quem
quod laudas ob ea, quae adhuc fecit, plane probo ; sunt
enim laudanda, si modo contra alienam potentiam,
non pro sua suscepit eas actiones ; cum vero iudicas
tantum illi non modo licere, sed etiam a te ipso tribu-
endum esse, ut rogandus sit, ne nolit esse nos salvos,
nimium magnam mercedem statuis—id enim ipsum
illi largiris, quod per illum habere videbatur res publica—, neque hoc tibi in mentem venit, si Octavius
illis dignus sit honoribus, quia cum Antonio bellum
gerat, iis qui illud malum exciderint, cuius istae reliquiae sunt, nihil, quo expleri possit eorum meritum,
tributurum umquam populum Romanum, si omnia
8 simul congesserit.   Ac vide, quanto diligentius homines metuant, quam meminerint : quia Antonius vivat
atque in armis sit, de Caesare vero, quod fieri potuit
ac debuit, transactum est neque iam revocari in
integrum potest, Octavius is est, qui quid de nobis
iudicaturus sit exspectet populus Romanus, nos ii
sumus, de quorum salute unus homo rogandus videatur.   Ego vero, ut istoc revertar, is sum, qui non

Furthermore, see to it that your splendid achieve- 7
ments, past and present, in Antony's case, be not
transformed from a source of honour for a heroic spirit
into one of a reputation for timidity.   For if Octavius
takes your fancy, the man to whom you would have
me apply for security, people will think that you were
not shunning a master, but were seeking a more
friendly master.   Your praise for what he has hitherto
done has my unfeigned approval; for his actions call for
praise, provided always that he has undertaken them
to break another man's power, not to further his own.
But when you conclude that so much power should
not only be for him to take, but should be presented
to him by yourself, so that one must ask him not to
declare himself against our safety, you fix the price
of the bargain too high (for you lavish upon him that
very authority which he was thought to have pro-
cured for the state), and this does not enter your
mind, that if Octavius is worthy of any high office
because he is waging a war with Antony, the Roman
people will never be able to bestow a full measure
of recompense upon those who removed the bane of
which this is the residue, if in one act it heaps all it
has on the shoulders of one man.

And observe how much more insistent is men's 8
sense of fear than their memory: seeing that Antony
is still alive and in arms, but in Caesar's case, what
could and should have been done has been accomplished once for all and cannot now be reversed,
Octavius is the man on whose decisions what to do
with us the Roman people must wait, and we are the
men for whose safety, it would seem, application
must be made to one individual !   No—to return to
what you said—, I am the sort of man who would

modo non supplicem, sed etiam coërceam postulantes,
ut sibi supplicetur, aut longe a servientibus abero
mihique esse iudicabo Romam, ubicumque liberum
esse licebit, ac vestri miserebor, quibus nec aetas
neque honores nec virtus aliena dulcedinem vivendi
9 minuere potuerit.   Mihi quidem ita beatus esse vide-
bor, si modo constanter ac perpetuo placebit hoc
consilium, ut relatam putem gratiam pietati meae ;
quid enim est melius quam memoria recte factorum
et libertate contentum neglegere humana ? Sed certe
non succumbam succumbentibus nec vincar ab eis,
qui se vinci volunt, experiarque et tentabo omnia
neque desistam abstrahere a servitio civitatem nostram.   Si secuta fuerit quae debet fortuna, gaude-
bimus omnes ; si minus, ego tamen gaudebo.   Quibus
enim potius haec vita factis aut cogitationibus
traducatur quam iis, quae pertinuerint ad liberandos
10 cives meos ?   Te, Cicero, rogo atque hortor, ne de-
fatigere neu diffidas, semper in praesentibus malis
prohibendis futura quoque, nisi ante sit occursum,
explores, ne se insinuent, fortem et liberum animum,
quo et consul et nunc consularis rem publicam vindi-
casti, sine constantia et aequabilitate nullum esse
putaris.   Fateor enim duriorem esse condicionem
spectatae virtutis quam incognitae : bene facta pro

not merely refuse to make entreaty, but would put under restraint those who demand that entreaty be made to them. Or else I shall hold myself far aloof from those who accept servitide, and shall find Rome for myself wherever a man may still be free; and I shall feel sorry for you, whose love of sweet life neither your age nor your high position, nor the example of courage which others set you, will be able to curtail.

For my part I shall be happy in my own eyes if 9 only I hold firmly and without a break to this resolve, that I shall deem myself repaid in gratitude for my devotion to my country. For what is better than the memory of righteous deeds and disregard of human exigencies in the pure enjoyment of liberty ? But assuredly I shall not submit myself to the submissive, nor take defeat from those who court defeat ; and I shall essay and adventure everything, and shall never cease to draw our community out of the reach of servitude. If our efforts meet with the fortune which they deserve, we shall all be glad ; if otherwise, *I* shall be glad even so. For what actions or reflections could better occupy this life of ours than those relating to the liberty of my fellow-citizens ?

Cicero, I beg and admonish you, do not flag or lose 10 heart ; and while you ward off present evils always cast a searching glance upon future ones too, lest they steal in upon you while there is none to cope with them in advance. Understand once for all that the courageous and free spirit with which you championed the state as consul, and now as a consular, goes for nothing without a firm purpose and an even temperament. I grant you that merit well-tried has a more exacting task than merit undiscovered. We

debitis exigimus, quae aliter veniunt, ut decepti ab iis, infesto animo reprehendimus. Itaque resistere Antonio Ciceronem, etsi maxima laude dignum est, tamen, quia ille consul hunc consularem merito prae-
11 stare videtur, nemo admiratur. Idem Cicero, si flexerit adversus alios iudicium suum, quod tanta firmitate ac magnitudinine animi direxit in exturbando Antonio, non modo reliqui temporis gloriam eripuerit sibi, sed etiam praeterita evanescere coget —nihil enim per se amplum est, nisi in quo iudicii ratio extat—, quia neminem magis decet rem publicam amare libertatisque defensorem esse vel ingenio vel rebus gestis vel studio atque efflagitatione omnium. Quare non Octavius est rogandus, ut velit nos salvos esse : magis tute te exsuscita, ut eam civitatem, in qua maxima gessisti, liberam atque honestam fore putes, si modo sint populo duces ad resistendum improborum consiliis.

XXVI (I. 18)

M. CICERO S. D. M. BRUTO

Romae, A.U.C. 711

1 Cum saepe te litteris hortatus essem, ut quam primum rei publicae subvenires in Italiamque exer-
730

require of it a high performance as of right, and
when things fall out otherwise we assail men with
reproaches for the deception they have practised on
us. Therefore Cicero's defiance of Antony calls for
the highest praise, yet because it is assumed that
the historic consul is morally bound to set the standard for to-day's consular, no one is impressed.

But if the same Cicero should defer to others in **11**
his convictions, which he applied so resolutely and in
such a grand manner when he bundled Antony out,
he will find that he not only has thrown away his
reputation for the future, but will also ensure that his
past achievements shall be blotted out—for nothing
is great in itself that does not bear the plain mark
of reasoned judgement—; because no one man is
better fitted to be a patriot and to champion liberty
with wise thoughts or brave deeds, or with the devotion and the imperious call to leadership of the entire
community. For these reasons we must *not* beg
Octavius to deign to keep us safe. No, no! You
must rouse yourself up, and realize that the state
which was the scene of your greatest achievements
will enjoy its freedom and honour on these terms
alone, if leaders are forthcoming for the people in
making a stand against the policies of reprobates.

XXVI (I. 18)

CICERO TO BRUTUS

Rome, July 27, 43 B.C.

Having repeatedly urged you in my letters to come **1**
to the rescue of the state as soon as possible, and to

citum adduceres, neque id arbitrarer dubitare tuos necessarios, rogatus sum a prudentissima et diligentissima femina, matre tua, cuius omnes curae ad te referuntur et in te consumuntur, ut venirem ad se a. d. VIII. Kal. Sextiles : quod ego, ut debui, sine mora feci. Cum autem venissem, Casca aderat et Labeo et Scaptius. At illa rettulit quaesivitque, quidnam mihi videretur, arcesseremusne te atque id tibi conducere putaremus, an tardare ac commorari te 2 melius esset. Respondi id, quod sentiebam, et dignitati et existimationi tuae maxime conducere te primo quoque tempore ferre praesidium labenti et inclinatae paene rei publicae ; quid enim abesse censes mali in eo bello, in quo victores exercitus fugientem hostem persequi noluerint et in quo incolumis imperator, honoribus amplissimis fortunisque maximis, coniuge, liberis, vobis affinibus ornatus, bellum rei publicae indixerit ? Quid dicam " in tanto senatus populique consensu," cum tantum resideat intra muros mali ? 3 Maximo autem, cum haec scribebam, officiebar dolore, quod, cum me pro adulescentulo ac paene puero res publica accepisset vadem, vix videbar, quod promiseram, praestare posse. Est autem gravior et difficilior animi et sententiae, maximis praesertim in rebus, pro altero quam pecuniae obligatio : haec enim solvi potest et est rei familiaris iactura tolera-

***

ᵃ Lepidus.

bring your army to Italy, and believing as I did that
your intimates were in full agreement with me, I
was asked by a woman of great capacity and energy,
your mother, whose every care centres on you and
is wholly exercised on your behalf, to meet her on
July 25. This I promptly did, as in duty bound.
On my arrival I found Casca there and Labeo and
Scaptius. But *she* put the question and invited my
opinion : were we to give you a call, and were we to
decide that this was in your interests, or was it better
for you to hold back and make no move ?

I told her in reply what I felt, that it was in the 2
highest interests of your exalted rank and reputation
to bring support at the earliest possible moment to the
free state, which is losing its foothold and on the verge
of collapse. For what calamity, think you, is lacking
in a war in which the victorious armies have refused
to pursue a fleeing enemy, and a general[a] with his
forces intact, endowed with the highest public dis-
tinctions and with an ample fortune, with a wife and
children and a marriage connexion with you, has
declared war upon the state ? Why should I say
" with such unanimity among Senate and people,"
seeing that so much evil disposition still lurks within
the walls ?

But what grieves me most sorely at the time of 3
writing is that when the state accepted me as surety
for this stripling—one might almost call him a boy—
I hardly seemed in a position to make good my promise. You see, it is a more serious and arduous risk,
especially on an issue of paramount importance, to
engage on behalf of another one's soul and one's
sentiment than to pledge one's money ; for a money
pledge can be redeemed, and the forfeiture of one's

bilis ; rei publicae quod spoponderis, quemadmodum
solvas, si is dependi facile patitur, pro quo spopon-
4 deris ? Quamquam et hunc, ut spero, tenebo multis
repugnantibus : videtur enim esse in eo indoles, sed
flexibilis aetas multique ad depravandum parati, qui
splendore falsi honoris obiecto aciem boni ingenii
praestringi posse confidunt. Itaque ad reliquos hic
quoque labor mihi accessit, ut omnes adhibeam
machinas ad tenendum adulescentem, ne famam sub-
eam temeritatis : quamquam quae temeritas est ?
Magis enim illum, pro quo spopondi, quam me ipsum
obligavi, nec vero paenitere potest rem publicam
me pro eo spopondisse, qui fuit in rebus gerundis cum
5 suo ingenio, tum mea promissione constantior. Maximus autem, nisi me forte fallit, in re publica nodus est
inopia rei pecuniariae : obdurescunt enim magis co-
tidie boni viri ad vocem tributi, quod ex centesima
collatum impudenti censu locupletium in duarum
legionum praemiis omne consumitur ; impendent
autem infiniti sumptus cum in hos exercitus, quibus
nunc defendimur, tum vero in tuum—nam Cassius
noster videtur posse satis ornatus venire. Sed et

family property is to be borne, but political obligations, how are you to discharge them, if the person on whose behalf you went bail is ready and willing to make a call on you for full payment?

And yet, so I hope, I shall keep my hold even on 4 him, in spite of opposition from many quarters. For he seems to have good natural qualities, but he is pliable at his age, and many are prepared to pervert him : they are confident that the keen edge of his sound character can be blunted by dangling before him the glitter of high office falsely won. So this task has been imposed upon me on top of all the others, that I must bring to bear every device by which I may hold back the young man, lest I be saddled with a reputation for rashness. And yet wherein does the rashness lie? For the obligation rested rather upon the person for whom I stood surety than upon myself; and indeed the state cannot regret that I pledged myself on behalf of a man who owes it as much to my guarantee as to his own character that in the campaign he has been comparatively steadfast.

But, unless I happen to be mistaken, the most 5 knotty problem in affairs of state is the lack of financial resources. For men of goodwill shut their ears more and more each day to the call of taxation ; because of brazen under-valuations by the well-to-do, the proceeds of the one-per-cent are being entirely swallowed up by the bonuses for two legions. Moreover we are confronted with unlimited expenditure, both on the armies here, by which we are defended for the present, and also on your forces ; for it seems as if our friend Cassius could arrive here with a sufficient equipment. But these and many other

N

haec et multa alia coram cupio, idque quam primum.
6 De sororis tuae filiis non exspectavi, Brute, dum
scriberes : omnino ipsa tempora—bellum enim ducetur
—integram tibi causam reservant ; sed ego a principio, cum divinare de belli diuturnitate non possem,
ita causam egi puerorum in senatu, ut te arbitror e
matris litteris potuisse cognoscere, nec vero ulla res
erit umquam, in qua ego non vel vitae periculo ea
dicam eaque faciam, quam te velle quaeque ad te
pertinere arbitrer.   vi. Kal. Sextiles.

matters I want to talk over with you face to face, and that at the earliest possible moment.

I did not wait for you, Brutus, to write about your 6 sister's children. Altogether, the mere state of the times (for the war will be a long one) is keeping their case open against your return. But from the outset, when I could not foretell the long duration of the war, I pleaded the case of the boys in the Senate with such force as I believe you may have been able to ascertain from your mother's letters. Indeed there will never be any affair in which I shall not, even at the risk of my life, speak and act in the way which I shall judge to be in accord with your wishes and in your interest. July 27.

[QUINTUS CICERO]
HANDBOOK OF
ELECTIONEERING

WITH AN ENGLISH TRANSLATION BY
MARY ISOBEL HENDERSON, M.A.

VICE-PRINCIPAL AND FELLOW OF SOMERVILLE COLLEGE, OXFORD,
AND UNIVERSITY LECTURER IN ANCIENT HISTORY

INTRODUCTION TO THE
COMMENTARIOLUM PETITIONIS

From mid-65 to mid-64 B.C. Marcus Tullius Cicero was campaigning for election to a consulship of 63. Of his six competitors two were formidable. Both were " nobles " (*i.e.*, of consular ancestry). C. Antonius, who *c.* 77 had evaded trial for plundering Greece, was desperate for office and money, and talked of raising a slave rebellion if he failed.[a] L. Sergius Catilina, who had bribed a court to acquit him of misgovernment in Africa, did not launch his rebellion until 63, after a second defeat, but he was known to be capable of violence.[b] A notorious killer in Sulla's proscriptions, he was suspected of some part in an abortive plot of 66 B.C. which had by now leaked out ; Cicero, attacking his rivals in the pre-election speech *In toga candida*, hinted darkly at these current rumours.[c] In alarm the leading nobles turned to Cicero, a " new man " or commoner, who had at first expected little help from them.[d] Against their authority he had carried the appointment of Pompey to the command which still kept him away in the east. In general repute he was reckoned " Popular," as opposed to the aristocratic " Optimates." But these were rhetorical labels, and implied no rigid political

[a] *In toga cand.*, Asconius p. 78 Kiessling-Schoell.
[b] *In toga cand.*, Asconius 76 ; Sallust, *Cat.* 18, 23 (unreasonably doubted because the speech of *Cat.* 20 is fictitious).
[c] *In toga cand.*, Asconius 82.
[d] Cic. *Ad Att.* i. 2. 2.

alignments. Cicero was favoured by the class of his origin, the wealthy Knights, including the big contractors of public revenue ; his connexions with the Italian *bourgeoisie* were wide ; his influence could unite the stable elements of society in the election itself and in any danger to come ; and the Roman nobility were intelligent enough to recognize the mental power and fire that matched him with Catiline's versatile energy. Their judgement was endorsed. Cicero headed the poll ; Antonius narrowly beat Catiline for the other consulship. "

The " Handbook of Electioneering " (as it calls itself) or canvassing either is, or pretends to be, addressed to Marcus Cicero by his younger brother Quintus during this canvass. The question of its authenticity starts from the transmission of the text.[a] It is preserved with Letters *ad Familiares*, but is not contained in our oldest and best manuscript, the Codex Mediceus 49.9. In other manuscripts it occurs after the spurious " Letter of Cicero to Octavian." These facts do not prove that it is spurious, but they place burden of proof equally upon those who accept the authorship of Quintus and those who ascribe it to some later ancient writer. There is no presumption in favour of either.

Although it has the usual epistolary superscription, the document is not a letter but a treatise. At the end Marcus is asked to improve it, as if for publication. Its flat-footed pedagogic style, broken by one ineptly rhetorical patch, is disappointing in the brother whose diction Marcus praised for simple elegance, and whose four extant letters are at least

[a] For the stemmatology see W. S. Watt, *Ciceronis Epistulae* III (Oxford Classical Texts), pp. 180 ff.

lively.[a] Letters, however, cannot provide a proper stylistic criterion for a treatise ; and we have no other prose of Quintus to compare.

More specific arguments have been based on verbal reminiscence. Several passages in the handbook correspond so closely to extant passages of Marcus' lost invective *In toga candida* that one of the two indubitably lifted them from the other.[b] Nearly all these correspondences fall in the rhetorical patch, *Comm.* 8-12 ; and the abrupt stylistic switch would be easier to explain if the handbook were a later work drawing on Marcus' invective. The alternative is to suppose that Quintus capriciously garnished his treatise with some few rhetorical flourishes which, by a lucky chance, came in useful for the impromptu invective of Marcus. This hypothesis seems the less probable of the two ; yet it is not to be rigorously excluded.

Such factual items as the handbook contains might be common knowledge both to Quintus and to a later student of Marcus' speeches.[c] It has been

[a] Cic. *De or.* ii. 10 ; *Ad fam.* xvi. 8, 16, 26, 27.

[b] § 2 : . . . consulatu putari : *In toga cand.*, Asconius 76-77. § 8 : . . . certare non posse : *In toga cand.*, Asconius 74. § 9 : . . . Tanusiorum : compare Asconius 75, summarizing *In toga cand.* (but the list of names has a variant). § 10 : . . . dextra secuerit : *In toga cand.*, Asconius 78. § 10 : . . . manu tulerit : *In toga cand.*, Asconius 80. § 10 : . . . suspicionem relinqueret : *In toga cand.*, Asconius 82. § 12 : . . . sicas destringere : *In toga cand.*, Asconius 83. Further coincidences with speeches may or may not be accidental— § 9 : . . . Quam ob rem ? : *Pro Murena* 73. § 9 : . . . in caede civium : *De har. resp.* 42. § 34 : . . . facultatis habiturus : *Pro Mur.* 44. § 35 : . . . pluris veniunt : *Pro Mur.* 44.

[c] The few details not known to ourselves (mostly in *Comm.* 8-10) might come from *In toga candida* or other lost works.

argued that no later writer would have omitted the
abortive plot of 66 B.C., as the handbook does—
whereas Quintus might, theoretically, have written
before the story leaked.[a] But in fact, most imperial
writers do omit this dim affair ; and an imperial
reader of *In toga candida* would be little impressed by
the brief and oblique allusion to a plot which never
matured.[b] The plot is indispensable only in modern
books ; for antiquity, the argument from silence is
negative.

Positive errors have not been demonstrated ; nor
have doubts been dispelled. Almost certainly (for
instance) the handbook dates Marcus' defence of
Q. Gallius before the election, against the weighty
authority of Asconius.[c] It appears unaware of the
distinction between the genuine Sodalities—religious
or social clubs—and the gangs for electoral bribery
which usurped the name of Sodality, probably not
before 58 B.C.[d] It implies that Marcus had defended
ex-consuls, which he is not known to have done before
63 B.C.[e] It denounces Catiline for the same misdeeds,
including [perhaps] incest with a sister, for which
Marcus denounced Clodius in similar words.[f] The

---

[a] Something, however, was rumoured by July/August,
65 B.C. (Cic. *Pro Sulla* 81).

[b] *In toga cand.*, Asconius 82, beginning " praetereo "
(" I pass over " . . .) ; Asconius supplies the omitted data.
See further *Journ. Rom. Stud.*, 1950, pp. 13 f.

[c] *Comm.* 19 ; Asconius 78. [But see on this J. P. V. D.
Balsdon, in *C.Q.* N.S. xiii (1963), p. 249.—*E.H.W.*]

[d] *Comm.* 19. See further *Journ. Rom. Stud.*, 1950, p. 12.

[e] *Comm.* 2. See R. G. M. Nisbet, *Journ. Rom. Stud.* (1961),
pp. 84-87 (also arguing derivation from *In toga candida*
76-77).

[f] *Comm.* 9 ; *cf.* Cic. *De har. resp.* 42. [But it is doubtful
whether incest is meant in *Comm.* 9. See p. 756.—*E.H.W.*]

reply that incest was a commonplace of invective
would be more relevant if the *commentariolum* were a
speech ; it does nothing to allay suspicion of the
manual's invective repertory. None of these points,
indeed, can be carried to the length of formal proof,
but their cumulative effect is disquieting in a document of dubious transmission.

The question remains : why was the handbook
written ? Manuals addressed as letters were common
in Greek, and two Latin works of Ciceronian date are
cited as parallels. About Varro's *commentarius* of
71 B.C., instructing Pompey in senatorial procedure,
no details are known[a] ; but Marcus Cicero's letter of
59 B.C. to Quintus, on the duties of a provincial governor, has some general likeness to the *commentariolum*.
In particular, both confess that the recipient has
nothing to learn from them[b] ; and therefore the
triteness of the handbook's information is no argument
against its authenticity. Yet Marcus wrote his letter
with a practical purpose—to console Quintus for being
kept in Asia, and exhort him to improve his ways as a
governor. More simply, he wrote because Quintus
was abroad. But in 65/64 Quintus was in Italy, and
presumably with his brother canvassing.[c] At this
time, a plausible reason for pestering Marcus with
platitudes on electioneering is hard to conceive. The
handbook itself seems uncertain of its own purpose ;
it hints at publication, yet includes some items which

[a] Gell. xiv. 7 describes a more general treatment written
thirty or forty years later, after the *commentarius* was lost.

[b] *Comm.* 1 and 58; Cic. *Ad Q.F.* i. 1. 18. (*Cf. Ad Q.F.*
i. 2 for Marcus' more outspoken criticism of Quintus.)

[c] Aedile 65, private senator 64. Had he been prevented
from his canvassing duty, he must surely have referred to the
fact.

could not be published without damage to both brothers.[a]

Alternatively, the *commentariolum* may have been suggested to a later writer by the letter of 59. That the subject should occur to a forger or an essayist would not be surprising. The election of 64 was among the chosen topics of Ciceronian fakes ; bogus replies to *In toga candida* from Antonius and Catiline were circulating more than a century later.[b] Exercises impersonating historical characters on set occasions were taught and practised keenly in higher education.[c] A favourite type was the letter of advice to a great man from a counsellor ; and the picture of Quintus as his brother's counsellor had been painted for posterity by Marcus himself.[d] The theme and the literary interest were ready to hand at any time down to (say) Trajan's reign. What some scholars doubt is whether an imitator could have avoided transparent blunders. Others would attribute higher standards of accomplishment to the ancient art of literary impersonation (*prosopopoeia*).[e]

In the present division of opinion, simple observation may be more useful than argument. Whether Quintus wrote it or not, the *commentariolum* is, as it claims to be, an academic composition, undertaken " for the sake of bringing into one focus, by logical classification, matters which in real life seem dis-

---

[a] *e.g.*, *Comm.* 5, 19, 35, 42, 45-47, 52.

[b] Asconius 84.

[c] Quintilian iii. 8. 48-70, and see further below, p. 794. On supposititious letters, see Sykutris, P.-W. Suppl. V, 202-203 (in art. " Epistolographie ").

[d] Cic. *Post red. in sen.* 37 ; *De or.* i. 4 ; *Ad Q.F.* i. 1. 43.

[e] Compare R. Syme, *Sallust*, p. 324 (discussing the parallel dispute over the *Suasoriae* ascribed to Sallust).

connected and indeterminate." [a]   In the scholastic
tradition, it multiplies categories beyond necessity.[b]
Its practical advice is superfluous, as it admits, and
often inept or naïve : for instance, Marcus is to tell
the " Optimate " nobles (who detested Pompey) that
he had posed as " Popular " only to get Pompey's
support.[c] As it also implies, it is written in leisured
circumstances.[d] Its comments and aphorisms, though
sometimes vivacious, lack the sense of urgency.
Marcus, in two letters of 65 B.C., reveals the personal
pressures and shifting odds within the electorate,
which he later compared to the deep sea surge [e] ;
the handbook presents a blueprint of the perfect
canvass in which every good citizen will vote for
Marcus. Whatever its date, the attempt to reduce a
Roman election to terms of an armchair exercise is
deliberate and successful.

[The author in § 58 refers to his work as *commentariolum petitionis*. This title or designation appears
as *Commentarium Consulatus Petitionis* in the better
MSS., as *De Petitione Consulatus* in inferior MSS., which
also say that the work is Quintus Cicero's addressed
to his brother Marcus.

That the author was not Quintus Cicero was argued
long ago by A. Eussner, *Comment. Pet. examinatum*

[a] *Comm.* 1.
[b] *E.g.*, in *Comm.* 34, the senseless distinction between
salutatores, *deductores*, and *adsectatores* ; or, in *Comm.* 49,
the still more ludicrous preoccupation with *distributio*.
[c] *Comm.* 5. For Marcus' very different view of the absent
Pompey's standpoint see Cic. *Ad Att.* i. 1. 2, with D. R.
Shackleton Bailey's comment.
[d] *Comm.* 58.
[e] Cic. *Ad Att.* i. 1 and 2 ; *Pro Planc.* 15.

atque emendatum, Würzburg, 1872, and by G. L. Hendrickson, in *Amer. Journ. of Philol.* xiii (1892), pp. 200-212, and *The Comm. Pet. attributed to Q. Cicero*, Univ. of Chicago, 1904 ; and the attribution was defended by others (see, *e.g.*, R. Y. Tyrrell and L. C. Purser, *The Correspondence of Cicero*, I, ed. 3, 1904, pp. 116-132. Recently it was defended vigorously by E. H. Clift, *Latin Pseudepigrapha*, Baltimore, 1945 and supported by R. Till in *Historia*, xi (1962), pp. 315-338. But Mrs. Henderson (of whose arguments Till does not take account), in *Journ. of Roman Studies*, xl (1950), pp. 8-21, presented a cogent case against it (cp. R. G. M. Nisbet, " *The Comm. Pet.* : Some arguments against authenticity," in *Journ. of Roman Studies*, li (1961), pp. 84-87 ; W. S. Watt, *M. Tull. Cic. Epp.* Vol. III, 1958, p. 179). Her arguments were criticized by J. P. V. D. Balsdon in *Classical Quarterly*, lvi = N.S. xiii (1963), pp. 242-250, and we now have what she wrote, by way of introduction to the *Comm. Pet.*, for the Loeb Classical Library. She had modified her attitude. In any case the matter must be left undecided.

For the text we rely on the following codices :

Harleianus 2682 (in the British Museum), 11th cent. (H)

Berolinensis Lat. fol. 252 (at present in Tübingen), 12th cent. (F)

Palatinus Lat. 598 (in the Vatican), 15th cent. (D)

Parisinus Lat. 14761, 15th cent. (V)

W. S. Watt takes account also of :

Canonicianus Class. Lat. 210 (at Oxford), 15th cent. (B)

There are a number of other MSS. of the same class

as V and B. The whole tradition is derived from a lost archetype (X).

The text of Books ix-xvi of Cicero's *Epistulae ad Familiares* is based on the same tradition and also on the very old and good Codex Mediceus 49.9 which does not include the *Commentariolum Pet.*

SELECT BIBLIOGRAPHY FOR THE *COMMENTARIOLUM*
AND FOR THE *EPISTULA*

A. Eussner, *Commentariolum Petitionis examinatum atque emendatum.* Würzburg, 1872.

H. Sjögren, *Epistulae ad Quintum fratrem, Comm. Pet.,* etc. Leipzig, 1914.

W. S. Watt, *M. Tulli Ciceronis Epistulae* Vol. III. . . . Accedunt Commentariolum Petitionis et Pseudo-Ciceronis Epistula ad Octavianum. Oxford, 1958.

Rosa Lamacchia, *Pseudo-Ciceronis Epistula ad Octavianum.* Rome, 1967 ; [*M. Tulli Ciceronis*] *Epistola ad Octavianum.* Florence, 1968.

G. L. Hendrickson in *Amer. Journ. of Philol.* xiii (1892), pp. 200 ff. ; and *The Comm. Pet. attributed to Q. Cicero.* Decenn. Publ. of the Univ. of Chicago, 1st Ser. VI, 1904.

R. Y. Tyrrell and L. C. Purser, *The Correspondence of Cicero*, I³, 1904, pp. 116 ff.

H. Sjögren, in *Eranos*, 1913, pp. 112 ff.

W. S. Watt, in *Classical Quarterly*, N.S. viii (1958), pp. 25 ff.

Rosa Lamacchia, in *Stud. It. Fil. Class.* xxxv (1963), pp. 228 ff.

M. I. Henderson, in *Journ. of Rom. Stud.* xl (1950), pp. 8 ff.

R. G. M. Nisbet in *Journ. of Rom. Stud.* li (1961), pp. 84 ff.

J. P. V. D. Balsdon in *Classical Quarterly*, N.S. xiii (1963), pp. 242 ff.—[*E. H. W.*]]

COMMENTARIOLUM PETITIONIS

QUINTUS MARCO FRATRI S. D.

1. 1   Etsi tibi omnia suppetunt ea quae consequi ingenio
aut usu homines aut diligentia[1] possunt, tamen amore
nostro non sum alienum arbitratus ad te perscribere
ea quae mihi veniebant in mentem dies ac noctes
de petitione tua cogitanti, non ut aliquid ex his novi
addisceres,[2] sed ut ea quae in re dispersa atque
infinita viderentur esse ratione et distributione sub
uno aspectu ponerentur.   Quamquam plurimum
natura valet, tamen videtur in paucorum mensum
negotio posse simulatio naturam[3] vincere.

2   Civitas quae sit cogita, quid petas, qui sis. Prope[4]
cottidie tibi hoc ad forum descendenti meditandum
est[5] : " Novus sum, consulatum peto, Roma est."

Nominis novitatem dicendi gloria maxime suble-
vabis. Semper ea res plurimum dignitatis habuit ;
non potest qui dignus habetur patronus consularium
indignus consulatu putari. Quam ob rem quoniam ab
hac laude proficisceris et quicquid es ex hoc es, ita pa-

----

[1] *var. lect.* intelligentia.

[2] addisceres *Lambinus* : addiscerem.

[3] naturam *ed. Romana* : naturarum. *Puteanus transfers
the sentence* quamquam . . . vincere *to § 42, after* videare.

[4] *Variously altered by scholars.*

[5] est *Tydeman* : sit.

----

[a] [In her translation Mrs. Henderson used " commoner "

HANDBOOK OF ELECTIONEERING

QUINTUS TO HIS BROTHER MARCUS

ALTHOUGH you are furnished with all that men can 1. 1
acquire by ability, experience, or application, I
thought it in keeping with our affection to write in
full to you what has been coming into my mind as I
think day and night about your canvass—not that
you would learn anything new from it, but for the
sake of bringing into one focus, by logical classification, matters which in real life seem disconnected and
indeterminate. Though nature is strong indeed, yet
an assumed personality can, it seems, overcome the
natural self for an affair of a few months.

Consider what city this is, what is it you seek, who 2
you are. Every day or so, as you go down to the
Forum, you must repeat to yourself : " I am ' new ' ᵃ;
I seek the consulship ; this is Rome."

For your status as a " new man " you will compen-
sate chiefly by your fame as a speaker. Great prestige
has always attached to this ; an advocate deemed
worthy to defend ex-consuls cannot be thought unworthy of the consulship. Therefore—since you
start with this repute, and are what you are because

to render *novus homo* (the first member of any *gens* or family
to gain curule office). I have substituted " new man," the
alternative rendering which she herself gives in her Introduction to the *Commentariolum*.—*E.H.W.*]

ratus ad dicendum venito quasi in singulis causis iudi-
3 cium de omni ingenio futurum sit. Eius facultatis ad-
iumenta, quae tibi scio esse seposita, ut parata ac
prompta sint cura, et saepe quae ⟨de⟩ Demosthenis
studio et exercitatione scripsit Demetrius recordare.
Deinde ⟨fac⟩ ut amicorum et multitudo et genera ap-
pareant ; habes enim ea quae ⟨qui⟩ novi habuerunt ?—
omnis publicanos, totum fere equestrem ordinem,
multa propria municipia, multos abs te defensos
homines cuiusque ordinis, aliquot conlegia, praeterea
studio dicendi conciliatos plurimos adulescentulos, cot-
tidianam amicorum adsiduitatem et frequentiam.
4 Haec cura ut teneas commonendo[1] et rogando et omni
ratione efficiendo ut intellegant qui debent tua causa,
referendae gratiae, qui volunt, obligandi tui tempus
sibi aliud nullum fore. Etiam hoc multum videtur
adiuvare posse novum hominem, hominum nobilium
voluntas et maxime consularium ; prodest, quorum
in locum ac numerum pervenire velis, ab iis ipsis illo
5 loco ac numero dignum putari. Ii rogandi omnes sunt
diligenter et ad eos adlegandum est persuadendum-
que est iis nos semper cum optimatibus de re publica
sensisse, minime popularis fuisse ; si quid locuti po-
pulariter videamur, id nos eo consilio fecisse ut nobis
Cn. Pompeium adiungeremus, ut eum qui plurimum
posset aut amicum in nostra petitione haberemus aut
6 certe non adversarium. Praeterea adulescentis nobilis

---

[1] commonendo *Koch* : commendo *or* commendando.

---

[a] See Cic. *De div.* ii. 96 : by practising, Demosthenes
learned to pronounce R.   [b] See Introduction, pp. 740, 746.

of it—present yourself as well prepared for your speeches as if all your intellectual powers were to be judged on each single case. Take care that the aids 3 to eloquence, which I know you have in reserve, are ready to hand; and often remind yourself what Demetrius wrote of Demosthenes' efforts and exercises.[a] Then, see to it that you show off both the number and the variety of your friends, for how many " new men " have had as many as *you* have ?— all the contractors of public revenues, virtually all the Order of Knights, many boroughs in your pocket, many men of all ranks whom you have defended at law, several Colleges ; also, large numbers of young men drawn to you by the pursuit of oratory, and a crowd of friends in daily and constant attendance. See that you hold on by admonitions, requests, or 4 any other means of making it clear that there will never be another chance for those who owe you a debt to thank you, or for the well-disposed to put you under an obligation to themselves. Further, a " new man " can be greatly helped by the good will of nobles, and especially of the ex-consuls ; it is an advantage that those whose position and company you wish to attain should think you worthy of that position and company. They must all be diligently 5 canvassed, and you must send friends to persuade them that our political sympathies have always been with the " Optimates " ; we have been far from " Popular " in politics [b] ; if we ever appear to have spoken in a " Popular " way, we did it with the purpose of attaching Gnaeus Pompey to ourselves, in order to have him, with his very great power, as a friend in our canvass, or at least not an opponent. Take pains, besides, to acquire young nobles, or 6

elabora ut habeas, vel ut teneas studiosos quos habes ;
multum dignitatis adferent. Plurimos habes ; perfice
ut sciant quantum in iis putes esse. Si adduxeris ut
ii qui non nolunt cupiant, plurimum proderunt.[1]

2. 7 Ac multum etiam novitatem tuam adiuvat quod
eius modi nobiles tecum petunt ut nemo sit qui audeat
dicere plus illis nobilitatem quam tibi virtutem pro-
desse oportere. Nam P. Galbam et L. Cassium
summo loco natos quis est qui petere consulatum
putet ? Vides igitur amplissimis ex familiis homines,
8 quod sine nervis sint, tibi paris non esse. At Antonius
et Catilina molesti sunt. Immo homini navo,[2] in-
dustrio, innocenti, diserto, gratioso apud eos qui res
iudicant, optandi competitores ambo a pueritia sicarii,
ambo libidinosi, ambo egentes. Eorum alterius bona
proscripta vidimus, vocem denique audivimus iurantis
se Romae iudicio aequo cum homine Graeco certare
non posse, ex senatu eiectum scimus optimorum[3]
censorum existimatione, in praetura competitorem
habuimus amico Sabidio et Panthera, cum[4] ad tabulam quos poneret non haberet (quo tamen in magistratu amicam quam domi palam haberet de machinis
emit) ; in petitione autem consulatus caupones[5] omnis
compilare per turpissimam legationem maluit quam
9 adesse et populo Romano supplicare. Alter vero, di

---

[1] *Facciolati proposed* proderit.
[2] navo *Puteanus* : novo.
[3] optimorum *Eussner* : optima vero.
[4] cum *Lambinus* : quom iam *Constans* : quam (quod . . .
habebat *B*).
[5] caupadoces *H¹ F* : Cappadoces *Buecheler*.

---

[a] See Asconius 72 ; Cic. *Pro Mur.* 17 ; *Ad Att.* i. 1. 1.
[b] Antonius (Asconius 75).

rather to keep the enthusiasm of those whom you
have acquired ; they will bring you great prestige.
You have acquired a large number ; make them
realize how important you think them. If you can
bring those who are not against you to be eager for
you, they will be most useful to you.

Another great help for your status as a " new 2. 7
man " is that your noble competitors are persons of
whom nobody would venture to say that they should
get more from their rank than you from your moral
excellence. Who would think that Publius Galba
and Lucius Cassius, high-born as they are, are candidates for the consulship ? [a] So you see that men of
the greatest families are not equal to you, because
they lack vigour. Or are Antonius and Catiline sup- 8
posed to be the trouble ? On the contrary, two
assassins from boyhood, both libertines, both paupers,
are just the competitors to be prayed for by a man of
energy, industry, and blameless life, an eloquent
speaker, with influence among those who judge in
the law-courts. Of those two, we have seen the
one [b] sold up by legal process ; we have heard him
declare an oath that he cannot compete in fair trial
in Rome against a Greek ; we know he was expelled
from the Senate by the decision of admirable censors.
He was a fellow-candidate of ours for the praetorship,
when Sabidius and Panthera were his only friends,
when he had no slaves left to auction off (but, in
that praetorship he did buy from the stands in the
slave-market a girl-friend to keep openly at home).
In consular candidature, rather than present himself
to solicit the votes of the Roman People, he preferred
a most wicked mission abroad, where he plundered
all the innkeepers. As to the other, good heavens ! 9

boni ! quo splendore est ? Primum nobilitate **eadem**
qua †Catilina†.[1] Num maiore ? Non. Sed virtute.
Quam ob rem? Quod Antonius[2] umbram suam metuit,
hic ne leges quidem, natus in patris egestate, educatus
in sororiis[3] stupris, corroboratus in caede civium, cuius
primus ad rem publicam aditus in equitibus R. occi-
dendis fuit (nam illis quos meminimus Gallis, qui tum
Titiniorum ac Nanneiorum[4] ac Tanusiorum capita
demetebant,[5] Sulla unum Catilinam praefecerat) ;
in quibus ille hominem optimum, Q. Caecilium, sororis
suae virum, equitem Romanum, nullarum partium,
cum semper natura tum etiam aetate iam quietum,
3. 10 suis manibus occidit. Quid ego nunc dicam petere
eum tecum consulatum qui hominem carissimum
populo Romano, M. Marium, inspectante populo
Romano vitibus per totam urbem ceciderit, ad bustum
egerit, ibi omni cruciatu lacerarit, vivo stanti collum
gladio sua dextera secuerit, cum sinistra capillum
eius a vertice teneret, caput sua manu tulerit, cum
inter digitos eius rivi sanguinis fluerent ; qui postea
cum histrionibus et cum gladiatoribus ita vixit ut
alteros libidinis, alteros facinoris adiutores haberet ;
qui nullum in locum tam sanctum ac tam religiosum
accessit in quo non, etiam si in aliis culpa non esset,

---

[1] C. Antonius *Manutius*. *The right name was ousted by*
Catilina, *which, as Watt suggests, may have been a gloss on*
alter. [2] C. Antonius *Corradus* : manius.
[3] sororiis *Watt* : sororis *B* : sorore *or* sororum.
[4] nanniorum *codices* (*F has* mannorum): Manliorum
Buecheler. [5] demetebant *Verburgius* : demebant.

---

[a] ["in debauchery of his sister," Mrs. Henderson. I trans-
late Watt's *sororiis* and assume that the reference is to the
relations of that sister with other men than her brother.—
E.H.W. But Watt agrees with Mrs. Henderson's interpretation.]

What is his claim to glory ? First, he has the same
noble birth [as Antonius]. Any greater nobility ?
No. But he has greater manliness. Why ? Only because Antonius is afraid of his own shadow, whereas
Catiline does not even fear the law. Born in his
father's beggary, bred in his sister's debauchery,[a]
grown up in civil slaughter, his first entry into public
life was a massacre of Roman Knights (for Sulla
had put Catiline in sole charge of those Gauls we
remember, who kept mowing off the heads of Titi-
nius and Nanneius and Tanusius and all). Among
them he killed with his own hands his sister's husband,
the excellent Quintus Caecilius, a Roman Knight, a
neutral in politics, a man always inoffensive by
nature and by that time also through advancing age.
Need I go on ? *He* to be running for the consulship 3. 10
with you—he who scourged Marcus Marius, the
Roman People's darling, all around the town before
the Roman People's eyes, drove him to the tomb,[b]
mangled him there with every torture, and with a
sword in his right hand, holding his head of hair in
his left, severed the man's neck as he stood there
alive, and carried the head in his hand, while rills of
blood flowed between his fingers ! And then he lived
with actors and gladiators as his accomplices, the
former in lust, the latter in crime—he who could not
enter any place so sacred and holy that he did not
leave it under suspicion of being polluted by his mere
wickedness, even if other people were guiltless ; who

[b] M. Marius Gratidianus, a partisan of the great Marius,
was killed in 82 B.C. by the Sullan Catiline at the tomb of
Catulus, who had been forced to suicide by the Marians in
87. The *commentariolum* omits the genitive Catuli (*Journ.
Rom. Stud.*, 1961, pp. 86 f.).

tamen ex sua nequitia dedecoris suspicionem relinqueret ; qui ex curia Curios et Annios, ab atriis
Sapalas[1] et Carvilios, ex equestri ordine Pompilios et
Vettios sibi amicissimos comparavit[2] ; qui tantum
habet audaciae, tantum nequitiae, tantum denique in
libidine artis et efficacitatis, ut prope in parentum
gremiis praetextatos liberos constuprarit ? Quid ego
nunc tibi de Africa, quid de testium dictis scribam ?
Nota sunt, et ea tu saepius legito ; sed tamen hoc
mihi non praetermittendum videtur, quod primum ex
eo iudicio tam egens discessit quam quidam iudices
eius ante illud iudicium fuerunt, deinde tam invidiosus
ut aliud in eum iudicium cottidie flagitetur. Hic se
sic habet ut magis timeant,[3] etiam si quierit, quam
11 ut contemnant,[3] si quid commoverit. Quanto melior
tibi fortuna petitionis data est quam nuper homini
novo, C. Coelio ! ille cum duobus hominibus ita nobi-
lissimis petebat ut tamen in iis omnia pluris essent
quam ipsa nobilitas, summa ingenia, summus pudor,
plurima beneficia, summa ratio ac diligentia petendi;
ac tamen eorum alterum Coelius, cum multo inferior esset genere, superior nulla re paene, superavit.
12 Qua re tibi, si facies ea quae natura et studia quibus
semper usus es largiuntur, quae temporis tui ratio
desiderat, quae potes, quae debes, non erit difficile
certamen cum iis competitoribus qui nequaquam
sunt tam genere insignes quam vitiis nobiles[4] ; quis

---

[1] Scapulas *Puteanus.*
[2] comparavit *Squarzaficus* : comparavit.
[3] timeant . . . contemnant *Tydeman* : -at . . . -at.
[4] *Perhaps* notabiles.

got as his closest friends from the senate-house men like Curius and Annius, from the auctioneers' halls men like Sapala and Carvilius, from the Order of Knights men like Pompilius and Vettius ; who has such impudence, such wickedness, and besides such skill and efficiency in his lust that he has raped children in smocks practically at their parents' knees. Need I write now to you of Africa and the statements of the witnesses ? All *that* is well known ; read it yourself, again and again. Yet this, I think, I should not leave out—that he came out of that trial as impoverished as some of his jury were before that trial, and so hated that there are daily clamours for another prosecution against him.[a] His condition is such that, so far from ignoring him if he makes trouble, people fear him even if he is doing nothing. How much 11 better luck has fallen to you in your canvass than to C. Coelius, another " new man," a while ago ![b] He stood against two men of the highest nobility, yet whose nobility was the least of their assets—great intelligence, high conscience, many claims to gratitude, great judgement and perseverance in electioneering ; yet Coelius, though much inferior in birth and superior in almost nothing, defeated one of them. So for you, if you do what you are well endowed for 12 doing by nature and by the studies which you have always practised—what the occasion demands, what you can and should do—it will not be a hard contest with these competitors who are by no means as eminent in birth as they are notable in vice. Can

[a] Catiline was tried in July/August, 65 B.C. for misgovernment in Africa and acquitted through bribery.
[b] C. Coelius Caldus, consul in 94 B.C. with L. Domitius Ahenobarbus (the unsuccessful noble is unknown).

enim reperiri potest tam improbus civis qui velit uno
suffragio duas in rem publicam sicas destringere ?

4. 13 Quoniam quae subsidia novitatis haberes et habere
posses exposui, nunc de magnitudine petitionis dicendum videtur. Consulatum petis, quo honore nemo
est quin te dignum arbitretur, sed multi qui invideant;
petis enim homo ex equestri loco summum locum
civitatis atque ita summum ut forti homini, diserto,
innocenti multo idem ille honos plus amplitudinis
quam ceteris adferat. Noli putare eos qui sunt eo
honore usi non videre, tu cum idem sis adeptus, quid
dignitatis habiturus sis. Eos vero qui consularibus
familiis nati locum maiorum consecuti non sunt suspicor tibi, nisi si qui admodum te amant, invidere.
Etiam novos homines praetorios existimo, nisi qui tuo
beneficio vincti sunt, nolle abs te se honore superari.

14 Iam in populo quam multi invidi sint, quam multi
consuetudine horum annorum ab hominibus[1] novis
alienati, venire tibi in mentem certo scio ; esse etiam
non nullos tibi iratos ex iis causis quas egisti necesse
est. Iam illud tute circumspicito, quod ad Cn. Pompei gloriam augendam tanto studio te dedisti, num
quos tibi putes ob eam causam esse ⟨non⟩ amicos.[2]

15 Quam ob rem cum et summum locum civitatis petas
et videas esse studia quae tibi adversentur, adhibeas
necesse est omnem rationem et curam et laborem et
diligentiam.

5. 16 Et petitio magistratuum divisa est in duarum

---

[1] hominibus *Squarzaficus* : honoribus.
[2] esse ⟨non⟩ amicos *Lambinus* : ⟨non⟩ esse amicos
Turnebus : esse inimicos *Petreius*.

there be a citizen so vile as to want to unsheathe, with one vote, two daggers against the State?

Having explained what compensations for your 4. 13 status as a " new man " you have or could have, I think I should speak of the importance of this canvass. You seek the consulship, and there is nobody who does not think you worthy of the office, but many who envy you. You, by origin a Knight, seek the highest place in the body politic—the highest, and to a brave, accomplished, and upright man this office brings far more dignity than to any others. Do not think that those who have held the office will fail to see how much prestige will be yours when you have reached it. Men of consular families who have not risen to the position of their ancestors envy you, I suspect, unless they are very fond of you ; and I think " new men " of praetorian standing, unless attached to you by your kindnesses, do not want to be surpassed by you in rank. Then, how many among 14 the people are envious, how many, in the fashion of these years, are averse to " new men," is a point which occurs to you, I am quite sure ; and a good many must be angry with you in consequence of the cases that you have pleaded. Then, turn your thoughts to this : do you not think that certain people will be less than friendly because of your devoted efforts to glorify Pompey ? [a] Therefore, 15 since you seek the highest place in the body politic, and since you see that there are interests opposed to you, it is necessary to apply all your judgement and care and effort and attentiveness.

Canvassing for magistracies is classified as atten- 5. 16

[a] See Introduction, pp. 740, 746, and Cicero's speech *De imperio Cn. Pompei* (66 B.C.).

rationum diligentiam, quarum altera in amicorum
studiis, altera in populari voluntate ponenda est.
Amicorum studia beneficiis et officiis et vetustate et
facilitate ac iucunditate naturae parta esse oportet.
Sed hoc nomen amicorum in petitione latius patet
quam in cetera vita ; quisquis est enim qui ostendat
aliquid in te voluntatis, qui colat, qui domum ventitet,
is in amicorum numero est habendus. Sed tamen qui
sunt amici ex causa iustiore cognationis aut adfinitatis
aut sodalitatis aut alicuius necessitudinis, iis carum
17 et iucundum esse maxime prodest. Deinde ut quisque
est intimus ac maxime domesticus, ut is amet ⟨et⟩
quam amplissimum esse te cupiat valde elaborandum
est, tum ut tribules, ut vicini, ut clientes, ut denique
liberti, postremo etiam servi tui ; nam fere omnis
sermo ad forensem famam a domesticis emanat
18 auctoribus. Deinde sunt instituendi cuiusque generis
amici : ad speciem, homines inlustres honore ac
nomine (qui, etiam, si suffragandi studia non navant,
tamen adferunt petitori aliquid dignitatis) ; ad ius
obtinendum, magistratus (ex quibus maxime consules,[1] deinde tribuni pl.) ; ad conficiendas centurias,
homines excellenti gratia. Qui abs te tribum aut
centuriam aut aliquod beneficium aut habeant aut ut
habeant sperent, eos prorsus magno opere et compara
et confirma ; nam per hos annos homines ambitiosi

---

[1] consules *Squarzaficus* : consul.

---

[a] Here used in its proper sense of a religious or social club.
[The author may simply mean "ties of friendship."—*E.H.W.*]
[b] The Roman citizen body was divided into local tribes.
which were also voting units.

tiveness to two objects, the one concerned with securing support of friends, the other with securing favour of the People. The endeavours of friends should be enlisted by kindnesses and observance of duties and old acquaintance and affability and natural charm. But that word " friends " has a wider application in a canvass than in the rest of life, for anybody who shows you some good will, or cultivates your society, or calls upon you regularly, is to be counted as a " friend." Still, it is very useful to be on affectionate and pleasant terms with those who are friends on more genuine grounds—ties of blood or marriage, fellowship in a Sodality,[a] or some other bond. Next, all those who are nearest and most in 17 your family circle must with every effort be brought to feel affection and wish you all possible success ; so too must your fellow-tribesmen,[b] neighbours, and clients, then your freedmen, and finally even your slaves, for the talk which makes one's public reputation generally emanates from sources in one's own household. Then, you must set up friends of every 18 sort : for show, men of illustrious career and name (who bring a candidate some prestige, even if they do not take an active interest in canvassing) ; to maintain your legal rights, magistrates (especially the consuls ; next the tribunes of the People) ; for getting the votes of the centuries,[c] persons of exceptional influence. Take special pains to recruit and retain those who have from you, or hope to have, control of a tribe or a century, or some other advantage ; for in these days, electioneering experts have

[c] The centuries were the group-units of voting in the major form of assembly (how they were integrated with the tribes is uncertain).

vehementer omni studio atque opera elaborarunt[1] ut
possent a tribulibus suis ea quae peterent impetrare ;
hos tu homines, quibuscumque poteris rationibus, ut
ex animo atque [ex illa][2] summa voluntate tui studiosi
19 sint elaborato. Quod si satis grati homines essent,
haec tibi omnia parata esse debebant, sicuti parata
esse confido. Nam hoc biennio quattuor sodalitates
hominum ad ambitionem gratiosissimorum tibi obli-
gasti, C. Fundani, Q. Galli, C. Corneli, C. Orchivi ;
horum in causis ad te deferendis quid tibi eorum
sodales receperint et confirmarint scio, nam interfui ;
qua re hoc tibi faciendum est, hoc tempore ut ab his
quod debent exigas saepe commonendo, rogando,
confirmando, curando ut intellegant nullum se umquam aliud tempus habituros referendae gratiae ;
profecto homines[3] et spe reliquorum tuorum officiorum
et[iam] recentibus beneficiis ad studium navandum
20 excitabuntur. Et omnino, quoniam eo genere ami-
citiarum petitio tua maxime munita est quod ex
causarum defensionibus adeptus es, fac ut plane iis
omnibus quos devinctos tenes discriptum ac disposi-
tum suum cuique munus sit ; et quem ad modum nemini illorum molestus nulla in re umquam fuisti, sic
cura ut intellegant omnia te quae ab illis tibi deberi
6. 21 putaris ad hoc tempus reservasse. Sed quoniam tribus
rebus homines maxime ad benevolentiam atque haec
suffragandi studia ducuntur,[4] beneficio, spe, adiunc-

---

[1] elaborarunt *Turnebus* : laborarunt *or* laborant.
[2] *Deleted by Watt.*
[3] hi omnes *Buecheler.*
[4] adducuntur *Lambinus.*

---

[a] Here " Sodality " is used in its usurped sense of a gang
for electoral bribery. [But *sodalitates* here may mean
religious fellowships or simply mean ordinary friendships.

worked out, with all their eager will and resources,
how to get what they want from their fellow-tribesmen.
Work by any means you can to make these persons
sincere and whole-hearted supporters of your cause.
However, if people were grateful enough, all this 19
should have been arranged for you, as I am sure it
has ; for in these last two years you have laid under
obligation four Sodalities run by men of great
influence in electioneering,[a] C. Fundanius, Q. Gallius,
C. Cornelius, and C. Orchivius. I know (for I was
present) what the members of the Sodalities undertook and assured for you when they entrusted you
with the briefs for these four. So what you have to
do is to exact from them on this occasion what they
owe you by frequent admonitions, requests, assur-
ances, making it clear that they will never have
another chance to thank you. They will surely be
spurred to active interest by the hope of your good
offices in future and by your recent services. In 20
general, since your campaign is amply supported by
the kind of friendship which you have acquired by
defending cases, make quite sure that a particular
duty is apportioned and assigned to each of all whom
you have laid under obligation ; and since you have
never before troubled any of them for anything, make
it clear that you have kept in reserve for this occasion
all your claims to what in you opinion they owe you.
Now, since men are brought to good will and this 6. 21
interest in electoral support by three things in particular—benefits received, expectations, and spon-

Cp. J. P. V. D. Balsdon in *C.Q.*, N.S. xiii, p. 247.—*E.H.W.*]
Cornelius, defended by Marcus in 65 B.C., ran a gang of this
kind (Cic. *Pro Corn.*, Asconius 67 ; *Ad Q.F.* ii. 3. 5 ; *In
Vat.* 5).

tione animi ac voluntate, animadvertendum est quem
ad modum cuique horum generi sit inserviendum.
Minimis beneficiis homines adducuntur ut satis causae
putent esse ad studium suffragationis, nedum ii
quibus saluti fuisti, quos tu habes plurimos, non
intellegant, si hoc tuo tempore tibi non satis fecerint,
se probatos nemini umquam fore ; quod cum ita sit,
tamen rogandi sunt atque etiam in hanc opinionem
adducendi ut, qui adhuc nobis obligati fuerint, iis
22 vicissim nos obligari posse videamur. Qui autem spe
tenentur, quod genus hominum multo etiam est[1]
diligentius atque officiosius, iis fac ut propositum[2] ac
paratum auxilium tuum esse videatur, denique ut
spectatorem te suorum officiorum esse intellegant
diligentem, ut videre te plane atque animadvertere
23 quantum a quoque proficiscatur appareat. Tertium
illud genus est studiorum[3] voluntarium, quod agendis
gratiis, accommodandis sermonibus ad eas rationes
propter quas quisque studiosus tui esse videbitur,
significanda erga illos pari voluntate, adducenda amicitia in spem familiaritatis et consuetudinis confirmari
oportebit. Atque in his omnibus generibus iudicato
et perpendito quantum quisque possit, ut scias et
quem ad modum cuique inservias et quid a quoque
24 exspectes ac postules. Sunt enim quidam homines in
suis vicinitatibus et municipiis gratiosi, sunt diligentes
et copiosi qui, etiam si antea non studuerunt huic
gratiae, tamen ex tempore elaborare eius causa cui
debent aut volunt facile possunt ; his hominum
generibus sic inserviendum est ut ipsi intellegant te
videre quid a quoque exspectes, sentire quid accipias,

---

[1] etiam est *Gruter* : etiam si.
[2] promptum *suggested by Ernesti.*
[3] studiosorum *Koch* : *Buecheler deletes.*

taneous personal attachment—we must consider how
to deal favourably with each of these categories. Very
small benefits induce men to think that they have
sufficient cause to support a canvass—much more
would those (and you have a large number thus in
your debt) whom you have saved from ruin understand that if they do not do their duty by you on this
special occasion, nobody will ever respect them ; but
even so, you must solicit them and also bring them to
believe that we in our turn may be obliged to those
who have hitherto been obliged to us. As to those 22
who are attached to us by their expectations—a far
more painstaking and devoted category of persons
—make them perceive that your help is ready at hand
for them ; also let them see that you are watching
their services carefully, that you look and notice
exactly how much comes of each of them. The third 23
category, of the voluntary helpers, will have to be
encouraged by thanks, by adapting what you say to
the considerations why each person will appear keen
for your interests, by indicating that you return
their good will, by carrying the acquaintance to a
hope of close intimacy. In all these categories,
judge and ponder each man's capacity, in order to
know how you should cultivate him and what you
should expect or demand of him. For there are men 24
of influence in their own neighbourhoods and towns,
persistent and prosperous persons who, even if they
have not felt inclined to exercise their influence
before, still can easily make efforts at a moment's
notice for someone to whom they are indebted or
well disposed. In cultivating these kinds of men,
let them understand that you know what to expect
of each, realize what you get, and remember what

o

meminisse quid acceperis. Sunt autem alii qui aut
nihil possunt aut etiam odio sunt tribulibus suis nec
habent tantum animi ac facultatis ut enitantur ex
tempore ; hos ut internoscas videto, ne spe in aliquo
maiore posita praesidi parum comparetur.

7. 25 Et quamquam partis ac fundatis amicitiis fretum ac
munitum esse oportet, tamen in ipsa petitione amicitiae permultae ac perutiles comparantur ; nam in
ceteris molestiis habet hoc tamen petitio commodi :
potes honeste, quod in cetera vita non queas, quoscumque velis adiungere ad amicitiam, quibuscum si
alio tempore agas ut te utantur, absurde facere
videare, in petitione autem nisi id agas et cum multis
26 et diligenter, nullus petitor esse videare. Ego autem
tibi hoc confirmo, esse neminem, nisi si aliqua necessitudine competitorum alicui tuorum sit adiunctus, a
quo non facile si contenderis impetrare possis ut suo
beneficio promereatur se ut ames et sibi ut debeas,
modo ut intellegat te magni se aestimare,[1] ex animo
agere, bene se ponere, fore ex eo non brevem et
suffragatoriam sed firmam et perpetuam amicitiam.
27 Nemo erit, mihi crede, in quo modo aliquid sit, qui
hoc tempus sibi oblatum amicitiae tecum constituen-
dae praetermittat, praesertim cum tibi hoc casus
adferat, ut ii tecum petant quorum amicitia aut con-
temnenda aut fugienda sit, et qui hoc quod ego te
hortor non modo adsequi sed ne incipere quidem
28 possint. Nam qui[2] incipiat Antonius homines adiungere atque invitare ad amicitiam quos per se suo
nomine appellare non possit ? mihi quidem nihil

---

[1] magni se aestimare *Koch*. *The* mss. *vary*.
[2] qui *Gesner* : quid.

you have got. But there are others who count for nothing or who are actually disliked by their fellow-tribesmen, and have not the spirit or talent for improvisation. Be sure to distinguish these, lest by placing too great a hope in somebody you may get too little help.

Again, while you should be supported and fortified 7. 25 by friendships already formed and established, many useful friendships are acquired in the canvass itself, since a canvass, for all its nuisances, has the convenience that you can make friends of any people you wish without disgrace, which you cannot do in the rest of life. If at some other time you were to exert yourself to court friendship with them, you would seem to act in bad taste ; but in a canvass you would be thought a very poor candidate if you did not so act and with vigour too in connection with many such people. But *I* assure you that there is nobody (unless 26 closely connected with one of your competitors in some way) whom you cannot easily induce, if you try, to earn your affection and obligation to him by doing you a good turn—that is, if he conceives that you value him highly, that you are sincere, that it is a good investment for him, that the result will not be a brief vote-catching friendship but a solid and permanent one. Believe me, there will be nobody, in so 27 far as he is of the least intelligence, who will miss this opportunity offered to him of setting up a friendship with you, especially as chance gives you competitors whose friendship is to be despised or shunned, and who cannot even begin—let alone accomplish—what I am urging you to do. For how should Antonius begin to 28 attach or invite to his friendship people whom he cannot call by their names without a prompter ? To

stultius videtur quam existimare esse eum studiosum
tui quem non noris. Eximiam quandam gloriam et
dignitatem ac rerum gestarum magnitudinem esse
oportet in eo quem homines ignoti nullis suffragantibus
honore adficiant ; ut quidem homo nequam,[1] iners,
sine officio, sine ingenio, cum[2] infamia, nullis amicis,
hominem plurimorum studio atque omnium bona
existimatione munitum praecurrat, sine magna culpa
8. 29 neglegentiae fieri non potest. Quam ob rem omnis
centurias multis et variis amicitiis cura ut confirmatas
habeas. Et primum, id quod ante oculos est, senatores equitesque Romanos, ceterorum ⟨ordinum⟩
omnium[3] navos homines et gratiosos complectere.
Multi homines urbani industrii, multi libertini in foro
gratiosi navique versantur ; quos per te, quos per
communis amicos poteris, summa cura ut cupidi tui
sint elaborato, appetito, adlegato, summo beneficio
30 te adfici ostendito. Deinde habeto rationem urbis
totius, conlegiorum omnium,[4] pagorum, vicinitatum ;
ex his principes ad amicitiam tuam si adiunxeris, per
eos reliquam multitudinem facile tenebis. Postea
totam Italiam fac ut in animo ac memoria tributim
discriptam[5] comprensamque habeas, ne quod muni-
cipium, coloniam, praefecturam, locum denique Italiae
ne quem esse patiare in quo non habeas firmamenti
31 quod satis esse possit, perquiras et investiges homines
ex omni regione, eos cognoscas, appetas, confirmes,
cures ut in suis vicinitatibus tibi petant et tua causa
quasi candidati sint. Volent te amicum, si suam a te
amicitiam expeti videbunt ; id ut intellegant, ora-

---

[1] homo nequam *Gulielmius* : homine quam *or* hominem
quam.   [2] summa *suggested by C. G. Schütz.*
   [3] ⟨ordinum⟩ omnium *Buecheler* : ordinum *suggested by*
Petreius : hominum.   [4] montium *Mommsen.*
   [5] discriptam *C. F. W. Mueller* : descriptam.

my mind, nothing is so silly as to think that a man
whom you do not know is your eager supporter. It
needs outstanding renown, prestige, and achievements to make strangers, if no one solicits them to
do so, confer an honour upon one. A lazy good-for-
nothing, with no sense of duty, no brains, a bad name,
and no friends, cannot outpace a man supported by
the favour of most people and the approbation of all,
unless gross negligence is to blame. Therefore, take 8. 29
care to secure all the centuries through many friends
of different sorts. First—and this is obvious—draw to
yourself senators, Roman Knights, active and influential men of all other ranks. Many energetic city folk,
many influential and active freedmen are about the
Forum ; as many as possible should be most diligently brought by yourself or by mutual friends to
desire your success ; pursue them, send agents to
them, show them how you esteem the benefaction.
Then, reckon up the whole city—all the Colleges,[a] 30
the suburbs, the environs ; if you strike a friendship
with the leading men from among their number, you
will easily, through them, secure the masses that
remain. After that, comprehend in your mind and
memory the whole of Italy divided into its tribal
divisions, and let there be no town, colony, rural
district, or indeed any place in Italy where you have
not a sufficiency of support ; inquire and seek out 31
men everywhere, get to know them, pursue them,
secure them, see that they canvass their localities
for you and act like candidates on your behalf. They
will want you as a friend if they see that you are
anxious for their friendship ; pursue the object of

[a] Trade guilds   the term was also used as cover for the
electoral gangs.

tione ea quae ad eam rationem pertinet habenda consequere. Homines municipales ac rusticani, si nomine nobis noti sunt, in amicitia se esse arbitrantur; si vero etiam praesidi se aliquid sibi constituere putant, non amittunt occasionem promerendi. Hos ceteri et maxime tui competitores ne norunt quidem, tu et nosti et facile cognosces, sine quo amicitia esse

32 non potest. Neque id tamen satis est, tametsi magnum est, si non sequitur[1] spes utilitatis atque amicitiae, ne nomenclator solum sed amicus etiam bonus esse videare. Ita cum et hos ipsos, propter suam ambitionem qui apud tribulis suos plurimum gratia possunt, studiosos in centuriis habebis et ceteros qui apud aliquam partem tribulium propter municipi aut vicinitatis[2] aut conlegi rationem valent cupidos tui

33 constitueris, in optima spe esse debebis. Iam equitum centuriae multo facilius mihi diligentia posse teneri videntur : primum ⟨oportet⟩[3] cognosci equites (pauci enim sunt), deinde appeti (multo enim facilius illa adulescentulorum ad amicitiam aetas adiungitur). Deinde habes[4] tecum ex iuventute optimum quemque et studiosissimum humanitatis ; tum autem, quod equester ordo tuus est, sequentur illi[5] auctoritatem ordinis, si abs te adhibebitur ea diligentia ut non ordinis solum voluntate sed etiam singulorum amicitiis eas centurias confirmatas habeas. Nam studia adulescentulorum in suffragando, in obeundo, in

---

[1] consequatur *VB*, *rightly ?*
[2] vicinitatis *Petreius* : civitatis.   [3] *Added by Watt.*
[4] habeto *Eussner.*   [5] alii *Hendrickson.*

---

[a] Eminent Romans kept a *nomenclator* to remind them of the names of persons they met.

making them understand that point by using discourse appropriate to the purpose. Small-town and country folk think themselves our friends if we know them by name ; and if indeed they think they are are also gaining some protection for themselves, they lose no opportunity of deserving it. To the rest, especially to your competitors, they are total strangers, whereas *you* know them or will easily get to know them—without which there can be no friendship. Yet merely to know them, though important, is not [32] enough unless it is followed by the hope of advantage and friendship, so that you are seen to be a good friend and not only a recollector of names.[a] So, when those whose own electioneering ambition has gained them most influence with their tribesmen are busy for you in the centuries—and when you have established, as persons desirous of your interests, those others who carry weight with some of their tribesmen by reason of their home town, district, or College—then your hopes should be high. And the [33] centuries of Knights can, I think, be secured much more easily, with care. First you should get to know the Knights (there are not many)[b] ; then, try hard to win them (young men of that age are much more easily attached as friends). Further, you have with you those of the best breeding and highest culture among the young generation ; and then, as the Order of Knights is on your side, they will follow the Order's authority, if you take the trouble to secure its centuries not only by the general good will of the Order, but by individual friendships. Young men's enthusiasm in winning support, visiting electors, carrying

[b] At the lowest accepted reckoning, there were 1,800. The whole passage is obscure, and has been much disputed.

nuntiando, in adsectando mirifice et magna et honesta
sunt.

9. 34   Et, quoniam adsectationis mentio facta est, id quoque curandum est ut cottidiana cuiusque generis et
ordinis et aetatis utare ; nam ex ea ipsa copia coniectura fieri poterit quantum sis in ipso campo virium
ac facultatis habiturus.   Huius autem rei tres partes
sunt : una salutatorum [cum domum veniunt],[1] altera
35 deductorum, tertia adsectatorum.   In salutatoribus,
qui magis vulgares sunt et hac consuetudine quae
nunc est ⟨ad⟩[2] pluris veniunt, hoc efficiendum est ut
hoc ipsum minimum officium eorum tibi gratissimum
esse videatur ; qui domum tuam venient, iis significato te animadvertere (eorum amicis qui illis renun-
tient ostendito, saepe ipsis dicito) ; sic homines saepe,
cum obeunt pluris competitores et vident unum esse
aliquem qui haec officia maxime animadvertat, ei se
dedunt, deserunt ceteros, minutatim ex communibus
proprii, ex fucosis firmi suffragatores evadunt.   Iam
illud teneto diligenter, si eum qui tibi promiserit
audieris fucum, ut dicitur, facere aut senseris, ut te id
audisse aut scire dissimules, si qui tibi se purgare volet
quod suspectum esse arbitretur, adfirmes te de illius
voluntate numquam dubitasse nec debere dubitare;
is enim qui se non putat satis facere amicus esse nullo
modo potest.   Scire autem oportet quo quisque animo
sit, ut et quantum cuique confidas constituere possis.
36 Iam deductorum officium quo maius est quam salutatorum, hoc gratius tibi esse significato atque ostendito, et, quod eius fieri poterit, certis temporibus

---

[1] *Deleted by Orelli.*   [2] *Added by Watt.*

---

[a] The distinction between these categories is nugatory.

news, and attending on you is amazingly important, and confers credit on you.

And now that I have mentioned attendance, you 9. 34 must take care to have it daily, from all sorts and ranks and ages, for the very numbers will give an idea of the resources of strength you will have at the poll itself. This subject falls into three parts : the first, callers at your house ; the second, escorts from your house ; the third, attendants in general.[a] The 35 callers are a more promiscuous crowd, and in the fashion of today visit more than one candidate. You must make even this small service of theirs appear to be very gratifying to you ; indicate that you notice who comes to your house (tell it to friends of theirs who will repeat it to them, and often tell them yourself). So, callers who visit several of the candidates, seeing that one of them takes special notice of this service, often devote themselves to him, desert the rest, and gradually emerge as his own men instead of everybody's, solid supporters instead of double-faced. Now retain this carefully : if anybody has committed himself to you, and you hear or see that he is (as they say) double-crossing you, pretend not to have heard or noticed it ; and if anybody, thinking that you suspect him, tries to clear himself, assure him that you have never doubted his good faith nor have any right to doubt it ; for nobody can be a friend if he thinks that he does not come up to standard. You should know how each man is disposed towards you, so that you can decide, accordingly, how much confidence to place in each. Now as to the 36 escorts, inasmuch as their services are more important than those of the callers, indicate clearly that they are more gratifying to you, and so far as possible,

descendito ; magnam adfert opinionem, magnam dig-
37 nitatem cottidiana in deducendo frequentia. Tertia
est ex hoc genere adsidua adsectatorum copia. In ea
quos voluntarios habebis, curato ut intellegant te sibi
in perpetuum summo beneficio obligari ; qui autem
tibi debent, ab iis plane hoc munus exigito,[1] qui per
aetatem ac negotium poterunt, ipsi tecum ut adsidui
sint, qui ipsi sectari non poterunt, suos necessarios in
hoc munere constituant. Valde ego te volo et ad rem
pertinere arbitror semper cum multitudine esse.
38 Praeterea magnam adfert laudem et summam dignitatem, si ii tecum erunt qui a te defensi et qui per te
servati ac iudiciis liberati sunt ; haec tu plane ab his
postulato ut, quoniam nulla impensa per te alii rem,
alii honestatem, alii salutem ac fortunas omnis obtinuerint,[2] nec aliud ullum tempus futurum sit ubi tibi
referre gratiam possint, hoc te officio remunerentur.
39   Et quoniam in amicorum studiis haec omnis oratio
versatur, qui locus in hoc genere cavendus sit praetermittendum non videtur. Fraudis atque insidiarum et
perfidiae plena sunt omnia. Non est huius temporis
perpetua illa de hoc genere disputatio, quibus rebus
benevolus et simulator diiudicari possit ; tantum est
huius temporis admonere. Summa tua virtus eosdem
homines et simulare tibi se esse amicos et invidere
40 coegit.   Quam ob rem Ἐπιχάρμειον illud teneto,[a]
nervos atque artus esse sapientiae non temere credere,
et, cum tuorum amicorum studia constitueris, tum

---

[1] exigito *conjectured by Orelli* : exigitur.
[2] obtinuerint *C. F. W. Mueller* : obtinuerunt.

---

[a] Quoted in Greek by Marcus, *Ad Att*. i. 19. 8.

go down to the Forum at regular hours ; a large company of daily escorts makes a great impression and adds great prestige. The third item under this 37 heading is the supply of full-time attendants. To those who are volunteers, make it clear that you are forever in their debt for a very great kindness. To those who owe you this service, insist absolutely that any who are not too old or too busy should regularly attend on you themselves, and that those who cannot themselves do so should appoint their relatives to this duty. I am very anxious that you should always have a crowd about you ; I think it important to the occasion. Further, it will bring you great credit and high 38 prestige if you have around you those whom you have defended, who have been preserved and saved from condemnation by you. Demand of them plainly that since it is due to your unpaid efforts that they have retained their property, or their reputation, or their life and all their fortunes, and since there will never be another chance for them to thank you, they should repay you by this service.

Now, since all this discourse of mine is concerned 10. 39 with the zealous aid of friends, I think that I should not omit to say what point under this heading requires caution. All things are full of deceit, snares, and treachery. This is not the time for the whole long argument on this heading—how genuine good will can be distinguished from counterfeit ; this is the time for a warning only. The excellence of your moral nature has impelled the same persons both to feign friendship for you and to bear you envy. Hold fast, 40 therefore, to the old saying of Epicharmus that the bone and sinew of wisdom is, Never trust rashly [a] ; and as you assemble the zealous aid of your friends,

etiam obtrectatorum atque adversariorum rationes et
genera cognoscito. Haec tria sunt : unum quos
laesisti, alterum qui sine causa non amant, tertium
qui competitorum valde amici sunt. Quos laesisti,
cum contra eos pro amico diceres, iis te plane purgato,
necessitudines commemorato, in spem adducito te in
eorum rebus, si se in amicitiam contulerint, pari studio
atque officio futurum. Qui sine causa non amant, eos
aut beneficio aut spe aut significando tuo erga illos
studio dato operam ut de illa animi pravitate deducas.
Quorum voluntas erit abs te propter competitorum
amicitias alienior, iis quoque eadem inservito ratione
qua superioribus et, si probare poteris, te in eos ipsos
competitores tuos benevolo esse animo ostendito.

11 41 Quoniam de amicitiis constituendis satis dictum est,
dicendum est de illa altera parte petitionis quae in
populari ratione versatur. Ea desiderat nomencla-
tionem, blanditiam, adsiduitatem, benignitatem,
12 rumorem, speciem[1] in re publica. Primum id quod
facis, ut homines noris, significa ut appareat, et auge
ut cottidie melius fiat ; nihil mihi tam populare neque
tam gratum videtur. Deinde id quod natura non
habes induc in animum ita simulandum esse ut natura
facere videare ; nam comitas tibi non deest ea quae
bono ac suavi homine digna est, sed opus est magno
opere blanditia, quae, etiam si vitiosa est et turpis
in cetera vita, tamen in petitione necessaria est ;

---

[1] speciem *Lambinus* : spem.

get to know also the methods and types of your detractors and your opponents. The types are three : first, those whom you have hurt; second, those who do not like you, though they have no reason ; third, those who are close friends of your competitors. As to those whom you have hurt by defending a friend against them, exculpate yourself in full, reminding them of your personal obligations, and make them hope that, if they become friends of yours, you will do them equally zealous service in their own affairs. Those who do not like you, though they have no reason, you should endeavour to turn away from that perverse frame of mind by doing them a kindness, or promising one, or indicating your own affection for them. Those who are estranged from you by friendship with your competitors should be treated by the same methods as the others ; and if you can make them believe it, convey that you feel kindly towards your competitors themselves.

Now that enough has been said of instituting 11. 41 friendships, I must now speak of the other part of the canvass, which concerns method in dealing with the People. This requires a memory for names, an ingratiating manner, constant attendance, generosity, publicity, a fine political image. First, show off 42 your habit of *knowing people* so that it is obvious, and increase and improve it daily ; nothing, to my mind, is so popular and gratifying. Then, be determined that what you lack by nature should be so well simulated that it seems a natural act. You are not wanting in the pleasant manners proper to a kind and agreeable man, but what you urgently need is *ingratiation*, which may be a base fault in the rest of life, but in a canvass it is indispensable. For it is

etenim[1] cum deteriorem aliquem adsentando facit,
tum improba est, cum amiciorem, non tam vitu-
peranda, petitori vero necessaria est, cuius et frons et
vultus et sermo ad eorum quoscumque convenerit
sensum et voluntatem commutandus et accommo-
43 dandus est. Iam adsiduitatis nullum est praeceptum,
verbum ipsum docet quae res sit ; prodest quidem
vehementer nusquam discedere, sed tamen hic fructus
est adsiduitatis, non solum esse Romae atque in foro
sed adsidue petere, saepe eosdem appellare, non
committere ut quisquam possit dicere, quod eius
consequi possis, se abs te non [sit][2] rogatum et valde
44 ac diligenter rogatum. Benignitas autem late patet :
[et][3] est in re familiari, quae quamquam ad multitudinem pervenire non potest, tamen ab amicis ⟨si⟩
laudatur, multitudini grata est ; est in conviviis, quae
fac ut et abs te et ab amicis tuis concelebrentur et
passim et tributim ; est etiam in opera, quam per-
vulga et communica, curaque ut aditus ad te diurni
nocturnique pateant, neque solum foribus aedium
tuarum sed etiam vultu ac fronte, quae est animi
ianua ; quae si significat voluntatem abditam esse ac
retrusam, parvi refert patere ostium. Homines enim
non modo promitti sibi, praesertim quod a candidato
petant, sed etiam large[4] atque honorifice promitti
45 volunt. Qua re hoc quidem facile praeceptum est, ut
quod facturus[5] sis id significes te studiose ac libenter
esse facturum ; illud difficilius et magis ad tempus

---

¹ etenim *suggested by Petreius* : ea enim *Buecheler* : te enim.
² *Deleted by Watt.*   ³ *Deleted by Baiter.*
⁴ *var. lect.* longe.

vile when flattery is used to corrupt a man, but less execrable when used to conciliate friendship, and indispensable for a candidate, whose facial expression and conversation must be modified and adapted to the humour and the inclination of all whom he meets. Now, *attendance* needs no instructions ; the word 43 itself explains what it is. Never to leave town is very rewarding ; yet the gains from your personal attendance consist not merely in being at Rome and in the Forum, but in canvassing continuously, soliciting the same people many times, and, so far as possible, not letting anybody be in a position to say that that he has not been canvassed by you—and thoroughly and diligently canvassed too. Next, *generos- 44 ity* has a wide field—it is shown in the use of one's private means, for although this cannot reach the masses, the masses like hearing it praised by your friends ; it is shown in banquets, to which you and your friends should often convoke the people at large or tribe by tribe; also in rendering services, which you will widely advertise, and seeing that you are approachable day and night, not only through the door of your house but through your facial expression, which is the gate of the mind ; if it shows that your feelings are reserved and withdrawn, it hardly matters that your door is open. People want not only promises (especially in their demands from a candidate), but promises made in a lavish and complimentary way. And so—an easy rule—if you are 45 going to do what is asked, show that you will do it willingly and gladly ; but the next thing is harder, and accords better with your circumstances than

---

[5] facturus *with* f *deleted* V : acturus.

quam ad naturam accommodatum tuam, quod facere
non possis, ut id aut iucunde ⟨neges aut etiam non⟩[1]
neges ; quorum alterum est tamen boni viri, alterum
boni petitoris. Nam cum id petitur quod honeste aut
sine detrimento nostro promittere non possumus, quo
modo si qui roget ut contra amicum aliquem causam
recipiamus, belle negandum est, ut ostendas necessitudinem, demonstres quam moleste feras, aliis te id
rebus exsarturum[2] esse persuadeas. Audivi hoc dicere
quendam de quibusdam oratoribus, ad quos causam
suam detulisset, gratiorem sibi orationem ⟨eius⟩ fuisse
qui negasset quam illius qui recepisset ; sic homines
fronte et oratione magis quam ipso beneficio reque
capiuntur. Verum hoc probabile est, illud alterum sub-
durum tibi homini Platonico suadere, sed tamen tem-
pori tuo consulam. Quibus enim te propter aliquod
officium necessitudinis adfuturum negaris, tamen ii
possunt abs te placati aequique discedere ; quibus
autem idcirco negaris, quod te impeditum esse dixeris
aut amicorum[3] hominum negotiis aut gravioribus causis
aut ante susceptis, inimici[4] discedunt omnesque hoc
animo sunt ut sibi te mentiri malint quam negare. C.
Cotta, in ambitione artifex, dicere solebat se operam
suam, quod non contra officium rogaretur, polliceri
solere omnibus, impertire iis apud quos optime poni
arbitraretur ; ideo se nemini negare, quod saepe acci-
deret causa cur is cui pollicitus esset non uteretur,
saepe ut ipse magis esset vacuus quam putasset ; neque posse eius donum compleri qui tantum modo reci-

12. 46 (marginal)
47 (marginal)

---

[1] *Added by Watt following Purser and Constans.*
[2] exsarturum *Lambinus* : exaucturum *or* exacturum.
[3] amiciorum *Eussner.*
[4] ⟨i⟩ inimici *conjectured by Buecheler.*

with your character : whatever you cannot perform, decline gracefully or, better, *don't* decline. A
good man will do the former, a good candidate the
latter. If asked for something which we cannot decent-
ly or with impunity promise—if, for instance, somebody asks you to accept a brief against a friend—you
must refuse nicely, explaining your obligation to your
friend, declaring how sorry you are, assuring the man
that you will patch it all up in other ways. Somebody 12. 46
told me of certain advocates to whom he had referred
his case, that he was more gratified by the words of
the one who refused than by those of him who accepted ; and indeed, people are charmed more by
looks and words than by the substantial benefit
received. That, however, is fair enough ; the alternative course of *not* declining is rather difficult to
commend to a Platonist like you, but I am going to
have regard for your present circumstances. If you
tell people that you cannot help them because of
some personal duty to others, they may still go away
pacified and unruffled ; but if you refuse because you
are prevented (you say) by affairs of friends or by
previous or more important engagements, they go
away hating you ; they are all in the mood that they
had rather you lied to them than refused them. C. 47
Cotta,[a] a past master of electioneering, used to say
that (unless duty forbade a request) he used to
promise his help to all, but give it to those in whom he
expected he was making the best investment ; he
refused nobody because it often turned out, for some
reason, that the man to whom he had promised help
did not use it, or that he himself was less busy than
he expected ; if one undertook only what one could

---

[a] Consul 75 B.C. ; admired and often mentioned by Marcus.

peret quantum videret se obire posse ; casu fieri ut
agantur ea quae non putaris, illa quae credideris in
manibus esse ut aliqua de causa non agantur ; deinde
esse extremum ut irascatur is cui mendacium dixeris.

48 Id, si promittas, et incertum est et in diem et in pau-
cioribus ; sin autem [id]¹ neges, et certe abalienes et
statim et pluris ; plures enim multo sunt qui rogant
ut uti liceat opera alterius quam qui utuntur. Qua re
satius est ex his aliquos aliquando in foro tibi irasci
quam omnis continuo domi, praesertim cum multo
magis irascuntur iis qui negent quam ei quem videant
ea ex² causa impeditum ut facere quod promisit cupiat

49 si ullo modo possit. Ac ne videar aberrasse a distributione mea, qui haec in hac populari parte petitionis
disputem, hoc sequor, haec omnia non tam ad amicorum studia quam ad popularem famam pertinere :
etsi inest aliquid ex illo genere, benigne respondere,
studiose inservire negotiis ac periculis amicorum,
tamen hoc loco ea dico quibus multitudinem capere
possis, ut de nocte domus compleatur, ut multi spe
tui praesidi teneantur, ut amiciores abs te discedant
quam accesserint, ut quam plurimorum aures optimo

13. 50 sermone compleantur. Sequitur enim ut de rumore
dicendum sit, cui maxime serviendum est. Sed quae
dicta sunt omni superiore oratione, eadem ad rumorem
concelebrandum valent, dicendi laus, studia publicanorum et equestris ordinis, hominum nobilium volun-

---

¹ *Deleted by Puteanus.*
² ea *or* ea ex *codd.* : iusta *Lambinus.*

be sure to perform, one's house would be empty ; by chance, a case you didn't expect is tried, but one you thought you were busy with is not tried for some reason ; and finally, the anger of the man to whom one lied would be the last event in the series—for if 48 you do promise, the anger is uncertain, not immediate and occurs in fewer cases ; but if you refuse you are sure to rouse antagonism at once, and in more people ; since those who ask that they be allowed to employ the services of a person are many more than those who actually employ them. So it is better that some of these people should sometimes be angry with you in the Forum than all of them all the time in your house —especially as they are much angrier with those who refuse them than with a man who (as they see) has a reason for not fulfilling his promise, although he would want to do so if he possibly could.

(And, in case you think I have wandered from my 49 own classification of subject-matter by putting this argument into the part of the canvass concerning the People, my view is that all this pertains to Popular Reputation rather than to Zealous Aid of Friends. Although something of this latter category enters in —gracious answers, zealous service in friends' affairs or dangers—I am here speaking of ways to capture the masses, so as to fill your house before dawn, to hold many people in hope of your protection, to send them away better friends than they came, to fill as many ears as possible with excellent reports of you.)

The next required talking point is *publicity*, which 13. 50 you must court to the full. But for widespread publicity the strong points are those of my whole discourse above—your fame as an orator, the favour of the public revenue contractors and the Order of

tas, adulescentulorum frequentia, eorum qui abs te
defensi sunt adsiduitas, ex municipiis multitudo
eorum quos tua causa venisse appareat, bene ⟨te⟩
ut homines nosse, comiter appellare, adsidue ac diligenter petere, benignum ac liberalem esse loquantur
et existiment, domus ut multa nocte[1] compleatur,
omnium generum frequentia adsit, satis fiat oratione
omnibus, re operaque multis, perficiatur id quod fieri
potest labore et arte ac diligentia, non ut ad populum
ab his hominibus fama perveniat sed ut in his studiis
51 populus ipse versetur. Iam urbanam illam multitudinem et eorum studia qui contiones tenent adeptus
es in Pompeio ornando, Manili causa recipienda,
Cornelio defendendo ; excitanda nobis sunt quae
adhuc habuit nemo quin idem[2] splendidorum hominum voluntates haberet. Efficiendum etiam illud est
ut sciant omnes Cn. Pompei summam esse erga te
voluntatem et vehementer ad illius rationes te id
52 adsequi quod petis pertinere. Postremo tota petitio
cura ut pompae plena sit, ut inlustris, ut splendida, ut
popularis sit, ut habeat summam speciem ac dignitatem, ut etiam, si qua possit ⟨ratio⟩ne,[3] competitoribus tuis exsistat aut sceleris aut libidinis aut lar-
53 gitionis accommodata ad eorum mores infamia. Atque
etiam in hac petitione maxime videndum est ut spes
rei publicae bona de te sit et honesta opinio ; nec
tamen in petendo res publica capessenda est neque in
senatu neque in contione. Sed haec tibi sunt reti-

---

[1] ⟨de⟩ nocte *suggested by Malaespina.*
[2] quin idem *Manutius* : qui idem.   [3] ⟨ratio⟩ne *Watt* : ne.

---

[a] Manilius sponsored the bill of 66 B.C. for Pompey's
eastern command, p. 761, n. *a* ; Cornelius was another
Pompeian defended by Marcus (p. 764, n. *a*, p. 765).

Knights, the good will of the nobles, the crowd of young men about you, the attendance of clients defended by you, the numbers from Italian towns who have obviously come for your sake ; so that they say and believe that you know people well, solicit them courteously, canvass continuously and thoroughly, are a gracious and generous person ; and that your house is full long before dawn with crowds of all classes, you give satisfaction to everybody in what you say and to many in what you actually do, you achieve the result (so far as hard work, skill, and application can achieve it) that the People itself, instead of hearing at second hand from these acquaintances of yours, shares their devotion to you. You have already won over those city masses 51 and the favour of their political managers by advancing Pompey, by undertaking the case of Manilius and defending Cornelius [a] ; now we have to mobilize the support which nobody has ever possessed without the good graces of the highest personages. You have also to make everybody know that Pompey is a strong supporter of yours and that your success in this candidature would suit his plans extremely well.[b] Lastly, see that your whole canvass is a 52 *fine show*, brilliant, resplendent, and popular, with the utmost display and prestige ; and also, if it can be managed at all, that there should be scandalous talk, in character, about the crimes, lusts, and briberies of your competitors. Above all, it must be shown 53 in this canvass that high hopes and good opinions are entertained for your political future. Yet, during your canvass, you must not deal with politics either in the Senate or in political meetings of the People.

[b] See, however, Introduction, p. 746, n. *c*.

nenda : ut senatus te existimet ex eo quod ita vixeris
defensorem auctoritatis suae fore, equites R. et viri
boni ac locupletes ex vita acta te studiosum oti ac
rerum tranquillarum, multitudo ex eo quod dumtaxat
oratione in contionibus ac iudicio popularis fuisti te a
suis commodis non alienum futurum.

14. 54   Haec mihi veniebant in mentem de duabus illis
commentationibus[1] matutinis, quod[2] tibi cottidie ad forum descendenti meditandum esse dixeram : "Novus
sum, consulatum peto." Tertium restat : "Roma
est," civitas ex nationum conventu constituta, in qua
multae insidiae, multa fallacia,[3] multa in omni genere
vitia versantur, multorum adrogantia, multorum con-
tumacia, multorum malevolentia, multorum superbia,
multorum odium ac molestia perferenda est. Video
esse magni consili atque artis in tot hominum cuiusque
modi vitiis tantisque versantem vitare offensionem,
vitare fabulam, vitare insidias, esse unum hominem
accommodatum ad tantam morum ac sermonum ac
55 voluntatum varietatem. Qua re etiam atque etiam
perge tenere istam viam quam instituisti,[4] excelle
dicendo ; hoc et tenentur Romae homines et adliciun-
tur et ab impediendo ac laedendo repelluntur. Et
quoniam in hoc vel maxime est vitiosa civitas, quod
largitione interposita virtutis ac dignitatis oblivisci
solet, in hoc fac ut te bene noris, id est ut intellegas
eum esse te qui iudici ac periculi metum maximum
competitoribus adferre possis. Fac ut se abs te
custodiri atque observari sciant ; cum diligentiam
tuam, cum auctoritatem vimque dicendi, tum profecto

---

[1] commentationibus *Palermus* : commonitionibus *or* com-
motionibus.   [2] quod *Lambinus* : quas *Facciolati* : quo.
[3] multae fallaciae *Lambinus*.

Instead, you must keep in mind that the Senate should deem you, on your life's record, to be in future an upholder of its authority ; the Roman Knights and men of worth and substance, from your past life, to be devoted to peace and quiet times ; the masses, to be favourably inclined to their interests, since you have been " Popular " at least in your speeches in political meetings and lawcourts.

This is what occurred to me about those first two **14. 54** morning meditations, when I said that every day as you go down to the Forum you must repeat to yourself : " I am ' new ' ; I seek the consulship." There remains the third, " This is Rome "—a conglomerate of nations, in which there are many snares, intrigues, and vices of all sorts, many people's insolence, contumacy, malice, haughtiness, animosity and vexation to be borne. I see that among so many people of such great and various vices, it needs much judgement and skill to escape resentment, gossip, or treacherous attack, to be a man whose one personality has been adapted to such multifarious ways of behaving, speaking, or feeling. So, go steadily on by the path you **55** have chosen to tread, and be supreme in oratory ; this is what holds and attracts men in Rome, and keeps them off from hampering or harming you. Further, as the worst vice of this city is to forget moral worth when bribery enters in, know yourself— I mean, understand that you, of all people, can put the fear of prosecution and its dangers into your competitors. Let them know that they are under your watchful observation ; they will be terrified not only by your application, your authority and power as an

---

⁴ instituisti *Gruter* : instituisti.

56 equestris ordinis erga te studium pertimescent. Atque
haec ita te nolo[1] illis proponere ut videare accusationem iam[2] meditari sed ut hoc terrore facilius hoc
ipsum quod agis consequare. Et plane sic contende
omnibus nervis ac facultatibus ut adipiscamur quod
petimus. Video nulla esse comitia tam inquinata
largitione quibus non gratis aliquae centuriae renun-
57 tient suos magno opere necessarios. Qua re si ad-
vigilamus pro rei dignitate, et si nostros ad summum
studium benevolos[3] excitamus, et si hominibus studio-
sis[4] nostri gratiosisque[5] suum cuique munus discribi-
mus, et si competitoribus iudicium proponimus, se-
questribus metum inicimus, divisores ratione aliqua
coercemus, perfici potest ut largitio nulla fiat aut
nihil valeat.

58 Haec sunt quae putavi non melius scire me quam te
sed facilius his tuis occupationibus conligere unum in
locum posse et ad te perscripta mittere. Quae tametsi
scripta ita sunt ut non ad omnis qui honores petant
sed ad te proprie et ad hanc petitionem tuam valeant,
tamen tu, si quid mutandum esse videbitur aut
omnino tollendum, aut si quid erit praeteritum, velim
hoc mihi dicas ; volo enim hoc commentariolum
petitionis haberi omni ratione perfectum.

[1] te nolo *Watt* : nolo te *Buecheler* : te volo *or* volo **te.**
[2] iam accusationem *Lambinus* : accusationem tam.
[3] *Buecheler would delete* benevolos.
[4] *HF have* studiis : *Petreius conjectures* gratiosis.
[5] nostri gratiosisque *Gesner* : studiosisque nostri *Petreius* :
gratiosisque nostri.

orator, but also by the favour that you have with the Order of Knights. I do not want you so to present **56** these advantages to them as to give the impression that you are already contemplating a prosecution, but only, through their terror of one, to gain your end more easily.[a] Strive, then, with all your strength and talents to obtain what we are seeking. I see that no election is so polluted with bribery that some centuries do not return, without bribes, the candidates with whom they have a very special bond. So, if we **57** keep as alert as the high occasion demands, and if we stir up our well-wishers to the utmost zeal, and if we assign a particular task to each of our influential supporters, and if we set prosecution before the eyes of our competitors, strike alarm into the agents of bribery and somehow curb the distributors, we can achieve the result that bribery does not occur or has no effect.

Here it is ; I thought, not that I knew all this **58** better than you, but that, considering how busy you are, I could more easily pull it together into one whole and send it to you in writing. Although it is written in such a way that it applies not to all who are seeking office but to you in particular and to this canvass, still, please tell me if you think that anything should be changed or struck out altogether, or if anything has been left out. For I want this handbook of electioneering to be considered perfect in every way.

[a] Cic. *Pro. Mur.* 43 ; candidates should not be seen to intend a prosecution. It is not clear how Marcus is to frighten his competitors without appearing to intend one.

[CICERO]
LETTER TO OCTAVIAN

WITH AN ENGLISH TRANSLATION BY
MARY ISOBEL HENDERSON, M.A.

VICE-PRINCIPAL AND FELLOW OF SOMERVILLE COLLEGE, OXFORD
AND UNIVERSITY LECTURER IN ANCIENT HISTORY

INTRODUCTION TO THE
EPISTULA AD OCTAVIANUM

SINCE the sixteenth century this piece has been recognized as the work not of Cicero but of some rhetorician. Marcus Cicero's authorship is excluded by the cheapness of its style and thought; further tests are superfluous. It is not a letter (in spite of its epistolary superscription), but an invective comparable to the pseudo-Ciceronian *In Sallustium Crispum*. Both are samples of the school exercises constantly prescribed in imperial times, developing real or imaginary situations in the life of Cicero or other historical personages.[a]

The situation here imagined is set in 43 B.C., before Cicero's death on December 7, and after Octavian's alliance with Antony (probably in November). The author ignores the predominance of Antony at this stage; and on three matters of fact he is probably, though not certainly, in error.[b] Otherwise, while his picture is both imprecise and implausible, he seems to be aware of the outline of history. After Caesar was killed (March 15, 44 B.C.), the consul Antony

---

[a] *e.g.*, Seneca, *Suas.* vi. 14 : " The schoolmen are in the habit of reciting exercises on the theme ' Cicero deliberates whether he should burn his speeches if Antony promised to spare his life in return.' " See also Quintilian iii. 48-70.

[b] See pp. 804-806.

abolished the office of Dictator and allowed the assassins to hold their provincial commands, but quickly showed his ambition to succeed to Caesar's autocracy. He used—and forged—Caesar's note-books to disguise his control of public revenues and imperial government; he overrode the Senate's arrangement by swapping his own province of Macedonia for Cisalpine Gaul. Octavian, Caesar's eighteen-year-old nephew and adopted heir, had reached Italy in April. The name of Caesar gave him an unrivalled hold on the army's affections, and made him the only effective instrument of opposition to Antony—while he chose to act as loyal. Accordingly the Senate, on Cicero's advice, wooed him with extraordinary honours—a gilded statue, senatorial rank, the right to seek office ten years below the legal age, an *imperium* to legitimize his private army. In the spring of 43 he marched with the consuls to relieve the consul-elect, Decimus Brutus, who was besieged by Antony in Mutina. Antony, twice defeated, was declared a public enemy; Octavian, with the fallen consuls, was hailed as *Imperator* by the soldiers. But the soldiers were sick of civil war. Two other army contingents joined the defeated Antony; and the rescued Decimus Brutus was soon deserted by his troops, hunted and killed in the Alps. Meanwhile, on August 19, Octavian marched on Rome, demanded the vacant consulships for himself and a relative, and set up a court to try Caesar's assassins. Being now in a position to bargain, he led his troops to meet Antony and Lepidus, and came to the agreement which established the Triumvirate. The three proceeded in turn to Rome, and carried out proscriptions in which Cicero was killed.

[CICERO]

The " Epistula " is supposed to represent Cicero's reproaches of Octavian for his treachery. Cicero's genuine correspondence is not preserved after July 28, 43, when he suspected Octavian deeply, but had not yet seen the worst. For a glimpse of reality, however, the last two letters are worth reading (*Ad·Brut.* xxvi (=i. 18) ; *Ad fam.* x. 24). The later and highly tendentious version of Augustus is given in his *Res Gestae*, 1-2.

[For the text of the *Epistula ad Octavianum* we have not only the tradition of the manuscripts which contain also the *Commentariolum Petitionis* (H, F, D, V, B etc. of the X family—see p.· 747—they have the *Commentar.* after the *Epist.*), but in addition nearly all the codices on which we rely for Cicero's *Epistulae ad Atticum,* *Epistulae ad Quintum Fratrem,* and *Epistulae ad M. Brutum*—the Ω family, especially :—

Parisinus "Nouv. Fonds" 16248, 14th–15th cent. (G)
Landianus 8 (at Piacenza), 14th–15th cent. (H)
Palatinus Lat. 1510 (in the Vatican), 15th cent. (V)
Taurinensis Lat. 495 (at Turin), 15th cent. (O)
Parisinus Lat. 8538, written in 1419. (R)
Parisinus Lat. 8536, 15th cent. (P)
Mediceus 49.18 (at Florence), written in 1393. (M)

The last named is the oldest and best of its class, which is different from that of the preceding and contains many codices—B. Ullman, *The Origin and Development of Humanistic Script*, Rome, 1960, p. 28. All the MSS. of this family are descended from a lost archetype. Of the two families, Sjögren favoured X, but Watt prefers Ω with good reason. *Cf.* W. S. Watt, *M. Tulli Cic. Epistulae* Vol. III, pp. 186 ff. We now have also *Pseudo-Ciceronis Epistula ad Octavianum*:

LETTER TO OCTAVIAN

R. Lamacchia recognovit, Roma, 1967 [M. T. Ciceronis scripta omnia quae extant critico apparatu instructa, consilio et auctoritate Collegi Ciceronianis studiis provehendis]. Also [*M. Tulli Ciceronis*] *Epistola ad Octavianum.* Introduzione, testo critico e commento a cura di Rosa Lamacchia. Firenze, 1968. [*E.H.W.*]}

PSEUDO-CICERONIS
EPISTULA AD OCTAVIANUM

CICERO OCTAVIANO SALUTEM

1 Si per tuas legiones mihi licitum fuisset, quae
nomini meo populoque Romano sunt inimicissimae,
venire in senatum coramque de re publica disputare,
fecissem, neque tam libenter quam necessario ; nulla
enim remedia quae vulneribus adhibentur tam faciunt
dolorem quam quae sunt salutaria. Sed quoniam cohortibus armatis circumsaeptus senatus nihil aliud
vere[1] potest decernere nisi timere (in Capitolio signa
sunt, in urbe milites vagantur, in Campo castra ponuntur, Italia tota legionibus ad libertatem nostram
conscriptis ad servitutem adductis equitatuque exte-
rarum nationum distinetur), cedam tibi in praesentia
foro curia et sanctissimis deorum immortalium templis
in quibus reviviscente iam libertate deinde rursus
oppressa senatus nihil consulitur, timet multa, assen-
2 titur omnia. Post etiam paulo temporibus ita
postulantibus cedam urbe, quam per me conservatam
ut esset libera in servitute videre non potero ; cedam
vita, quae, quamquam sollicita est, tamen, si profutura
est rei publicae, bona spe posteritatis me consolatur,
qua sublata non dubitanter occidam ; atque ita

[1] libere *Wesenberg.*

[CICERO'S] LETTER TO OCTAVIAN

HAD I been permitted by your legions, bitter enemies 1
of my name and of the Roman People, to come into
the Senate and contend with you face to face concerning the Republic, I should have done so willingly,
or rather, of necessity ; for none of the remedies
applied to wounds hurts as much as those that heal.
But as the Senate is hedged around with armed
cohorts and can in its decrees honestly express nothing but fear (ensigns are on the Capitol, soldiers
roam the City, bivouacs are being pitched in the
Campus, all Italy is distraught with legions recruited
for our liberties but brought to enslave us, and with
cavalry of foreign nations), I will give place to you for
the present, and withdraw from the Forum, the Senate
House, the most holy temples of the immortal gods,
where liberty just reviving has been crushed again,
where the Senate is consulted on nothing, fears many
things, says yes to everything. Then, a little later, 2
when the times demand it, I shall withdraw from the
City, which I preserved to be free and cannot behold
in slavery ; I shall withdraw from life ; it is a troubled
life, yet if it is destined to be of service to the Republic, it comforts me with the good hope of posterity's
praise (if that hope is removed, I will perish without

[CICERO]

cedam ut fortuna iudicio meo, non animus mihi
defuisse videatur. Illud vero, quod et praesentis
doloris habet indicium et praeteritae iniuriae testimonium et absentium sensus significationem, non
praetermittam, quin, quoniam coram id facere pro-
hibeor, absens pro me reque p. expostulem tecum.
Atque ita dico " pro me," si quidem mea salus aut
utilis rei publicae est aut coniuncta certe publicae
saluti. Nam, per deum immortalium fidem, nisi forte
frustra eos appello quorum aures atque animus a
nobis abhorret, perque Fortunam populi Romani,
quae, quamquam nobis infesta est, fuit aliquando
propitia et, ut spero, futura est, quis tam expers
humanitatis, quis huius urbis nomini ac sedibus usque
adeo est inimicus ut ista aut dissimulare possit aut
non dolere aut, si nulla ratione publicis incommodis
mederi queat, non morte proprium[1] periculum vitet ?

3   Nam ut ordiar ab initio et perducam ad extremum
et novissima conferam primis, quae non posterior dies
acerbior priore et quae non insequens hora antece-
dente calamitosior populo Romano inluxit ? M. Antonius, vir animi maximi (utinam etiam sapientis consili
fuisset !), C. Caesare fortissime sed parum feliciter a
rei publicae dominatione semoto[2] concupierat magis
regium quam libera civitas pati poterat principatum.
Publicam dilapidabat pecuniam, aerarium exhau-
riebat, minuebat vectigalia, donabat civitates immunitate et nationes[3] ex commentario ; dictaturam

[1] *var. lect.* propria.

800

hesitation). And I shall withdraw in a manner which will show that it was fortune which failed me in my policy, not fortitude which failed me in myself. But, as a sign of present grief, a witness of past injury, and a token of the feelings of absent friends, I shall not miss the occasion of remonstrating with you in absence (since I am forbidden to do so in person) on my own account and on the Republic's. (I say " on my own account " in case my safety is of any use to the Republic, or at least relevant to its safety.) By the troth of the immortal gods (unless I appeal in vain to gods whose ears and hearts are turned from us), and by the Fortune of the Roman People (which, though hostile now, once favoured us and will again, I hope), I ask : Is there any man so uncivilized, or so antagonistic to this City's name and abodes, that he could dissemble this state of affairs or feel no grief, or, if he could by no means cure the public ills, could fail to escape from his personal danger by death ?

To begin at the beginning and carry on to the end— to compare the latest events with the first—has not each day dawned more bitter than the last for the Roman People, each succeeding hour more disastrous than the one before ? When, by a most brave act with no luck to follow, Caesar was removed from his despotic rule of the Republic, Mark Antony, a man of high courage (would that his judgement had been wise as well !) coveted a pre-eminence more regal than a free country could endure. He played ducks and drakes with public funds, drained the treasury, decreased the revenue, exempted cities and peoples from taxation on the authority of Caesar's private

---

² summoto *in margin of Lambinus' edition.*
³ immunitate, nationes ⟨civitate⟩ *Lamacchia.*

gerebat, leges imponebat, prohibebat dictatorem
creari, legibus senatus consultis[1] ipse repugnabat
in senatu, provincias unus omnis concupierat. Cui
sordebat Macedonia provincia quam victor sibi sump-
serat Caesar, quid de hoc sperare aut exspectare nos
4 oportebat ? Exstitisti tu vindex nostrae libertatis ut
tunc quidem optimus (quod utinam neque nostra nos
opinio neque tua fides fefellisset !), et veteranis in
unum conductis et duabus legionibus a pernicie
patriae ad salutem avocatis subito prope iam adflic-
tam ac prostratam rem publicam tuis opibus extulisti.
Quae tibi non ante quam postulares, maiora quam
velles, plura quam sperares, detulit senatus ? dedit
fascis ut cum auctoritate defensorem haberet, non ut
imperio se adversum armaret ; appellavit imperatorem hostium exercitu pulso tribuens honorem, non
ut sua caede reversus[2] ille fugiens exercitus te
nominaret imperatorem ; decrevit in foro statuam,
5 locum in senatu, summum honorem ante tempus. Si
quid aliud est quod dari possit, addet ; quid aliud est
maius quod velis sumere ? Sin autem supra aetatem,
supra consuetudinem, supra etiam mortalitatem tuam
tibi sunt omnia tributa, cur aut ut ingratum crudeliter
aut ut immemorem benefici tui scelerate circum-
scribis senatum ? Quo te misimus ? a quibus rever-
teris ? Contra quos armavimus ? quibus arma cogitas

---

[1] legibus senatus consultis *Aldus* : legibus senatus con-
sulti *or* consulto *or* legibus s. c. *most* mss.

[2] reversus *Watt* : rursus *or* ausus *or* caesus.

---

[a] After defeating Pompey and the Republican forces at
Pharsalus (48 b.c.). [But the author's statement is doubtful.]
[b] See W. S. Watt, *Class. Quart.* 1958, p. 29. The army
hailed Octavian as *imperator* not after a victory in war (as
was customary) but after its massacre of Senators in Rome.

notebook ; he was acting as dictator and laying down laws, but he forbade election of a dictator, and in the Senate he resisted laws and senatorial decrees. He coveted all the provinces for himself alone. What were we to hope or expect from one who disdained Macedonia, a province which the victorious Caesar took to himself ? [a] You arose to vindicate our liberty, 4 a great patriot as you then were (would that my judgement and your perfidy had not deceived me !) ; you concentrated the veterans, recalled two legions from destroying their country to saving it, and at once by your resources raised up the Republic, then almost shattered and prostrated. Was there anything that the Senate did not grant you before you asked, on a bigger scale than you wanted, in more quantity than you hoped ? It gave you the Fasces to authorize you as its defender, not to arm you with official power against itself. It called you *Imperator* to honour you for putting the enemy's army to flight, not in order that this fleeing army, returned from its massacring of the Senate, should then name you *Imperator*. [b] It decreed you a statue in the Forum, a seat in the Senate, high office before the legal age. If there is 5 anything more that it can give, it will add that too ; what else bigger would you want to take? Or if everything has been conferred on you beyond what is due to youth, to tradition, even to your own mortal nature, why do you curtail the Senate so cruelly, as if it were ungrateful, or, should I say, so wickedly, as if it had forgotten your services ? Whither did we send you, and from whom are you now returned ? Against whom did we arm you, and now

inferre ? A quibus exercitum abducis ? [et] quos adversus aciem struis ? Cur hostis relinquitur, civis hostis loco ponitur ? Cur castra medio itinere longius ⟨ab⟩ adversariorum castris et propius urbem moven-

6 tur ? Cogit illorum spes aliquid nos timere. O me numquam sapientem et aliquando id quod non eram frustra existimatum ! quantum te, popule Romane, de me fefellit opinio ! O meam calamitosam ac praecipitem senectutem ! o turpem exacta demen- tique aetate canitiem ! Ego patres conscriptos ad parricidium induxi, ego rem publicam fefelli, ego ipsum senatum sibi manus adferre coegi, cum te Iunonium puerum et matris tuae partum aureum esse dixi ; at te fata patriae Paridem futurum praedice- bant,[1] qui vastares urbem incendio, Italiam bello, qui castra in templis deorum immortalium, senatum in

7 castris habiturus esses. O miseram et in brevi tam celerem et tam variam rei publicae commutationem ! quisnam tali futurus ingenio est qui possit haec ita mandare litteris ut facta non ficta videantur esse? quis erit tanta animi facilitate qui, quae verissime memo- ria propagata fuerint, non fabulae similia sit existi- maturus ? Cogita enim Antonium hostem iudicatum, ab eo circumsessum consulem designatum eundem- que rei publicae parentem, te profectum ad consulem liberandum et hostem opprimendum hostemque a te fugatum et consulem obsidione liberatum, deinde

---

[1] praedicebant *Lambinus* : praedicabant.

---

[a] There is no record that Cicero ever talked any such nonsense, but apocryphal stories that he had a dream linking Octavian with Jupiter or Juno were later told (Suetonius, *D.A.* 94 ; Dio xlv. 2 ; Plutarch, *Cic.* 44).

whom do you mean to attack? From whom are you leading the army astray, against whom are you drawing up its ranks? Why is the enemy abandoned, and the citizen put in the enemy's place? Why is your camp, in mid-march, moved farther from the opposing camp, nearer to the City? Because of the 6 enemy's hopes, we must needs have some fear. Ah me, I was never wise, and was once vainly believed to be what I was not! O People of Rome, how you were deceived in your opinion of me! O my ruined and decrepit old age! O the disgrace to my grey hairs, my life concluding in dotage! It was I who led the Fathers of the Senate to the slaughter of their fatherland; I who betrayed the Republic; I who forced the Senate itself to suicide, when I called you Juno's favourite boy and the golden offspring of your mother [a]—but the Fates foretold that you would be the Paris of your country, to devastate Rome with burning and Italy with war, to hold your camp in the temples of the immortal gods, and the Senate in your camp. How pitiable, how swift and complex has been 7 the change of the Republic in this brief time! Who will ever have the genius to write an account of it which sounds like fact and not fiction? Who will be intelligent enough not to think that these events, though most faithfully preserved in memory, are like stories? Imagine: Antony, declared a public enemy, laying siege to the Consul Designate, the Father of his country [b]; yourself setting out to liberate the consul and crush the enemy; the enemy put to flight and the consul liberated from siege by

[b] Decimus Brutus was never given the rare official title of *Pater Patriae*, but the author may mean it in a loose metaphorical sense.

paulo post fugatum illum hostem arcessitum tamquam coheredem mortua re publica ad bona populi
Romani partienda, consulem designatum rursus in-
clusum eo ubi se non moenibus sed fluminibus et
montibus tueretur. Haec quis conabitur exponere ?
quis credere audebit ? Liceat semel impune peccare,
8 sit erranti medicina confessio. Verum enim dicam :
utinam te potius, Antoni, dominum non expulissemus
quam hunc reciperemus ! non quo ulla sit optanda
servitus, sed quia dignitate domini minus turpis est
fortuna servi ; in duobus autem malis cum fugiendum
maius sit, levius est eligendum. Ille ea tamen exora-
bat quae volebat auferre, tu extorques ; ille consul
provinciam petebat, tu privatus concupiscis ; ille ad
malorum salutem iudicia constituebat et leges ferebat,
tu ad perniciem optimorum ; ille a sanguine et
incendio servorum Capitolium tuebatur, tu cruore et
flamma cuncta delere vis. Si qui dabat provincias
Cassio et Brutis et illis custodibus nominis nostri
regnabat, quid faciet qui vitam adimit ? si qui ex
urbe eiciebat tyrannus erat, quem hunc vocemus qui
9 ne locum quidem relinquit exsilio ? Itaque si quid
illae maiorum nostrorum sepultae reliquiae sapiunt,
si non una cum corpore sensus omnis uno atque
eodem consumptus est igni, quid illis interrogantibus
quid agat nunc populus Romanus respondebit aliquis
nostrum qui proximus in illam aeternam domum

---

[a] Although, in § 7, the author had clearly referred to the
alliance of November, 43, between Antony and Octavian,
which restored Antony to primacy, he here represents Antony
as an outcast and Octavian as dominant.

[b] In 44 Antony had suppressed the demagogue Hero-

you—and then, a little after his flight, that same enemy fetched in as joint heir with yourself, on the demise of the Republic, to share in the Roman People's property; and the Consul Designate hemmed in again where he had no walls to defend him, but only rivers and mountains. Who will attempt to relate such things, and who will dare to believe them? Now, let me go unpunished for a first offence; for that mistake let a confession be my medicine. I will speak truth, Antony: would that we had not driven out your despotism, rather than take in Octavian's![a] Not that any servitude is desirable; but the fate of a slave is rendered less humiliating by the quality of his master, and of two evils the greater is to be shunned, the lesser chosen. Antony gained by entreaty what he wanted to carry off; you do it by extortion. Antony sought a province as consul; you covet one as a private person. Antony's courts and laws were established for the benefit of bad characters; yours for the ruin of the best. Antony protected the Capitol from bloodshed and burning by slaves[b]; you want to wipe out everything in blood and fire. If he who gave provinces to Cassius and Brutuses,[c] and those guardians of the Roman name, was a despot, what will the man who killed them be? If he, who ejected them from Rome, was a tyrant, what shall we call the man who did not even leave them room for exile? And so, if those buried remains of our ancestors have any understanding—if the mind of man is not consumed on one and the same pyre as the body—what shall the next of us to pass into that eternal home reply to them when they ask, How fares the

philus, who posed as a descendant of Marius and instigated popular riots.   [c] [Crete to Marcus, Gaul to Decimus.]

discesserit ? aut quem accipient de suis posteris
nuntium illi veteres Africani, Maximi, Pauli, Scipiones ? quid de sua patria audient quam spoliis
triumphisque decorarunt ? an esse quendam annos
XVIII natum, cuius avus fuerit argentarius, adstipulator
pater, uterque vero precarium quaestum fecerit, sed
alter usque ad senectutem ut non negaret, alter a
pueritia ut non posset non confiteri ; eum agere
rapere rem publicam, cui nulla virtus, nullae bello
subactae et ad imperium adiunctae provinciae, nulla
dignitas maiorum conciliasset eam potentiam, sed
forma per dedecus pecuniam et nomen nobile con-
sceleratum impudicitia dedisset, veteres[1] vulneribus
et aetate confectos Iulianos gladiatores, egentis
reliquias Caesaris ludi, ad rudem compulisset, quibus
ille saeptus omnia misceret, nullis parceret, sibi
viveret, qui tanquam in dotali matrimonio[2] rem
publicam testamento legatam sibi obtineret ? Audient
duo Decii servire eos civis qui ut hostibus imperarent
victoriae se devoverunt ; audiet C. Marius impudico
domino parere nos, qui ne militem quidem habere
voluit nisi pudicum ; audiet Brutus eum populum
quem ipse primo, post progenies eius a regibus liber-

'0

---

[1] <qui> veteres *Wesenberg.*
[2] *Lamacchia suggests* patrimonio.

---

[a] *Adstipulatores* hung around the money market in the
Forum, offering themselves as witnesses or guarantors of
contracts for a small fee. Octavian's father became a senator
and praetor, but to impute base occupations in childhood
was within the conventions of rhetorical abuse.

[b] *Rudem* is ironically substituted for *gladium*, apparently meaning that the gladiators were too old to have any
weapon but the *rudis*—a wooden sword given to them on
retirement.

[c] The Decii, father and son, were credited with acts of

Roman People now ? What news of their descendants
will they hear, those ancient Africani, Maximi,
Pauli, Scipiones ? What will they hear of their own
country, which they adorned with spoils and triumphs?
That there is an eighteen-year-old, whose grandfather was a money-changer and his father a tout
witness,[a] both indeed plying a precarious trade—but
the one down to old age so that he could not deny it,
the other from childhood so that he could not help
but confess it ; and he is pillaging the Republic—he,
who established that claim to power not by courage,
by any provinces conquered in war and annexed to
the empire, by any high rank of his ancestors. On
the contrary, his good looks brought him, through
shame, money and a noble name disgraced by lewd-
ness ; he impelled the old Julian gladiators, worn out
by wounds and age, the beggarly relics of Caesar's
training-school, to take up their wooden swords [b] ;
surrounded by them, he spreads universal chaos,
sparing none and living for himself, as if the Republic
were bequeathed into his possession as a marriage
settlement. The two Decii will hear that those 10
citizens, for whose dominion over foes they vowed
their lives to Victory,[c] are now enslaved ; Marius,
who did not want any common soldier even unless he
was chaste,[d] will hear that we submit to an unchaste
master ; Brutus will hear that the people whom he
first, and his descendant after him, freed from Kings [e]

devotio—vowing their lives in return for victory and then
getting themselves killed—in 340 and 295 B.C. respectively.

[d] An apocryphal story of Marius' insistence on morality in
his army was already known to Cicero (*Pro Mil.* 9).

[e] Lucius Junius Brutus, who according to Roman tradition expelled Tarquinius Superbus in 509 B.C., and Marcus
Junius Brutus the assassin of Caesar.

avit, pro turpi stupro datum in servitutem. Quae
quidem si nullo alio, me tamen internuntio celeriter
ad illos deferentur ; nam si vivus ista subterfugere
non potero, una cum istis vitam simul fugere decrevi.

is given over into slavery as payment for a base debauch. All this news shall quickly be conveyed to them by myself, if by no other intermediary ; for if I cannot escape alive from these circumstances, I am resolved to escape from life at the same time as I escape from them.

CHRONOLOGICAL ORDER OF THE LETTERS

based on the order fixed in R. Y. Tyrrell and L. C. Purser, *The Correspondence of M. Tullius Cicero*, vol. vii., Dublin, 1901 (by kind permission of the Board of Trinity College, Dublin).

ABBREVIATIONS

A = *Epistulae ad Atticum.*
F = *Epistulae ad Familiares.*
Q.Fr. = *Epistulae ad Quintum Fratrem.*
Br. = *Epistulae ad M. Brutum.*

B.C.

68	A i. 5, 6, 7 ?
67	A i. 9, 8, 10, 11
66	A i. 3, 4
65	A i. 1, 2
64	[*Q. Cic. de petit. consul.*]
63	F xiii. 76 ?
62	F v. 7, 1, 2, 6
61	A i. 12, F v. 5, A i. 13, 14, 15, 16, 17
60	A i. 18, 19, 20, ii. 1, 2, 3, Q.Fr. i. 1
59	A ii. 4, 5, 6, 7, 8, 9, 12, 10, 11, 13, 14, 15, 16, 17, 18, 19, 20, 21, 22, 23, 24, 25, Q.Fr. i. 2, F xiii. 42, 41 ; also 43 ? (before 58 B.C. ; so also xiii. 44, 45, 46)
58	A iii. 3, 2, 4, 1, 5, 6, F xiv. 4, A iii. 7, 8, 9, Q.Fr. i. 3, A iii. 10, 11, 12, 14, 13, Q.Fr. i. 4, A iii. 15, 16, 17, 18, 19, 20, F xiv. 2, A iii. 21, 22, F xiv. 1, A iii. 23, F xiv. 3, A iii. 24, 25
57	A iii. 26, 27, F v. 4, A iv. 1, 2, 3, Q.Fr. ii. 1, F vii. 26 ; also xiii. 51 ?
56	F i. 1, 2, 3, 4, 5a, Q.Fr. ii. 2, A iv. 4, Q.Fr. ii. 3, F i. 5b, 6, Q.Fr. ii. 4, 5, A iv. 4a, 5, F v. 12, A iv. 6, 7, 8, F v. 3, i. 7, xiii. 6a, 6b, Q.Fr. ii. 8 (= 6), A iv. 8a

813

ORDER OF THE LETTERS

55 F i. 8, Q.Fr. ii. 9 (= 7), A iv. 10, 9, Q.Fr. ii. 10 (= 8),
    A iv. 11, 12, F vii. 2, 3, 1, xiii. 74, 40, A iv. 13

54 F v. 8, Q.Fr. ii. 11 (= 9), 12 (= 10), F vii. 5, Q.Fr. ii.
    13 (= 11), F vii. 6, 7, A iv. 14, Q.Fr. ii. 14 (= 12),
    F vii. 8, Q.Fr. ii. 15a (= 13), 15b (= 14), A iv. 15, 16,
    Q.Fr. ii. 16 (= 15), iii. 1, A iv. 17 (part) plus 18
    (part), F vii. 9, 17, Q.Fr. iii. 2, 3, 4, A iv. 18 (part),
    Q.Fr. iii. 5 plus 6, 7, F vii. 16, Q.Fr. iii. 8, A iv. 19
    (part), 17 (part), Q.Fr. iii. 9, F i. 9, vii. 10, i. 10,
    xiii. 49, 60, 73

53 F ii. 1, vii. 11, ii. 2, 3, vii. 12, 13, 14, 18, 15, ii. 4, 5, 6,
    xiii. 75 ; also xvi. 13 ?, 14 ?, 15 ?, 10 ?, 16 ?

52 F v. 17, 18, iii. 1, vii. 2

51 F iii. 2, A v. 1, 2, 3, 4, 5, 6, 7, F iii. 3, viii. 1, A v. 8,
    F iii. 4, A v. 9, F viii. 2, 3, A v. 10, F xiii. 1, A v. 11,
    F ii. 8, A v. 12, 13, 14, F iii. 5, viii. 4, A v. 15, 16, 17,
    F viii. 5, 9, xv. 3, iii. 6, xv. 7, 8, 9, 12, A v. 18, F xv. 2,
    A v. 19, F xv. 1, iii. 8, viii. 8, ii. 9, 10, viii. 10, ii. 7,
    A v. 20, F vii. 32, xiii. 53, 56, 55, 61, 62, 64, 65, 9 ;
    also 47 ?

50 F xv. 4, 10, 13, 14, viii. 6, 7, iii. 7, ii. 14, ix. 25, xiii. 59,
    58, iii. 9, A v. 21, F xiii. 63, A vi. 1, F xiii. 54, 57,
    ii. 11, A vi. 2, F ii. 13, 18, xiii. 2, 3, iii. 10, ii. 19, 12,
    A vi. 3, F iii. 11, xv. 5, viii. 11, A vi. 4, 5, 7, F viii. 13,
    ii. 17, 15, xv. 11, iii. 12, A vi. 6, F iii. 13, xv. 6,
    viii. 12, 14, A vi. 8, 9, F xiv. 5, A vii. 1, F xvi. 1, 2,
    3, 4, 5, 6, 7, 9, A vii. 3, 4, 5, 6, 7, 8, 9

49 F xvi. 11, v. 20, A vii. 10, 11, 12, F xiv. 18, A vii. 13,
    13a, F xvi. 14, A vii. 14, 15, F xvi. 12, A vii. 16,
    F xvi. 8, A vii. 17, 18, 19, 20, 21, 22, 23, 24, viii. 11a,
    vii. 25, viii. 12b, vii. 26, viii. 1, 11b, 12c, 12d, 2, 12a,
    3, 11c, 6, 4, 5, 7, 8, 9, 10, 11, 11d, 12, F viii. 15,
    A viii. 15a, 13, 14, 15, 16, ix. 1, 2, 12a, 3, 5, 7a, 6, 6a,
    7c, 7b, 4, 7, 8, 9, 10, 11a, 11, 12, 13a, 13, 14, 15, 16,
    17, 18, 19, x. 1, 2, 3, 3a, 4, 9a (= F viii. 16),
    A x. 5, 8a, 8b, 6, F iv. 1, A x. 7, F iv. 2, 19, A x. 8, 9,
    F ii. 16, A x. 10, 11, 12, 12a, 13, 14, 15, 16, 17, 18,
    F xiv. 7

48 A xv. 1, 2, F viii. 17, ix. 9, xiv. 8, A xi. 3, F xiv. 21,
    A xi. 4, F xiv. 6, 12, A xi. 5, F xiv. 19, A xi. 6, F xiv.
    9, A xi. 7, F xiv. 17, A xi. 8

47 A xi. 9, F xiv. 6, A xi. 10, 11, 12, 13, 14, 15, 16, 17,

F xiv. 11, A xi. 18, F xiv. 15, A xi. 25, 23, F xiv. 10, 13, A xi. 19, 24, F xiv. 24, 23, A xi. 20, 21, 22, F xiv. 22, xv. 15, xiv. 20, 21 ; also xiii. 48 ?

46 F xiii. 10, 11, 12, 13, 14, xi. 1, xiii. 29, v. 21, A xii. 2, F ix. 3, 2, 7, 5, vii. 3, vi. 22, ix. 4, A xii. 5c, 3, 4, F ix. 6, A xii. 5, F ix. 16, 18, vii. 33, ix. 20, vii. 27, 28, ix. 19, 26, 17, 15, xiii. 68, iv. 13, 15, 8, 7, 9, vi. 6, 13, 12, 10a, 10b, xii. 17, iv. 3, 4, 11, ix. 21, vi. 14, A xii. 6a, 6b, 7, 8, 11, F vii. 4, ix. 23, A xii. 1, F xiii. 66, 67, 69, 70, 71, 72, 17, 18, 19, 20, 21, 22, 23, 24, 25, 26, 27, 28a, 28b, 78, 79, vi. 8, 9, v. 16, **xv. 18** ; also xii. 20 ?, xiii. 52 ?

45 F xv. 16, vi. 7, 5, 18, iv. 14, 10, ix. 10, vi. 1, 3, 4, **xv. 17**, 19, ix. 13, xiii. 16, A xii. 13, 14, 15, 16, 18, 17, 18a, 19, 20, xiii. 6, F iv. 5, A xii. 12, 21, 22, 23, 24, 25, 26, 27, 28, 29, 33, 30, 32, 31, 34, 35 ?, F xiii. 15, **v. 13**, vi. 21, iv. 6, vi. 2, ix. 11, 36, 37, 37a, 38, 38a, 39, 40, F v. 14, A xii. 42, F v. 15, A xii. 41, 43, 44, 45 ?, xiii. 26, xii. 46, 47, 48, 50, 49, 51, 52, 53, xiii. 1, 2, 27, 28, 29, 2a, 30, 31, 32, xii. 5a, F iv. 12, A xiii. 4, 5, 33, 6a, 8, 7, 7a, xii. 5b, F vi. 11, A xiii. 9, 10, 11, 12, 13, 14, 15, 16, 17, 18, 19, 21a, F ix. 22, A xiii. 20, 22, 33a, 23, F xiii. 77, v. 9, A xiii. 24, 25, F ix. 8, A xiii. 35, 36, 43, F. vi. 20, A xiii. 44, 34, F vi. 19, A xii. 9, F xvi. 22, A xii. 10, xiii. 21, F xvi. 17, A xiii. 47a, F xvi. 19, A xiii. 48, 37, 38, 39, 40, 41, 45, 46, 47, F vii. 24, A xiii. 49, 50, F vii. 35, A xiii. 51, F xii. 18, 19, xiii. 4, 5, 7, 8, v. 11, vii. 29, v. 10b, A xiii. 52, F ix. 12, A xiii. 42, F xiii. 30, 31, 32, 33, 34, 35, 36, 37, 38, 39, xvi. 18, 20

44 F vii. 30, viii. 50, v. 10a, vii. 31, xii. 21, vi. 15, **xi. 1**, **vi. 16, xv. 20**, A xiv. 1, 2, 3, 4, 5, 6, 7, 8, F vi. 17, A xiv. 9, 10, 11, 12, 13a, 13b, 13, 14, 15, 16, 17a (= F ix. 14), F xii. 1, A xiv. 17, 19, 18, 20, 21, 22, xv. 1, 1a, 2, 3, 4, 4a, F xii. 16, A xv. 6, 5, 7, F xi. 2, A xv. 8, 9, 10, 11, 12, 16, 16a, 15, 17, 18, 19, 20, 21, F xvi. 23, A xv. 22, 23, 24, 14, 25, F vii. 21, 22, xi. 29, A **xv. 26**, 27, 28, xvi. 16, 16a, xv. 29, xvi. 1, 5, 4, 2, 3, F vii. 20, A xvi. 6, F vii. 19, A xvi. 16b, 16c, 16d, 16e, 16f, F xi. 3, A xvi. 7, F xi. 27, 28, xvi. 21, x. 1, 2, xii. 22 (1-2), 2, xvi. 25, xi. 4, 6 (1), xii. 3, 23, A xv. 13, **xvi. 8, 9, 11, 12, 10, 13a, 13b, 13c, 14,**

815

ORDER OF THE LETTERS

F xvi. 24, A xvi. 15, F xi. 5, x. 3, xi. 7, 6 (2-3),
ii. 22 (3-4), xvi. 26, 27, x. 4

43 F x. 5, xi. 8, xii. 24, 4, x. 28, ix. 24, xii. 5, 11, 7, x. 31, xii.
25a, x. 6, 27, xii. 28, 26, 27, 29, x. 7, 8, 10, xii. 6, Br.
ii. 1, 3, 2, F x. 12, Br. ii. 4, F x. 30, Br. ii. 5, i. 2,
sects. 4-6, i. 3, sects. 1-3, F x. 9, Br. i. 3, sect. 4, F xi.
9, 11, 13b, xii. 25b, Br. i. 5, F x. 14, xi. 10, 11, xii.
12, x. 13, xi. 13a, 15, 21, sects. 1-6, Br. i. 4, sects.
1-3, F x. 21, Br. i. 4, sects. 4-6, F xi. 12, x. 34a, 18,
xi. 18, Br. i. 6, 1, 2, sects. 1-3, F x. 17, xi. 19, x. 34,
sects. 3-4, xi. 20, 23, x. 19, 25, 16, xii. 15, sects. 1-6,
14, x. 20, 35, Br. i. 8, F xi. 16, 17, x. 33, Br. i. 11, 17,
F xii. 15, xi. 26, 21, 24, x. 23, 32, Br. i. 10, F xii. 8,
30, xi. 13, sects. 4-5, xii. 13, Br. i. 9, F xi. 25, xii. 9,
Br. i. 7, F xi. 15, x. 22, 26, Br. i. 13, F xii. 10, x. 29,
xi. 32, Br. i. 12, 14, 15, 16, 18, F x. 24

INDEX OF NAMES I

CICERO'S LETTERS TO QUINTUS

(The references are to the Book, Letter, and Section or Sections)

817

INDEX OF NAMES I

818

INDEX OF NAMES I

INDEX OF NAMES I

INDEX OF NAMES I

INDEX OF NAMES II
CICERO'S LETTERS TO BRUTUS

(The serial number of the letters follows that of the text)

822

INDEX OF NAMES II

INDEX OF NAMES III

COMMENTARIOLUM PETITIONIS

(The references are to Sections)

INDEX OF NAMES IV
EPISTULA AD OCTAVIANUM

(The references are to Sections)

Printed in Great Britain by R. & R. Clark, Limited, *Edinburgh*

THE LOEB CLASSICAL LIBRARY

VOLUMES ALREADY PUBLISHED

LATIN AUTHORS

AMMIANUS MARCELLINUS. J. C. Rolfe. 3 Vols.

APULEIUS: THE GOLDEN ASS (METAMORPHOSES). W. Adlington (1566). Revised by S. Gaselee.

ST. AUGUSTINE: CITY OF GOD. 7 Vols. Vol. I. G. E. McCracken. Vol. II. W. M. Green. Vol. III. D. Wiesen. Vol. IV. P. Levine. Vol. V. E. M. Sanford and W. M. Green. Vol. VI. W. C. Greene. Vol. VII. W. M. Green.

ST. AUGUSTINE, CONFESSIONS OF. W. Watts (1631). 2 Vols.

ST. AUGUSTINE: SELECT LETTERS. J. H. Baxter.

AUSONIUS. H. G. Evelyn White. 2 Vols.

BEDE. J. E. King. 2 Vols.

BOETHIUS: TRACTS AND DE CONSOLATIONE PHILOSOPHIAE. Rev. H. F. Stewart and E. K. Rand. Revised by S. J. Tester.

CAESAR: ALEXANDRIAN, AFRICAN AND SPANISH WARS. A. G. Way.

CAESAR: CIVIL WARS. A. G. Peskett.

CAESAR: GALLIC WAR. H. J. Edwards.

CATO AND VARRO: DE RE RUSTICA. H. B. Ash and W. D. Hooper.

CATULLUS. F. W. Cornish; TIBULLUS. J. B. Postgate; and PERVIGILIUM VENERIS. J. W. Mackail.

CELSUS: DE MEDICINA. W. G. Spencer. 3 Vols.

CICERO: BRUTUS AND ORATOR. G. L. Hendrickson and H. M. Hubbell.

CICERO: DE FINIBUS. H. Rackham.

CICERO: DE INVENTIONE, etc. H. M. Hubbell.

CICERO: DE NATURA DEORUM AND ACADEMICA. H. Rackham.

CICERO: DE OFFICIIS. Walter Miller.

CICERO: DE ORATORE, etc. 2 Vols. Vol. I: DE ORATORE, Books I and II. E. W. Sutton and H. Rackham. Vol. II: DE ORATORE, Book III; DE FATO; PARADOXA STOICORUM; DE PARTITIONE ORATORIA. H. Rackham.

CICERO: DE REPUBLICA, DE LEGIBUS. Clinton W. Keyes.

THE LOEB CLASSICAL LIBRARY

CICERO: DE SENECTUTE, DE AMICITIA, DE DIVINATIONE. W. A. Falconer.

CICERO: IN CATILINAM, PRO MURENA, PRO SULLA, PRO FLACCO. New version by C. Macdonald.

CICERO: LETTERS TO ATTICUS. E. O. Winstedt. 3 Vols.

CICERO: LETTERS TO HIS FRIENDS. W. Glynn Williams, M. Cary, M. Henderson. 4 Vols.

CICERO: PHILIPPICS. W. C. A. Ker.

CICERO: PRO ARCHIA, POST REDITUM, DE DOMO, DE HARUSPICUM RESPONSIS, PRO PLANCIO. N. H. Watts.

CICERO: PRO CAECINA, PRO LEGE MANILIA, PRO CLUENTIO, PRO RABIRIO. H. Grose Hodge.

CICERO: PRO CAELIO, DE PROVINCIIS CONSULARIBUS, PRO BALBO. R. Gardner.

CICERO: PRO MILONE, IN PISONEM, PRO SCAURO, PRO FONTEIO, PRO RABIRIO POSTUMO, PRO MARCELLO, PRO LIGARIO, PRO REGE DEIOTARO. N. H. Watts.

CICERO: PRO QUINCTIO, PRO ROSCIO AMERINO, PRO ROSCIO COMOEDO, CONTRA RULLUM. J. H. Freese.

CICERO: PRO SESTIO, IN VATINIUM. R. Gardner.

[CICERO]: RHETORICA AD HERENNIUM. H. Caplan.

CICERO: TUSCULAN DISPUTATIONS. J. E. King.

CICERO: VERRINE ORATIONS. L. H. G. Greenwood. 2 Vols.

CLAUDIAN. M. Platnauer. 2 Vols.

COLUMELLA: DE RE RUSTICA, DE ARBORIBUS. H. B. Ash, E. S. Forster, E. Heffner. 3 Vols.

CURTIUS, Q.: HISTORY OF ALEXANDER. J. C. Rolfe. 2 Vols.

FLORUS. E. S. Forster; and CORNELIUS NEPOS. J. C. Rolfe.

FRONTINUS: STRATAGEMS AND AQUEDUCTS. C. E. Bennett and M. B. McElwain.

FRONTO: CORRESPONDENCE. C. R. Haines. 2 Vols.

GELLIUS. J. C. Rolfe. 3 Vols.

HORACE: ODES AND EPODES. C. E. Bennett.

HORACE: SATIRES, EPISTLES, ARS POETICA. H. R. Fairclough.

JEROME: SELECT LETTERS. F. A. Wright.

JUVENAL AND PERSIUS. G. G. Ramsay.

LIVY. B. O. Foster, F. G. Moore, Evan T. Sage, A. C. Schlesinger and R. M. Geer (General Index). 14 Vols.

LUCAN. J. D. Duff.

LUCRETIUS. W. H. D. Rouse. Revised by M. F. Smith.

MANILIUS. G. P. Goold.

MARTIAL. W. C. A. Ker. 2 Vols. Revised by E. H. Warmington.

MINOR LATIN POETS: from PUBLILIUS SYRUS to RUTILIUS NAMATIANUS, including GRATTIUS, CALPURNIUS SICULUS,

THE LOEB CLASSICAL LIBRARY

NEMESIANUS, AVIANUS, with "Aetna," "Phoenix" and other poems. J. Wight Duff and Arnold M. Duff.

OVID: THE ART OF LOVE AND OTHER POEMS. J. H. Mozley. Revised by G. P. Goold.

OVID: FASTI. Sir James G. Frazer. [by G. P. Goold.

OVID: HEROIDES AND AMORES. Grant Showerman. Revised

OVID: METAMORPHOSES. F. J. Miller. 2 Vols. Vol. I revised by G. P. Goold.

OVID: TRISTIA AND EX PONTO. A. L. Wheeler.

PETRONIUS. M. Heseltine; SENECA: APOCOLOCYNTOSIS. W. H. D. Rouse. Revised by E. H. Warmington.

PHAEDRUS AND BABRIUS (Greek). B. E. Perry.

PLAUTUS. Paul Nixon. 5 Vols.

PLINY: LETTERS, PANEGYRICUS. B. Radice. 2 Vols.

PLINY: NATURAL HISTORY. 10 Vols. Vols. I-V. H. Rackham. Vols. VI-VIII. W. H. S. Jones. Vol. IX. H. Rackham. Vol. X. D. E. Eichholz.

PROPERTIUS. H. E. Butler.

PRUDENTIUS. H. J. Thomson. 2 Vols.

QUINTILIAN. H. E. Butler. 4 Vols.

REMAINS OF OLD LATIN. E. H. Warmington. 4 Vols. Vol. I (Ennius and Caecilius). Vol. II (Livius, Naevius, Pacuvius, Accius). Vol. III (Lucilius, Laws of the XII Tables). Vol. IV (Archaic Inscriptions).

SALLUST. J. C. Rolfe.

SCRIPTORES HISTORIAE AUGUSTAE. D. Magie. 3 Vols.

SENECA: APOCOLOCYNTOSIS. Cf. PETRONIUS.

SENECA: EPISTULAE MORALES. R. M. Gummere. 3 Vols.

SENECA: MORAL ESSAYS. J. W. Basore. 3 Vols.

SENECA: NATURALES QUAESTIONES. T. H. Corcoran. 2 Vols.

SENECA: TRAGEDIES. F. J. Miller. 2 Vols.

SENECA THE ELDER. M. Winterbottom. 2 Vols.

SIDONIUS: POEMS AND LETTERS. W. B. Anderson. 2 Vols.

SILIUS ITALICUS. J. D. Duff. 2 Vols.

STATIUS. J. H. Mozley. 2 Vols.

SUETONIUS. J. C. Rolfe. 2 Vols.

TACITUS: AGRICOLA AND GERMANIA. M. Hutton; DIALOGUS. Sir Wm. Peterson. Revised by R. M. Ogilvie, E. H. Warmington, M. Winterbottom.

TACITUS: HISTORIES AND ANNALS. C. H. Moore and J. Jackson. 4 Vols.

TERENCE. John Sargeaunt. 2 Vols.

TERTULLIAN: APOLOGIA AND DE SPECTACULIS. T. R. Glover; MINUCIUS FELIX. G. H. Rendall.

VALERIUS FLACCUS. J. H. Mozley.

3

THE LOEB CLASSICAL LIBRARY

Varro: De Lingua Latina. R. G. Kent. 2 Vols.
Velleius Paterculus and Res Gestae Divi Augusti. F. W. Shipley.
Virgil. H. R. Fairclough. 2 Vols.
Vitruvius: De Architectura. F. Granger. 2 Vols.

GREEK AUTHORS

Achilles Tatius. S. Gaselee.
Aelian: On the Nature of Animals. A. F. Scholfield. 3 Vols.
Aeneas Tacticus, Asclepiodotus and Onasander. The Illinois Greek Club.
Aeschines. C. D. Adams.
Aeschylus. H. Weir Smyth. 2 Vols.
Alciphron, Aelian and Philostratus: Letters. A. R. Benner and F. H. Fobes.
Apollodorus. Sir James G. Frazer. 2 Vols.
Apollonius Rhodius. R. C. Seaton.
The Apostolic Fathers. Kirsopp Lake. 2 Vols.
Appian: Roman History. Horace White. 4 Vols.
Aratus. Cf. Callimachus: Hymns and Epigrams.
Aristides. C. A. Behr. 4 Vols. Vol. I.
Aristophanes. Benjamin Bickley Rogers. 3 Vols. Verse trans.
Aristotle: Art of Rhetoric. J. H. Freese.
Aristotle: Athenian Constitution, Eudemian Ethics. Virtues and Vices. H. Rackham.
Aristotle: The Categories. On Interpretation. H. P. Cooke; Prior Analytics. H. Tredennick.
Aristotle: Generation of Animals. A. L. Peck.
Aristotle: Historia Animalium. A. L. Peck. 3 Vols. Vols. I and II.
Aristotle: Metaphysics. H. Tredennick. 2 Vols.
Aristotle: Meteorologica. H. D. P. Lee.
Aristotle: Minor Works. W. S. Hett. "On Colours," "On Things Heard," "Physiognomics," "On Plants," "On Marvellous Things Heard," "Mechanical Problems," "On Invisible Lines," "Situations and Names of Winds," "On Melissus, Xenophanes, and Gorgias."
Aristotle: Nicomachean Ethics. H. Rackham.
Aristotle: Oeconomica and Magna Moralia. G. C. Armstrong. (With Metaphysics, Vol. II.)
Aristotle: On the Heavens. W. K. C. Guthrie.

THE LOEB CLASSICAL LIBRARY

ARISTOTLE : ON THE SOUL, PARVA NATURALIA, ON BREATH. W. S. Hett.

ARISTOTLE : PARTS OF ANIMALS. A. L. Peck : MOVEMENT AND PROGRESSION OF ANIMALS. E. S. Forster.

ARISTOTLE : PHYSICS. Rev. P. Wicksteed and F. M. Cornford. 2 Vols.

ARISTOTLE : POETICS ; LONGINUS ON THE SUBLIME. W. Hamilton Fyfe ; DEMETRIUS ON STYLE. W. Rhys Roberts.

ARISTOTLE : POLITICS. H. Rackham.

ARISTOTLE : POSTERIOR ANALYTICS. H. Tredennick ; TOPICS. E. S. Forster.

ARISTOTLE : PROBLEMS. W. S. Hett. 2 Vols.

ARISTOTLE : RHETORICA AD ALEXANDRUM. H. Rackham. (With PROBLEMS, Vol. II.)

ARISTOTLE : SOPHISTICAL REFUTATIONS. COMING-TO-BE AND PASSING-AWAY. E. S. Forster ; ON THE COSMOS. D. J. Furley.

ARRIAN : HISTORY OF ALEXANDER AND INDICA. 2 Vols. Vol. I. P. Brunt. Vol. II. Rev. E. Iliffe Robson.

ATHENAEUS : DEIPNOSOPHISTAE. C. B. Gulick. 7 Vols.

BABRIUS AND PHAEDRUS (Latin). B. E. Perry.

ST. BASIL : LETTERS. R. J. Deferrari. 4 Vols.

CALLIMACHUS : FRAGMENTS. C. A. Trypanis ; MUSAEUS : HERO AND LEANDER. T. Gelzer and C. Whitman.

CALLIMACHUS : HYMNS AND EPIGRAMS, AND LYCOPHRON. A. W. Mair ; ARATUS. G. R. Mair.

CLEMENT OF ALEXANDRIA. Rev. G. W. Butterworth.

COLLUTHUS. Cf. OPPIAN.

DAPHNIS AND CHLOE. Cf. LONGUS.

DEMOSTHENES I : OLYNTHIACS, PHILIPPICS AND MINOR ORATIONS : I-XVII AND XX. J. H. Vince.

DEMOSTHENES II : DE CORONA AND DE FALSA LEGATIONE. C. A. and J. H. Vince.

DEMOSTHENES III : MEIDIAS, ANDROTION, ARISTOCRATES, TIMOCRATES, ARISTOGEITON. J. H. Vince.

DEMOSTHENES IV-VI : PRIVATE ORATIONS AND IN NEAERAM. A. T. Murray.

DEMOSTHENES VII : FUNERAL SPEECH, EROTIC ESSAY, EXORDIA AND LETTERS. N. W. and N. J. DeWitt.

DIO CASSIUS : ROMAN HISTORY. E. Cary. 9 Vols.

DIO CHRYSOSTOM. 5 Vols. Vols. I and II. J. W. Cohoon. Vol. III. J. W. Cohoon and H. Lamar Crosby. Vols. IV and V. H. Lamar Crosby.

DIODORUS SICULUS. 12 Vols. Vols. I-VI. C. H. Oldfather. Vol. VII. C. L. Sherman. Vol. VIII. C. B. Welles. Vols.

IX and X. Russel M. Geer. Vols. XI and XII. F. R. Walton. General Index. Russel M. Geer.

DIOGENES LAERTIUS. R. D. Hicks. 2 Vols. New Introduction by H. S. Long.

DIONYSIUS OF HALICARNASSUS : CRITICAL ESSAYS. S. Usher. 2 Vols.

DIONYSIUS OF HALICARNASSUS : ROMAN ANTIQUITIES. Spelman's translation revised by E. Cary. 7 Vols.

EPICTETUS. W. A. Oldfather. 2 Vols.

EURIPIDES. A. S. Way. 4 Vols. Verse trans.

EUSEBIUS : ECCLESIASTICAL HISTORY. Kirsopp Lake and J. E. L. Oulton. 2 Vols.

GALEN : ON THE NATURAL FACULTIES. A. J. Brock.

THE GREEK ANTHOLOGY. W. R. Paton. 5 Vols.

THE GREEK BUCOLIC POETS (THEOCRITUS, BION, MOSCHUS). J. M. Edmonds.

GREEK ELEGY AND IAMBUS WITH THE ANACREONTEA. J. M. Edmonds. 2 Vols.

GREEK MATHEMATICAL WORKS. Ivor Thomas. 2 Vols.

HERODES. Cf. THEOPHRASTUS : CHARACTERS.

HERODIAN. C. R. Whittaker. 2 Vols.

HERODOTUS. A. D. Godley. 4 Vols.

HESIOD AND THE HOMERIC HYMNS. H. G. Evelyn White.

HIPPOCRATES AND THE FRAGMENTS OF HERACLEITUS. W. H. S. Jones and E. T. Withington. 4 Vols.

HOMER : ILIAD. A. T. Murray. 2 Vols.

HOMER : ODYSSEY. A. T. Murray. 2 Vols.

ISAEUS. E. S. Forster.

ISOCRATES. George Norlin and LaRue Van Hook. 3 Vols.

[ST. JOHN DAMASCENE]: BARLAAM AND IOASAPH. Rev. G. R. Woodward, Harold Mattingly and D. M. Lang.

JOSEPHUS. 9 Vols. Vols. I-IV. H. St. J. Thackeray. Vol. V. H. St. J. Thackeray and Ralph Marcus. Vols. VI and VII. Ralph Marcus. Vol. VIII. Ralph Marcus and Allen Wikgren. Vol. IX. L. H. Feldman.

JULIAN. Wilmer Cave Wright. 3 Vols.

LIBANIUS : SELECTED WORKS. A. F. Norman. 3 Vols. Vols. I and II.

LONGUS : DAPHNIS AND CHLOE. Thornley's translation revised by J. M. Edmonds ; and PARTHENIUS. S. Gaselee.

LUCIAN. 8 Vols. Vols. I-V. A. M. Harmon. Vol. VI. K. Kilburn. Vols. VII and VIII. M. D. Macleod.

LYCOPHRON. Cf. CALLIMACHUS : HYMNS AND EPIGRAMS.

LYRA GRAECA. J. M. Edmonds. 3 Vols.

LYSIAS. W. R. M. Lamb.

THE LOEB CLASSICAL LIBRARY

MANETHO. W. G. Waddell; PTOLEMY: TETRABIBLOS. F. E. Robbins.

MARCUS AURELIUS. C. R. Haines.

MENANDER. F. G. Allinson.

MINOR ATTIC ORATORS. 2 Vols. K. J. Maidment and J. O. Burtt.

MUSAEUS: HERO AND LEANDER. *Cf.* CALLIMACHUS: FRAGMENTS.

NONNOS: DIONYSIACA. W. H. D. Rouse. 3 Vols.

OPPIAN, COLLUTHUS, TRYPHIODORUS. A. W. Mair.

PAPYRI. NON-LITERARY SELECTIONS. A. S. Hunt and C. C. Edgar. 2 Vols. LITERARY SELECTIONS (Poetry). D. L. Page.

PARTHENIUS. *Cf.* LONGUS.

PAUSANIAS: DESCRIPTION OF GREECE. W. H. S. Jones. 4 Vols. and Companion Vol. arranged by R. E. Wycherley.

PHILO. 10 Vols. Vols. I-V. F. H. Colson and Rev. G. H. Whitaker. Vols. VI-X. F. H. Colson. General Index. Rev. J. W. Earp.

Two Supplementary Vols. Translation only from an Armenian Text. Ralph Marcus.

PHILOSTRATUS: THE LIFE OF APOLLONIUS OF TYANA. F. C. Conybeare. 2 Vols.

PHILOSTRATUS: IMAGINES; CALLISTRATUS: DESCRIPTIONS. A. Fairbanks.

PHILOSTRATUS AND EUNAPIUS: LIVES OF THE SOPHISTS. Wilmer Cave Wright.

PINDAR. Sir J. E. Sandys.

PLATO: CHARMIDES, ALCIBIADES, HIPPARCHUS, THE LOVERS, THEAGES, MINOS AND EPINOMIS. W. R. M. Lamb.

PLATO: CRATYLUS, PARMENIDES, GREATER HIPPIAS, LESSER HIPPIAS. H. N. Fowler.

PLATO: EUTHYPHRO, APOLOGY, CRITO, PHAEDO, PHAEDRUS. H. N. Fowler.

PLATO: LACHES, PROTAGORAS, MENO, EUTHYDEMUS. W. R. M. Lamb.

PLATO: LAWS. Rev. R. G. Bury. 2 Vols.

PLATO: LYSIS, SYMPOSIUM, GORGIAS. W. R. M. Lamb.

PLATO: REPUBLIC. Paul Shorey. 2 Vols.

PLATO: STATESMAN, PHILEBUS. H. N. Fowler; ION. W. R. M. Lamb.

PLATO: THEAETETUS AND SOPHIST. H. N. Fowler.

PLATO: TIMAEUS, CRITIAS, CLITOPHO, MENEXENUS, EPISTULAE. Rev. R. G. Bury.

PLOTINUS. A. H. Armstrong. 6 Vols. Vols. I-III.

THE LOEB CLASSICAL LIBRARY

PLUTARCH : MORALIA. 16 Vols. Vols. I-V. F. C. Babbitt. Vol. VI. W. C. Helmbold. Vol. VII. P. H. De Lacy and B. Einarson. Vol. VIII. P. A. Clement, H. B. Hoffleit. Vol. IX. E. L. Minar, Jr., F. H. Sandbach, W. C. Helmbold. Vol. X. H. N. Fowler. Vol. XI. L. Pearson, F. H. Sandbach. Vol. XII. H. Cherniss, W. C. Helmbold. Vol. XIII, Parts 1 and 2. H. Cherniss. Vol. XIV. P. H. De Lacy and B. Einarson. Vol. XV. F. H. Sandbach.

PLUTARCH : THE PARALLEL LIVES. B. Perrin. 11 Vols.

POLYBIUS. W. R. Paton. 6 Vols.

PROCOPIUS : HISTORY OF THE WARS. H. B. Dewing. 7 Vols.

PTOLEMY : TETRABIBLOS. Cf. MANETHO.

QUINTUS SMYRNAEUS. A. S. Way. Verse trans.

SEXTUS EMPIRICUS. Rev. R. G. Bury. 4 Vols.

SOPHOCLES. F. Storr. 2 Vols. Verse trans.

STRABO : GEOGRAPHY. Horace L. Jones. 8 Vols.

THEOPHRASTUS : CHARACTERS. J. M. Edmonds ; HERODES, etc. A. D. Knox.

THEOPHRASTUS : DE CAUSIS PLANTARUM. G. K. K. Link and B. Einarson. 3 Vols. Vol. I.

THEOPHRASTUS : ENQUIRY INTO PLANTS. Sir Arthur Hort. 2 Vols.

THUCYDIDES. C. F. Smith. 4 Vols.

TRYPHIODORUS. Cf. OPPIAN.

XENOPHON : ANABASIS. C. L. Brownson.

XENOPHON : CYROPAEDIA. Walter Miller. 2 Vols.

XENOPHON : HELLENICA. C. L. Brownson.

XENOPHON : MEMORABILIA AND OECONOMICUS. E. C. Marchant ; SYMPOSIUM AND APOLOGY. O. J. Todd.

XENOPHON : SCRIPTA MINORA. E. C. Marchant and G. W. Bowersock.

DESCRIPTIVE PROSPECTUS ON APPLICATION

CAMBRIDGE, MASS.   LONDON
HARVARD UNIV. PRESS   WILLIAM HEINEMANN LTD